"I love writing lyrics. For years scarcely a day passed whose low descending sun did not see me at my desk trying to find some rhyme for 'June' that would not be 'soon,' 'moon,' 'tune' or 'spoon.'"
—**P. G. Wodehouse**

"He is the 'best' writer of our time: the best living writer of English."
—**Hilaire Belloc**

"Before Larry Hart, only P. G. Wodehouse had made any assault on the intelligence of the song-listening public. . . . Larry always said he was 'inspired' by Wodehouse."
—**Richard Rodgers**

"You are the lyric writer I most admire. . . . Over the years I have held you as the model of light verse in the song form. I believe I know more of your phrases than you would remember yourself."
—**Howard Dietz**

"[Wodehouse's lyrics] had the great virtue which Gilbert's lyrics have and which, I am told, the comic verses of Molière and Aristophanes also have: they say things as simply as you would say them in commonplace speech, yet they sing perfectly. There was nothing he wanted to say that he couldn't say to music."
—**Gilbert Seldes**

"One day, in fifty, a hundred years time, the words of Porter, Hart, Wodehouse, Gershwin, Coward, maybe a few of my own, will be published, recited, analyzed, codified."
—**Johnny Mercer**

"What he did for the musical theatre still matters today, and more important, still entertains today."
—**Tim Rice**

"Wodehouse's talent in this field has never been fully recognized. As far as I'm concerned, no one wrote more charming lyrics than he in the period from just before World War I to the Twenties."
—**Ira Gershwin**

"Wodehouse is the father of the modern theatre lyric and it is a true delight to read as well as sing his marvelous creations. Ira Gershwin idolized him and it is easy to understand why."
—**Michael Feinstein**

"Not only are the lyrics witty and skillful on their own terms, but they help open up a window to the Princess Theater shows, a primary influence in the development of the American musical. For it was these shows, done in a smaller theater, which pioneered the [first steps toward] integration of song and text and, by a stretch of the imagination, the first tentative glimmer of what was to become, one day, Off-Broadway."
—**Tom Jones** (*The Fantasticks*)

"With his great sense of the *play* of words, Wodehouse lit the way to literate lyrics for all who followed."
—**Steve Ross**

"No one did more to make the mould into which so many people were to pour their talent."
—**Adolph Green**

"My favourite song? My first favourite is my own *Bitter Sweet* waltz, which I think delicious; failing this slightly egotistical opinion, I would say the good old *Rain* song from *Oh, Boy!* by my dear Mr. Kern."
—**Noël Coward**

THE COMPLETE LYRICS OF
P. G. WODEHOUSE

Like you read about in books.

We collar ev'rything on which we lay our hooks.

If you leave your door unlocked, we come inside

But we never could be lawyers, for we've

some proper pride.

2.

We're crooks, crooks

Like you read about in books.

We're strong on intellect, though maybe not

on looks

We have done a lot of things which we regre

But we've never sunk so low as to be friends

of La Follette.

in books.

Guy Bolton, P. G. Wodehouse and Jerome Kern at work in the Princess Theatre.

THE COMPLETE LYRICS OF P. G. WODEHOUSE

EDITED BY BARRY DAY

Editorial Consultant: Tony Ring

THE SCARECROW PRESS, INC.
Lanham, Maryland • Toronto • Oxford
2004

SCARECROW PRESS, INC.

Published in the United States of America
by Scarecrow Press, Inc.
A wholly owned subsidiary of
The Rowman & Littlefield Publishing Group, Inc.
4501 Forbes Boulevard, Suite 200, Lanham, Maryland 20706
www.scarecrowpress.com

PO Box 317
Oxford
OX2 9RU, UK

British Library Cataloguing in Publication Information Available

Library of Congress Cataloging-in-Publication Data

Wodehouse, P. G. (Pelham Grenville), 1881–1975.
    [Songs. Texts]
    The complete lyrics of P.G. Wodehouse / edited by Barry Day.— 1st
        p. cm.
    Includes bibliographical references (p.   ) and index.
    ISBN 0-8108-4994-1 (hardcover : alk. paper)
    1. Popular music—Texts. 2. Musicals—Excerpts—Librettos.
  I. Day, Barry. II. Title.
ML54.6.W54 D29 2004
782.42164'0268—dc21   2003013116

Dedicated to *Evelyn D'Auzac*,
who first had the thought

and editorial consultant *Tony Ring*,
who did so much to turn it into reality

CONTENTS

• Act 2—Opening Chorus • Just A Voice To Call Me Dear • Half A Married Man
• Man, Man, Man • (Let's Build) A Little Bungalow in Quogue • Will You Forget?
• Act 3—Opening Chorus • Why Can't They Hand It To Me? • Gypsy, Bring Your
Fiddle (The Lilt of a Gypsy Strain) • Act 3—Finale

ACKNOWLEDGMENTS

A project like this stretches over a period of years and involves the help and encouragement of numerous people. I would like to thank the following. They know what they did . . .

In alphabetical order . . .

Louis Aborn (Tams Witmark); The Berg Collection at the New York Public Library; Ken Bloom; Andrew R. Boose (for permission to use Kern material); Marguerite Bolton Bundres (Guy's daughter); Sir Edward Cazalet; Hal Cazalet; Maryann Chach (Shubert Archive); Eric Comstock; Lorna Dallas; Lee Davis; Michael Dorr; Rosalind Fayne, my indefatigable assistant (*sine qua non*); Mark Trent Goldberg (Gershwin Estate); Mark Horowitz (Library of Congress); Barrie Ingham; Marty Jacobs (Museum of the City of New York); Kathryn Johnson (British Library); Simon Jones; Robert Kimball (that father lode of knowledge on musical theatre); Wendy Leshner (Universal Music US); Richard Mangan (Mander & Mitchenson Collection); John McGlinn; the late Robert Montgomery and Peter H. Felcher (Cole Porter Estate); Jay Morganstern (Warner/Chappell US); Norman Murphy; Dave Olsen (Warner/Chappell US); Alan Pally (New York Library for the Performing Arts at Lincoln Center); Ross Plotkin and Lynn Weber (Taylor Trade Publishing); Linda Shaughnessy (A. P. Watt); Caroline Underwood (Warner/Chappell UK); Debbie Williams (formerly Universal Music UK).

INTRODUCTION

When you know that someone wrote about a hundred books and died with another one unfinished on his bedside table, it's almost impossible to conceive that he could have found the time to do anything else of consequence. Which is presumably why so few of P. G. Wodehouse's countless admirers are aware that 'Plum' also had a hand in 19 plays (more than, say, Lonsdale or Maugham) and was involved in the libretto or lyrics (and frequently both) for almost 40 musical comedies between 1905 and 1934. (He had five shows running simultaneously on Broadway in 1917 alone.) There are more libretti by Wodehouse, for instance, than there are by Gilbert.

Had he not made such an overwhelming impact with his written words, therefore, Wodehouse would have rated a significant place in both English and American theatrical history for his use of the spoken and sung word.

From around 1915 until the outbreak of World War II, he shuttled across the Atlantic, somehow managing to balance his prolific output so as to satisfy his bigamous twin muses. He himself was in no doubt that the one positively sustained the other and, surprisingly, it was the theatre that affected the fiction. He described his early novels as "musical comedies without the music" and thought of them in terms of "acts, chorus numbers, duets and solos." "The only way to write a popular story is to split it up into scenes, and have as little stuff between the scenes as possible." It gives one an excuse to re-read the novels once more with that new perspective.

It also gives fresh insight into the way he deployed character within a cast-iron plot construction. A principal character, for instance, must be given enough "big scenes" to justify his star stature. ("If this were a musical comedy, we should have to get Leslie Henson to play this part and if he found that all he had was a scene in act one, he would walk out.")

Wodehouse's theatrical achievement—aided and abetted by his principal collaborators, writer Guy Bolton and composer Jerome Kern—was no less than to pick up the lyrical torch lit by W. S. Gilbert and use it to light the way to the modern musical, picking his way through the debris of the overblown imported operetta en route. Without his apparently casual pioneering efforts, it is no exaggeration to say that later exponents of popular theatre music in the 1920s and later—talents such as the Gershwins, Rodgers and Hart, and Cole Porter—might never have fulfilled their true potential.

It could be argued that Wodehouse was fortunate in that he was familiar with both cultures—English and American—but then that bi-cultural confidence was a by-product of the fact that he found he could operate with ease in either. The real reason for his success was that the man possessed an incredible ear for the nuance of language and enjoyed nothing more than adapting to circumstance and the discipline of a deadline.

His witty literacy in the crafting of a lyric stems straight from Gilbert, that colossus who bestrode Victorian comic opera—but with one significant difference which was to make *all* the difference. Gilbert's lyrics invariably preceded Sullivan's music, which made them scan like verse. Clever as the words were, they moved along at a predictable pace on railway tracks. Kern, who was no fan, referred to his "versifying to music."

Wodehouse turned the convention of then popular song on its head by taking existing music and showing that it was perfectly possible to fit clever but conversational phrasing to any melody. Gilbert, for instance, could never have written:

What bad luck! It's
Coming down in buckets

Its very unexpected incorrectness is precisely what catches the ear. Gilbert probably turned in his grave but what Wodehouse achieved in this and other rule-breaking rhymes was to move from the "poeticism" of his predecessor to the colloquialism of the modern song lyric. He was also to begin the process that Ira Gershwin later perfected—the fitting of words, mosaic-fashion, to existing tunes.

No lyricist, unaided, would have written the line:

I love him, because he's—I don't
    know—
Because he's just my Bill.

The "I don't knows" were necessitated by Kern's three extra notes but it was Wodehouse's "conversational" skills that gave the final line its haunting memorability.

Kern invariably provided the melody first—as George Gershwin was to do for Ira—which Wodehouse infinitely preferred.

"W. S. Gilbert always said that a lyricist can't do decent stuff that way. But I don't agree with him. I think you get the best results by giving the composer his head and having the lyricist follow him. For instance, the refrain of one of the songs on *Oh, Boy!* began: 'If every day you bring her diamonds and pearls on a string'—I couldn't have thought of that if I had done the lyric first. Why, dash it, it doesn't scan. But Jerry's melody started off with a lot of little twiddly notes, the first thing emphasized being the 'di' of 'diamonds' and I just tagged along after him. Another thing. . . . When you have the melody, you can see which are the musical high spots in it and can fit the high spots of the lyric to them. Anyway, that's how I like working, and to hell with anyone who says I oughtn't to."

Perhaps it was not surprising that Wodehouse found that lyric writing came so easily. Although he was by no means a musician in any real sense, he clearly had a sense of the musical.

Wodehouse scholar David Jasen likens his literary style to ragtime:

> Although apparently wild and uncontrolled, with its syncopation and intricate secondary notes, ragtime was precise and needed to be precisely executed. . . . Plum's dialogue is akin to the cross-current in syncopation. His distortion of famous quotations intermingled with cliches is a direct parallel to the secondary improvisation which is basic to ragtime.

Kern was the key to Wodehouse's greatest achievements. As that perceptive critic, the late Benny Green observed—"while Kern achieved many masterpieces without Wodehouse, Wodehouse achieved none without Kern." The two men first worked together as early as 1906 but it was the

eight years between 1916 and 1924 that marked their mature collaboration. It produced ten shows, several of which helped define the direction the American—and, in due course, the English—musical theatre was to take.

That course was charted by the integration of plot, character, and song. More and more the songs not only defined an aspect of the character but also helped the plot along, instead of holding it for ransom while an interpolated specialty number was performed. "A thing on which we prided ourselves," Bolton would recall "was the integration of numbers and books. I would write a scene and hand it to Plum and next morning find half the scene gone and its content expressed in a lyric."

Rodgers and Hammerstein's *Oklahoma!* (1943) is popularly supposed to mark the dawn of the integrated musical—and, admittedly, it did include the dimension of dance—but the *handful* of mini-musicals that the "trio of musical fame," Bolton and Wodehouse and Kern, wrote for the Princess Theatre in New York between 1916 and 1918 *were* truly the first to brush away the cobwebs of Hapsburg operetta and tell stories about contemporary people, however stylized, speaking—and singing—the language of the day.

Strangely, Wodehouse has never received the credit due for his groundbreaking efforts—hence this book. His literary reputation, which grew exponentially from the 1920s, distracted attention from these more collaborative efforts, as far as the general public was concerned. Fortunately, his fellow professionals were not so myopic. Larry Hart declared himself to be "inspired" by Wodehouse's craft, while castigating others who failed to use "interior rhymes, feminine rhymes, triple rhymes and false rhymes" and settled for nothing but "juxtapositions of words like 'slush' and 'mush.'"

His partner, Richard Rodgers, was no less complimentary. Johnny Mercer was to include him in his list of the six lyricists who would be studied in the twenty-first century. Howard Dietz considered him "the lyric writer I most admire," while Alan Jay Lerner was convinced that Wodehouse and his two partners had "inaugurated" the American musical. But perhaps the greatest admirer was his lifelong friend, Ira Gershwin. The two men collaborated intermittently but corresponded for the rest of Wodehouse's life, returning to the subject of lyrics and the musical theatre again and again. Shortly before he died Wodehouse was writing to Gershwin, appalled at the demise of two recent Broadway productions that had recently sunk to the tune of more than a million dollars. On his Christmas card he wrote—"Ira, we are well out of it."

It would be nice to report that Wodehouse reciprocated his colleagues' professional admiration but, by and large, he did not.

He felt that Cole Porter had "no power of self-criticism. He just bungs down anything, whether it makes sense or not just because he has thought of what he feels is a good rhyme." The result, he felt, was "terribly uneven. He gets wonderful ideas, but he will strain for rhymes regardless of sense." There was something about Porter's personal style that colored the professional perception—"I always feel about Cole's lyrics that he sang them to Elsa Maxwell and Noël Coward in a studio stinking of gin and they said—'Oh, Cole, *darling*, it's just too marvellous.' Why can't he see that you must have a transition of thought in a lyric just as in dialogue?"

On one thing at least, though, he agreed with Coward. Porter's lyrics for *Kiss Me, Kate* were just too *too*. . . . "Cole is brilliant but what a dirty-minded son of a bachelor. That 'Too Darned Hot' lyric is simply filthy." Coward himself he considered "a great lyric writer. It seems a bit unfair for a man to write the words *and* the music. His rhymes are so good."

With regard to Lorenz Hart, he was clearly of two minds. At one point he is saying that Hart "was always good. If there is a bad lyric of his in existence, I have not come across it. It seems to me he had everything. He could be ultra-sophisticated and simple and sincere.

And his rhyming, of course, was impeccable. But the great thing about his work was that, as somebody once wrote, he was the first to make any real assault on the intelligence of the songwriting public. He brought something quite new into a rather tired business."

Later—1950, after a revival of *Pal Joey*—he would take a diametrically opposite point of view. Perhaps too much exposure to Hart's slick cynicism had finally ruffled the Wodehouse feathers. "I can't see him as a lyricist at all. He has no charm whatsoever, and all those trick rhymes of his, which the intelligentsia rave about . . . are the easiest things in the world to do. Ira is worth ten of him." Throughout his life he would maintain that Gershwin was "the best of the bunch," a bunch in which he also picked out Howard Dietz for special mention ("I had no idea he was such a wizard").

Looking at the body of his lyrical work—or, indeed, his fiction, for that matter—the choice of Gershwin as a fellow spirit is not surprising. In the best sense of the phrase, both of them were simple souls who believed in conveying simple, often romantic, sentiments in simple words. Their ingenuity—their genius, even—lay in the artfully artless way they managed to arrange them within the discipline of the lyric form and—in both their cases—to the preordained rhythms they

were given to work with. Both were true romantics capable of avoiding both hyperbole and banality while picking their way over well-trodden ground.

When teamed with their natural partners—Kern in Wodehouse's case and George in Ira's—both could create surprisingly moving results.

Here's Wodehouse in "What I'm Longing To Say" from *Leave It To Jane*:

Somehow, whenever I'm with you
    I never
Can say what I'm longing to say.
When it's too late and you're not near
    me,
I can find words, but you're not there
    to hear me.
That's why, when we are together
I just talk of the weather,
Simply because,
When I'm with you, I never
Can say what I'm longing to say.

. . . or this from *Oh, Boy!* of the same year, as the young lovers look back on what they've missed:

I was often kissed 'neath the mistletoe
By small boys excited with tea.
If I'd known that you existed
I'd have scratched them and resisted,
    dear,
But I never knew about you, oh, the
    pain of it,
And you never knew about me.

The other string to Wodehouse's bow, of course, was his comedy material, which can obviously be traced back to William Schenk Gilbert but—just as relevantly—forward to Porter and Coward. It could reasonably be claimed that Wodehouse invented the "patter" song as it applied to the stage musical, adapting the music hall "turn" to the requirements of a given comic character in the plot.

A particular favorite was the comic burglar and, starting with his very first performed song, "Put Me In My Little Cell," he is constantly extolling the supposed domestic joys of prison life.

Another was the historical pseudo-biography, promoting the merits of "Napoleon," "Sir Galahad," "Joan of Arc," "Julius Caesar" or "Cleopatterer." Listening to these you are hearing anticipatory echoes of what Porter would come up with in "Solomon" or Coward in "Josephine."

> Napoleon was a homely gink,
> He hadn't time to doll up,
> But though he looked like thirty cents,
> He packed an awful wallop.
> And all the kings of Europe,
> When they came to know his habits,
> Pulled up their socks and ran for blocks,
> He got them scared like rabbits.

There are other themes to which Wodehouse returns again and again—just as there are in his fiction. One of them is the Battle of the Sexes.

In almost all the shows, although hero and heroine—after the obligatory misunderstanding—end up in fond embrace, there is likely to be one of the comic characters bemoaning the fact that women are predators and marriage a snare and a delusion. From *Oh, Lady! Lady!!* (1918):

> It's a hard, hard world for a man
> For he tries to be wise and remain aloof
>   and chilly,
> But along comes something feminine
>   and frilly,
> So what's the use?
>
> Though long you've been a gay and
>   giddy bachelor,
> There'll come on the scene a girl not
>   like the rest.
> You'll notice something in her eye that
>   fills you with dismay;
> You'll find that when you're with her
>   you can't think what to say.
> That's a sure, sure sign
> You have ceased to be a rover
> And your single days are over.
> You had best begin rehearsing
> For the better-and-the-worsing . . .

. . . or from *The Girl Behind the Gun* (1918):

> But women haven't any sense of pity
> For, if they had, the bride would stop
>   and think,

She'd say: "Why should I marry this
    poor fathead?
What have I got against the wretched
    gink?"
But no! She fills the church with her
    relations,
Who would grab him by the coat tails if
    he ran;
All his pals have been soft-soaped,
And his best man he's been doped.
Women haven't any mercy on a man!

. . . from *Sitting Pretty* (1924):

For some girl's going to come and
    grab you
Sooner or late! Just wait! Yes, in a while
With frozen smile along the aisle you'll
    stagger –
That wedding cake will soon be sitting
    grimly
Upon the plate

. . . from *The Nightingale* (1927):

He bid goodbye to all his weeping
    friends,
Just gasps, "I will" and then the trap
    descends.
Poor thing, some girl has got him,
Poor lamb, he doesn't know.
He'll never get another chance to talk,
He's got it where the bottle gets the
    cork.
He looks up as he places on the ring,
All the choir boys start to sing,
Poor stiff, that's another one gone.

For the much-married Bolton, misogyny was to become a professional stock-in-trade, which often took on a bitter tone in later work. For Wodehouse, happily married to the same woman for over sixty years, it was presumably—like the mother-in-law joke—simply a good comic wheeze.

It has often occurred to me that writers of lyrics give more away about themselves than they perhaps realize—possibly because the constraints of the novel, essay or poem form are whatever the novelist, essayist or poet chooses them to be, whereas the lyricist is concentrating so hard on the disciplines of thirty-two bars of music and a handful of words which must fall into a certain pattern of rhythm and emphasis that he may lose a little personal 'editorial' control.

Coward, for instance, lets us see more of his "secret heart" in his lyrics than in any of his overt but carefully-edited autobiographical writing. Wodehouse does something similar. It is strange to see the man who never lets the purple of passion, let alone sex, sully so much as one of many thousands of his pages of fiction writing lyrically—and often movingly—of what it feels like to be in love. Even stranger, poking knowing fun at sexual mores in a song such as "Polly Believed In Preparedness" or "Saturday Night," it's easy to argue that he was merely playing with an established conventional form of song, just as one might parody Chaucer or create a new limerick, once one knew the literary formula to follow. Nonetheless, it gives one to wonder whether Wodehouse was quite the *parfait gentil* knight he would have us believe . . . or whether he was not in his public persona—as John Osborne said of Coward—his own finest creation.

In 1954 Wodehouse gave us his own account of his years in the theatre. It was called *Bring On The Girls* and it was ostensibly a collaboration with his old sparring partner, Guy Bolton, although it reads like pure Wodehouse. Of Bolton he wrote later that they had done "twenty-three shows together and met every freak that ever squeaked and gibbered along the Great White Way."

Many of them do their squeaking and gibbering in this autobiographical narrative that takes their story up to 1934, but a word of warning is needed here . . .

These are recollections in the relative tranquility of twenty years later and—like the later published letters—"edited" for posterity. As Wodehouse suggested to Bolton in 1946 prior to writing the book:

I think we shall have to let truth go to the wall if it interferes with entertainment. And we must sternly repress any story that hasn't a snapper at the finish. . . . That is what

we want to avoid in this book—shoving in stuff just because it happened. Even if we have to invent every line of the thing, we must have entertainment.

We must shove in every possible "of those times" descriptions we can think of. This will be up to you, as I am so constituted that I never notice what is going on around me and, if asked, would say that there have been no changes in New York since 1916.

Later (1952), he would add:

Brooding over the book, I believe we ought to carry on aziz to end on *Oh, Boy!* tour and then transpose *Oh, My Dear!* And *Oh, Lady! Lady!!*, so as to make *Oh, Lady! Lady!!* come after *Oh, My Dear!* I want to get *Oh, My Dear!*, *Kitty Darlin'*, *Miss 1917* . . . and *Rose of China* into one year. We shall thus get a funny "failure" chapter, which will take the curse off the monotonous run of successes. Then we can get the happy ending by having *Oh, Lady! Lady!!* and *Leave It To Jane* come after this bunch of flops.

Why not end the book with the crash of 1929 and show us both cleaned out? We discuss the situation and feel that we must face it bravely. You tell me the *Going Greek* plot . . . and we end the book with you writing on a blank sheet of paper:

GOING GREEK
Book by Guy Bolton,
Lyrics by P. G. Wodehouse

And after publication he would write to his friend Denis Mackail:

> It's an odd book. Of course, the things we say happened to us didn't really but they did happen to somebody and are all quite true. . . . Anyway, we have avoided that awful "We opened in Phil. with the following cast—that sterling actor George Banks as the Prince . . ." which make theatrical reminiscences so boring.

But, then, we don't need to rely entirely on pseudo-autobiography, when we have the incidental truth of the novels and stories to tell us how Wodehouse *really* remembered The Great White Way . . . the norm above which he sought to rise. The observations are funny only because they are so patently true.

On the popular song:

> It was sure-fire, he said. The words . . . were gooey enough to hurt, and the tune reminded him of every other song-hit he had ever heard. There was, in Mr. Blumenthal's opinion, nothing to stop the thing selling a million copies.
> —*Quick Service* (1940)

The song itself was almost certainly of the "Back Home In Tennessee," "My Mammy," or "Sonny Boy" (1928) variety—the last of which Wodehouse used to devastating effect in "Jeeves and the

Song of Songs" (1929). In the earlier episodic novel *Indiscretions of Archie* (1921), he has an aspiring songwriter audition "It's A Long Way Back To Mother's Knee":

> One night a young man wandered
>   through the glitter of Broadway.
> His money he had squandered. For a
>   meal he couldn't pay.
> He thought about the village where his
>   boyhood he had spent,
> And yearned for all the simple joys with
>   which he'd been content.
> He looked upon the city, so frivolous
>   and gay,
> And, as he heaved a weary sigh, these
>   words he then did say:
>
> "It's a long way back to mother's knee,
>   mother's knee, mother's knee,
> It's a long way back to mother's knee,
> Where I used to stand and prattle
> With my teddy bear and rattle.
> Oh, those childhood days in Tennessee
> They sure look good to me!
> It's a long, long way back, but I'm gonna
>   start today!
> I'm going back,
> Believe me, oh,
> I'm going back,
> (I want to go,)
> Back—
> I'm going back on the seven-three
> To the dear old shack where I used
>   to be!
> I'm going back to my mother's knee."

He went back to his mother on the
    train that very day:
He knew there was no other who could
    make him bright and gay:
He kissed her on the forehead and he
    whispered, "I've come home!"
He told her he was never going any
    more to roam.
And onward through the happy years,
    till he grew old and grey,
He never once regretted those brave
    words he once did say:
"It's a long way back to mother's
    knee . . . etc."

Then there was the question of the
plot. The show will almost certainly be
called *The (Something) Girl* or possibly
The Girl From (Somewhere). Supposing,
for the sake of argument, it was *The Girl
From Brighton*:

> The situation was as follows: the
> hero, having been disinherited by his
> wealthy and titled father for falling
> in love with the heroine, a poor
> shop-girl, has disguised himself
> (by wearing a different colored
> neck-tie), and has come in pursuit
> of her to a well-known seaside
> resort, where, having disguised her-
> self by changing her dress, she is
> serving as a waitress in the Rotunda,
> on the Esplanade. The family butler,
> disguised as a Bath-chair man, has
> followed the hero, and the wealthy
> and titled father, disguised as an

Italian opera singer, has come to the
place for a reason which, though
extremely sound, for the moment
eludes the memory. Anyhow, he is
there, and they all meet on the
Esplanade. Each recognizes the
other, but thinks himself unrecog-
nized. Exeunt all, hurriedly, leaving
the heroine alone on the stage. It is
a crisis in the heroine's life. She
meets it bravely. She sings a song
entitled 'My Honolulu Queen,'
with chorus of Japanese girls and
Bulgarian officers."

       —"Bill the Bloodhound" from
       The Man With Two Left Feet (1917)

I should perhaps mention one further idiosyncrasy that makes attribution
of song to show a little more complex
than usual.

It's by no means unusual for a
show to undergo revisions during its
lifetime—in try-out, during the run,
on tour—but the Wodehouse-Bolton
shows have an added dimension of
complexity to them.

In later years a restless Guy Bolton
was constantly nudging Wodehouse to
see if there was the possibility of one
or other of their old hits being revived.
Leave It To Jane and *Oh, Kay!* were
indeed brought back during their
joint lifetimes.

But even after Wodehouse's death
there was to be another round of

re-writing. Bolton's papers contain multiple versions of such shows as *Oh, Lady! Lady!!* and *Oh, My Dear!*, for instance, in which the plots differ significantly from the original. Sometimes new characters are added and in one case the score has been rearranged, so that it now includes hit songs from several of the other shows. To complicate matters even further, most of these versions are undated!

To save on endless footnotes and cross-references, I have worked from what appears to be the "core" version and then appended the songs that were used somewhere in the show's original run. Where there are significant variations in different versions of a lyric, I have included them, but where the change involved only the occasional word, I have usually omitted the variation for the sake of readability. For the same reason, where different versions of the song have variations in the way the lines break, I have settled for what seems more sensible to me. I have also used punctuation that makes for easier reading. If that gives the purist reason to swing the occasional lead pipe—so be it.

With that in mind, let us begin. . . .

MISCELLANEOUS SONGS

(1904-1915)

There is no hard evidence that would date P. G. Wodehouse's first attempt at lyric writing. A friend of his, one Kenneth Duffield, claimed that it was when Wodehouse once visited him up at Cambridge and wrote:

MY GRASSY CORNER GIRL (QUEEN)

She's my Grassy Corner Girl,
Shy and sweet.
And my heart is in a whirl
When we meet.
Just we two in my canoe,
With none to come between;
But we're never quite alone,
We've Cupid for our Chaperone.
She's my little Grassy Corner Queen.

(It has been claimed that it was subsequently used in *The Hon'ary Degree* at the New Theatre, Cambridge, in June 1907, but the libretto of the show in the British Library does not include it.)

SERGEANT BRUE (1904)

A Musical Farce

Presented by Frank Curzon at the Strand Theatre, London, in June 1904 and subsequently transferred to the Prince of Wales Theatre (152 performances).

BOOK
Owen Hall

LYRICS
J. Hickory Wood

MUSIC
Liza Lehmann

The play was also presented by Charles B. Dillingham at the Knickerbocker Theatre, New York, on April 24, 1905.

STAGE DIRECTOR
Herbert Gresham

MUSICAL DIRECTOR
Watty Hydes

ROYAL STRAND THEATRE.

Sole Proprietor & Manager ... ... Mr. FRANK CURZON

EVERY EVENING at 8.
Mr. FRANK CURZON'S COMPANY
IN
"SERGEANT BRUE"
(Of the "C" Division.)
A Musical Farce by OWEN HALL.

Music by Madame LIZA LEHMANN.　　　Lyrics by J. HICKORY WOOD.

Sergeant Brue	(of the "C" Division)	...	Mr. WILLIE EDOUIN
Michael Brue	(his Son)	...	Mr. FARREN SOUTAR
Aurora Brue ...	(his Daughter)	...	Miss ALICE HOLLANDER
Daisy	(Servant)	...	Miss JESSICA LAIT
Mabel Widgett ...			Miss NINA WOOD
Vivienne Russell ...			Miss NELLIE SEYMOUR
Louise Clair	...	...	Miss KITTY ASHMEAD
Eva Graham	...	...	Miss DOROTHY DREW
'Arriet ...			Miss VALÉRIE de LACY
Gerald Treherne ...	...	...	Mr. ARTHUR APPLEBY
Matthew Habishom	... (a Solicitor) ...		Mr. EDWARD KIPLING
Inspector Gorringe	... . (of the "C" Division)		Mr. DONALD DALMUIR
Mr. Lambe ...			Mr. PEET LESLIE
Erskine Murray ...	... ...	...	Mr. HARRY LAMBART
Captain Bay ...			Mr. MICHAEL SANTLEY
Mr. Crank ...	(Magistrate at Crawlborough Street)		Mr. FRED LACEBY
Crookie Scrubbs ...	(a Criminal)		Mr. ARTHUR WILLIAMS
Lady Bickenhall ...			Miss MILLIE LEGARDE

Other Characters by Mesdames Violet Lorraine, Zilla Gray, Phyllis Allen, Hellen Holland, Ethel Wilson, Lillie Maxwell, Clara Dow, Kitty Rawlinson, &c. Messrs. G. Franklin, H. Warren, Leslie Gaze & Cecil Kingsley.

ACT I.	...	...	...	Michael Brue's Hairdressing Saloons
		(Three Months Elapse).		
ACT II. ...	...	...	...	The Green Park Hotel
ACT III. Scene 1.		...	Crawlborough Street Police Court
Scene 2.		...	...	75, Berkeley Square

The Scenery by JULIAN HICKS.
There will be 10 minutes interval between the 1st & 2nd Acts, and 5 minutes between 2nd & 3rd Acts.

Musical Director	...	...	...	...	Mr. FREDERICK ROSSE
Stage Manager ...	...	...	...	...	Mr. J. B. WATSON
Assistant Stage Manager				...	Mr. E. SHALE

The Music of "Sergeant Brue" is published by HOPWOOD & CREW, Ltd., New Bond Street, W.
"So did Eve" is published by FRANCIS, DAY & HUNTER, Charing Cross Road, W.C.
Dresses by "VIOLA," 27, Albemarle Street, W.
Millinery by VIOLETTE, 4, Lower Seymour Street, W.　　Men's Costumes by MORRIS ANGEL & SONS.
Wigs by CLARKSON.　　The Furniture and Upholstery by JAMES S. LYONS.
Floral Decorations by M. GUGGENHEIM, 305, Goswell Road.
The Pictures in the Theatre lent by SAMUEL COOMBES, "The Old Picture Shop," 175, Strand.

MATINEE EVERY WEDNESDAY and SATURDAY at 2.15.

PRICES—Private Boxes, £2 2s. and £3 3s.　　Stalls, 10s. 6d.　　Dress Circle, First Two Rows, 7s. 6d.; other Rows, 6s.　　Upper Circle, 4s.　　Pit, 2s. 6d.　　Gallery, 1s.
BOX OFFICE (Mr. H. FRY) OPEN 10 to 10.　　Telephone, 1791 Gerrard.
Doors Open at 7.30.　　Commence at 8.

Business Manager	...	...	...	...	Mr. SEYMOUR HODGES

Extract from the Rules made by the Lord Chamberlain:—(1) The name of the actual and responsible Manager of the Theatre must be printed on every play bill. (2) The public can leave the Theatre at the end of the performance by all exit and entrance doors, which must open outwards. (3) Where there is a fire-proof screen to the proscenium opening, it must be lowered at least once during every performance, to ensure its being in proper working order. (4) Smoking is not permitted in the auditorium. (5) All gangways, passages and staircases must be kept free from chairs or any other obstructions, whether permanent or temporary.

SYNOPSIS

Sergeant Samson Brue of 'C' Division is a policeman of no more than average intelligence. His son, Michael, has a barber's shop, his daughter Aurora is a nurse and the Sergeant himself wishes himself rich and fantasizes about Lady Bickenhall, an unattainable Goddess beyond the reach of normal policemen.

Whilst celebrating his 43rd birthday with his children a solicitor arrives with the news that Brue is heir to a fortune worth about £10,000 a year (in 1904 money), left by his brother Benjamin, who went to the colonies and made good. The only fly in the otherwise unsullied ointment is that he will never get the capital unless he becomes an Inspector.

He becomes friendly with a notorious jail-bird, "Crookie" Scrubbs who, having been caught with his hand in the barber-shop till, volunteers to help Brue become an Inspector, and immediately becomes responsible for most of the Sergeant's mishaps. In trying to assist him to an important capture of burglars, for example, he merely causes the arrest and appearance in court of the unfortunate policeman.

Lady Bickenhall, aware that she will only get to share Brue's fortune if the required promotion is secured, compromises her position and her evidence enables him to escape the charge. The magistrate, releasing Brue, nevertheless expresses the hope that he will be dismissed from the force. Lady B contrives that a gambling party be held on Brue's own premises in Berkeley Square, and that he shall lead the raiding party. Amongst the players round the gaming table he finds the very magistrate before whom he had appeared on the charge of burglary and the Home Office civil servant with whom he was in cahoots.

What we do know is that his first lyric to be performed on the professional stage was in this "musical farce" and was a parody of a well known song, "Put Me In My Little Cell." The program credits the music to Madame Liza Lehmann and the lyrics to J. Hickory Wood (a name worthy of a Wodehouse character). Wodehouse was asked to contribute an additional lyric by actor/manager Owen Hall, for which he received the somewhat garbled credit of "G. E. Wodehouse" on the published sheet music. Despite that, he confided to his diary: "Encored both times. Audience laughed several times during each verse. This is fame."

It is impossible to say precisely where the lyric fitted into the plot, since the song was not included in the published score (1904) or the libretto. It was presumably added to the show later in its run, when it was sung by a Mr. T. A. Shale, who does not feature in the program. When the show transferred later in the year Mr. Shale is mentioned under "Other characters played by. . . ." All that is known is that the song was copyrighted in 1905.

The theme of the song—the joys of prison life to the habitual prisoner—was to become a recurrent one in his later work. "Dear Old Prison Days" (*Oh, Lady! Lady!!*), "We're Crooks" (*Miss 1917*), "Dartmoor Days" (*The Golden Moth*), "Tulip Time in Sing-Sing," and "Dear Old-Fashioned Prison of Mine" (*Sitting Pretty*) being variations on the same theme.

The comic aspect of criminal life remained a constant element of a Wodehouse plot on both stage and page. A high percentage of the stories and libretti were to feature a comic burglar—and occasionally a larcenous couple, such as Chimp Twist, Spike Mullins, Spink, Phipps and Soapy and Dolly Molloy, Soapy Sid, Aileen Peavey and Eddie Cootes. And all of this at least twenty years before Damon Runyon . . .

PUT ME IN MY LITTLE CELL

(Crookie Scrubbs)

1.

When you've got to earn your living with your
    fingers,
When you're looking out for someone to garrote,
Then the memory of prison somehow lingers
Where you get your morning cocoa piping hot,
Where you didn't have to pay for board and
    lodging,
Where your meals were always ready on the nail,
When in Bow or Piccadilly Little Mary aches
    for skilly
Then you miss the quiet comfort of a gaol.

Put me in my little cell.
Rock me off to sleep.
Leave a warder watching at the door.

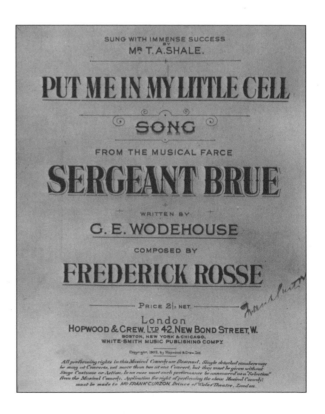

Leave, oh leave a warder.
Call me in the morning,
Bring me breakfast while I wait,
As you used to do when I was "in" before,
When I was "in" before.

2.

There are pleasant little spots my heart is
    fixed on,
Down at Parkhurst or at Portland on the sea.
And some put up at Holloway and Brixton
But—Pentonville is good enough for me.
And Dartmoor is so breezy and romantic
That you're sorry when they let you out
    on bail,
When you've worked till you are droppin'
From a week or two of hoppin'
Then you miss the quiet comforts of a gaol.

Put me in my little cell
Do not make a noise
If, oh if you want me,
If you want me, knock upon the door.
Let my days be sweetened
With a round of honest toil
As they used to be when I was "in" before,
When I was "in" before.

3.

Down at Wormwood Scrubbs the air's a bit
    relaxin',
So they feed you up on chicken broth and tea.
And the Chaplain or the Doctor for the axin'
Will advise a little sojourn by the sea.
When you find that breaking stones is not the
    proper
Sort of task for one whose health is on the fail,
When they start you making boots for
Some poor copper who has cause to
Curse the day he helped to clap you into gaol.

Put me in my little cell
Let my job be soft,
Tell, oh tell the guv'nor that,

My heart with grief and pain is tore.
Say it's all a blunder
That I'm not the chap they want,
But I'm like a bloke that once was "in"
    before,
That once was "in" before.

Even though Wodehouse only contributed
the one song, he was clearly impressed by
another number called "Under A Panama,"
which contains the lines:

> Bill says to Lu, "Think how happy
>   we'd be,
> Down by the Congo;
> We'd live on love 'neath a bamboo
>   tree" —
> Lulu replies, "Not me!"

The theme of primitive love was to recur several
times later in songs such as "Desert Island"
(*See You Later* 1918) and "Bongo On the Congo"
(*Sitting Pretty* 1924).

THE BEAUTY OF BATH (1906)

Presented by Charles Frohman with Seymour Hicks and Ellaline Terriss at the Aldwych Theatre, London, on March 19, 1906, and transferred to the Hicks Theatre (subsequently renamed the Globe) in December 1906 (287 performances).

BOOK　　Seymour Hicks and Cosmo Hamilton
LYRICS　　Chas. H. Taylor
MUSIC　　Herbert E. Haines

SYNOPSIS

It's the end of the first act on the first night of a new play at the Mascot Theatre. The audience includes Sir Timothy Bun and his Lady, together with their twelve adopted daughters, the 'Bath Buns'; Lord Quorn and his fiancée, Truly St. Cyr, the actress; the widow, Mrs. Alington; Viscount Bellingham and his daughter, the Hon. Betty Silverthorne. Betty falls violently in love with the star, Alan Beverley, to the disgust of her father.

Some time earlier, Mrs. Alington had sent a photograph of Betty to her sailor son Dick (Lieut. Richard Alingham), who has more than a passing physical resemblance to Mr. Beverley, and Dick had fallen in love with the photograph. He arrives home that evening, rushes to the theatre and meets his mother and Betty. Since in the play Mr. Beverley was also wearing sailors' clothes, Betty assumes Dick to be Beverley.

Meanwhile Lord Belllingham, who has also met Dick, assumes him to be the actor and seeks to cure what he believes to be his daughter's infatuation by inviting Dick (as Beverley) to a ball the following night at Bellingham House, on condition that he insult Betty in return for a huge fee. Dick, of course, is only too happy to promise that Betty should be discouraged from speaking to actors. Others invited to the ball are the Bath Buns, Mrs. Alington and Beverley (as Dick Alington) and Beverley's girl, Dorothy.

When Dick (as Beverley) arrived at the ball he was introduced to the various guests, and then admitted he very seldom went into Society. Keeping his word, he creates a terrible disturbance, but Betty is too clever to be taken in. Not only had she realized the similarity between the two men but she had seen through her father's plot as well. Betty was quite happy with her Dick and, since Beverley already had a sweetheart of his own, it may be assumed that he was happy with the outcome as well. "The Frolic of A Breeze" was the last major song, reflecting the fact that not only Betty and Dick but Alan Beverley and his Dorothy, and Lord Quorn and his actress Truly had all passed through troubled waters to reach a rather calmer path to the altar.

THE ALDWYCH THEATRE.

| Proprietor | .. | .. | .. | " | .. | .. | SEYMOUR HICKS. |
| Sole Lessee & Manager | .. | .. | .. | .. | .. | | CHARLES FROHMAN. |

Licensed by the Lord Chamberlain to Charles Frohman, Aldwych Theatre, Aldwych, W.C.

TO-NIGHT AND EVERY EVENING at 8. MATINEE SATURDAY at 2.

CHARLES FROHMAN presents

ELLALINE TERRISS & SEYMOUR HICKS

IN A NEW MUSICAL PLAY BY

SEYMOUR HICKS and COSMO HAMILTON.

Lyrics by CHAS. H. TAYLOR.   Music by HERBERT E. HAINES.

"THE BEAUTY OF BATH."

◆

Lieut. Richard Alington, R.N	.. .. ..	..	SEYMOUR HICKS
Viscount Bellingham	.. .. ..	..	WILLIAM LUGG
Lord Quorn	.. .. (Betty's Cousin)	..	LAURENCE CAIRD
Mr. Beverley..	.. .. .. (an Actor)..		STANLEY BRETT
Sir Timothy Bun	.. .. (of Bath)..	..	.. MURRAY KING
Hon. Mortimer Gorst	.. ..	..	CECIL KINNAIRD
Tattersal Spink	.. ..	..	.. BERT SINDEN
Hon. Charles Templeton ..	.. .. ..		REGINALD KENNETH
The Earl of Orpington	.. ..	..	E. W. ROYCE
Lemon Goodge (Programme Boy at the Mascot Theatre)			MASTER VALCHERA
Mrs. Alington	.. (Alington's Mother)	..	ROSINA FILIPPI
Hon. Dorothy Quorn	.. (Quorn's Sister)	..	BARBARA DEANE
Miss Truly St. Cyr ..	.. (an Actress)	..	MAUDI DARRELL
Mrs. Goodge (in service at Bellingham House)			SYDNEY FAIRBROTHER
Lady Bun	.. .. ..(Sir Timothy's Wife)	..	MOLLIE LOWELL
The Countess of Orpington (née Amelia van Paulk)	..		VERA MORRIS
The Comtesse Therese Rosemere	.. ..	..	RENEE DE MONTEL
Lady Delbeck	.. ..	..	MARGUERITE LESLIE
Countess of Chandon ..	.. ..	..	GEORGIE READ
Jane Topit	.. .. .. (Betty's Maid) ..	..	TOPSY SINDEN

Hot Bun	..	.. ..	..MAY GATES
Iced Bun	..	.. ..	.. LILLIE McINTYRE
Spice Bun	..	..	.. KITTY MELROSE
Plum Bun	..	..	CLAIRE RICKARDS
Rice Bun	..	..	.. HILDA HARRIS
Crumb Bun	..	..	MARION LINDSAY
Penny Bun	..	The twelve Bath Buns ..	PAULINE FRANCIS
Youngest Bun ..		..	AGNES HODGKINSON
Currant Bun	..	..	ENID LESLIE
Cross Bun	..	..	.. MABEL WATSON
Seed Bun	..	..	MABEL ELLIS
Home Made Bun		.. ..	.. ELSIE KAY

AND

The Hon. Betty Silverthorne (The Beauty of Bath)   ELLALINE TERRISS

Solo Dances in Act II. by TOPSY SINDEN and BERT SINDEN.

ACT I. The Foyer of the Mascot Theatre, London (ON A FIRST NIGHT).
ACT II. The Ball Room at Bellingham House, London (NEXT EVENING).

Scenery by WALTER HANN.

The Play produced by SEYMOUR HICKS.

The Dances and Choral Effects arranged by EDWARD ROYCE.

Miss Ellaline Terriss' dresses designed and the 'Picture' and other costumes of Act II. arranged and supervised by WILHELM.

Dresses executed by Miss FISHER, B. J. SIMMONS & Co., and MORRIS ANGEL & SON. Dresses in Act I. by Mdme. HERBERT. Miss Ellaline Terriss' 1st Act dress and cloak made by "LUCILLE," Hanover Square, W.

Electrical effects by T. J. DIGBY.

Wigs by W. CLARKSON.   Gloves by BARNARD'S.

Jet Ornaments by CHAS. PACKER & Co.

Jewellery by R. WHITE & SON.   Furniture by WOLFE & HOLLANDER.

The music published by HOPWOOD & CREW, Ltd., 42, New Bond Street, London, W.

MATINEE EVERY SATURDAY at 2.

| Stage Director | ... | ... | ... | ... | ... | EDWARD ROYCE |
| Musical Director | | | | | | KARL KIEFERT |

General Manager .. (For Charles Frohman) .. **W. LESTOCQ.**

PRICES : Private Boxes £4 4s., £2 2s. and £1 11s. 6d. Stalls, 10s. 6d. Balcony, 7s. 6d., 6s. and 5s. Upper Circle, 5s. and 4s. Pit, 2s. 6d. Gallery, 1s.

Telephone 2315 Gerrard.

Business Manager .. .. .. **OSCAR BARRETT, Junr.**

Extract from Rules made by the Lord Chamberlain.—1. The name of the actual and responsible Manager of the Theatre must be printed on every play-bill. 2. The Public can leave the Theatre at the end of each performance by all exit and entrance Doors, which must open outwards. 3. Where there is a fire-proof screen to the proscenium opening, it must be lowered at least once during every performance, to ensure its being in proper working order. 4. Smoking is not permitted in the Auditorium. 5. All gangways, passages, and staircases must be kept free from chairs, or any other obstructions whether permanent or temporary.

It was to be two years after *Sergeant Brue* before Wodehouse found the first real sign of the fame he had been ironically proclaiming to his diary.

Seymour Hicks (1871–1941) was well established on the London stage as a light comedian and sometime playwright and impresario, usually in partnership with his wife and co-star, Ellaline Terriss (1871–1971). In 1906 he was to appear in his own collaboration with Cosmo Hamilton, *The Beauty of Bath*, supervised by the anglophile American producer Charles Frohman (1861–1915).

Another new member of the Frohman-Hicks team was the young American composer Jerome D. Kern (1885–1945). For the past couple of years he had been mastering the art of "interpolation." A producer—such as Alfred Butt or George Edwardes (1852–1915)—would commission a show, then hire other song writers to add individual songs to strengthen it. By 1905 Kern was under a three-year contract to Frohman to produce a dozen songs a year and *The Beauty of Bath* was one of his routine assignments. "Dr. Tinkle-Tinker" (as he was called) was to work with a young humorist called Wodehouse, who was employed as a newspaper columnist and also turning out literate light verse six times a week on a variety of topics.

For "Oh, Mr. Chamberlain"—a satire on Joseph Chamberlain's tariff protection policies—they shared the lyrical credit. The song was, in fact, a revised version of a number used in the previous year's *Catch Of The Season*. Kern had written a number of lyrics of his own in these early years before leaving that particular chore to others. (During his career he was said to have collaborated with over seventy different lyricists.)

With a political incorrectness that persisted throughout his career, he positively disliked the universally admired Gilbert & Sullivan. ("They are so monotonous . . . saccharine and tinkling.")

Hicks himself sang their first number, which Wodehouse recalled as being "a pretty poor effort all round, but Jerry's melody was so terrific that the number used to get six or seven encores every night and I spent most of the next year writing encore verses"—for which Hicks paid him £2 a week for the rest of the show's run. (His diary of professional earnings for January 1906 shows he received £2 for a lyric in *The Catch of the Season*, a musical comedy, but no further details are recorded.)

By his own account he worked for Hicks—first at the Aldwych, then at the Hicks when it opened in December 1906—until December of the following year. At that point he moved to join George Edwardes at the Gaiety, where the long running *Girls of Gottenberg* was in preparation.

OH, MR. CHAMBERLAIN!

(Lyrics by P. G. Wodehouse and Jerome Kerns)

(Music by Jerome Kern)

1.
Who is the man who's got a hand in ev'rything
    you see?
Who is the man whose name you hear wherever
    you may be?
He's in the papers ev'ry day as doing this or that;
Last week, one learns, he gave John Burns a
    brand new bowler hat.

Chorus:
It's Mister Chamberlain, it's Joey Chamberlain
He's in the air no matter where you chance to go
He's Alfred Austin's "ghost" and writes *The
    Winning Post*!
Did our Brum Chum, popular, perky Joe.

2.
Wherever you go you'll find the name is ringing
    in your head.

You think of it at breakfast, and
    you dream of it in bed,
And clergymen at weddings,
    very often, so they say,
Are heard to ask the bride if she
    will honour and obey.

Chorus:
Our Mister Chamberlain, our Joey
    Chamberlain,
He's in the air no matter where
    you chance to go.
He runs the Times Book Shop and
    invented Maizy-pop,
Did our Brum Chum, popular
    perky Joe.

3.
He plays for Aston Villa just by
    way of keeping fit,
He runs the mile in four-fifteen
    and wrestles Hackenschmidt,
He sleeps a couple of hours a
    week, and works right round
    the clock,
He wrote *The Master Christian*
    and *Oh! Stop Your Tickling,
    Jock!*

Chorus:
Did Mr. Chamberlain, our Joey
    Chamberlain,
He makes things buzz whatever he does;
    he's never slow.
The clever man today who'll make Mister
    Horner pay
Is our Brum Chum, popular, perky Joe

The second song from the show was also a
    revised version of a song from *Catch of the
Season* (1905).

Miss ELLALINE TERRISS.

THE PLAY PICTORIAL
The BEAUTY OF BATH
No. 45 Vol. 7
WITH WHICH ARE INCORPORATED 'THE PLAY' 'THE PLAY-SOUVENIR' 'THE STAGE SOUVENIR'
MONTHLY 6D NET
[This Journal is supplied to the Trade on terms which do not allow of any discount on the published price.]

THE FROLIC OF A BREEZE

Lyrics by P. G. Wodehouse
and F. Clifford Harris

Music by Jerome Kern

1.
There was once a breeze from over the seas
Came travelling to London for a lark
And as it blew, there came in view
An unemploy'd procession in the Park.
He watch'd them march to the Marble Arch,
And puffing unexpectedly he grinn'd:

"Here's a job," said he, "It seems for me,
They are wanting someone here to raise the
    wind!"

Oh, whee up! The wayward wind was blowing
With a vigour that was owing
To its generous anxiety to please,
But the men forgot their manners
When it blew away their banners,
And they said a lot of things about the breeze
Quite a lot of snappy things about the breeze!

2.

A motor raced at a fearful pace
Beyond the speed permitted by the law;
And dogs in rows turned up their toes,
And chickens got hysterics by the score
But an eagle eye was there to spy,
And a watch had timed the chauffeur in his
    course,
For behind a tree stood X twenty-three
The most energetic liar in the Force.

Oh, whee up! The wayward wind was blowing,
Like the wind the car was going,
And police traps had been placed behind the
    trees,
But in court next day the chauffeur
Said "I couldn't drive her slow. For
I was blown along too quickly by the breeze,
Blown at eighty miles an hour by the breeze!"

3.

A steamship roll'd in the river cold
And it didn't seem to know which way to go;
It was drawing near to bump the pier
When suddenly the breeze began to blow,
The vessel heel'd, a passenger reel'd
And fell into the water on the spot,
"Hi, save that man," yelled the skipper, "if you can,
He's the only blooming passenger we've got."

Oh, whee up! The wayward wind was blowing
And the weather look'd like snowing,

And the water was at forty-two degrees,
But he answer'd with a shiver
I feel safer in the river,
Than aboard a penny steamer in the breeze,
On a County Council steamer in the breeze!

"The Frolic of A Breeze" was duly published
in the vocal score but the show's libretto
in the British Library includes another lyric
bearing Wodehouse's initials, which does not
appear to have been used, but since Wodehouse
and Kern were reported to have produced *three*
songs, this was presumably the third.

BEHIND THE SCENES

When the curtain has descended,
And the comedy is ended,
And the audience to their homes have gone away,
I hate to feel it's finished
For my interest's undiminished
In the doings of the people in the play.
Is the hero still as winning as he was at the
    beginning?
Does the heroine continue to attract?
Is the villain still a nuisance
With his plotting and his sinning
When none of them have really got to act?

Oh, to peep behind the scenes!
Is there trouble till the hero intervenes?
Are her eyes like 'stars in Heaven'

After twenty past eleven?
Oh, I wish I had a peep behind the scenes.

There were once two politicians,
Both in very high positions
And they somehow couldn't manage to agree.
Till, after consultation inner,
Said the one, "Well, come to dinner
And talk it over quietly with me."
But there's nobody who knows if
Arthur spoke his mind to Joseph

Or if Manchester he mentioned by
    the way.
And his views on Mr. Horridge
I would willingly disclose, if
I had only heard what he had got to say.

Oh, to peep behind the scenes.
Do you think they talked about the
    might-have-beens?
Or, when they were left together
Did they just discuss the weather?
Oh, I wish I'd had a peep behind
    the scenes.

We read in all the papers
Of the County Council's capers,
When they went across to France the
    other day,
How, when travelling though the city,
If a girl they met was pretty,
They would kiss her—in a diplomatic
    way.
And each gay and gallant rover
Was undoubtedly in clover;
But what nobody can throw a
    light upon
Is how *did* their wives receive them
When they came again to Dover,
And met them at the station later on?

Oh, to peep behind the scenes!
Were they told to tell their tales to the Marines?
Did they feel that little use is
To be had from lame excuses?
Oh, I *wish* I could have seen behind the scenes!

THE FROLIC OF THE BREEZE.

The Names of the
ladies are the Misses—

STANDEN, LESLIE,
CARTER, DAVISON,
STOREY, JAMES,
BORELLI, BATEMAN
and LAWS.

A STEAMSHIP rolled in the river cold,
    And it didn't seem to know which way to go.
It was drawing near to bump the pier
    When suddenly the breeze began to blow ;
The vessel heeled, a passenger reeled,
    And fell into the water on the spot.
"Hi, save that man," yelled the skipper,
    "If you can,
He's the only blooming passenger we've got !"

Oh, wee up ! the wayward wind was blowing,
And the weather looked like snowing,
And the water was at forty-two degrees.
But he answered, with a shiver,
"I feel safer in the river,
Than aboard a penny steamer in the breeze,
On a County Council Steamer in the breeze."

Tattersall Spink—MR. BERT SINDEN.

It would be another ten years before Wodehouse and Kern collaborated again but the foundations for their later ground-breaking relationship were now firmly in place.

Hicks clearly liked Wodehouse's work enough to ask him to contribute to two more shows the following year. By this time he was close friends with both Hicks and Terriss—a friendship that survived even the fact of his buying his first car, Hicks's exotic Darracq, and piloting it into a hedge on his maiden flight.

In an interview in the late 1940s Hicks recalled part of another Wodehouse lyric from one of those early shows of nearly fifty years before. It seems more than coincidental that it should have been called . . .

THE MOTOR CAR

What is the thing that helps to keep the
    population small?
What is it makes us run like hares and jump
    a six-foot wall?

What is it makes the skunk turn pale and feel
    that life is flat?
And murmur sadly, "What's the use, I can't
    compete with that?"
It is the motor-car, it is the motor-car,
If you exceed the legal speed you have
    to pay,
You get on very well, till it blows you
    up to—(BANG)

When you motor down to Brighton for
    the day.

Years later Terriss recalled that "he was always like a rather large boy, with an open and happy nature . . . and I should think he still remains the same."

As part of his apprenticeship with Hicks, Wodehouse worked on *My Darling* (1907).

MY DARLING (1907)

Presented by Seymour Hicks at the Hicks Theatre, London, on March 1, 1907 (61 performances).

BOOK   Seymour Hicks
LYRICS   Charles Taylor
             (Additional lyrics by Evelyn Baker and P. G. Wodehouse)
MUSIC   Herbert E. Haines

Although Wodehouse is not credited in the libretto in the British Library, there is internal evidence that he contributed to three songs—although the credit in each case goes to one "G. P. Wodehouse."

    The subject of the first was to become a recurring theme in later shows . . .

TO LIVE A SIMPLE LIFE (THE SIMPLE LIFE)

I have been told Society today
Is giving up high life and prodigal display
To let its taste be guided
Along the path provided
By Nature, long 'ere Adam found a wife.
So I've come here with expectations high
To note the way it makes the merry moments
    fly,
And hear the kind of laghter
That brings no headache after,
In point of fact, to seek the Simple Life.

What a most refreshing place the world is going
    to be
When we're back to Nature and the ways of
    Arcadee.
Eden without apple-trees, when all the world
    and wife,
With certain items up-to-date, can lead the
    Simple Life.

In the dear old days of long ago,
When ev'ry one you met was natural, you know,
For dress they did not care much,
And no one used to wear much,
Except perhaps a rabbit skin cut low,
And if you go to the Opera today,
You'll see in dress we are as natural as they.
An ancient Grecian Goddess
Would like the modern bodice
We're going back to Nature all the way.

What a most refreshing place the world is going
    to be,
When we are back to Nature and the ways of
    Arcadee.
Dress bills, now la Milo's come, will lead no
    more to strife
We'll need a coat of paint to live the Simple Life.

THE GLOW-WORM

In the wilds of Epping Forest, once a little glow-
   worm glowed
And he wanted to see London, but he didn't
   know the road;
So he asked a friendly Bunny, who said: "Right
   ahead! But note,
My father went there once and someone stole his
   overcoat,

And if you ask the ducks and geese and all the
   hens about you'll learn
That many people go to town, but none of them
   return."
Said the giddy little glow-worm: "I'm going there
   tonight,
And observation I'll avoid by switching off my
   light."

So the giddy giddy glow-worm
Took his little lantern down,
Found the batteries all right,
To the bunny said "Goodnight,"
And started off for London
Started off for London.
Started off for London Town.

To Parliament he went, and from the Strangers'
   Gallery,
He strained his little eyes, for there were lots of
   things to see;
The Members sat beneath in rows; and some of
   them were boys,
And sev'ral of the rest had on cloth caps and cor-
   duroys.
To these, he saw, the Premier was especially
   polite
If they looked cross at what he said, he got a
   nasty fright.
They did not catch the Speaker's Eye: but quite
   informally
Just whistled though their fingers, and
   exclaimed, "Here, what price me?"

And the giddy giddy glow-worm
Said, "If this is what they do,
I shouldn't care to be
An unfortunate M.P.
I would rather live inside the Zoo."

Repeat

Upon the Thames Embankment next the Glow-
   worm cast an eye;
He stopped and watched the steam-boats and
   the trams go rolling by
And he noticed with astonishment that ev'ry one
   that passed
Had always fewer passengers on board it than
   the last.
He asked a London sparrow if he knew how it
   was done,
And the sparrow answered promptly:
"It's like this, my dear old son.
As to why these trams were started, there has
   been a lot of talk,
But it's just because the Council's men have
   grown too fat to walk!"

And the giddy giddy glow-worm
Answered "Well, if that is so,
If they don't mind what they spend,
Where's their wasting going to end?
That's what ev'ry one would like to know"
Ev'ry one would like to know.

Repeat

CALICO

(Charles H. Taylor and G. P. Wodehouse)

Now Mary was apprenticed to a Draperee
At a shop in Upper Tooting
She daily measured calico for lingerie,
For the swells of Upper Tooting.
The terrible monotony so worked upon her head
She dreamt of doing nothing else when she went
   off to bed.

She sat up in her slumber, and mechanically said:
"Four and a half at seven three."

Oh, yes, she sat up in her sleep,
And most politely she would say,
White goods were selling very cheap,
And was there anything more today?
She did a rapid mental sum
And, trained by practice long,
Reached out a finger and a thumb
And another cotton sheet went . . .

Her little brother Willie had two maiden aunts
Dear old girls, and I've been told once
They set to work and made for him a pair of
    pants
From a pair of father's old ones.
They fitted him so tightly that he hadn't room
    to grow;
He wore then to a party and he feasted high
    and low;
The buttons held out pluckily, but something
    had to go;
When little Willie joined the dance.

Oh, yes, he joined in a quadrille,
For his dancing he was proud
All went on beautifully till
He to his partner turned and bowed.

Then came a period of gloom,
And people looked askance;
And all the talk of all the room
Was dear little Willie Watson's . . .

Now Mary's Cousin Annie was a laundry maid;
Daily scrubbed the clothes and wrung them.
Some funny games the breezes with the
    garments played,
When upon the line she hung them.
But Annie was a careless girl, and often made a
    mess,
By sending certain articles to quite the wrong
    address.
The consequent annoyance isn't easy to
    express;
But customers remarked Oh! . . .

Oh, yes, she hovered round the tub,
But couldn't recollect things long,
Nighties and other things she'd scrub,
Then send them home again all wrong.
Young men into the laundry rushed,
Demnding "What are these?"
Poor girl! She turned away and blushed
And she never said a word but . . .

The fruitful partnership with Hicks and
Terriss continued later that same year.

THE GAY GORDONS (1907)

A Play with Music

Presented by Seymour Hicks/Charles Frohman at the Aldwych Theatre, London, on September 11, 1907 (229 performances).

BOOK   Seymour Hicks
LYRICS   Arthur Wimperis, C. H. Bovill, P. G. Wodehouse, and Henry Hamilton
MUSIC   Guy Jones

CAST	
Seymour Hicks, Ellaline Terriss, Fred Emney,	Zena Dare, A. W. Baskcomb

SYNOPSIS

The scene is the Scottish Highlands on the day beloved of sportsmen, August 12. The shooting party from Melrose Castle includes Peggy Quainton, heiress to the American millionaire Andrew Quainton, occupier of the castle and owner of the shoot.

Peggy has original thoughts on the subject of marriage. Her wealth has tempted many suitors whom she has rejected. She wants to be loved for herself by an honest, handsome and brave man, who knows nothing of her position and prospects. In a moment of wild inspiration and girlish irresponsibility she changes places with Victoria Siddons, daughter of the peripatetic Punch and Judy show, who acts as "help" to widow Janet McCleod, tenant of the cottage.

Mrs. McCleod is in a state of suppressed excitement, for her foster-son, Angus Graeme, a private in the Highland Regiment, the Gay Gordons, is expected. Angus, clad in tartan and kilt, appears, and the first person he meets is Peggy in disguise. They are immediately attracted to each other. Peggy is delighted with her soldier and plays the part of "help" to perfection. Angus learns that she scorns titles and would on no account marry a man who had one.

Angus then learns from his foster-mother of the circumstances surrounding his birth, and the family solicitor Archibald Speedy (of Speedy, Wait & Shift in Edinburgh) arrives with papers conclusively proving his right to the Earldom of Melrose and its lands.

At the start of Act II Angus is disappointed to hear that the Punch and Judy caravan appears to have left, and assumes that Peggy has gone with them. He instructs Speedy to start giving away his newly discovered fortune, worth £150,000 per annum, which leads into the song "Now That My Ship's Come Home."

He then goes to meet Quainton at the castle and invites him to stay on with his family as Angus's guest. Quainton would be all in favor of his marrying Peggy and when a message reaches Angus identifying his girl as Quainton's daughter, the two of them plan to disguise his earldom from her until everything is settled.

They arrange for another Private from the regiment to take his place. When next Peggy and Angus meet, she reveals who she is and says that it is not deceit to pretend to be someone else if what you say is sincere—to love is to forgive. She tells Angus she loves him because he is just "You, You, You."

Victoria Siddons's father then lets the cat out of the bag as to Angus's identity. Peggy threatens to return to America, but on hearing from Angus that when he first wooed her he did not know he was an Earl, she relents and marries him after all.

NOW THAT MY SHIP'S COME HOME

Angus: I'm going to be a Brewster, spending thousands every day

Chorus: You've seen him in the play

Angus: I mean to chuck the stuff away,
I'll have my trousers and my coats
All warmly lined with ten pound
    notes;
And pals in need shall all be freed
From all financial cares.

Chorus: You'll find us on the stairs!

Angus: I'll settle all your cares.

Chorus: If you are going to
swim the Channel,

Angus: I'll provide your Bovril
    free.
If you are captured
    by Raisuli,
Simply drop a line
    to me.
I'll make everybody
    happy
From the Mile End
    Road to Rome,
I'll buy the earth and
    give it to Winston,

Chorus: Now that my ship's
come home.

Chorus: (Repeats)

Angus: The Servant's
Compensation Act is
certainly a bore

Chorus: A rotten kind of law!

Angus: We used to get on very well before,
If Jane or Mary slipped and fell,
We kissed the place to make it well;
But now they say we've got to pay
A lot of money too.

Chorus: We're feeling rather blue,

Angus: But I will see you through

Chorus: If your best butler on a sick bed,

Angus: Through smoking your cigars
should be,

If your head housemaid strains
    a tendon
While sitting on a policeman's knee,
If your new cook sings hymns and
Fractures her collar bone,
I'll pay the million or so that they'll
    fine you,

Chorus: Now that my ship's come home

Chorus: (Repeats) If your best butler . . .
    they'll fine you

Angus: For Mister Haldane I will buy some
    soldiers made of lead

Chorus: He'll like it if you do.

Angus: Some jokes for Mister Plowden, too,
    I'll buy a knighthood now, I'm rich
    For Marie Lloyd and Little Tich;
    And I shall stop the motorbus
    For making such a row.

Chorus: The smell's a nuisance too.

Angus: It's rather like the Zoo.

Chorus: I'll keep the House of Peers from
    starving,

Angus: When abolished by C.B.
    I'll bribe the German bands and
      organs
    Not to play the "Zuyder Zee"

THE NEW EARL ENTERTAINING HIS FRIENDS

Angus: "I will buy you everything you want, now that my ship's come home"

Seymour Hicks (*Angus Graeme*) and "friends."

Suffragettes shall have new faces,
Then they can sell their own.
I'll buy a new coat of paint for
      La Milo.

Chorus: Now that my ship's come home.

Chorus: (Repeats) I'll keep . . . come home

YOU, YOU, YOU

Peggy: The Perfect Man is a wonderful man,
He's tall and dark and dashing.
His hands and feet are small and neat,
His eyes are large and flashing.
With a long moustache, and curling
      lip,
And a chest so strong and massive;
And a chin like the ram of a
      battleship
He's stately and impassive.

Refrain: Well, nobody could call you that, dear;
And nobody could praise your eyes.
It wouldn't be the truth to say you're
      handsome,
For you wouldn't hope to win a
      beauty prize.
Then some might call you rather
      stumpy:
You're not the perfect man, it's true.
But I don't mind that. I love you, for
It's you, you, you.

The Perfect Man is a wonderful man,
His teeth are strong and pearly:
A giant mind is his combined
With hair that's crisp and curly.
He's of lofty rank; and his name
      one sees
As a leader of the Smart Set.

But a girl doesn't love just for things
      like these
The man on whom her heart's set.

Refrain: It's not because your feet are tiny,
It's not because your hair's so neat,
It's not because you never get
      excited,
And you never seem to suffer from
      the heat.
It's not because when you are
      worried,
You simply sit and smile and coo,
No! the reason that I love you is
It's you, you, you.

By now he was beginning to strike the writing balance that would carry him through the next two decades. Apart from his day job on the *Globe*, which he had started on an occasional basis in 1901, Wodehouse was producing a steady stream of the fiction that was to make his name with the general public. Since the turn of the century he had published a series of school stories—*The Pothunters* (1902), *A Prefect's Uncle* and *Tales of St. Austin's* (both 1903), *The Gold Bat* (1904) and *The Head of Kay's* (1905).

In 1906 he graduated into general fiction with *Love Among the Chickens* and the game, one might say, was afoot.

So—by 1909—was his career as one of the first of the transatlantic commuters. By now his work was being published in both countries, although England remained his true base of operations.

In 1914 he was offered the chance by an old *Globe* colleague, Charles Bovill, to collaborate on a revue for the prestigious Empire Theatre. The two had written lyrics for *The Gay Gordons* and felt their styles would coalesce. The result was *Nuts and Wine*, for which they wrote both lyrics and sketches. Since it is impossible at this date to determine precisely who wrote what, all material extant in the British Library text has been included. Despite generally enthusiastic reviews, the show was not a success, closing after only a few performances.

The experience, however, did teach Wodehouse one valuable lesson—the requirements of the hit or miss revue format called for a great deal of material, which the prolific Plum was happy to supply. Once again his name caused initial problems. The program insisted it was "G. P. Wodehouse," while the Lord Chamberlain's Office representative sent to license the show made matters worse by insisting that it was the work of "G. P. Woodhouse," while reporting that it was a "sprightly impudent revue, rather happy in its good-humoured chaff with the crazes of today."

THE
ALDWYCH THEATRE.

Sole Lessee and Manager   ...   .   CHARLES FROHMAN.

Licensed by the Lord Chamberlain to Charles Frohman, Aldwych Theatre, Aldwych, W.C.

WEDNESDAY EVENING, SEPTEMBER 11th, at 8,
CHARLES FROHMAN
PRESENTS
(SEYMOUR HICKS' Production)
ELLALINE TERRISS
AND
SEYMOUR HICKS
IN
"The Gay Gordons"
A Play with Music, in Two Acts.

Book by SEYMOUR HICKS.   Music by GUY JONES.

Lyrics by ARTHUR WIMPERIS, C. H. BOVILL, P. G. WODEHOUSE, and HENRY HAMILTON.

Angus Graeme...	SEYMOUR HICKS
Nervy Nat	FRED EMNEY
Edmund Siddons	A. W. BASKCOMB
Andrew Quainton	WILLIAM LUGG
John Smith	LAURENCE CAIRD
The Marquis of Dalesbury	CECIL KINNAIRD
Viscount Belstairs	KENNETH MACLAINE
Lord Elmington	ARTHUR ROYD
Lord Meilsham	MERVYN DENE
Archibald Speedy	J. C. BUCKSTONE
Corporal	WILL BISHOP
Janet McCleod...	ROSINA FILIPPI
Victoria Siddons	ZENA DARE
Charlotte Siddons	SIDNEY FAIRBROTHER
Mary McCleod...	BARBARA DEANE
Lady Millicent Graeme of Lockalt	KATIE BUTLER
Lady Graeme of Lockalt	VERA MORRIS
A Peasant Woman	GEORGINA DELMAR
AND	
Peggy Quainton	ELLALINE TERRISS

Guests :—Misses Aime Dixon, Pauline Francis, May Gates, Rena Goldie, Hilda Harris, Elsie Kay, May Kennedy, Ruby Kennedy, Dorrie Keppel, Marion Lindsay, Claire Rickards, Doris Stocker, Sylvia Storey, Mabel Watson.

Act I.   -   -   -   A Moor in the Highlands on "The 12th."
(R. C. McCleery.)

Act II.   -   -   -   Tent in the Gardens of Meltrose Castle.
(Philip Howden and R. C. McCleery.)

THE PLAY PRODUCED BY SEYMOUR HICKS

The Dances and Choral Effects arranged by EDWARD ROYCE.

Dresses specially designed by WILHELM.   Executed by LUCILLE LIMITED, MADAME HERBERT, MISS FISHER and MISS NASH.

Uniforms by MORRIS ANGEL and B. J. SIMMONS & Co.

Flowers by MADAME DE COURCY.

The Guns used in the Piece supplied by WILLIAM EVANS (Gunmaker to H.R.H. the Duke of Connaught), 63, Pall Mall, S.W.

Acting Manager ...		T. AYNSLEY COOK
Stage Manager ...	For Seymour Hicks	EDWARD ROYCE
Musical Director ...		FRANK E. TOURS

MATINEE EVERY SATURDAY AT 2.15.

General Manager   (For Charles Frohman)   ...   W. LESTOCQ

PRICES : Private Boxes, £4 4s., £2 2s. and £1 11s. 6d.   Stalls, 10s. 6d.

Balcony, 7s. 6d., 6s. and 5s.   Upper Circle, 5s. and 4s.

Pit, 2s. 6d.   Gallery, 1s.

Telephone 2315 Gerrard.   Doors open at 7.30 ; Matinees at 1.45.

BOX OFFICE (MR. L. MALONEY) OPEN 10 TO 10.

Manager   ..   ...   (For Charles Frohman)   ...   A. L. LEVERING

*Extract from Rules made by the Lord Chamberlain.—*1. The name of the actual and responsible Manager of the Theatre must be printed on every play-bill. 2. The Public can leave the Theatre at the end of each performance by all exit and entrance Doors, which must open outwards. 3. Where there is a fire-proof screen to the proscenium opening, it must be lowered at least once during every performance, to ensure its being in proper working order. 4. Smoking is not permitted in the Auditorium. 5. All gangways, passages, and staircases must be kept free from chairs, or any other obstructions whether permanent or temporary.

NUTS AND WINE (1914)

A New and Original Revue

Presented by Oscar Barrett Jr. at the Empire Theatre, London, on January 4, 1914 (7 performances; this is the most often quoted number but the existence of a theatre program dated in March suggests that the run may have been slightly longer).

BOOK	C. H. Bovill and P. G. Wodehouse
LYRICS	C. H. Bovill, P. G. Wodehouse and Guy Jones
MUSIC	Frank E. Tours and Melville Gideon
	Director Julian Alfred

CAST

R. G. Knowles, Maidie Hope, Violet Lloyd, Albert Le Fre, Babette,

Eric Thorne, Phyllis Bedells, Dorothy Monkman

SYNOPSIS

The basic plot—if such it can be called—which links several surrealistic situations is that Mr. Punch returns to England to find many of its fundamental institutions changed out of all recognition.

Eton, for instance, is the "New Eton," reduced to only three classes—those in Music Hall, Tango and Agriculture. The Chorus of Eton Boys, Mothers, Cousins and Aunts celebrate.

THE FOURTH OF JUNE

Eton! Eton!
Greatest school on earth,
World renowned
As a training ground
For boys of noble birth.
Eton! Eton!
Where squads of learned men
Severely strain
The bulging brain
Of England's Upper Ten.

But in the grinding round
Of ceaseless education,
An interval is found
For rest and recreation.
We would not shirk
Other work
But 'ere we sink or swoon,
We deem it best
To take a rest
Upon the Fourth of June.

The Fourth of June.
That's the one great day
When fathers, mothers,
Aunts and cousins
Come in dozens—
Beneath the trees they stray,
All the afternoon,
The whole world you meet on
The Fourth at Eton,
The Fourth, the Fourth of June . . .

By some illogical logic of plot the teacher of the tango class turns out to be musical star Gertie Millar.

MY TANGO MAID

Dusky eyes, I know the secret of your tenderest sighs,
With surprise I read the answer in your wonder-ful eyes.

Long ago, I knew the message of the breezes that blow
Sweet and low,
I heard you sighing to me.
Senor, I love you so.
From afar I love to serenade you with my guitar,
Guiding star, Oh, let me tell you what a treasure you are.

Dearest maid, to bear my heart to you I'm almost afraid,
Ever glad, Oh, won't you echo softly,
"I love you, my Tango Maid."

My Tango Maid,
Oh, won't you listen to my love serenade?
I'm yearning for you alone,
Don't you know my soul is burning,
My Tango Maid?
In all the blossoms of the garden arrayed,
My heart has strayed
To you, my Tango Maid.

We now meet the Marquess of Hoxton, head of the Music Hall Class.

THE MUSIC HALL CLASS

We're the Music Hall Class. What ho!
Every trick of the trade we know.
Take it from us, although we hate to brag,
We do patter and dances which
Simply terrify Little Tich.
We're the lads for the back chat and the gags.

We know the business from soup to nuts,
Now you Stolls and Alfred Butts,
We're the fellows you simply must engage
We leave all the rest behind,
Aw'fully funny, but quite refined,
Give us a chance and we shall be the rage.

Refrain:

Etonians, Mothers, Aunts and Cousins
We are the lads
To make a hit,
Study our ads,
We're simply IT.
If real red hot stars you're out to find
Bear us in mind.
We're just the kind
Give us a chance
To make our name,
Patter or dance, it's all the same.
All the other comics will go out of business
When we get in the game.

Hoxton now has a solo to express his state of mind in the new order of things.

I'VE LOST MY DUCK

I'm one of the sons of Britannia
But at present I'm right out of luck;
Such a misfortune's enough to unman yer,
I've just lost my little pet duck.
Talk of eggs! She could lay them in
    hundreds,
She'd have laid you a carpet if asked
My word! But that duck was a wonder.
But alas! I have lost her at last!

I've lost my pretty little duck
Who used to go "Quack, quack"
Oh, dear, whatever shall I do?
Her bill was yellow and her tail was blue
And strange to say
My neighbour, Mr. Black
Has been equally unlucky,
So we're both looking for a ducky
That goes "Quack, quack, quack, quack!"

Next a Chorus of Boys and Flappers sing.

DON'T DO ANYTHING UNTIL YOU HEAR FROM ME

Hello, are you there?
Gerrard O.O.O?
I can't hear a word you say.
How the line does buzz today.
Yes, I've got the number. Whoa!
Don't go.
Hello, is that you?
Don't you go away.
Please don't cut us off, Exchange
We've got something to arrange.
That's all I want to say.

Don't do anything till you hear from me.
Don't see anyone till I ring you up tomorrow
    morning
I've got many things to tell you when you're free
So don't do anything until I telephone
And make an appointment.
Wait till you hear from me.

Mr. Punch now visits the offices of the *New News*—a paper that has now absorbed *The Times*—and meets its revolutionary new editor, Mr. George L. Washington of Pittsburgh, grandson of you-know-who. Punch asks him if he is a married man.

Washington: No sir. I have enough troubles
              of my own. Single men have
              marriage to look forward to—
              married men only death.

Then—for no apparent plot reason—he sings.

TWO TO TOOTING

I've a story sad to tell
Which will illustrate quite well
We must be very careful what we say
For the language that we speak

Often sounds a lot like Greek
When words get twisted in a funny way.
Once a lady went insane
Simply trying to catch a train
For Tooting where the tooties love
    to toot.
At the station to a clerk
She was overheard to remark—
"Two to Tooting for the Two-Two train."

"Two to Tooting," said the lady to
    the youth
Who was selling tickets for the train.
"Tum-tiddley-um," he replied
And then was mum
For he thought that she had water on
    the brain.
"Two for the toot-toot to Tooting,"
    then she cried.
"Tiddley-um ti, tiddley-um," she heard
    him shout.
"Two to Tooting" was her cry.
"Tiddley-um," was his reply
While the train steamed out.

Later on there came a man
From a well-known Scottish clan
To bonnie Scotland he was keen to go.
With his family of three
Bound for Forfar—that's N.B.
As every booking office clerk should know.
But this youth was rather dense
And devoid of common sense
And the same misunderstanding came again
When the Scot pulled out his purse,
And exclaimed in accents terse—
"Four for Forfar by the four-four train."

"Four for Forfar," said the Scotsman to the youth
Who was not quite certain what to do.
"Hi tiddley-hi," he replied with a sigh,
For he thought the Scot was simply fou the noo.
"Four for Forfar," yelled the angry passenger
"Yip-i-addy and pip-pip," he heard him shout.

"Four for For." The Scotsman cried,
"Tiddley-umpty," he replied
As the train rolled out.

Fictional and "real" characters intermingle. We now meet Lady Teazle (of Sheridan's *School for Scandal*).

THE LADY JOURNALIST

If you're inclined to stray far from the
    primrose way
You should display a preference.
Look out! There's someone who sees everything
    you do,
Takes notes for future reference

She only wants a tale fit for the London *Mail*
And a page of print to tell it on.
Your cupboard you may lock, but still you'll get
    a shock
For she'll bring out the skeleton.

Lady Journalist,
In her net you will get by and by
If she's on your trail
To escape her X-ray eye
Mind what you're about.
She's a sleuth for the truth, not a doubt.
And you'll find your little capers
Under headlines in the papers
If you don't look out.

She gets her paragraphs from the domestic staffs
Of leaders of Society
The cook reports on improper goings-on
At a bob per impropriety.
Your faithful butler, too, has got his eye on you
As you eat your breakfast cereal.
He murmurs with delight—"Yes, drunk again
    last night."
For he knows that's good material

The song was dropped and replaced with:

NOT A WORD

Don't let me go any farther
But if you will come to my school
I'll teach you how to handle
The spiciest scandal.
According to regular rule
I have classes for gentlemen only,
But don't be afraid you'll be seen,
For those who take these'll
Find dear Lady Teazle
Provides a most adequate screen.

Not a word! Not a word!
The parrot's a talkative bird,
But Alfonso the page

Always covers the cage.
Not a word!
As I learnt from Mama,
When in doubt, *cachez-ça*
Not a word!

Don't let it go any farther,
I've heard there's a certain M.P.
(Though it's quite on the Q.T.)
So keen on his duties
He never gets home until three.
He stays there for every division,
No word of a speech will he lose,
But so goes the story
Our friend—though a Tory
On some things has Liberal views.

Not a word! Not a word!
He gets home each day, I have heard.
"All night sittings," says he.
Yes, on somebody's knee.
Not a word!
If a pair he can't reach
He's content with a peach.
Not a word!

Don't let it go any farther
But living just over the way
Is a little grass widow
Who certainly did owe
Much more than she ever would pay.
But now all her bills have been settled
And she's never lonely or bored,
For her kind Uncle Willie
Has turned up from Chile,
So virtue has met its reward.

Not a word!
Uncle Jim's turned up also, I've heard
But she must be discreet
For the two never meet.
Not a word!
And her new mat has got
'Welcome' on it—eh, what?
Not a word!

The music hall star Gaby Delys enters, "wearing no clothes at all." The Lord Chamberlain's censor, who had cheerfully passed the rest of the script, noted anxiously that this stage direction will, of course, need to be adjusted!

GABY

Men of me are always chattering
Tales unflattering
They keep scattering.
I don't mind their little malices
If the palace is
Full!
What I wear
Makes you stare
But I really do not care
If you see
Little Me
In my *robe de nuit*.

For I am Gaby
I don't care,
I'm at my best
When I'm undressed.
I am not shabby
I am there
For you
To view—
That's Gaby.

ext a Trio:

WILL YOU SING THIS GLEE WITH ME?

Will you sing this glee with me?
Will you sing this glee with me?
Will you harmonise?
Let the music rise
To the topmost top, top C?

If you'll sing this glee with me,
I shall not feel so forlorn
Now the words you know
Let your voices go—
"Hail, smiling morn, smiling morn, smiling
morn."

WHERE DID YOU GET THAT GIRL?

I'm a lonesome Johnnie Warner
Standing in a corner
On a sunny day
Eating my heart away
Because I have no girl.
Over by that table
Stands a girl named Mabel
With a fellow who—
I once knew.
My brain is in a whirl
Ah, Mabel winks her eye
And I am going to cry.

Where did you get that girl?
Oh, you lucky devil,
Where did you get that girl?
Tell me on the level,
Have you ever kissed her?
If she has a sister,
Lead me, lead me, lead me to her, mister
Gee, but I wish I had a girl,
I'd love her, I'd love her
If she's here long I'm liable
To give away my Bible
Where! Where! Where did you get that girl?

Here's a snappy flapper
With a chappy dapper
Looking bright and gay.
I'll make a play to catch
Her before she flies.
Goodness, now they're coming,
Business will be humming.
So gather round,

Girls, you're found.
You may gaze into my eyes
But don't you dare to wink
Or I'll shriek aloud and think—
Where did you get that girl?

George Washington meets the symbolic figure of Truth and they sing a duet about
a Wodehouse *bête noir* of the period—the wily
Welshman, David Lloyd George.

THE CHANCELLOR OF
THE EXCHEQUER

I'm not a Member. No, not I
Of your belted Aristocracy
In the Strand, Piccadilly, Rotten Row or the Cut.
If Taffy's Budget then I should read
Then I am stranded on the beach
In the Strand, on your uppers—stony broke—
    busted
Then we'll all go Tango teasing
We will, by George!
Of a tax on land why make a fuss?
It still remains but a penny on a bus
In the Strand for the Chancellor of the Exchequer

To pay the extra taxes, I
Must take my Moët Extra Dry
In the Strand, Lockharts—Romano's—outside
If there's another bit on the income stuck
My income I intend to chuck!
In the Strand—Waterloo—Water-loss! What ho!
And racing men will suffer—they will, poor
    things
For racing comes as a matter of course
There's a bit upon the backer
Put a bit upon a horse
In the Strand for the Chancellor of the Exchequer.

Lloyd wrote his scheme and he will not
    smudge it
And he won't budge an inch

Not an inch from his Budget
When it comes
We must pay
Or be presented at the Court.

Though a cycle tax our hearts would harrow,
I'd stick to the wheel for I'd shove along a barrow
In the Strand—no change—on change—
    change here
Oh, take the tax off glucose
Oh, do! Please do!
Be kind to the thirsty, beery men
It's a tanner on the barrel and a penny on the can
In the Strand for the Chancellor of the
    Exchequer

Why don't they tax all pastry cooked,
For on pastry I have never looked.
Yes, put a tax on pastry—if not, why not?
The contents of each pastry cart,
A penny on a pancake and twopence on a tart
In the Strand for the Chancellor of the
    Exchequer.

Why not tax all domestic pets,
Alligators and Suffragettes?
Whether for good or only now and then,
House boats, hotels, flats, Abodes of Love—
These attacks on a Tax on Taxis
Flags up
So are the roads.
There's a tax on Stocks and Shares, should be
But let Marconigrams go free, do you see
For the Chancellor of the Exchequer.

On the decks of the New Mayflower yacht
the passengers sing in unison:

BARCAROLLE

'Neath smiling skies
The ocean lies
At rest like some lagoon,
As on we steal

Beneath our keel
The whispering waters croon.
Through golden days
We lie and laze
Beneath the blue above
Life seems one long
Delightful song,
A song of love.

After we fare
To regions where,
Grey, gaunt and mist empearled,
To flout the skies
The cliffs arise
That guard the long lost world.
The journey done,
Our haven won
(If Fate will be but kind)
When we explore
Its fabled shore
There love we'll find.

A character called Mrs. Newlywed sings:

HAVANA ANNA

In the Bay
Once a boat fast at her anchor lay
And her Captain, they say
Met Havana Anna
On the quayside one day.
One look sealed his fate
And then early or late
'Neath her lattice with a mandoline,
He came to play.
He'd call up to his love—
"Look down, dear, from above."

"I sigh for you
I'd die for you,
Havana Anna,
That's what I would do.
Come what may

I'll be true to you.
I yearn for you, I burn for you,
Havana Anna.
Love me if you can,
Fairest one,
Rarest one,
Havana Anna."

The script then appends a number of songs which were presumably intended as later additions. In view of the revue's short run, it's unlikely that the material was ever used.

I'D LIKE TO LIKE A GIRL LIKE YOU

My mind is in a quandry and I don't know what
   to do,
I'm up against a problem and a mighty hard
   one, too.
The time has come for me to marry,
Still I'm all at sea
I don't know what girl is the girl
That's all the world to me.
There's Cinderella, Stella, Della, Mabel sweet
   and shy,
For any one of these dear girls I'd lay me down
   and die.

I'd like a graceful girl like May,
She's just the proper height and style
I'd like a girl demure like Carrie,
With her tantalizing, roguish smile.
I'd like a girl neat like Betty
But I must confess I'm up against a wall
For I can't tell which girl
Of all the girls I like
That I'd like to like the best of all.

He then tried his hand at a London song— a subject he was to refine later in "London, Dear Old London" (*The Cabaret Girl* 1922).

DON'T PUT THE
BLAME ON LONDON

Don't you say one word against dear old
    London,
London, you can take from me, is it!
If you've done things which you should have
    left undone,
London's to blame not the least little bit,
You'd have done just the same wherever
    you lit.

Don't put the blame on her name,
It's a shame, for old London's all right.
Guess London West—is the best
Got the rest beaten right out of sight.
You'd have done things that are just as silly
Anywhere else but in Piccadilly.
She is not what upset you.
Any old place would get you.
Don't put the blame on London Town.

OH, THAT YANKIANA RAG

A dance *à la Americain*
By each Parisian
Is thought to be the proper thing.
It's so entrancing
When you're dancing,
In Paris you'll hear everywhere,
When you go over there.
Those tunes from Dixie Land—Yankee-land,
They think ragtime is simply grand.
This kind of dance you'll see them do,
When they strike up the band.

Oh, oh, that Yankiana Rag, rag, rag,
With a dreamy motion *à la Matchiche*
Dancing with an ever lovin', lovin' peach.
Look up into my eyes, *ma belle chérie*,
Honey-bug, throw yourself away,
Whenever the band starts in to play. Oh, that
    Yankiana Rag.

RIDING IN A LONDON BUS

Such is life on a merry little trip
When riding on a London bus.
Such is the strife and the flips and the slips
That make the public cuss!
Starting—stopping,
Ladies shopping,
Dogs out for the air.
Jerking, lurching,
People searching
For the proper fare.

Wait on the curb for an hour or so
Oh, the joys of the L.G.O.
Pull up—"Full Up!"
"Take the next!"
Shake downs—break downs—
People vexed!
Delays—who pays
For appointments missed?

No wonder people talk
What with all this what-do-you-call-this . . .
Let's get out and *walk*.

WHAT DO YOU MEAN,
YOU LOST YOUR DOG?

I've got a dog called Rover,
Here, Rover
Come, Rover.
He roams around all over,
Just home three times a day.
I'll bet he hears me whistling,
See the neighbours are listening.
"What do you mean, you lost your dog?"
I hear the neighbours say.
Has anybody here seen Rover?
I'm looking for him all over.
He's a hunting dog alright,
He keeps me hunting day and night
This is what I worry over.

Say, my whistle's getting dry.
It seems as if I hear that mongrel whine
"Woof! Woof! Woof! Woof! Woof!"
I should worry like a tree
And have someone training me.
Where's the dog, gone, dog gone, dog of mine?

I'm looking around for Rover,
Here, Rover
Come, Rover.
I got him up in Dover
A hundred miles away.
Wait till he comes, I'll chain him,
I'll train him,
I'll brain him.
"What do you mean, you've lost your dog?"
Again I hear them say.

WE'RE ALL GOING
ROUND TO FATHER'S

We'll all go round to Father's,
Father's one of the best.
If we're away for a single day,
Father gets depressed.
Tell the cabman where to stop,
Open the door of Father's shop,
Isn't it nice to have a pop
Like Father?

WE'RE LEAVING ENGLAND

We are going far away
From our rotten native land,
We've had just all we can stand.
In the London of today
Classic Art's too often banned,
A dancer they resent
Who shows her—temperament.
And however well I speak
They forget me in a week.
What good is that to me?

And it merely made them smile
When I went to Ellis Isle,
Because I wasn't all I ought to be.
As far as I can see
Old England simply isn't worth a——

Chorus: (We believe you)
So we're clearing out of England,
We shall never see it more.
With the tear drops in our eyes
We have said our last good-byes.
We have drunk our final toddies
At the bar and Oddy's
And we're clearing out of England,
So farewell, our native shore.

Good-bye, England, we are leaving you.
We wish we'd left before.
Though we hate to make a fuss,
You're a bit too thick for us.
We are going where the clerics
Do not suffer from hysterics
When they look in at a music-hall.
Farewell, our native shore
In the land which we are seeking
Telephones don't make you sore,
As our London service does.

With that intermittent buzz,
In the country which we go to
They don't give you Gerrard 02
When you ask for Hop 123
So, farewell our native shore.

We are rather fond of dancing
But it's now become a bore
For this Argentine affair
Is enough to bleach your hair.
It's an epileptic spasm,
So we're going where no one has 'em.
We will leave the Tango tanging.
So farewell our native shore!

THE PRINCESS PERIOD
(1916–1918)

Goodbye, Mister Willie Shakespeare—goodbye, tragedy, too.
Goodbye, gloomy melodrama, finished with you.
We want a play that is light and gay before us,
We want a Princess cast and a Princess chorus.
What could be sweeter, I say,
Than a musical comedy play?
I love a musical comedy, musical comedy glow,
The colors blending in scenes unending,
Set to a truly hilarican, purely American go.
I love those wonderful, beautiful, cutey and cuteyful girls,
I love those rollicking, frolicking Rosy and Dollycan pearls.
You feel your blood a-tingaling, senses mingaling
Right from your head to your toe,
That's why you go to a musical comedy show.

—Lyric by Alfred Bryan (1919)

Musical comedy, the most glorious words in the English language.

—Producer Julian Marsh in *42nd Street*

Musical comedy is the Irish stew of the drama. Anything may be put into it,
with the certainty that it will improve the general effect.

—"Bill the Bloodhound" from The *Man With Two Left Feet* (1917)

Musical comedy is not dashed off. It grows—slowly and painfully, and each step
in its growth either bleaches another tuft of the author's hair or removes it from
the parent skull altogether.

—P. G. Wodehouse

Musical comedy was my dish, the musical-comedy theatre my spiritual home. I
would rather have written *Oklahoma!* than *Hamlet*. (Actually, as the records show,
I wrote neither, but you get the idea.)

—P. G. Wodehouse

Writing musical comedies is like eating salted almonds—you can always manage
one more.

—P. G. Wodehouse

He (Bingo Little) always reminds me of the hero of a musical comedy who takes the centre of the stage, gathers the boys round him in a circle, and tells them all about his love at the top of his voice.

—Bertie Wooster
"The Pride of the Woosters Is Wounded"
from *The Inimitable Jeeves* (1923)

Every time these three (Bolton & Wodehouse & Kern) gather together, the Princess Theatre is sold out for months in advance. . . . I like the way they go about a musical comedy. I like the way the action slides casually into the songs. I like the deft rhyming of the song that is always sung in the last act by two comedians and a comedienne. They are my favourite indoor sports.

—Dorothy Parker

It is my opinion that the musical numbers should carry on the action of the play, and should be representative of the personalities who sing them. . . . In other words, songs must be suited to the action and the mood of the play.

—Jerome Kern

The whole growth of our musical comedy can be seen through the growth of integration.

—Leonard Bernstein

I've always maintained and I always will maintain that for pure lunacy nothing can touch the musical comedy business. Alice in Wonderland is nothing to it.

Have you felt that, too? That's exactly how I feel. It's like a perpetual Mad Hatter's Tea Party.

—Wally Mason and Jill in *Jill the Reckless* (1921)

Wodehouse once told me that the greatest challenge (and greatest worry) to him in lyric writing was to come across a section of a tune requiring

The *Princess* team: Coproducer Morris Gest, Wodehouse, Guy Bolton, coproducer and Princess Theatre cofounder Ray Comstock, and Jerome Kern.

three double rhymes. . . . When I finally wound up with "wings on—strings on—things on," that was *that*, and I felt like a suddenly unburdened Atlas.

—Ira Gershwin (*Lyrics On Several Occasions*)

The year 1914 was a turning point in more ways than one. On the battlefields of Broadway several primal forces came together. One of them was caused by the war itself. Overnight the Viennese operetta with its emphasis on European settings began to seem a little unpatriotic. Why should we be celebrating the artistic and emotional values of the obvious enemy? Truth to tell, the vogue had probably just about run its course anyway, but there was definitely now a need for something new. Why not something with good all-American values?

Two youngish producers—Ray Comstock and Morris Gest—were beginning to make their mark in management by building up a string of provincial theatres. They managed to get a toehold in New York when Comstock also became manager of a Shubert theatre—a 299-seat jewelbox of a house at 104 West 39th Street, built in 1913 on the site of an old livery stable and called The Princess. (The rather odd number of seats was explained by the fact that stringent fire laws applied to theatres holding 300 or more, but for one holding a mere 299) . . .

Something was wrong with the place. It was too small with its fourteen rows, a single central aisle, a small balcony and two boxes. Nothing seemed to run there. The Shuberts were on the verge of closing it when Comstock formed an unlikely alliance with the formidable Bessie Marbury. A successful literary and actors' agent, specializing in imported talent, the lady was junoesque to the point of being statuesque—Wodehouse once described her as "dear, kindly, voluminous" and recalled an argument she had with the diminutive Comstock as being a "nose to bosom" altercation. Miss Marbury also had a

big idea—think small! Small was also intimate; with the right kind of show you could create a personal interaction between cast and audience. Less *could* be more.

The format she and Comstock devised was minimalist in the extreme. The standard operetta had something like a dozen sets; the Princess shows would have *two*, one for each of the two acts. Of course, there would be girls but no more than twelve instead of anything up to a hundred, and the orchestra would be limited to eleven, whereas forty was by no means unusual. "Midget musical comedy" was the description Wodehouse and Bolton were to coin to describe this new *genre*.

Shows would be written specially for the venue, and the stories would be contemporary, to keep costuming at a minimum, and the talent—on both sides of the footlights—would be young and keen to prove something. Established talent, they both knew all too well, could be both temperamental and expensive. No budget was to exceed $7,500, whereas a Broadway "book" show averaged $50,000.

As the year turned, so did Bessie Marbury—to Jerome Kern.

Up to this point in his career much of Kern's work in the musical theatre had been as an interpolator—an unsatisfactory occupation with an interesting genesis:

At the beginning of the century, before the American theatre found its distinctive voice, most of the shows were either British imports or adaptations of operettas. In neither case was the transition as simple as it might appear.

The British musicals were so devised that nothing significant was allowed to happen for the first hour, so that the rich patrons might arrive late without missing anything. The Viennese operettas, on the other hand, were written for operatic voices and much of the material was unsuitable for the lighter "show voices" of the American talent that would be performing it. In either case, the shows literally "came up short" and required the padding—however irrelevant to the plot it might often appear—of the interpolator's art.

It was, at least, a way to get your songs heard and your name known.

Kern—with his writing partner, Guy Bolton (1884–1979)—had already demonstrated his desire to innovate within a form that had become overly-stylized. Why should a show stop dead while someone sang a totally unconnected number? Why couldn't the words and music flow seamlessly from the plot and actually *develop* the storyline? The two men had already tried their hand at something of the sort in parts of *Ninety In the Shade* (1915) and were now given a free hand to experiment with their first Princess show, *Nobody Home*, later that same year.

Rodgers and Hammerstein's *Oklahoma!* (1943) is generally credited as being the first "integrated" musical, and certainly it did add dance to the equation, but the first attempt to create a genuine artistic synergy by integrating book, music and lyrics began right on West 39th Street in 1915 with Kern and Bolton.

Kern could honestly claim—and was not backward about doing so—that he was the bridge between the Viennese-y and the start of genuine (Jewish) American popular theatre music. To that degree he, more than anyone else, gave American musical theatre a distinctive voice and created the transition from operetta to musical comedy.

Nobody Home ran for six months at the Princess, then toured for the next two years or so. Comstock and Marbury now chose the subject to replace it, an adaptation of a straight play, to be called *Very Good Eddie*. Despite Kern's objection, the management team decided to leave the work of adaptation to the original author, and early previews proved the decision to be disastrous. To everyone's relief, Guy Bolton was called in to "doctor" the book.

While all this was going on, Plum Wodehouse was blithely continuing his writing career. Several novels had been published—*A Gentleman of Leisure* (1910), *The Prince and Betty* (1912), *The Little Nugget* (1913), *The Man Upstairs* (1914) and *Something Fresh* (1915), the first of the Blandings Castle novels and the first novel he had serialized in the *Saturday Evening Post*—and he had already introduced the world to two of his main characters, Psmith ("the P silent as in "pshrimp") and Jeeves. He was now also on the staff of the American edition of *Vanity Fair* and it was in his capacity as its theatre critic that he found himself attending the Broadway opening of *Very Good Eddie* on December 23rd, 1915.

From the back of the theatre Bolton and Kern watched the show unfold. Much of it worked as well as they could have hoped, with one exception—the lyrics. In one of the front rows the critic from *Vanity Fair* appeared to be enjoying himself hugely, even though in his diary Wodehouse recorded that he "enjoyed it in spite of lamentable lyrics."

It was to be a case of the hour and the man coinciding. Recalling their earlier collaboration on *The Beauty of Bath*, Kern introduced Wodehouse to Bolton—by some published accounts on that opening night, by others slightly later. Correspondence files, however, reveal a draft (unsigned) contract for Wodehouse to provide lyrics for a musical version of a Bolton play entitled *Fully That* dated November 20th, 1915, suggesting their acquaintance predated that December evening. (Further "evidence" is the announcement in the *Dramatic Mirror* [November 27th, 1915] of the forthcoming production, which mentioned Bolton, Wodehouse & Kern by name.) Whenever and whatever the occasion, all that mattered was that three complementary talents, mutually obsessed with creating new musical theatre, had found one another and were about to make a little history.

But before they did, a small diversion. . . .

NINETY IN THE SHADE (1915)

Presented at the Knickerbocker Theatre, New York, on January 25, 1915 (40 performances).

BOOK Harry B. Smith (and Guy Bolton)
MUSIC Jerome Kern (in part)

The significance of this show is simply that (a) it appeared before *Very Good, Eddie* and (b) it contained a song with lyrics by Wodehouse. So either Kern and Wodehouse had resumed their collaboration somewhat earlier than the story of the meeting at the Princess would suggest or—less plausibly—the song was left over from the earlier period and Kern simply retrieved it as yet another interpolation. Whatever the explanation, the song was to turn up again in *Oh, Boy!* (1917) as "A Package of Seeds" with the lyric credit shared with Herbert Reynolds.

A PACKET OF SEEDS

Beautiful girls are so scarce, I have found,
There never seems half enough to go 'round.
I've often wished that in gardens they grew,
Warmed by the sunshine and wet by the dew.

Refrain:
If I'd a garden where girlies would grow,
You'd find me there with my spade and my hoe,
My little garden I never would leave,
I'd work from daybreak until the eve,
Daytime and night I would cheerfully toil—
To kill the blight and encourage the soil,
And when at last I had cleared it of weeds,
I'd go and buy me a packet of seeds.

All through the winter they'd lie there below,
Snugly tucked under a mantle of snow.
April at last rain and sunshine would bring,
    (warmth & showers)
And all my flowers would bloom in the Spring.

Refrain:
Primrose and Myrtle and Lily, I'd see,
They'd be there growing for no-one but me.
Delightful creatures, a garden of girls,
With fairest features and lovely curls.
All round my garden in raptures I'd roam,
I'd stay all day there and never go home.
I can't imagine what more a man needs
Than lots of grounds and a packet of seeds.

It would not be long before *New Yorker* wit
George S. Kaufman would enshrine the
legend in rhyme. . . .

    This is the trio of musical fame:
    Bolton and Wodehouse and Kern:
    Better than anyone else you can name,
    Bolton and Wodehouse and Kern.
    Nobody knows what on earth they've been
        bitten by.
    All I can say is I mean to get lit an' buy

Orchestra seats for the next one that's
        written by
Bolton and Wodehouse and Kern

If they had read that on the morning of their
first meeting with Ray Comstock, they would
have laughed hollowly—and in unison.

It was *not* encouraging. The trio—accompanied by Bessie Marbury—went along early in January 1916 and presented him with two ready-made ideas for Princess shows.

The first was a Cinderella story of a girl who washes dishes but dreams of becoming a star; their working title was *The Little Thing*. The other was about a young man who marries against his rich aunt's wishes—*Oh, Boy!*

Comstock rejected both of them. He wanted the team to work on adapting a lugubrious straight play into a musical, and it was that or nothing. They took nothing and left. In rejecting *The Little Thing* Comstock had just had the dubious honor of turning down the opportunity to produce what, in greatly changed form, would become Ziegfeld's *Sally*—one of the longest running musicals in American theatre history.

But that would have to wait until 1920, after other shows for two very different but equally hardnosed Broadway managers. Bolton & Wodehouse & Kern first turned to the man who predated the Shuberts as the "Czar of Broadway." If you had a show to put on, the chances were it would be put on in a Klaw & Erlanger theatre.

The diminutive producer Abraham Lincoln Erlanger (1860–1930) was a legend in his own lifetime. Size was undoubtedly a preoccupation with Erlanger and he surrounded himself with objects on a massive scale. He suffered from what we would now call a Napoleon complex and artifacts of "the little corporal" abounded. Later—in *Have A Heart*—Wodehouse and Kern would pin him down in a song entitled "Napoleon" and, later still, Wodehouse would re-create him as

Isaac Goble of Goble & Cohn—but for now they just had to listen.

Erlanger's first *dictat* was that the title of the proposed show—*Little Miss Springtime*—as it was called in its Philadelphia preview—be changed forthwith. "We don't have nothing little at the New Amsterdam Theatre," he said—and *Miss Springtime* it duly became, although some sheet music had already appeared using the original title.

"He had been brought up in the lower-browed school of musical comedy, where you shelved the plot after the opening number and filled the rest of the evening by bringing on the girls in a variety of exotic costumes, with some good vaudeville specialists to get the laughs. Mr. Goble's idea of a musical piece was something embracing trained seals, acrobats, and two or three teams of skilled buck-and-wing dancers, with nothing on the stage, from a tree to a lampshade, which could not suddenly turn into a chorus-girl. The austere legitimateness of *The Rose of America* gave him a pain in the neck. He loathed plot, and *The Rose of America* was all plot.

"Why, then, had the earthy Mr. Goble consented to associate himself with the production of this intellectual play? Because he was subject, like all other New York managers, to intermittent spasms of the idea that the time is ripe for a revival of comic opera. Sometimes, lunching in his favourite corner of the Cosmopolis grill-room, he would lean across the table and beg some other manager to take it from him that the time was ripe for a revival of comic opera—or more cautiously, that pretty soon the time was going to be ripe for a revival of comic opera. And the other manager would nod his head and thoughtfully stroke his three chins and admit that, sure as God made little apples, the time was darned soon going to be ripe for a revival of comic opera. And then they would stuff them-

selves with rich food and light big cigars and brood meditatively."

—Jill the Reckless (1921)

"Here, a composer who had not got an interpolated number in the show was explaining to another composer who had not got an interpolated number in the show the exact source from which a third composer who had got an interpolated number in the show had stolen the number which he had got interpolated. There, two musical comedy artists, who were temporarily resting were agreeing that the *prima donna* was a dear thing but that, contrary as it was to their life-long policy to knock anybody, they must say that she was beginning to show the passage of years a trifle and ought to be warned by some friend that her career as an *ingénue* was a thing of the past."

—Jill the Reckless (1921)

The comfort level of Goble and his ilk rises appreciably when Wally Mason, the show doctor in the novel, comes up with lyrics like these:

PULLMAN PORTERS ON PARADE

Just see them Pullman porters,
Dolled up with scented waters
Bought with their dimes and quarters.
See, here they come! Here they come!
Oh, see those starched-up collars,
Hark how their captain hollers,
"Keep time, keep time."
It's worth a thousand dollars
To see those tip-collectors,
Those upper-berth inspectors,
Those Pullman porters on parade.

Then he knows he is dealing with the tried and true.

MISS SPRINGTIME (1916)

(Originally LITTLE MISS SPRINGTIME)

Presented by Klaw & Erlanger at the New Amsterdam Theatre, New York, on September 25, 1916 (227 performances).

BOOK	Guy Bolton (Based on *Zigeuner Primas*)
LYRICS	P. G. Wodehouse and Herbert Reynolds (There are several more songs in the libretto, but I have included only those which Wodehouse wrote or in which he had a hand.)
MUSIC	Emmerich Kalman and Jerome Kern
SCENERY	Joseph Urban

John E. Hazzard Sari Petrass George MacFarlane Charles Meakins Georgia O'Ramey Jed Prouty

"MISS SPRINGTIME," NOW BEING PRESENTED AT THE NEW AMSTERDAM

CAST

Paul:	Marto/Varady:
CHARLES MEAKINS	GEORGE MACFARLANE
Robin:	Maimie: GEORGIA O'RAMEY
JOHN E. HAZZARD	Dustin: JED PROUTY
Rozika: SARI PETRASS	Block: PERCY WOODLEY

SYNOPSIS

The setting is in the town of Pilota. Paul, the editor of the local paper, and his friend Robin, chairman of the local Entertainment Committee, are serenading Rozika, with whom Paul is in love ("Throw Me a Rose"). Robin has invited Signor Marto, the famous opera singer, back to his home town as a P.R. event. The local girls complain of a shortage of men in the town ("This is the Existence"). Rozika, in particular, anticipates Marto's arrival. An aspiring singer herself, she hopes he will discover her ("Cinderella"). Robin now receives word that Marto will not be coming. In desperation he persuades Varady, an itinerant gypsy photographer, to impersonate the singer, not realizing that Varady is Marto travelling incognito. Maimie now arrives. A former fiancée of Robin's . . .

Robin: You returned my letters but you kept the diamond ring.
Maimie: Well, my love for you had died, but my feelings had not changed towards the ring.

. . . she is now married to Dustin, a rich American.

Rozika sings for "Marto" and he promises to find her work in Budapest. Although she is in love with Paul, the pull of her career is greater. Wouldn't it be wonderful if they could *all* go to the big city? ("My Castle in the Air"). Rozika is happy with the way things are turning out but Maimie is less enchanted ("Saturday Night"). Things seem to have been better in the good old days. Look what's happened to the theatre, for instance ("Melodrama Burlesque").

Rozika arrives at the Budapest Opera but immediately feels out of place and wishes she had never left home. By this time Robin and Marto are also in love with her. She tells Robin that she is in love with Paul, which causes him a little rueful self-evaluation ("All Full of Talk"). Marto offers to fulfil his promise to make her a star but, instinctively, he knows what she will choose when he tells her she must follow her heart.

THROW ME A ROSE

(Paul and Robin)

(Lyrics by P. G. Wodehouse and Herbert Reynolds)

Paul:

Love, to my song and sigh
Let your eyes unclose,
And from your lattice high
Throw me a rose.
Throw me the one you kept
Closest to your breast,
That all contented slept, by your lips
    caressed.
Near to my heart shall its petals unfold,
Token of love that can never, no never,
    grow cold
Love, let your lattice in kindness
    unclose,
Bid me contented be; throw me a rose.

Robin:

(Spoken)
How do you expect to wake the
    girl up if you sing her a
    lullaby?
Keep your lullabies till after you
    are married. You may need
    them then.
Rosi, wake up!

(Sings)
Lady, just to show you,
There are certain men who
    know you,
I will throw you
Bits of wisdom from my level
    head.
I know you are stringing
This poor fellow here who's
    singing,
While you're clinging
Wide awake, dear, to your
    little bed.
Lady, dear, throw the man a rose,

Hit him, if you want to, on his
    poor cold nose,
But don't think you are stringing two,
One of us is onto you.
Stop your kidding, do his bidding,
Quit your doze—
Getting out of bed's a task,
Still it's not so much to ask,
Just to sling a man one rose.

Both:

Throw me a rose,
One crimson rose,
Red as the sky
When sunset glows.
Rosika, dear,
Your lattice unclose,
Throw me, love, a red, red rose.

Repeat

THIS IS THE EXISTENCE

(Robin and Girls)
(Lyrics by P. G. Wodehouse
and Herbert Reynolds)

Robin: Though some jealous people tell us
That our town's not up-to-date,
In this pretty little city
We have one attraction great—
One which lends a fascination
That has ne'er been known to fail;
For our female population
Is much larger than the male.

Girls: If our census books you should
examine
You will find of men there is a
famine.

Robin: That is why I give you this advice
Don't forget our rural paradise
If you want a pleasant holiday
Step this way
And I will bet—you will come here
to stay.

Girls: *(Spoken)*
Yes, if you do, you'll always find us near,
and you'll feel
So good you'll want to cheer, and tell
them—
With your kind assistance, this is the
existence,
I'm in pretty soft down here.

Robin: Girls will meet you here and greet
you
As you're getting off the train,
They'll surround you till I'm bound you
Swear you won't go back again.
Each is prettier than the other,
And you murmur softly, "Gee,
Goodbye, home and goodbye,
mother,
You have seen the last of me."

Robin: So take a friendly native's good
advice
Don't neglect our rural paradise.
If you want a pleasant holiday,
Step this way and I'll bet you'll
Come here to stay.

Girls: Well

Robin: In Pilota etiquette is clear
When you see a pretty girl appear,
Go to it.
And when you've kissed her,
Rush and kiss her sister
That's the local rule down here.

CINDERELLA

(Once Upon a Time)

(Rozika)

Once upon a time, they say,
Poor Cinderella lived a lonely life,
Till Dame Fortune sent her way
A Fairy Prince who chose her for his wife.
Little Cinderella knew
A life no duller than my own must be.
I sat and moped
And pined and hoped
But never found a prince
To come and rescue me.
I've never even spied . . .
That great big world outside
Whose voice to me is calling,
Ever calling.

I can hear the thunder
Of that great big world of wonder
Like a voice out in the distance
That is calling me,
Growing ever stronger
As it bids me wait no longer,
Beating down my poor resistance,
As it shouts, 'Be free'
'Come away,' I can hear it say,

'Taste the joys and beauties that the world
   can give,'
Night and day that voice I hear
Ringing, singing in my ear,
Calling to me, 'Leave this gloomy round
   of care,
Come where Fame's awaiting you,
Roses in your path they'll strew,
In that great big world out there.'

MY CASTLE IN THE AIR

(Rozika and Boys)

(Music by Jerome Kern)

Rozika: I've a wond'rous castle that I've
          never lived in yet
         Built so many years ago in days
          that I forget.
         It has no stone battlements and
          great big wooden beams,
         Its walls and its bars are the
          dust of the stars,
         And its gate the gate of
          dreams.

Refrain: Come out there for a visit.
         I've lots of rooms for friends
         And if you ask "Where is it"?
         It's where the rainbow ends.
         It's somewhere there in
          Fairyland,
         Where there's never cloud
          or care.
         We'll have joy and laughter, mirth
          and song,
         And we'll all be happy as the day
          is long,
         In the shelter of my castle,
         Of my castle in the air.

         Ev'ry thing is perfect that you'll find
          there when you go,
         Just beyond the Milky Way and
         where the moonbeams grow,

No one ever worries there, for
   ev'rything goes right
The sky's always blue and no lover's
   untrue,
And your life's one long delight.

SATURDAY NIGHT

(A Very Good Girl on Sunday)

(Maimie Stone and Girls)

(Music by Jerome Kern)

Maimie: This is a wicked world, you'll find,
        so take my words to heart.

Time's apt our good intentions to
      diminish,
Just try to bear in mind it doesn't
      matter how you start
So much as how you finish.
I knew a little lady once, who meant
      extremely well
But she couldn't keep it up—and fell.

Refrain
Girls: She was a very good girl on Sunday,
Not quite so good on Monday,
On Tuesday, she was even worse,
On Wednesday and Thursday—
      good night, Nurse!
She seemed to lose by Friday
All sense of what was right.
She started out quite mild and meek,
But her virtue seemed to spring a leak,

She kept getting worse, all thro'
      the week,
And, oh, you Saturday night!

Maimie: She knew that men were wicked for
      her grandmamma had said,
That Satan was the master who
      employed them,
And so she made a rule that that
      should never turn her head,
She vowed that she'd avoid them,
But ev'ry time, she tried it, to her
      mind this thought would spring
"Am I passing up a darned good
      thing?"

Refrain
Girls: She wouldn't look at a man on Sunday,
She'd peep at him on Monday,

Section of Wodehouse manuscript for *All Full of Talk*.

On Tuesday, she took off the lid,
On Wednesday and Thursday,
   Oh, you kid!
She seemed to lose by Friday
All sense of what was right,
Most any time she met a guy,
She would pass along with
   downcast eye,
And say with a blush: "No Sir,
   Good bye,
But come 'round Saturday night."

The ills that lurk in alcohol she
   clearly understood
She feared the sweetest cocktail and
   the dry 'un.
She knew that drinking grape juice
   would make her as pure and good
As William Jennings Bryan.
But every time she thought of this,
   a still small voice would say,
"But who *wants* to be like William J?"

Refrain: She wouldn't drink anything on
      Sunday,
     She'd take a sip on Monday,
     On Tuesday she'd indulge in beer,
     On Wednesday and Thursday—
      whoops, my dear!
     She seemed to lose by Friday
     All sense of what was right,
     She started out to hit the trail,
     But her efforts seemed of no avail,
     So they brought her cocktails in a pail
     To save time Saturday night.

MELODRAMA BURLESQUE

(The Old-Fashioned Drama)

(Maimie, Dustin and Robin)

Maimie: I hate the feeble plays that are the
      fashion nowadays.

Dustin: The modern drama never has a punch.

Robin: Whenever I have sat in a front seat
      to watch a matinée
     I've wished I hadn't hurried over
      lunch,
     I find no satisfaction when there's talk
      instead of action.

Dustin: Oh, the things they put on nowadays
     are mud.

Robin: I like to look at something tough,
      where someone pulls the peppy
      stuff,
     And wants to swim in some one
      else's blood!

Refrain   When the villain lured the heroine at
      midnight to the mill
     Did we shudder?

Dustin: Yes, we shuddered!

Robin: See me shud!

All: He was not a pleasant persing,
     With his plotting and his cursing,
     But we liked him just because he
      wanted blood.

     I like the dramas where the husband
      finds the guilty pair

Maimie: And told them he knew all about
     their crime

Robin: Gee! While he'd be persuing 'em,
      I'd swallow all my chewing gum,
     I'd be so darned excited all the
      time.

Maimie: We saw the husband enter with a
      loaded pistol center.

Robin: And we knew that he had nipped
      them in the bud.

Dustin: He cried "Ah ha, I'll have your life
           For I saw you kiss my wife"
           And started in to have the fellow's
               blood.

All: He would raise his automatic
           With a glitter in his eye.
           And we shuddered with the accent on
               the shud,
           And we sympathized with hubby
           Though his conduct was not clubby
           But we like his honest zeal for
               shedding blood.

Dustin: "Now villain, say your prayers, for I've
               caught you unawares,
           The man who put my home upon
               the blink."

Robin: "You wrong me, Lord Cholmondelay
           Although I hugged her fondelay,
           Your wife is far more purer than
               you think."

Dustin: You cut a sorry figure, stage direction
               pulls the trigger

Robin: Some business of collapsing with
               a thud.

Maimie: "Now, see what you have done,
               you clam,
           You've gone and killed my brother,
               Sam
           And got our nice new rug all over
               blood."

All: Yes, the drama was the drama when
               we did that sort of thing,
           How we shuddered with accent on
               the shud
           We were sorry for the victim and the
               way that fate had tricked him
           But we did enjoy our little bit of
               blood, blood, etc.

ALL FULL OF TALK

(When You're Full of Talk)

(Robin)

Some people think the worst
    sensation anyone can know
Is being all dressed up and having
    got no place to go.
I'd rather be that way, with not a
    thing on earth to do
Than be all full of talk with no one
    there to talk it to.

Refrain: When you've lots to say, and there
               is no one around,
           You feel that you've been laid upon
               the shelf
           You have to sit and suffer
           While life keeps on getting
               tougher,
           For you can't say "Have another"
               to yourself.
           Your voice gets a rest, tucked away
               inside your chest,
           Till you've quite forgotten how it
               used to sound
           You could find some compensations
           In your wife's hard up relations
           When you're full of talk and want
               to get it from your system
           And you find that there is no one
               around.

           I often think how sad and
               lonesome Adam must
               have been,
           Alone inside the Garden till his
               (before) Eve came on the
               scene,
           It must have made him mad when
               he went out to take a walk
           And couldn't find a single thing
               that knew the way to talk.

Refrain:

He had lots to say, but there was
no one around,
Just animals and trees and other
junk.
The lion and the puma
Haven't got a sense of humor,
And you can't tell snappy stories to
a skunk,
You can't get a laugh from a
leopard or giraffe,
No wonder Adam bit his nails and
frowned
He could not tell chimpanzees his
Brand new stock of Ford car
wheezes,

He was full of talk and tried to get
it from his system
But he found that there was no
one around.

Alternative:

When Adam was a bachelor
A lonely life he had
But when he was a married man
His lot was just as bad.
Directly Eve came on the scene
He shouted out at last
And started in to try and talk
But found himself outclassed.
He had lots to say
But when Eve was around

He never got a chance of being
    bright
From the moment when he's waken
For his morning eggs and bacon
Till he put the cat outside last
    thing at night
She would not stop at all
Talking fashions for the fall,
She said she wished to be correctly
    gowned
And she'd argue whether fig
    leaves
Should be medium or big leaves.
He was all full of talk
Adam had no chance when Eve
    was around.

Another verse in Wodehouse's notebook—

When you're full of talk and there's
    no one around,
You get kind of low and
    melancholyish.
Ocean waves have animation,
But they've got no conversation
And you can't tell funny stories to
    the fish.
I'd be happy in a garrett,
If only I had a parrot,
Provided on the whole its views
    were sound,
But what's giving me the willies
Till I'm feeling fit to kill is
Being full of talk when there's no
    one around.

Like so many musical comedies of the period, the piece had its origins in Central European operetta. Emmerich Kalman's music was first heard in Leo Stein & Bela Jenbach's *Czardasfurstin* (1916) and subsequently in *The Gypsy Princess* (1921) with book by one Arthur Miller and lyrics by Arthur Stanley.

Fortunately, Bolton & Wodehouse's Anglo-American attack blew some of the cobwebs away and Kern's interpolations added a lyrical quality to the sugar confection.

Theatre Magazine called it "good all through, vernal and blithesome, as good as anything of its kind and better than anything done for years." Even though Kern had only played his familiar interpolating role, it could be said to be the team's first hit.

Not that the Broadway critics were such a key factor as they subsequently became. As Wodehouse later recalled: "Those were the days. None of this modern nonsense about 'We'll have to wait and see what the critics think of us.' [Erlanger said,] 'It will run at the New Amsterdam for a year and as soon as I have the New York opening off my hands, I shall organize a Western company.' Just like that. And the West was the West then. A full season in Chicago, fifty-two one-week stands, a third season of three-nighters, and Erlanger was more or less right. *Miss Springtime* ran for 230 performances—a very long run for those days—and was an even bigger success in Chicago. It went on touring for several years."

It certainly pleased at least one of its co-authors, who was by this time producing not only lyrics and libretti for several shows a season, as well as novels and short stories, but—for a while, at least—carrying out his journalistic chores. There was one surrealistic moment when part of his many duties at *Vanity Fair* involved him in reviewing his own theatrical work!

I feel a slight diffidence about growing enthusias-tic about *Miss Springtime*, for the fact is that, hav-ing contributed a few little lyrical bijoux to the above (just a few trifles, you know, dashed off in the intervals of more serious work) I am drawing a royalty from it which has already caused the wolf to move up a few parasangs from the Wodehouse doorstep. Far be it from me to boost—from sordid and commercial motives—a theatrical entertainment whose success means the increase of my meat-meals per week from one to two, but candor compels me to say that *Miss Springtime* is a corker. It is the best musical play in years.

Comstock had now seen the light—or perhaps the reflection from *Miss Springtime*—and was now ready to give the trio their head for the first Princess show. Well, not *quite* their head. He still wouldn't hear of *The Little Thing* but *Oh, Boy!* sounded better every time he heard it—so much so that he signed the contract before they'd even delivered the script.

But before they could settle to that, there was one final prior commitment that Bessie Marbury had made on their joint behalf. They owed a show to Colonel Henry Savage, another martinet to rival Erlanger. He sported something of a limp, which Bolton and Wodehouse later attributed to his having been "shot in the foot by some indignant author."

Whether he knew it or not, Savage was a lucky man. Bolton & Wodehouse & Kern were a theatrical phenomenon waiting in the wings. He was to have the advantage of their first full collaboration. A few short months later the price would most definitely go up.

HAVE A HEART (1917)

The Up-to-the-Minute Musical Comedy

Presented by Henry W. Savage at the Liberty Theatre, New York, on January 11, 1917 (78 performances) after a tryout in Atlantic City, Reading (Pennsylvania) and Wilmington (Delaware).

BOOK
Guy Bolton and P. G. Wodehouse

LYRICS
P. G. Wodehouse

MUSIC
Jerome Kern

CAST

Henry, the elevator boy: BILLY B. VAN

Ted Sheldon, a gilded youth: DONALD MACDONALD

Lizzie O'Brien: MARJORIE GATESON

Det. Baker of the Blueport Police: EUGENE KEITH

Rutherford Schoonmaker (Ruddy), Proprietor of Schoonmaker Dept. Store: THURSTON HALL

Capt. Charles (Chuck) Owen, a confidence man: ROY GORDON

Peggy Schoonmaker, his ex-wife: EILEEN VAN BIENE

Mrs. Pyne, Peggy's Aunt: FLAVIA ARCARO

Matthew Pyne, her husband: JAMES BRADBURY

Dolly Brabazon, a moving picture Star: LOUISE DRESSER

Yussuf, the entertainer: JOSEPH DEL PUENTE

SYNOPSIS

At Schoonmaker's department store, the sales girls feel rushed off their feet ("Shop"). Ted is trying to get a job there to be near Lizzie, who works there, but in reality is a Pinkerton agent tracking down forged currency. She, too, believes in the work ethic ("I'm So Busy"), while Ruddy Schoonmaker, the store's owner, can only think of his employees' welfare ("Have a Heart"). Ruddy is estranged from his wife, Peggy, who is being wooed by Owen, the forger who is circulating the dud money. Ruddy has apparently had a fling with the flamboyant Dolly Brabazon, but can't get over Peggy and tells her so ("And I Am All Alone"). He then hears that Dolly is arriving, expecting to marry him. Everyone has their troubles and Ted invites the Girls to share theirs with him ("I'm Here, Little Girls, I'm Here"). In desperation, Ruddy bribes Henry, the lift boy, to take Dolly out to dinner ("Bright Lights"). Peggy and Ruddy now run into each other and it's clear they are still in love ("The Road That Lies Before"). They decide to elope . . . (Act 1 Finale).

Everybody finds themselves at the Ocean View Hotel, where the cabaret is in full swing ("Samarkand"). Ruddy and Peggy arrive and the Girls tease her for being an obvious newlywed ("Honeymoon Inn"). She doesn't mind—she has her man back ("My Wife—My Man"). Dolly instructs Henry on how to recognize true love ("It's a Sure, Sure Sign"). Lizzie arrives with Ted still in pursuit ("You Said Something"). Peggy finds that Dolly is in the hotel but wants to be able to trust Ruddy.

Peggy: I want somebody to talk to, somebody who'll never tire of me,
              Like my dear dream playmate of long ago . . .

("Peter Pan"). Complications arise over the counterfeit currency and Ruddy is about to be wrongly arrested but Henry diverts the Detective. An awed Ruddy tells him—"You're a young Napoleon!" ("Napoleon"). Peggy is on the point of leaving with Owen. To celebrate his success he gives her a bouquet of flowers, including her favourite daisies ("Daisy"). To tie up the many loose ends of the plot, Dolly proves Owen the forger and explains that her only involvement with Ruddy was to provide "evidence" in the intended divorce. All ends happily—if a little abruptly!

SHOP

(Salesgirls)

Girls: It's time we were firm and lodged
     a strong complaint,
This sort of thing would try the
     temper of a saint.
We snatch a minute off to ease the
     cruel strain
And someone comes along, and
     makes us work again.

Refrain: Yes, that's the way! It's always the
     same,
Ev'ry day! It's really a shame.
Our little chats we have to stop
When we hear some one shouting
     "Shop!"
We're oppressed! It's simply not
     right,
Get no rest from morning till night.
It's a bore, this serving in a store.
Don't think we can stand it much
     more.

I'M SO BUSY

(Lizzie and Ted)

(Lyrics by P. G. Wodehouse and Schuyler Greene)

Lizzie: I've always said that the man I
     would wed
Must be one who would work all
     the time.
One with ambition,
Who'd make it his mission
To win a position sublime.
One whose chief pleasure would be
Making a fortune for me;
One who would toil all the day,
Down in the Market and say:

Refrain

Lizzie, Lizzie I'm so busy,
Don't know what to do.
Goodbye dear, I'm off to the Street,
Can't stop now, I'm cornering wheat,
I shall keep on till I'm dizzy
Till the deal goes through.
Lizzie, I'm so busy
I'm making a pile for you.

Ted: Don't be deceived, if you've ever
     believed
That my taste for hard labor is
     small.
Stifle the lurking
Idea that I'm shirking,
I never stop working at all.
I may have loafed in the past,
But I am busy at last,
I've found employment and I'm
Working away all the time.

Refrain: Lizzie, Lizzie, I'm so busy,
Busy loving you.
That's the job that suits me the best,
Though I never get any rest.
I shall keep on till I'm dizzy,
But I shan't get through.
Lizzie, I'm so busy
So, won't you get busy, too?

HAVE A HEART

(Ruddy)

A girl in a department store has quite a wretched
     time of it
I shouldn't care to have her job myself.
It seems to me a foolish way
To have to spend the whole damn (live long) day,
Stuck up behind a counter, hauling what-nots off
     the shelf.

I hate your strict employers, who are nutty about
  discipline,
Who run a store with punishment and fine.
Why pick on some poor little thing
Who's been out all night tangoing,
Because she gets to work at one o'clock instead
  of nine?

Refrain:

Have a heart! Have a heart!
Remember she is human just like you.
Wouldn't you regard with loathing,
Hats and coats and under-clothing,
If you hadn't got to bed till half-past two?
A shop girl (salesgirl) in the city is deserving of
  your pity,
Of pleasure life for her is not a whirl
So I'm making it my mission
To improve her sad condition,
And like Heaven, I'll protect the working-girl.

Each girl in my employment, on arriving in the
  morning is
Provided with refreshments on a tray.
It costs but little to supply
Dill pickles and Martinis dry,
Which put her in a mood to face the labors of
  the day.
If later she should grow fatigued, she totters to
  the reading room
Or staggers to a moving picture show
Or in the Rest-Room she may get
A soda or a cigarette;
These simple acts of kindness seem a lot to her,
  you know.

Refrain:
Have a heart! Have a heart!
Recollect a salesgirl isn't a machine.
Ev'ry day with much completeness
I am scatt'ring light and sweetness,
So she gets a chance to rest her aching bean.

I'm leader of the Movement for Effecting an
  Improvement,
The battle flag of freedom I unfurl.
She grows weary selling (showing) corsets,
If she never lies down or sits,
So, like Heaven, I'll protect the working-girl.

AND I AM ALL ALONE (I SEE YOU THERE)

(Ruddy and Peggy)

(Lyrics by Jerome Kern and P. G. Wodehouse)

Ruddy: Morning and night, I find no rest
       from the pain
     That comes because I can't forget you.
     All of the time you come to haunt
       me again
     Just as you were when first I met you.

     I see you there just as you used to be
     So sweet and fair, you stand and gaze
       at me.
     Your form is girlish in its slenderness,
     You've got a mother's smile of
       tenderness.
     I hear your laugh, it's like an April
       morn,
     I see you cry (weep), a tiny pearl
       is born
     I breathe your name, and find the
       vision has flown
     And I am all alone.

Peggy: If I were there, would you be good
       to me?
     If I were there, just as I used to be—
     We tried it once, you know, without
       success,
     How soon it changed, our dream of
       happiness.
     Our joy soon passed—it could not
       last, we've seen

So don't let's think of all that might
    have been—
For far behind us lies the love we've
    known.

I'M HERE, LITTLE GIRLS, I'M HERE

(Ted and Girls)

Ted: Ladies, I'm here just to be good
        to you,

Girls: That's true.

Ted: So will you say if there is anything
        I can do?

Girls: There's one thing we'll call your
        attention to.

Ted: I'll correct it, if you will give the
        clue.

Girls: Oh, you.

Ted: Rely on me. A friend and helper,
        I want to be.

Girls: We need, as you will no doubt agree
    A lot of cheerful society.

Ted: I quite understand, leave that to me,
    I'll just make a note, you see.

Girls: Yes, our life is rather flat.

Ted: Let me make a note of that.

Girls: Will you help if you can?

Ted: Ladies, I'm your man
    When you want a cozy chat,
    I'll drop in and comfort that.

Girls: Do! Do!

Ted: Whenever you're feeling blue.

Girls: Sometimes we feel so lonely.

Ted: As I can see,

Girls: If you would only . . .

Ted: Leave that to me. I'll drop in and
        comfort you,
    I want to be good to you.
    Trust me! In future, I'll be near,
    So please don't get down-hearted.
    Bear this in mind:
    I'm here, little girls, I'm here.

Girls: Life, for us, is quite the reverse of gay.

Ted: No play?

Girls: With all our Jacks and Freds and
        Billies so far away

Ted: I must own it does seem a trifle gray

Girls: No amusement, think of it, all
        the day!

Ted: I say!
    If that is so, it seems to me that I'm
        not *de trop*.

Girls: We'll find you such a relief, you know,
    When things have started to get too
        slow.

Ted: Oh yes, we'll have lots of fun,
        although
    Most careful how far we go.

Girls: You're the nicest man in town.

Ted: Let me get that jotted down.

Girls: If we gave you a kiss,
        Would it be amiss?

Ted: Why, I shouldn't even frown.
        I want to be good to you.

Girls: Do! Do!

Ted: Whenever you want me to.

Girls: Sometimes we feel deserted.

Ted: That well may be.

Girls: But if we flirted . . .

Ted: Leave that to me, I want to be good
            to you.
        Trust me! In future, I'll be near
        If you require flirtation,
        Just make a note:
        I'm here, little girls, I'm here.

BRIGHT LIGHTS

(Dolly and Henry)

Dolly: How I love to go out to some live spot,
        Where there's light and an orchestra
            plays.

Henry: Where you hand the head waiter
            a five spot,
        Or you don't get a table for days

Dolly: Where the gowns are all up to the
            minute,
        And where ev'rything's lovely
            and gay—

Henry: And the night's gone before you
            begin it;
        So you finish things up through
            the day.

Refrain

Both: Come with me where there are bright
            lights,
        Where the white lights gleam and
            glow.
        Where the festive ukulele
        Tinkles gaily,
        Let us go.
        We will sup with one another
        Till the merry morning chime.
        Say goodbye to home and mother,
        We'll be gone a long, long time.

Dolly: We will drink the champagne that
            is fizzy,
        Then, some dancing I'd adore.

Henry: All the people will whisper: "Who
            is he?"
        When they see me come (crawl) out
            on the floor.

Dolly: Do you think you could get through
            some one-steps,
        Or at dancing are you quite a dunce?

Henry: It is true that I've never yet done
            steps,
        But, ah gee! I'll try anything once!

Refrain

THE ROAD THAT LIES BEFORE

(Ruddy and Peggy)

Ruddy: If there's nothing more to say,
        If things can't be mended—

Peggy: Well, the chapter's ended,
        Let's say goodbye.

Ruddy: Wait, though. I've some things
            of yours,
        I had best return them.

Peggy: What! You didn't burn them?

Ruddy: Burn them? Not I!
These souvenirs of you,
Were once a lover's token
But now our vows are broken,
There's only this to do
This little glove which once you used
to wear
I'll now give back to you.

Peggy: No, keep it.

Ruddy: You used to use this once to bind
your hair
I'll give it back to you.

Peggy: No, keep it

Ruddy: The love that once you gave me
I now give back to you

Peggy: No, please keep that too.

Ruddy: Then our first kiss I'll now give back
to you

(They kiss)

Peggy: Once more Love's path we'll try
Together—you and I.
The road that lies before
Is dark and hard to see.
What e'er fate holds in store,
Try it with me! Try it with me!
What though we missed it once
We did not understand
Better today we know the way,
So let us set out hand in hand,
Love for our path a light we'll make
Shining to guide the steps we take.

FINALE—ACT 1

Girls: Just think of it, Ruddy has really
eloped,
Poor dear old Schoony has fled

Men: He's taking the deuce of a chance,
Think of the dance
She's going to lead the man after
they're wed
They used to be spliced to each other
before,
Marvellous nerve, the chap (man)
shows.
Now will they be wretched once more,
Or will their life become *Couleur
de Rose*?

All: Goodness knows.

Uncle &
Aunt: Lizzie, Lizzie do get busy
Tell us what to do.

Owen: *(Spoken)*
I can't think what you're about.

Lizzie: Oh, please, cut it out!

All: Lizzie, Lizzie, say, where is he?
What's the use of you?
That game we must be balking,
Don't let's stand here talking:
Do something, somebody!
Telephone everywhere!
Let's be quiet and cool.

(To Henry)
Can't you do anything?
Don't stand gaping there
(Why do you stop up there?)
Oh! the poor little fool!

Henry: Have a heart! Jiminy Christmas!
Have a heart!
(Gee! You girls are always picking on
a man!)
Can't you see I'm doing everything
I can
If you'll kindly keep your distance,

I might be of some assistance.
Remember, girls, you're dealing with
  a man

(To Aunt)
(Can that "Clara Kimball Young"
  stuff
Be a man!
Don't you see I'm doing everything
  I can?)

All: Have a heart! Have a heart!
You must go and make inquiries in
  the town.
You won't find out where your
  niece is
If you pull the boy to pieces;
So get in the lift, and let him take
  you down.

Though they fancy just as you did,
That pursuit they have eluded.
They will probably have tarried
At the parson's to get married,
There are slips between the lips,
  though, and the cup.

Henry: Don't imagine that I'm shirking
But the darn thing isn't working
The machinery has got all tangled up

All: Can't you start the thing on "High,"
  boy?
Was there ever such an inefficient
  pup?
What has happened to the elevator?
  Golly!
Has it stuck?
And all the while it's getting later,
What a rotten bit of luck.
Can't you start the thing on high,
  boy?
You can do it if you try, boy.
Was there ever such an inefficient pup?

Henry: Going up! Going up!

Uncle: He's doing it on purpose.

Owen: Schoonmaker bribed him to help
  them get away.

Lizzie: Someone has stopped the escalators,
(Auto horn is heard under stage)

Henry: Hark! The merry note of Klaxon—
  they're off.

Owen: Quick! Look out of the window.
  Can you see them?

All *(Except Principals)*:
Yes—
We see them there, just as they used
  to be
A happy pair. They go contentedly.
The motor hums a merry bridal tune
As they begin their second
  honeymoon
Without a care for what may lie
  before,
Resolved to dare whate'er may be
  in store.
And whether it be good or ill,
How ever it may chance,
The sun will shine upon them still,
The sunshine of romance.
Whatever Fate may bring,
Its blows can hold (have) no sting,
As in the days when we would sing:

Ruddy: I see you there, just as you used to be,
So sweet and fair, you stand and gaze
  at me.
Your form is girlish in its slenderness,
You have a mother's smile of
  tenderness.
I see you smile. It's like an April
  morn,

Each time you weep, a tiny pearl
    is born.
I breathe your name, and find the
    vision has flown.
And I am all alone.

OPENING CHORUS—ACT 2

SAMARKAND

(Yussuf, Boys and Girls)

Boys &
Girls: The weary sun has fled, and the day
        is o'er
The moon reigns in his stead over sea
    and shore.
The soothing shadows fall like a cool
    caress.
And darkness covers all, bringing
    happiness.
Who knows what woes may come
    tomorrow?
Sad tomorrow may be.
But fill your glasses high, and bid care
    goodbye.
Tomorrow is a long way off, you see!

Men: Cigarettes, cigars and coffee!

Yussuf: Of the very finest these!

Men: Cigarettes, cigars and coffee!

Yussuf: At your service, if you please!

Girls: So let's be gay,
Let soft music play
Beneath the ray
Of moonlight so bright.
Though troubles may

Men: Return with the day!

Girls: Be happy tonight.

Yussuf: The moon that shines up there,
Shines on my native land.
My heart is far away in Samarkand
Long ago in Samarkand, such nights
    I've known.
In that garden where I stand and wait
    alone.
In the moonlight wan and pale,
Singing with the nightingale—
"Sulima, your lover stands below."

Girls &
Boys: Oh, that scented garden, long ago.

Yussuf: "Show your face and let it dim the
    jealous moon.
With your beauty, turn the night to
    flaming noon.
See how brightly yonder star
Glitters down from Heaven's bar;
Your bright eyes will gleam more
    brightly far,
My Sulima!"
The nightingale
Took up the tale.
We sang together there
To Sulima the fair.
Soft breezes fanned
The list'ning land,
While the nightingale and I
Sang out our love beneath the silver
    sky,
When the moon shone down on
    Samarkand

HONEYMOON INN
(THE HONEYMOON HOTEL)

(Peggy and Ensemble)

Peggy: Out beyond the far horizon,
There's a place I've not set eyes on,
Where a happy haven
Wedded lovers may win.

"Ah, Say! Have A Heart"

"Napoleon"

(And I, Take After
Nap)

Billy B. Van (*Henry*) and Girls.

Covered deep with honeysuckles,
Near a stream that laughs and
    chuckles
Bathed in golden sunshine,
Stands the Honeymoon Inn.

Refrain: Life's always May there,
For sweethearts who stray there,
Away from the bustle and din.
All days are gay there

And no days are gray there.
When you're at the Honeymoon
    Inn
You live on bread and cheese and
    kisses
You know that this is
The thing to do.
I'd go and stay there,
I'd spend every day there,
If only the way there I knew.

Happy lovers there are able (There
    each happy couple's able)
To hold hands beneath the table,
If they're caught embracing
There is no one to grin.
No one pays the least attention;
Kissing is a great invention
Ev'rybody does it
At the Honeymoon Inn.

MY WIFE—MY MAN

(Peggy and Ruddy)

Ruddy: Is this just a dream once more?
    Just the dream I dreamt before?
    Oh, the sad time I've had,
    Peggy dear, away
    From you,

Peggy: *(Teasingly)*
    Oh, yes, I believe you were glad
    Of the holiday,
    It's true.
    Confess!

Ruddy: Why, it drove me half mad
    I could find, I swear,
    No plan
    Of life.

Peggy: *(With feeling)*
    Was it really so bad?
    Did you really care? My man!

Ruddy: My wife!

Refrain
Peggy: There's only just we two
    In all the world, you see.
    For I was made for you
    You, dear, for me—you, dear, for me.
    And life may bring us joy,

And life may bring us pain;
Cruel or kind, we shall not mind
Now we're together once again.
Gladness and grief alike we'll share,
Grief will be joy, if you are there.

Peggy: Ruddy, dear, do you fear
    That perhaps you may
    Regret?

Ruddy: Not I!
    Do you wish, now you're here,
    You were miles away?

Peggy: My pet!
    I'd die!

Ruddy: Can you trust me, dear,
    To be always true
    Through life?

Peggy: I can;
    All my doubts disappear
    As I cling to you.

Ruddy: My wife!

Peggy: My man!

Refrain
Peggy: The road that lies before
    Is dark and hard to see.
    Whate'er Fate holds in store,
    Try it with me! Try it with me!
    What though we missed it once,
    We did not understand.
    Better today, we know the way,
    So let us set out hand in hand.
    Love for our path a light will make
    Shining to guide the steps we take!

While they were preparing the show, Bolton was missing his wife, Marguerite. As a token he called the heroine Peggy—the diminutive of her name. Taking the coded love message one stage further Wodehouse included the lyric line—"Oh, the sad time I've had, Peggy dear, away from you."

IT'S A SURE, SURE SIGN

(Dolly)

I have a book I wouldn't lose for anything,
I might let you look,
But I should hold it tight.
It's crammed with information on each page
    to which you turn;
For instance, you'll discover, if your ears
    should burn,
It's a sure, sure sign
Some kind friend's begun to knock you
In a manner that would shock you.
It's a sure, sure sign.
Someone's got your reputation
Mixed up in their conversation.
Though they started saying lovely things
    about you,
They have finally decided you're a 'shine,'
And until the ear burn ceases
They'll be picking you to pieces,
It's a sure, sure sign.

Most any night, if you go to a restaurant
Where lights glitter bright,
You'll see a couple there.
He's asking her if she'd prefer some diamonds or
    a car,
And she replies she'd like them both, well, there
    you are!
It's a sure, sure sign.
And you're safe in saying 'Mister, that is not your
    little sister'
It's a sure, sure sign.
And the waiter, when he's waited,
Knows just how they are related.
If he urges her to order Lobster Newburg
And announces he intends to open wine,

If she answers 'Don't be silly!'
When he says 'Oh, call me Willy!'
It's a sure, sure sign.

Though long you've been a gay and giddy
    bachelor,
There'll come on the scene
A girl not like the rest.
You'll notice something in her eye that fills you
    with dismay;
You'll find that when you're with her you can't
    think what to say.
That's a sure, sure sign.
You have ceased to be a rover,
And your single days are over.
It's a sure, sure sign!
You had best begin rehearsing for the 'better-
    and-for-worse'-ing.
If she creeps beside you softly in the gloaming,
Whispers gently 'Don't you think the moon's
    divine?'
Keep your courage steady, Freddie,
For she's got the harpoon ready,
It's a sure, sure sign.

Our Uncle Sam's a nice polite old gentleman,
As meek as a lamb
When things are going right.
He'll stand for jokes from foreign folks until they
    get too rough,
But when he takes his coat off and says
    'That's enough!'
It's a sure, sure sign
There's trouble brewing
And there'll soon be something doing.
It's a sure, sure sign
That ambassadors and so on
Ocean trips are sure to go on.
Uncle Sammy doesn't go round hunting for
    them,
But he always knows just where to draw the line.
And when he breaks off relations
He's through with explanations,
It's a sure, sure sign.

Life nowadays is getting pretty serious,
In all sorts of ways
We're terribly oppressed.
Each day the price of eggs and ice gets higher
    ev'rywhere,
There's nothing much we can afford to eat
    but air.
It's a sure, sure sign
When you have to spend a nickel
For a peanut or a pickle;
It's a sure, sure sign
When you need a wealthy backer
If you're going to buy a cracker,
When you have to steal the kitten's milk for
    breakfast,
And the wafers from the goldfish when you dine,
Then the ultimate consumer's
Going to lose his sense of humour,
It's a sure, sure sign.

I'd like to sing from now right on to supper time,
But there's one thing one has to recollect;
If I'd my choice I'd use my voice
Till I was fit to drop.
But something seems to tell me
That it's time to stop.
It's a sure, sure sign
When the artistes in the offing
Look impatient and start coughing;
It's a sure, sure sign
When the audience, as you vex it,
Says "Look 'round and choose your exit";
When you see the stage director's glaring at you
In a way that sends cold shivers up your spine,
Then it's time to smile politely
And go off smiling brightly,
It's a sure, sure sign.

There is a mystery here in that the sheet music credits the lyric to one "R. P. Weston and Jerome Kern." Robert ("Bob") Patrick Weston (1878–1936) was an English author, songwriter and lyricist who was prolific on the London stage from around 1910 to 1924 and was responsible for "Anglicizing" many American imports—but there is nothing to suggest why he might have been involved in an exclusively American show as early as this unless, of course, he happened to be one of the more than seventy lyricists Kern was known to have worked with and the song had been originally written for another show. However, in view of the amount of mis-crediting that took place between production and publication—and because of the distinctly Wodehousean tone of the lyric—I have chosen to gamble on its authenticity. (If it isn't Wodehouse, it's still interesting as a period piece!)

YOU SAID SOMETHING

(Ted, Lizzie and Ensemble)

(Lyrics by Jerome Kern and P. G. Wodehouse)

Lizzie: All the men I know
        Fascinate me so.
        Oh, what romances
        I've built around them in my fancies.

Ted: I am not aware
        Why you think I care.

Lizzie: Why, surely you know, dear
        I was teasing. I love you, dear.

        You said something when you said
            you loved me.
        Oh, but I wonder for how long it
            will be.
        If you find one day you've altered
            your mind,
        I'd be forgiving, but simply could not
            go on living,
        Girls much prettier you'll find by
            the score.
        Will you regret you never met them
            before?
        You said something when you said
            you loved me—
        Say it a whole lot more.

Ted: All the girls I see
          Make a hit with me.
          Where'er I wander
          I love brunettes or something
          blonder.

Lizzie: I don't care a bit
          Where your heart may flit.

Ted: I am not aware
          Why you think I care;
          Why surely you knew, dear,
          I was teasing; I love you dear.

Lizzie: Why surely you knew, dear,
          I was teasing; I love you dear.

Refrain
Lizzie: You said something when you said
             you loved me,
          Oh, but I wonder for how long it
             will be.
          If you find some day, you've altered
             your mind
          I'd be forgiving, but simply could not
             go on living!
          Girls much prettier you will meet by
             the score.
          Will you regret you never met them
             before?
          You said something when you said
             you loved me—
          Say it a whole lot more.

PETER PAN

(Peggy)

When the birds say goodbye to the daylight
And with dewdrops the grass is pearled,
There's a song you can hear in the grey light,
That comes from the edge of the world.
Hark! There it is!
Rising—falling

Like a sob, like the moan of the breeze,
It is Youth and Romance that is calling—
Peter Pan's coming near through the trees.

How I wish that I were Wendy,
To be loved by Peter Pan.
We would fly up high
Through the moonlight sky.
He'd come right down and set me free,
And my bonds he'd sever,
Then, hand in hand, in the Never-Never-Land,
We'd be young forever.

Peter Pan, Peter Pan, can't you hear me?
Won't you fly down and help me, please?
Won't you play on your reed-pipe to cheer me,
In your home at the top of the trees?
There I would live,
Troubles forgetting,
Till the last fairy story is told.
Far away from the world and its fretting,
In the land where you never grow old.

Henry: Napoleon: That's who I am!
          Maybe it's a case of reincarnation

NAPOLEON

Napoleon was a little guy
They used to call him "Shorty"
He only stood about so high,
His chest was under forty.
But when folks started joshing him (But when
        folks started talking mean
His pride it didn't injure
He'd simply say: "Ah, fade away!"
("My Queen," he'd say to Josephine,)
He knew he had the ginger. ("The thing that
        counts is ginger.")

Napoleon, Napoleon, they thought him quite
       a joke
"Hey, take a slant at the little pill"

Was the line of chatter that they used to spill
But they couldn't (hold) faze Napoleon
When he started in to scrap
He was five feet high
But he was one tough guy
And I take after Nap!

Napoleon was a homely mutt (gink)
He hadn't time to doll up
And though he looked like thirty cents
He packed an awful wallop.
And all the kings of Europe
When they came to know his habits
Pulled up their socks and ran for blocks
He'd got them scared like rabbits.

Napoleon, Napoleon, he went out and got
    a rep,
He had a lot of 'em climbing trees
Though he only weighed a hundred in his
    B.V.D.'s
It was easy for Napoleon
And he wiped them off the map
He was not so tall
But could lick them all
And I take after Nap!

Napoleon was the ladies' pet
They liked to have him handy.
He used to blow in half his pay
On violets and candy.
He knew the game from soup to nuts
And he worked it on a system.
He'd meet a Queen at five fifteen
By six o'clock she's kissed him.

Napoleon, Napoleon, he had them hypnotized
    (The ladies thought him great)
They fell for him good and hard they did
When he came and handed them the "Oh,
    you kid."
All ladies loved Napoleon (They were wild
    about Napoleon)
For his work was full of snap

He was one good guy
    (He was sawn off short)
With a goo-goo eye
    (But he was one good (smooth) sport)
And I take after Nap!

Napoleon was a hard-up gink (mutt)
He'd not a million dollars
He used to ride around in Fords
He wore those paper collars. (But still he meant
    to make his pile)
He'd lunch and dine with emperors (And look
    how he succeeded,)
Whenever he was able
    (He made himself an Emperor,)
But just before the check arrived
    (Then grabbed the dough he needed)
Napoleon left the table.

Napoleon, Napoleon, they used to think him
    cheap.
They joshed him and they pulled his leg
They called him piker and a hard boiled egg.
But they couldn't faze Napoleon (But they
    didn't know Napoleon)
And he gave their wrists a slap
He was fond of dough (For he knew the
    trick,)
And he would not let go
    (And went and got rich quick,)
And I take after Nap!

Napoleon was a fat gazook
    (He got too fat. We all know that)
He never took to banting.
    (From portraits in the galleries)
And every time he walked up stairs
    (He never seemed to learn the knack)
He had to stand there panting,
    (Of laying off the calories)
But gee! That did not worry him
    (But though his waist was large, he faced)
When up against the foeman
    (And overcame all foemen.)

He knew that it's the brains that count
   (He knew quite well it's brains that tell)
And not a guy's abdomen.

Napoleon, Napoleon, they tried to get his goat.
They used to drop in at his flat
And leave him bottles of some anti-fat
But they couldn't faze Napoleon
He was not that sort of chap.
He was not so lean
But he'd got a swell-shaped bean
And I take after Nap!

Napoleon seldom mixed his drinks
His favourite glass was brandy.
He could not sleep unless they'd keep
The royal bottle handy.
And when they fixed his royal bath
He swore he'd not get in it
Until they sprayed his royal throat
With brandy once a minute.

Napoleon, Napoleon, the drink was by his hand
He'd stop his horse with the battle's roar
And loudly yell for one drink more.
It was the booze that saved Napoleon
From many an aimless zap
He could fight like sin
When he had four ports in
And I take after Nap!

The song was originally written for *Miss Springtime*. Since it is such a pointed dig at Abe Erlanger, Wodehouse may have decided discretion was preferable to valour and held it over for a non-Erlanger production!

DAISY

(Peggy and Girls)

Peggy: Back in the days of childhood
      When life was a joyful song.
       When skies were blue, and the world
         was all new,

      And when nothing at all went
        wrong.
As through the fields, I wandered
Weaving my daisy chain,
Gravely I'd pause, while I pondered
Crooning a nurs'ry refrain.

Refrain: Daisy, Daisy,
      Tell me all you know.
      Every time I pluck a petal
      Secrets you can show.
      Daisy, Daisy,
      Tell me all you see.
      There's a question you can settle:
      Does the one I love, love me?

Now I have grown much older
And life isn't half such fun,
A daisy-chain I shall never again
Sit and weave in the noonday sun.
But, when they bring me posies,
It's as it was before
Little I care for your roses—
I love the daisy far more.

Daisy, Daisy,
Tell me all you know
Every time I pluck a petal,
Secrets you can show.
Daisy, Daisy
Tell me all you see,
There's a question you can settle,
Does the one I love, love me?

The vocal score contains other numbers that do not appear to have been used in the final show. . . .

POLLY BELIEVED IN PREPAREDNESS

Ev'ry maiden today should know men thru
   and thru,

And it's never too soon to begin
To study their ways for each year nowadays
It gets harder to gather them in.
I once knew a girl who was prudence itself,
For she always was looking ahead;
She practised each glance and left nothing to
    chance
"Be prepared" was her motto, she said.

Refrain:
Polly believed in preparedness,
So when she put on a new dress,
She paid attention to things we won't mention;
You don't know they're there, but you guess.
Though her efforts were frequently wasted,
Still no trouble and forethought she spared,
For she said: "You can't know when the wind's
    going to blow,"
She liked to be prepared.

Now and then, some young man would drop in
    at her home
For a nice cozy afternoon chat.
She made preparations for such conversations
Before he had hung up his hat.
Young men, as you know, often let themselves go,
And are apt to say more than they mean;
So she felt the fitness of having a witness
To take a few notes of the scene.

Polly believed in preparedness
She knew what these meetings can be;
So she'd deposit her aunt in a closet,
And father behind the settee.
When men talked indiscreetly, how sweetly
    she'd smile,
As their fervor she shared,
In a corner, alone, stood a small dictaphone
She liked to be prepared.

THEY ALL LOOK ALIKE

In days gone by, I used to be
Inclined for men's society,

I would flirt and I would dance
Ev'ry time that I got the chance.
Athletic Jim taught me to swim,
Jack drove me in his car,
I'd stroll with Ned and golf with Fred,
What dear, good boys they are!
But now although, with one accord,
They try to please me, I'm just bored.

Refrain:
For they all look alike to me now
Yes, they all look alike to me now.
I used to feel as fond of them as I could be,
But ev'rything is changed somehow.
I meet an old acquaintance,
But no longer get a thrill,
I say, "How are you, Clarence?"
And he tells me he is Bill;
If I see a man on Sunday
I've forgotten him by Monday,
For they all look alike to me now.

Another cut song was set in the hotel. It was a trio for Henry, Dolly and the Maitre d'.

CAN THE CABARET

Henry: When you've picked out a nice little
           table for two

Dolly: And you sit just as close as you're able
           to do,

Henry: And you start to impart
           All the innermost secrets you have in
             your heart,

Dolly: Then the orchestra toots on his flutes,
           And the dancers are whirling around,

Henry: And the stately soprano beside the
           piano
           Drowns out ev'ry possible sound.

Dolly: And when there's a pause in the din.
The confounded waiter comes in.

Waiter: Madame would like more of ze butter?
Monsieur would like more of ze wine?
Ze lobster is utterly utter,
Ze salad exquisite, divine.

All: Alas, in these days of the cabaret craze,
You cannot converse when you dine.
If they'd only, only can the cabaret,
If they'd only send the jazz band far
away.
If they'd only try to quiet all the
syncopated riot,
We could sometimes have a word or
two to say.
If they'd load the ballad singers on
a dray,
And they'd drown 'em where the
flying fishes play,
We could start again to patter all the
good old spoony chatter,
If they'd only, only can the cabaret.

Henry: But the cabaret's running wherever
we eat

Dolly: And it seems we are never, no, never
to meet

Henry: Where a word can be heard,
Or a couple can murmur sweet
nothings absurd,

Dolly: For the quartette comes out with
a shout,
Singing songs that are eighty years
old.

Henry: While an old ladies' chorus goes
racing before us,
Our food and our passion grow cold.

Dolly: And just when that number is
through,
A cigarette boy comes in view.

Waiter: 'Cigars, cigarettes, souvenirs, Sir?
A doll for your girl? Treat her right!
A fine box of candy right here, Sir?
Aw, gee, they're all pikers tonight.'

All: Alas, in these days of the cabaret craze
The chance to make love isn't bright.
If they'd only, only can the cabaret,
If they'd send the Hula dancers on
their way,
We could breathe our passion fervent
While the crowd was unobservant,
And we wouldn't have to shout the
things we say.
If they'd string the fiddler up without
delay,
We'd be glad to let the angels hear
him play.
Yes, to rapture it would drive one,
And a girl could grab a live one,
If they'd only, only can the cabaret!

If there is any doubt about the influence of Wodehouse's lyrics on later writers, the young Noël Coward can be clearly seen to be one of his early acolytes. Not only was his first published song "The Story of Peter Pan" (1918) but in *London Calling!* (1923) he had a song called "Carrie Was A Careful Girl," which has more than an echo of "Polly"! Whereas Polly was inclined to "deposit her aunt in a closet/And father behind the settee," when Carrie invited a beau around "to have a little drink," she "had her Auntie Jessie underneath the kitchen sink."

Different versions of the libretto typically delete some of these songs and add others. In the 1918 copy on which the above is based, for instance, Peggy's "Peter Pan" was marked as "Out."

Once again numbers came and went in try-out. A song called "Come Out Of the Kitchen" (words and music by James Kendis and Charles Bayha) replaced "Polly Believed In Preparedness" (neither of which appears in this version) and "Bright Lights" replaced "That's The Life." "Why Can't It Happen To Me?"—sung by Ruddy and the Girls—gave way to a number for Peggy and the ensemble, "Daisy," although it did turn up later in *The Riviera Girl* as "Why Can't They Hand It To Me?"

On the subsequent tour, "Come Out Of the Kitchen" and "Peter Pan" were dropped and two new songs, "What Would You Do For $50,000?" and "Whirlwind Trot," were added.

Following the habit he would pursue through the rest of his career, Kern dug into his melody trunk. "Bright Lights" had Wodehouse words to the 1916 song, "Toodle Oo" and, since "I'm So Busy" credits both Wodehouse and Schuyler Greene (who wrote the previous lyric for "Toodle Oo"), the chances are that it was written for an earlier show-that-never-was.

The reviewers were beginning to get the point and although the reception was not over-effusive, the review that pleased the trio most was the one that concluded: "*Have A Heart* has a plot upon which Mr. Kern's music always has a direct bearing." As for Wodehouse, these lyrics "are good, but not so good as those which we wrote for *Miss Springtime*. A glittering exception, however, is "Napoleon."

Meanwhile—and very much in parallel—Bolton & Wodehouse & Kern were preparing their first show for Comstock. It would open on Broadway only five weeks later.

So the Princess phenomenon can be said to date from December 24th, 1916.

The show Ray Comstock had insisted on producing ended up being called *Go To It*—which audiences singularly failed to do. Since any Broadway producer worth the name is a pragmatist first and an idealist a long way after, Comstock sent for "the boys" post haste. How soon could they get—what was it called? *Oh, Boy?* into rehearsal? Five weeks? Fine, go to it. An unfortunate Freudian slip under the circumstances. So, script unread, score unheard, the show that was to break all previous box office records for a Broadway musical and create the genre called "The Princess Shows" was born.

It was with *Oh, Boy!* that Plum and Kern developed the *modus operandi* that suited them best and one that they would follow for the rest of their collaboration. Not being a musician himself, Plum preferred to work with a finished melody—and Kern was not going to argue with that. However, he did have one significant musical skill and that was an ability to whistle a tune accurately after he had heard it only once.

OH, BOY! (1917)

Presented by the Comstock-Elliott Company at the Princess Theatre, New York, on February 20, 1917 (475 performances), after a tryout at the Van Curler Opera House, Schenectady.

BOOK   Guy Bolton and P. G. Wodehouse
LYRICS P. G. Wodehouse
MUSIC Jerome Kern

Its 299-seat capacity made the theatre for *Oh, Boy!* immune to the city's fire laws that applied to theatres with 300 seats or more.

CAST

Briggs, George's valet:
CARL LYLE

Jane Packard:
MARION DAVIES

Polly Andrus:
JUSTINE JOHNSTONE

Jim Marvin:
HAL FORDE

George Budd:
TOM POWERS

Lou Ellen Carter:
MARIE CARROLL

Jackie Sampson:
ANNA WHEATON
(actress playing 'Modesty'
in *Experience*)

Constable Simms:
STEPHEN MALEY

Judge Daniel Carter:
FRANK McGINN

Mrs. Carter:
AUGUSTA HAVILAND

Miss Penelope Budd:
EDNA MAY OLIVER

A Club Waiter:
JACK MERRITT

Miss Lottie Limmut:
JEANETTE COOKE

Miss Iona Saxon:
PATRICE CLARKE

Miss Rhoda Byke:
EVELYN GRIEG

Miss Shella Ryve:
MARGARET MASON

Miss Inna Ford:
ANNA STONE

Miss Georgia Spelvin:
FLORENCE McGUIRE

Miss Wanda Farr:
KATHERINE HURST

Miss Anna Thrope:
ETHEL FORDE

Miss Billie Dew:
LILLIAN RICE

Miss Lotta Noyes:
KATHRYN RAHN

Miss Annie Olde-Knight:
LILLIAN LAVONNE

Miss B. Ava Little:
MARJORIE ROLLAND

Miss Delia Kards:
VERA MEYERS

Mr. Olaf Lauder:
AUSTIN CLARK

Mr. Ivan L. Ovanerve:
ALDEN GLOVER, Jr.

Mr. Will Hooper Rupp:
JOSEPH HADLEY

Mr. Phil Ossify:
CHARLES YORKSHIRE

Mr. Phelan Fyne:
RALPH O'BRIEN

Mr. Hugo Chaseit:
CLARENCE LUTZ

SYNOPSIS

While George is out his playboy friend Jim arrives with the Girls ("Let's Make a Night of It"). As they search for him, George arrives with his new bride, Lou Ellen ("You Never Knew About Me"). Jim teases George about his well known liking for the ladies ("A Package of Seeds"). A telegram announces that George's Quaker aunt and guardian, Aunt Penelope, is arriving. Fearing she may disapprove of the marriage and cut off George's allowance, they decide Lou Ellen should return home until the visit is over. Before she does, she and the Girls discuss what marriage is all about ("An Old-Fashioned Wife").

With the apartment empty once again, Jackie enters via the window (naturally) on the run from the law, only to be discovered by Jim. An amorous old gentleman called "Tootles" made a pass at her at the Country Club and somehow they both ended up attacking a passing policeman. When the pursuing policeman arrives, Jim pretends Jackie is Mrs. George Budd. When they are alone, he confesses his own attraction ("A Pal Like You"). He persuades her it is safe to stay in George's apartment and leaves. While Jackie is in the bedroom putting on Lou Ellen's pyjamas, George returns and writes a letter to his absent wife ("Letter Song"). George and Jackie inevitably meet and she offers to go but it has started to rain ("Till the Clouds Roll By").

Judge Carter—Lou Ellen's father—drops in to inspect the young man who is involved with his daughter. Luckily, he can't stay. The Girls arrive and find Lou Ellen's wedding finery ("A Little Bit of Ribbon"). They are joined by Jackie and Jim who celebrate the season with George ("The First Day of May"). Lou Ellen and her moralistic mother arrive and Jackie has to pretend to be George's Quaker aunt. The Girls offer to show her the town. (Act 1 Finaletto.) The Judge returns and Jackie recognizes him as "Tootles." He leaves for the Country Club and they all follow to resolve matters.

At the club Jim tells Jackie she is the only girl for him . . .

Jim: When I love a girl, I want to be the star—not just come on in the mob scenes.

Jackie: Isn't it funny? Give a man one smile and he thinks it hands him the right to scowl at every other male creature on your visiting list. ("Rolled Into One").

The Judge and Mrs. Carter enter. She is so shocked by recent events, she forbids George and Lou Ellen to speak to one another, except through her or her husband. This they find quite unfair ("Oh, Daddy, Please"). Jim and Jackie contemplate their future life together ("Nesting Time in Flatbush"). Lou Ellen decides the verbal embargo is not such a hindrance after all ("Words Are Not Needed").

Now George's real Aunt arrives. Before she can understand what is going on, the young people get her tipsy. Things are getting too much for all of them ("Flubby Dub the Cave Man"). Loose ends are rapidly tied up, forgiveness and forgetfulness are in the air. Jim and Jackie get engaged and Aunt Penelope blesses the union of George and Lou Ellen in time for a reprise of "Till the Clouds Roll By."

LET'S MAKE A NIGHT OF IT

(Jim and Boys and Girls)

Boys &
Girls: Creep along!
 Although it's very wrong
 To be here when we're
 Not invited . . .
 It makes us all the more excited—
 Not a sound!
 But let us prowl around,
 I can't help feeling that we've come where
 There may be someone hiding somewhere.

Girls: Sh-h, do be careful! Do be quiet
 Or we must run away.

Boys &
Girls: If we're caught by the proprietor,
 What are we to say?
 Like the Russian dancers, let's creep
 On our tip, tip toe

As we go
With stealth to and fro.

No, we'll not slink about!
Why should we think about
What the man may say?

Let's make a night of it—
Be gay in spite of it—
That's the wisest way.

I'll bet you ten to one
He won't mind.
He'll simply think it fun,
You will find.
He won't be hard on us,
He'll surely pardon us,
He won't spoil the party,
He won't be so silly and unkind
He can't be here at all
If he were near at all
He'd have heard the noise
He can't be here at all

To interfere at all
With our simple joys.

Boys: Don't let us hesitate
            He's not in.
            Come, for it's getting late
            Let's begin.

Boys &
Girls: Time is flying, so
            Use it while we may
            When the dawn is grey,
            Then we'll have to go,
            Let's make a night of it
            Let's make a night of it NOW!

            I bet you ten to one he won't mind,
            He'll simply think it fun, you will
                find.
            Leave it all to us, we know where
                to go
            We'll arrange it so, there's nothing
                to discuss
            We'll make a night of it
            We'll make a night of it now.

YOU NEVER KNEW ABOUT ME

(George and Lou Ellen)

George: We were children, once, long ago,
                dear,
            You and I—
            At the start our lives lay apart, as
            Lives will lie.
            Up I grew
            And I never knew
            That the world contained a darling
            Like you,
            Nor did you dream you would see
                little me, too,
            By and by

Refrain: I never knew about you, dear,

Both: And you never knew about me.
George: Life might have been Heaven,
            If I, then aged seven,
            Had but met you when you were
                three.
            We'd have made mud pies like
                affinities.
            We'd have known what rapture
                may be.
            I'd have let you feed my rabbit
            'Till the thing became a habit, dear!
            But I never knew about you.

Lou Ellen: Oh! What might it have been

George: And you never knew about me.

Lou Ellen: How I wish I'd known, dear, that
            One day you'd arrive—
            Just to feel I had an idea
            For which to strive—
            Had I known
            I'd meet you, my own,
            I would not have lived for pleasure
                alone;
            I was frivolous and gay, sad to say,
            When I was five.

Refrain
Both: I never knew about you, dear,
            And you never knew about me.

Lou Ellen: I never missed chances
            Of juvenile dances
            For my life was one mad spree.
            I was often kissed "neath the
                mistletoe"
            By small boys excited with tea.
            If I'd known that you existed,
            I'd have scratched them, and
                resisted, dear
            But I never knew about you

George: Oh! The pain of it
            And you never knew about me.

There was to be a touching Wodehousean
P.S. to this song. In his 1973 novel, *Bachelors
Anonymous*, it is said of the dull-as-ditchwater
lawyer Ephraim Trout that "as a child of eight
Mr. Trout had once kissed a girl of six under the
mistletoe at a Christmas party, but there his sex
life had come to an abrupt halt." Fifty-six years
later, it seems, a chord was struck . . .

A PACKAGE OF SEEDS

(Jim and Girls)

(The number was previously used in *Ninety In
the Shade* [1915].)

AN OLD-FASHIONED WIFE

(An Old-Fashioned Way)

(In the Good Old-Fashioned Way)

(Lou Ellen and Girls)

Lou Ellen: The modern wife leads a dreadful
             life—
             That seems the modern fashion:
             For wicked ways and cabarets
             She seems to have a passion.
             I never shall be up-to-date,
             That sort of thing I know I'd hate.

Refrain: So . . .
             I want to be a good little wife,
             In the good old fashioned way,
             I'll honor and obey,
             From home I will never stray.
             Although the thing that's smart is
             To be out all night at parties,
             I'll be sitting
             With my knitting
             In the good old-fashioned way.

             It's thought quite queer if they last
                 a year,
             These marriages that we know.
             You've hardly cried: "Here comes
                 the bride!"

Before she's off to Reno.
They'll have to change it, I suppose
From "Here she comes!" to "There
    she goes!"

Refrain: But . . .
             I want to be a good little wife
             In the good old-fashioned way.
             For ever and a day,
             Till our two heads are bent and
                 gray,
             Thru days serene and stormy
             There will be but one man for me,
             And we'll weather
             Life together
             In the good old-fashioned way.

(I WAS LOOKING FOR) A PAL LIKE YOU

(We're Going to Be Pals)

(Jim and Jackie)

Jim: You are such a pal,
             Don't know—never shall—
             Why you out-distance
             All other women in existence
             If you only knew,
             How I've longed for you.
             I never thought you would ever come
             What luck that brought you!

Refrain: Dozens and dozens of girls I have
                 met,
             Sisters and cousins of men in my set
             Tried to be cheerful
             And give them an earful
             Of soft sort of talk, but,
             Oh, gosh! the strain—something
                 fearful!
             Always found, after a minute or two,
             Just to be civil was all I could do.
             Now I know why I
             Could never be contented,
             I was looking for a pal like you.

Jackie: Oh, my friend in need,
You've been a friend indeed.
Saved me from danger
I can't believe you're just a stranger.
I've been waiting, too,
Years and years for you.
I shan't forget you
I mean to keep you now I've met you.

Refrain: I've known so many, such hundreds
of men;
Didn't like any—except now and
then.
Flirted a minute,
'Twas fun to begin it
But found out quite soon, there
Was nothing—nothing—nothing
in it.
Often and often I used to get blue,
Just went on flirting—for
something to do
Now I know why I'd
That sense of something missing:
I was looking for a pal like you.

LETTER SONG

(George)

Darling Lou Ellen, I'm writing this note to tell
you, dear,
All night through I'll be thinking of you, so have
no fear.
How I miss you, parted like this!
But I'll give your picture a goodnight kiss,
And I'll go to sleep and dream all the while
That you're still near.
I'll just dream about you, dear,
And you must dream about me.

Don't lie awake fretting,
There's no use regretting,
Things are sure to come right, you'll see.

Our misfortunes can't last forever, dear,
Glad again we're going to be—
Go to sleep and think how soon, dear,
We'll be on our honeymoon, dear.
And tonight I'll dream about you
And you must dream about me

TILL THE CLOUDS ROLL BY

(George and Jackie)

Jackie: I'm so sad to think that I have had to
Drive you from your home so coolly

George: I'll be gaining nothing by remaining,
What would Missus Grundy say?
Her conventions, kindly recollect
them!
We must please respect them duly.

Jackie: My intrusion needs explaining;
I feel my courage waning.

George: Please, I beg, don't mention it.
         I should not mind a bit,
         But it has started raining.

Refrain
Both: Oh, the rain comes a-pitter-patter,
         And I'd like to be safe in bed,
         Skies are weeping
         While the world is sleeping,
         Trouble heaping
         On (your/my) head.
         It is vain, to remain and chatter,
         And to wait for a clearer sky
         Helter-skelter
         I/you must fly for shelter
         Till the clouds roll by!

Jackie: What bad luck, it's coming down
             in buckets
         Have you an umbrella handy?

George: I've a warm coat—water proof—
             a storm coat,
         I shall be all right, I know,
         Later on, too, I will ward the
             grippe off,
         With a little nip of brandy.

Jackie: Or a glass of toddy draining.
         You'd find that more sustaining

George: Don't be worried, I entreat,
         I've rubbers for my feet
         So I don't mind it raining

Both: Oh, the rain comes a-pitter-patter, etc.

Wodehouse admitted that this song was "more or less a steal from an old German hymn." That didn't prevent it from being satirized by Rodgers & Hart in *The Rose of Arizona* sequence in *The Garrick Gaieties* (1926) in a song entitled "It May Rain When the Sun Stops Shining" . . .

We'll see a sunny day,
For love will find a way
Till the clouds go rolling by

At this point the several different versions of the libretto diverge slightly and what follows is a composite.

A LITTLE BIT OF RIBBON (RIBBONS AND LACES)

(Jane and Girls)

To a lingerie shop came a dainty little maid,
And they showed some pretty things to her,
They delighted her—what's more—
All the pretty things she saw,
Though I don't intend to tell you what they were.
"Mother says it's very wrong of me,"
She murmured to herself,
"Wasting money on delightful things like these."
For she tells me, don't you see,
There is nobody but me
Who is ever going to see them—
Yet, of course, one never knows.

For a little bit of ribbon,
And a little bit of lace,
And a little bit of silk that clings,
When together they are linking,
Always sets a fellow winking, (blinking)
And they also set him thinking things.

It's a useful combination for
Assisting a flirtation
If you want to get a man beneath your spell,
And although I'm hardly twenty
I believe I could do plenty—
With a little bit of ribbon,
And a little bit of lace,
And a little bit of silk as well.

'Neath a shady tree, in a hammock, I am told,
Sat a maid and a man one day,

For a hammock , there's no doubt,
When there's nobody about,
Holds a couple rather nicely, so they say.
Now a maiden in a hammock,
In a fashionable skirt,
Must be careful how she swings or she will find
That a little extra rock
Plays the dickens with her frock,
And it also plays the dickens
With a fellow's peace of mind.

For a little bit of ribbon,
And a little bit of lace,
And a little bit of silk that clings
When together they are linking
Always sets a fellow winking
And they also set him thinking things.

Now a little bird, it's said
Was in the branches overhead,
But when I asked him
What he saw, he wouldn't tell,
Though he said he'd like to mention
What attracted his attention
Was a little bit more ribbon
And a little bit more lace
And a little bit more silk as well.

Girls:
For a little bit of ribbon
And a little bit of lace
And a little bit of silk that clings
When together they are linking, etc.

Now a little bird, it's said,
Was in the branches overhead,
And when I asked him
What he saw, he wouldn't tell,
But to get him really going
All you need is to be showing . . .
Just a little bit of ribbon,
And a little bit of lace,
And a little bit of silk that clings

THE FIRST DAY OF MAY

(Jackie, Jim, and George)

Jim: Oh! Springtime is a happy season
Of which the poets make a fuss.
The pleasant sunshine brings the
  peas on
And ripens the asparagus.

George: As thro' the meadows green you
  ramble
You hear the lark's melodious lay

Jackie: While everywhere the lambkins
  gambol
In their boneheaded sort of way.
But Spring is dear to me because of
  Moving Day

Refrain
All: When Springtime is returning
You feel a yearning to roam
And the place is
Filled with packing cases,
Till there's no place
Like home
Your income is improving
And so you're moving away

George: And oh, joy! You're independent
Of the Swedish Superintendent

All: On the first day of May.

Jim: And then the place is in a fine way
With men who come in unawares
And do ju-jit-su with the Steinway
And catch-as-catch can with the
  chairs.

George: You hear a crash that turns you chilly
You say: "Good gracious, what was
  that?"

Jackie: And find they've dropped the stove
  on Willie,

Or stubbed their toe on
    James, the cat,
Or dump'd the chiffonier on father's
    Sunday hat.

Refrain: Oh, Springtime is a gay time
You spend the daytime
And night fighting battles
With your goods and chattels
Till you can't keep polite.
Cut glass you grind your heels on
You take your meals on
A tray
And you find the moving fellers
Swiped your box of Panatellas,

And you certainly are sure, oh
They've smashed Aunt Minnie's
    bureau,
And the maid is in a twitter,
Cos the dog got sore and bit her.

Oh yes, your income is improving
And so you're moving away.
And too late you'll find that maybe
You've gone and packed the baby
On the First Day of May

FINALETTO

(Jackie, Boys and Girls)

Jackie: Ladies and gentlemen,
Thee said a mouthful then,
Take me where you like,
Don't stand and make a fuss,
Let's get a move on us,
For the love of Mike—
I'm with you all the way—
I'm some sport!
Or, as I meant to say—
Time is short,
So don't thee hesitate—

Justine Johnstone (*far left*), Marion Davies (*third from left*), Hal Forde and Anna Wheaton (*fifth and sixth left*), Tom Powers facing Marie Carroll (*center*) and Edna May Oliver (*second from right*).

Don't thee procrastinate.
Show me your fair city, friends,
Of which I've heard such good
 report.

Boys &
Girls:
We'll show you round the town,
All round and up and down,
If you'll only wait!
We never hoped to find
You were the sporty kind,
This is simply great!
We'll take you ev'rywhere,
Far and near
We'll take you ev'rywhere
Don't you fear,
Leave it all to us,
We know where to go,
We'll arrange it, so
There's nothing to discuss.
We'll make a day of it,
We'll make a day of it
Now!

Jackie:
(To Mrs. Carter)
*(To the tune of "You Never Knew
 About Me")*
Thee never heard about me,
 friend,
And I never heard about thee.

George:
I'd have made some explanations in
The course of conversation
But it slipped from my mind,
 as things do.

Girls:
How peculiar!

George:
My memory is awful, it's true!

Girls:
Not a doubt of it

Lou Ellen:
Well, never mind, now's the time

Boys &
Girls:
Why, of course it is

Lou Ellen:
To show hospitality

Boys &
Girls:
To show hospitality.
Yes, we will show you
Round the town today,
We'll all be gay
During your stay.

Lou Ellen:
Or, if you'd rather
Chat with father,
That is just for you to say

Boys:
So if you'd rather,
Talk with father,
Or would he be in the way?

Boys &
Girls:
We'll show you round the town
All round and up and down,
If you'll only wait.
We never hoped to find
You were the sporty kind.
This is simply great,
We'll take you ev'rywhere
Far and near
We'll take you ev'rywhere
Don't you fear.
Leave it all to us!
We know where to go
We'll arrange it so
There's nothing to discuss.
We'll make a day of it!
We'll make a day of it!
Now!

Act 2 is set in the Country Club. Jim and the Boys and Girls are sitting around with the men in their polo gear. They sing "The Land Where the Good Songs Go." (At least, they did later in the run, when *Miss 1917*, the show in which the song originally appeared, had closed.)

ROLLED INTO ONE

(Jackie and Girls)

Jackie &
Girls:
Though men think it strange,
Girls should need a change
From their manly fascinations;
The fact is, this act is
A thing we're driven to.
You don't have much fun
If you stick to one,
Men have all such limitations.
Look 'round you, I'm bound you
Will find that this is true.

Refrain:
At the Op'ra
I like to be with Freddie,
To a musical show
I go
With Joe,
I like to dance with Ted
And golf with Dick or Ned,
And at the races
And other lively places,
Sam and Eddie are fun.
But I'm pining
'Till there comes in my direction,
One combining
Ev'ry masculine perfection;
Who'll be Eddie,
And Joe, and Dick and Sam and
Freddie,
And Neddie and Teddie
Rolled in one.

Solo:
Ev'rywhere you go
Men are useful, so
Just collect them where you find
them;
Catch twenty—that's plenty.
I don't think you'll need more.
If they say you flirt,
Don't be feeling hurt,

That's a way they have, don't
mind them.
They tell us they're jealous,
But that's what men are for.

OH, DADDY, PLEASE

(George, Lou Ellen and Judge)

Lou Ellen:
Oh, Daddy, please
Just hand on these
Few words to George for me.

Judge:
Wait, wait, my dear, please wait—
I've got to concentrate.

George:
Excuse me, sir
Just say to her
How faithful I will be.

Judge:
Oh, get out of my sight—
I've got my speech to write.

George &
Lou Ellen:
We are so sorry to
Keep interrupting you,
But your assistance
We are seeking
Now we're speaking
From a distance.

Special Refrain

Lou Ellen:
Please tell Georgie
I mean to be a good little wife
In the good old-fashioned way.
I'll honor and obey
From my home I'll never stray.
At nights I'll not be flitting
For I think 'twould be more
fitting
To be sitting
With my knitting
In the good old-fashioned way.

George: This favor, Judge,
           You cannot grudge
           Just tell Lou Ellen this . . .

Judge: I think I should allude
           To the high cost of food

Lou Ellen: Oh, listen, pray!
           What George may say
           I do not want to miss.

Judge: I'm certain if I do
           I'll get a cheer or two.

George &
Lou Ellen: Oh, won't you please attend?
           You are our only friend,
           And your assistance
           We are seeking
           Now we're speaking
           At a distance

(They both kneel)

George: Tell Lou Ellen
           I was so lonely,
           I lived all alone
           She is the only nice girl I have known
           Through my existence
           I've fought with such persistence
           As far as I could
           To keep women
           At a wholesome distance—
           Often and often I used to get blue,
           Just went on hoping,
           'Twas all I could do.
           Now I know why
           I could never like those others. I
           Was looking for a girl like Lou.

NESTING TIME IN FLATBUSH

(Jim and Jackie)

Jim: I've always liked the sort of songs
           You hear so much today

           Called "When it's something or
           other time"
           In some place far-away.
           Oh, "Tulip Time in Holland"
           A pleasant time must be—

Jackie: While some are strong for
           "Apple Blossom Time in
           Normandy"

Jim: But there's another time and place
           That makes a hit with me.

Refrain
Both: When it's nesting time in Flatbush
           We will take a little flat.

Jackie: With "Welcome" on the mat.

Jim: Where there's room to swing a cat
           I'll hang up my hat in our Flatbush
               flat
           Life will be so sweet with you.

Both: When it's nesting time in Flatbush
           In Flatbush Avenue.

Jackie: Our little home may have defects
           Like all these flats in town;
           It's safer (wiser) not to lean on
               the walls.

Jim: Because they might fall down.

Jackie: It's rather badly lighted
           Which makes it hard to see,
           And the neighbors play "Poor
               Butterfly" (the Gramophone)
           Each night till after three.

Jim: But it will be a paradise
           If shared, my love, with thee.

           When it's nesting time in Flatbush,
           As you heard me say before

Jackie: You will seek the janitor

Jim: With the girl whom I adore,
        Hand in hand, we'll soar to the
            seventh floor,
        (On the seventh floor, on the
            seventh floor)

Jackie: We will (And we'll) start to bill
        and coo

Both: When it's nesting time in Flatbush,
        In Flatbush Avenue

Additional chorus

Jackie: When it's nesting time in
            Flatbush
        We'll be happy, you and I.

Jim: With what raptures we will fly

Jackie: Our first rubber plant to buy.

Jim: I could not deny, I could not deny
        Such luxury to you.

Both: When it's nesting time in Flatbush,
        In Flatbush Avenue

Both: When it's nesting time in Flatbush,
        We will have our pictures 'took'

Jim: To put in a little book.

Jackie: For the visitors to look

Jim: If by hook or crook we secure a
            cook
        She shall see that picture, too,

Both: When it's nesting time in Flatbush
        In Flatbush Avenue

WORDS ARE NOT NEEDED

(Every Day)

(Lou Ellen and Boys)

Lou Ellen: A girl in love does not need words
                to say so
            To a man
            For love has a language of its own.

Boys: Can she learn it?

Lou Ellen: She can

Boys: Would he understand it?

Lou Ellen: Who?

Boys: Why, the chap she's talking to.
            If she didn't say a thing
            We don't see how he could

Lou Ellen: It's an easy thing to do!

Boys: It's an easy thing to do!

Lou Ellen: If every day he reads the
                message
            He sees in her eyes;
            If, when he gazes fondly in them
            She droops them and sighs;
            Then he will know she loves him
                dearly,
            What'ere may befall
            So, now you understand why
                words
            Are not needed at all.

Lou Ellen: Then flow'rs are quite a help
            For each means something,
            I am told.
            A rose may say, "I love you, dear!"

Boys: Yes, we know but
            That's old.

Can't you tell us
    something new?

Lou Ellen: That's an easy thing
              to do.

Boys: For the language of
              the flowers has
              been overdone

Lou Ellen: Jewels have their
              language, too.

Boys: Jewels have their
              language, too.

Lou Ellen: If ev'ry day he sends
              her diamonds
              Or pearls on a
                string,
              If ev'ry day, she gets
                a pendant
              Or bracelet or
                ring!
              Then she will know
                how very deeply
              In love he must be,
              When people love
                each other
              Words are not
                needed, you see

In some versions of the libretto the song is given to George and the Girls.

George: Life's too complicated. I wish we
              were back in the Golden Age

Jackie: Or the Bronze Age

Jim: Or the Stone Age

Jackie: My great big cave man!

Marion Davies

FLUBBY-DUB THE CAVE MAN

(Jackie, Jim and George)

Life today is so sad and grey
For the good old times have flown,
Things were better long, long ago
In the far off age of stone.
Then folks weren't always in a hurry,
All they said was—"I should worry."
Girls and men were happy then
And troubles were unknown.

Flubby-dub, the Caveman, lived the ideal life
Far from all this modern noise and care and
     strife.
He got up each morning with the sun

Took the dinosaurs for a run
When the rent collector called on quarter day
He got out his club and when men called for
 taxes
He'd just sharpen up his axes
Life was pretty soft for Flubby-dub.

Life they say in that distant day
Was so peaceful and serene
For the baby vampire hadn't come upon the
 screen (scene)
No one knew of the ukulele, so things went on
 jogging gaily
No one spent his last red cent for eggs and
 gasoline.

Flubby-dub the Caveman, lived the ideal life
Far from all this modern noise and care and strife
He was never trampled in the crush
Every evening in the uptown rush!
For in those delightful prehistoric days
Subways did not sub, and straps were not
 invented,
So that he was quite contented.
Life was pretty soft for Flubby-dub—the dub.

As with almost any show of this kind, numbers came and went both in tryout and even during the Broadway run. "A Package of Seeds" replaced "Ain't It a Grand and Glorious Feeling!" A song called "The Bachelor" ("That's the Kind Of Man I'd Like To Be") was replaced by "A Little Bit of Ribbon"—sung by the eighteen-year-old Marion Davies, later to become better known as the mistress of William Randolph Hearst. That number was also later dropped.

Originally the second act seems to have opened with "Koo-La-Loo" ("Ku-La-Loo" or "Down By the Kulaloo"—with a lyric by Anne Caldwell) but most surviving libretti suggest that it was subsequently replaced with "The Land Where the Good Songs Go," salvaged from *Miss 1917*. Immediately after the opening number came "Be A Little Sunbeam," which was quickly

replaced by a dance specialty for Dorothy Dickson and "Rolled Into One."

Toward the end of the Act, two early songs were eliminated to make room for "Flubby-Dub." "When the Orchestra is Playing Your Favorite Dance" was to turn up in *Leave It To Jane* (1917), while "Why Can't They Hand It To Me?" found its niche in *The Riviera Girl* (1917).

BE A LITTLE SUNBEAM

Say, have you heard of the Glad Game they play?
Try it yourself when you go home today.
Do not mind if Fate's unkind,
But simply grin and don't give in.
If troubles come, as they're certain to do,
Why should you care if they don't come to you?
Fate's blow you may defy,
If they soak some other guy.
Oh, be joyful, cheerful and serene
If poor father falls and busts his bean;
Don't be downcast, don't be sad,
Just be thankful you're not dad
As to fetch the Doc, you hurry,
Keep on shouting, "I should worry!"
If you try, you'll find that you can greet
Other people's troubles with a smile.
Cheer up! That's the only way,

Make each day Thanksgiving Day,
Be a little sunbeam all the while.
Though it's a tough little world, more or less,
Though all around you see folks in distress,
Don't feel sad, it's not so bad,
Each cloud you'll find,
Is silver lined.
If you are brave, and refuse to despair,
No matter how much your friends have to bear,
You'll find without a doubt
Plenty to be glad about.
If a mule kicks grandpa in the face,
Gladness is by no means out of place.
Just reflect it's painful, but
Grandpa was a homely mutt,

As to hospital you move him,
Say, "No doubt this will improve him."
Make him take a broad and cheerful view,
Sit beside his sick bed with a smile.
Point out just to keep him cool,
How it must have pleased the mule,
Be a little sunbeam all the while.

AIN'T IT A GRAND AND GLORIOUS FEELING!

Some days are bum days, but sometimes, there
    come days
When your luck's in from the start,
Days when the Jinx
Doesn't drive to the drinks
And Old Man Trouble has a heart.
When fate doesn't wait 'round the corner with
    a brick
And your stock goes up to par,
Things aren't this way very much, but say—
"Oh, Joy! Oh, Boy!" when they are!

Ain't it a grand and a glorious feeling,
When the world is fair and bright!
When nothing's gone wrong
From the breakfast gong,
Till you go to bed at night.
When you're able to say,
As you're hitting the hay,
"This is the end of a perfect day"
Ain't it a grand and glorious feeling
When you feel the world's all right!

THAT'S THE KIND OF MAN I'D LIKE TO BE (THE BACHELOR)

(George and Girls)

George: I don't know why, but I've always
    been shy:
    I feel a fool when a girl passes by:
    If her eyes look into mine,

I get cold shivers down my spine.
If I get cornered and can't run away,
I never know what the dickens to say:
My heart begins to thump,
And I look a perfect chump.
I've known men who weren't a bit
    like that.

Girls: So have we. It's a well-known variety.

George: Men who like to sit with girls and chat.

Girls: It's a type that has sought our society

George: Men who like to meet at lunch
    Twenty females in a bunch;
    Men who meet a girl on Sunday,
    And are holding hands by Monday.
    I have often envied them their nerve.

Girls: Though they don't always act with
    propriety

George: And their gift of rapid repartee:
    They don't sit there, red and dumb,
    Praying hard for death to come:
    That's the kind of man I'd like to be.

    I get no show, when to parties I go:
    People all think that I'm stupid and
        slow:
    Nowadays you've not a chance,
    Unless you dance the latest dance.
    I've had instructors who said they
        could teach:
    Hundreds of dollars I've handed to
        each:
    I do just what they say;
    But my feet get in the way.
    I've known men who keep it up all
        night.

Girls: So have we. It's a well-known variety

George: Men who trot with girls and hold
    them tight;

Girls: It's a type that has
         sought our society.

George: Men who grow
         excited, as
         Their pet jazz-band
         starts to jazz;
         At the dance they're
         perfect wizards:
         I admire these tango-
         lizards.
         I have often wished to
         be like them.

Girls: Though they don't
         always act with
         propriety

George: They've a skill which
         never comes to me
         All the fancy steps
         they do
         Not upon their
         partner's shoe
         That's the kind of
         man I'd like to be.

Raymond von Sickle and Eileen Wilson in *Oh, Boy!*

It's difficult to evoke the degree of success *Oh, Boy!* enjoyed when yesterday's numbers mean so little in today's terms. 475 performances in New York—more than half of them in the transfer to the 1,500-seat Casino Theatre and five companies on the road where the real money was to be made. One of them was still touring in 1922. Just over $29,000 to stage and a profit of $181,000 gave everyone cause for repeating the show's title frequently all the way to the bank.

As the *Times* summed it up: "You might call this a musical comedy that is as good as they make them if it were not palpably so much better." Wodehouse's lyrics—it was considered—"are shrewdly rhymed and have a rare lilt."

Ziegfeld, Erlanger, the Shuberts . . . all of them weighed in with offers for the trio's next show and, of course, Ray Comstock was asking what the next Princess show was to be and was ready with his own suggestion.

But first another short detour . . .

The show's Broadway success ensured a London production. British actor/producer George Grossmith signed a contract and the re-titled *Oh, Joy!* opened in 1919, marking the musical comedy debut of Beatrice Lillie. It was to be the first of four successful collaborations between Wodehouse and Grossmith—five if one includes *Sally*, in which Wodehouse's contribution was minor.

Someone who *almost* had the show on his *curriculum vitae* was the eighteen-year-old Noël Coward. He tells in *Present Indicative* of attending a mass audition at the Shaftesbury Theatre. "(The show) had been renamed, doubtless because the arrogant Americanism of *Oh, Boy!* might stir the English public's stomach to revolt." Coward was well into his set piece song when it became obvious "that Grossmith and Laurillard and all their myrmidons in the stalls were so immersed in conversation that not one of them was looking at me. I stopped dead and waited until their voices had died into silence. Then, with what I hoped was icy dignity, I said that I saw no point in singing to them if they continued to waste their time not listening to me."

The ever polite Grossmith insisted that Noël sing the song again and promptly hired him at the salary of twelve pounds a week. "The actual part I was to play would be decided upon later, but in the meantime I could rest assured that my remarkable talents should have full scope."

Whether Wodehouse and Coward ever met in later life is not recorded by either man, though Coward's early work as a lyricist shows clear evidence that he had studied Wodehouse's work. In his correspondence Wodehouse once observed that he liked Coward's "novels"—even though there was only the one, *Pomp and Circumstance*. He also refers to having read Coward's first volume of autobiography, the 1937 *Present Indicative*, which he enjoyed "but somehow I don't find myself liking him."

When Coward attended the first rehearsal some weeks later, however, the director (Austen Hurgon) disclaimed all knowledge of the arrangement. All the parts, large and small, were filled. Noël probably meant the chorus. Indeed, there was his name in the list. An irate young actor proceeded to storm the offices of Grossmith & Laurillard, where the latter only survived to produce another day by insisting that, while a mistake certainly seemed to have been made, someone of Noël's ability would be wasted in such a trifle. A firm commitment was made for a part in a forthcoming "straight" play. Exit affronted party, slightly mollified.

OH, JOY! (1919)

Presented by George Grossmith Jr. and Edward Laurillard at the Kingsway Theatre, London, on January 27, 1919 (167 performances).

CAST	
Briggs: HAL GORDON	Lou Ellen Carter: DOT TEMPLE
Jane Packard: ISABEL JEANS	Jackie Sampson: BEATRICE LILLIE
Polly Andrus: JUDITH NELMES	Constable Simms: FRED RUSSELL
Jim Marvin: BILLY LEONARD	Sir John Carter, J.P.: TOM PAYNE
George Budd: TOM POWERS	Lady Carter: DIANA DURAND
	Miss Penelope Budd: HELEN ROUS

For the London production Wodehouse did a small amount of "anglicization." For example, in "Till the Clouds Roll By" *grippe* became *flu*; the *First Day of May* became the dreaded *First Quarter Day*; and the moving man, *instead of stealing a box of Panatellas*, has *gone and swiped your best umbrella*.

"Nesting Time in Flatbush" became "Nesting Time in Tooting" (lyric missing) and there was a significant change to one particular number . . .

ROLLED INTO ONE

(Jackie)

Not so long ago
I was rather slow,
Just a little country bumpkin.
Though farming was charming,
I found it somewhat tame.
I could tell you now
How to milk a cow,
All the ways to snare a pumpkin,
To feed them,
Nay, breed them.
But, still, I'm not to blame.

In the morning
They used to call me early
In the rain or the snow,
Milking I'd go.
I used to chop the sticks
And then I'd feed the chicks.
And in the daytime
I hardly had a gay time,
For they'd teach me to hoe.
Of the rooster
I'd study all the habits
And I used to
Get acquainted with the rabbits.
Then at night time
I'd kiss my Uncle Joe
And mothers and brothers—
Then off to bed I'd go.

Now, don't think me loud,
If I like to crowd
And I'm fond of mild flirtations.
It's only when lonely
I ever feel depressed.
Give me lots of noise,
Let me meet the boys
For a bit of recreation.
When near them
I cheer them,
The truth must be confessed.

In the morning
I take a walk with Freddie,
Then to Bond Street I go
Shopping with Joe.
I always lunch with Jim—
I learn a lot from him.
And in the evening
I like to go with Benny
To a musical show.
And the chance is
I dine in Piccadilly.
At the dances,
Well, I like to dance with Willie.

Beatrice Lillie

And at night time,
When all the lights are low,
You must know
I just go
To bye-bye all alone.

Another song creates a slight puzzle. In *Oh, Boy!* George and Lou Ellen plead with her father to pass messages from one to the other in the song "Oh, Daddy, Please." In the UK version this same plot point is contained in a song that cannot be confirmed as a Wodehouse number. On the other hand, the original show had been such a hit that it is difficult to conceive of the boys replacing a perfectly good song with someone else's interpolation.

LOVING BY PROXY

(Lou Ellen, George and Sir John)

George: If I must speak through you,
Tell her my love is true.
Tell her I love her awfully,
Tell her my heart is lonely.
Say . . .

Father: Not a word!
It's quite absurd.
It's better far
To please Mama.

George: If love must be unspoken,
Give her this token—
No more I ask of you

Both: Loving by proxy, we're learning
today
Someone who's foxy must help you
to play.

George: My darling!

Lou Ellen: My dearest!

George: My sweetheart!

Father: Through me!

George: Give me a kiss by proxy.

Lou Ellen: By proxy.

Father: By proxy.

George: Loving a girl by proxy
Is the new game for three.

Lou Ellen: Here's what I dare not tell
    Say what he knows so well
    I will not leave him, never,
    My love will go on forever
    Say—

Father: I can't agree—
    Don't bother me.

Lou Ellen: Oh, say—

Father: I told you 'No'—
    He'd better go.

Lou Ellen: Why are you hard hearted?
    When we are parted,
    Who'll say one word for me?

Both: Loving by proxy, we're
     learning today
    Someone who's foxy must
     help you to play.

Etc. Reprise

A totally new song—which presumably was immediately prior to or even part of the Finale . . .

Beatrice Lillie and Billy Leonard: "Nesting Time in Tooting"

WEDDING BELLS

Why ask some ghastly female
All your earthly joys to share?
Why sacrifice your freedom?
I beg you to beware.

Wedding bells, wedding bells, when they chime,
Seem to say—'Run away, while you have time.'
We really can't agree,
For as far as we can see
When ringing,
They're bringing
Such happiness to me.

Though your dreams and your schemes are
  sublime,
Don't believe,
They deceive you—
It's a crime.
They'll say—'Wilt thou have this wife?'
Then they sentence you for life.
Lesson time,
Lesson time,
Lesson time.

You're just like silly mice
That take the bait with greatest ease.
They'll ask you, if you please,

Don't call our ladies 'Cheese.'
You're just the same as I was
But I found it out too late
Be strong and independent—
But then I know it's Fate.

Wedding bells, etc.

Though your dreams and your schemes are
    sublime,
Don't believe,
They deceive you—
It's a crime.
They'll say—'Why not take your cup?'

Do a bunk—your number's up!
Lesson time,
Lesson time,
Lesson time,

The trio's next assignment for Comstock was another adaptation—this time of a 1903 play called *The College Widow* by one George Ade. Although the show was intended to be a Princess production, that theatre was still happily occupied by *Oh, Boy!*, so Comstock placed it in the Longacre, a venue three times the size of the Princess—although it did finally play the Princess in a 1927 revival.

LEAVE IT TO JANE (1917)

Presented by William Elliott, Ray Comstock, and Morris Gest at the Longacre Theatre, New York, on August 28, 1917 (167 performances), after a tryout starting at Atlantic City, New Jersey, on July 30.

BOOK   Guy Bolton and P. G. Wodehouse (Based on the play *The College Widow* by George Ade)
LYRICS   P. G. Wodehouse
MUSIC   Jerome Kern

(The show was revived at the Princess Theatre in 1927 and had a major revival at the Sheridan Square Playhouse, New York, on May 25, 1959—928 performances.)

Oscar Shaw (*"Stub" Talmadge*) and the College Girls in *Leave It to Jane*.

CAST

'Stub' Talmadge, a busy undergraduate:
OSCAR SHAW

Billie Bolton, a half-back:
ROBERT G. PITKIN

Ollie Mitchell, a sophomore:
RULOFF CUTTEN

President Peter Witherspoon:
FREDERICK GRAHAM

Jane Witherspoon, his daughter:
EDITH HALLOR

Matty McGowan, a trainer:
DAN COLLYER

'Silent' Murphy, a center-rush:
THOMAS DELMAR

Flora Wiggins,
a prominent waitress:
GEORGIA O'RAMEY

Hiram Bolton, DD. LL.D:
WILL C. CRIMENS

Prof. Howard Talbot, a tutor:
ALGERNON GRIEG

Hon. Elam Hicks
of Squaintumville:
ALAN KELLY

Bub Hicks, a freshman:
OLIN HOWARD

Bessie Tanner, an athletic girl:
ANN ORR

SYNOPSIS

The campus of Atwater College where the Boys are singing the college football song ("Good Old Atwater"). But Coach McGowan is depressed because the team's stars won't be available for the big game against Bingham. We meet Stub and his girl friend, Bessie. Stub is ready for marriage, but Bessie's ideal is not quite his ("A Peach of a Life"). The girl the whole male population is in love with is Jane Witherspoon, the college President's vivacious daughter, who now arrives with her entourage ("Wait Till Tomorrow"). Witherspoon's friend Hiram Bolton arrives and bets Stub and the boys that Bingham will win—his son, Billy, an All-American star, is playing. Bessie chides Stub about his lack of get-up-and-go ("Just You Watch My Step").

Billy enters in search of his father and he and Jane are mutually smitten and this gives Stub and Bessie an idea—perhaps Jane can distract him ("Leave It To Jane"). Senator Hicks arrives with his son, Bub, who is to lodge with Flora, the campus man-eater, and her mother. Jane persuades Billy to stay over for the college dance that night. Bessie has no doubt he can be persuaded to stay indefinitely. After all, Jane is a siren ("The Siren's Song"). At the dance, while Billy waits for Jane, the orchestra plays his favourite waltz ("There It Is Again"). Jane comes to claim him and Flora reflects that the girl is a latterday Cleopatra—"A girl could get away with an awful lot of stuff in them days" ("Cleopatterer").

Billy decides not to go to Bingham after all. By staying at Atwater he will be near Jane ("The Crickets Are Calling").

The game is under way and Bingham is winning, causing Atwater supporters to redouble their encouragement ("Football Song"). To make a suitor jealous Flora pretends to be engaged to Bub, who is becoming more worldly by the minute ("Sir Galahad"). Billy wins the game for Atwater. Bessie is so thrilled with Stub's initiative in securing Billy that she promises to marry him ("The Sun Shines Brighter"). Now Bub is in love—but with Jane ("I'm Going to Find A Girl"). An angry Mr. Bolton tells Billy he must take a job in the family firm. Jane finds a downcast Billy, but when she explains that what started as a silly trick has turned into love, well . . .

GOOD OLD ATWATER (COLLEGE SONG)

(Boys)

Youth is a dream that will not last—
A stream that glides on, gay and glittering;
Bright for an instant—then it's past
And leaves but a sweet regret.
Ivy-clad walls against the sky,
And cool green elms where birds are twittering,
Soon we shall have to say goodbye—
But, though we go, we'll not forget.

Others will tread where we have been,
And live and laugh and hope in place of us:
Others will see what we have seen,
And fall 'neath the same soft spell.
Though to a world of joys and fears
Life whirls us off and leaves no trace of us,
Still we'll remember through the years
The dear old place we loved so well.

Good old Atwater,
To none we'll ever yield!

Opponents we will slaughter
Whene'er we take the field.
This is the song to sing 'em—
"Are we downhearted? *No!*
We're going to murder Bingham
And they haven't got a show!"

A PEACH OF A LIFE

(Stub and Bessie)

Stub: I feel a yearning whene'er I'm
        returning
    To *my* lonely bachelor gloom.
    The joint I inhabit is so dull and
        drab, it
    Is like getting back to a tomb.
    This thought comes often to me,
    How much more pleasant 'twould be,
    If some nice girl were near,
    My gray existence to cheer.

Refrain: It must be great to be married
    In spite of what some folks have said:

To loiter thro' life with a dear little
    wife
Who'd bring you your breakfast
    in bed.
She'd put on your slippers and bring
    you a book,
Then she'd go to the kitchen to speed
    up the cook,
While *you* took a nap on a cosy settee,
What a peach of a life that would be.

Bessie: I, too, can't smother, when back home
    with mother
A sort of kind of unrest
You're quite philanthropic to bring up
    a topic
I've wanted to get off my chest.
I'm tired of being alone,
I want a man of my own,
Life then couldn't be slow
And I'd be happy, I know

Refrain

Bessie: It must be great to be married
And hustle through life with your mate
Who'd get up at five for a ride or
    a drive
And start playing tennis at eight.
He would wake you in summer,
    when daylight was dim
Then you'd swing Indian clubs and
    go off for a swim.
By nine you'd be driving your ball
    from the tee,
What a peach of a life that
    would be!

Stub: At nine did you say
You would drive from the tee?

Bessie: Yes.

Stub: No! I don't think that life would
    suit me.

WAIT TILL TOMORROW

(Tomorrow Maybe!)

(Jane and Boys)

Boy: *(Spoken)*
Forget about the college. Concentrate
    on one of us

Jane: So many boys I see
Come making love to me,
Some young, some older,

Some shy, some bolder.
They yearn, they've often said,
For me to rest my head
Upon their shoulder.
Ah well,
Perhaps I may
But not today!

So—
Wait. Wait. Wait till tomorrow,
And should it chance that
    tomorrow
My love's no stronger,
Then—just wait a little longer.
Please, oh please, do not worry,
You know there's really no hurry,
So cheer up—you'll hear from me
Tomorrow—maybe.

Boys: Won't you use your common sense
When our love is so intense,
Is it right to keep us always
In suspense?

Jane: Now, listen, for it's true—(You're all
    so nice and kind,)
I'm fond of all of you. (I like you all,
    I find)
(To speak sincerely
The same—or nearly.)
One fine day, I've no doubt (But later
    on, no doubt)
Just *one* I'll single out
And love him dearly;
Which one I cannot say—(of course,
    today)
At least today.

(So) wait—wait—wait till tomorrow
Perhaps I'll tell you tomorrow
(That is, provided
Of course, that I've *quite* decided)
Though to keep you all guessing
Like this, I know is distressing,

So cheer up! You'll hear from me
Tomorrow, maybe!

Boys: Tomorrow—maybe!
We should think it very kind
If a moment you could find
Some day on this matter
To make up your mind.
But just use your commonsense,
Our love is so intense,
You ought to end this wild suspense!

Jane: (So) wait—wait, wait till tomorrow,
Perhaps I'll tell you tomorrow
(That is, provided
Of course, that I've quite decided)
Though to keep you all guessing
Like this, I know is distressing,
So cheer up! You'll hear from me
Tomorrow, maybe.

JUST YOU WATCH MY STEP

(Stub and Girls)

Bessie: I don't see why they let you loaf
    around the place.

Stub: Keep your eye on me, I'll be great
    some day.

Bessie: You know that everybody says you're
    a disgrace.

Stub: Gosh, how mad you'll be that you act
    this way.

Bessie: Real hard work is what you need
And you're hopeless, everybody has
    agreed.

Stub: Wait, some day I'll show a flash of
    speed.
(Spoken)   (I'm getting in wrong with
    everybody)

Girls: Oh, cheer up, Stubby, do—
           Don't let her bully you,
           You've lots of time to make us all
               quite proud of you.
           Don't be blue,
           We know you're going to be
               'hot-stuff' before you're
               through . . .

Stub: So far, I've not had my name written
               on the nation's roll of fame:
           Nobody I see makes a fuss of me.
           In a line crowds do not stand
           Waiting for a chance to shake my
               hand.
           Folks when I appear
           Don't get up and cheer.

Girls: But of chances for success
           The land's from North to South, full

Stub: Thank you for these cheering words
           Yes, girls, you've said a mouthful.

Chorus: Just you watch my step
           I've got push and pep.
           I'll win fortune and renown.

Girls: You'll win renown—

Stub: Though I've not started yet,
           Kindly don't forget
           You can't keep a good man down.

           All the wealthy men I know—
           Rockefeller, Henry Ford and Co.
           Once upon a time didn't have a dime.
           Morgan always touched the bunch,
           When it was his turn to pay the lunch
           With Carnegie at their pet automat.

Girls: Fortune's sure to smile
           Although at first she may be fickle

Stub: That's the stuff—
           Why, Heinz began his life without a
               pickle

Girls: Just you watch his step
           He's got push and pep.
           He'll win fortune and renown.

Stub: I'll win renown.

Girls: He'll land the sort of job
           They handed Charley Schwab
           You can't keep a good man down

Stub: Believe me, I'm a 'bear,'
           I'll be a millionaire—

Girls: Yes, in a year or two
           We'll come and visit you
           Upon your yacht or in your house on
               upper Fifth Avenue.
           We know you're going to be
               'hot-stuff' before you're
               through.

Stub: After you have made your name
           Dancing nowadays is quite a game.
           If you'd get rich quick,
           That's the only trick.
           I'd just like a little piece
           Of the money people pay Maurice—
           I would do it now,
           But I don't know how.

Girls: It's an easy thing to learn
           Why, anyone can do it.

Stub: Well, I need the money,
           So what-ho there, lead me to it—

Chorus: Just you watch my step
           I've got push and pep.
           I'll win fortune and renown, etc.

LEAVE IT TO JANE

(Bessie, Stub, Jane and Ensemble)

Bessie: Our gentle Jane,
When it comes to brain

Stub: Can make quite a show.

Jane: It's wicked, you know,
To flatter me so.

Stub: She's cooler than ice,
So take my advice
If you've a problem
Don't you think twice.

Refrain
Bessie &
Stub: Just—
Leave it to Jane,
Jane, Jane

Jane: I don't know why you should
Make me plot and plan for you.

Bessie: She is the girl with brain.

Jane: I always try to do everything I can
for you.

Bessie &
Stub: No problem you can wish on her
Gives her a strain,
She'll tackle gaily a score or more
daily
If something is on your mind.

Jane: And I can see that there is
Not a doubt of it!

Bessie &
Stub: Comfort you soon will find.

Jane: Leave it to me, I will soon
Get you out of it.

Bessie &
Stub: If you have started worrying,
Kindly refrain—

All: And just hand the whole thing
Over to Jane!

Jane: I've been that way
From a child, they say:

Stub: When she was but two,
Our Jane always knew
The right thing to do.

Bessie: Her tact and her sense
Were simply immense—

Stub: That's why we say with
           Fervor intense—

Refrain
Bessie &
Stub: Just—
           Leave it to Jane,
           No problem you can wish on her
           Gives her a strain.
           She'll tackle gaily
           A score or more daily,
           If something is on your mind,
           Comfort you soon will find
           If you have started worrying,
           Kindly refrain.
           Just hand the whole thing over
               to Jane.

The song is a revised version of "Whistling Dan" from *Ninety In the Shade* (1915).

THE SIREN'S SONG

(Jane, Bessie and Girls)

Jane: On an island far away,
           So the old world legends say,
           Sat wicked Sirens all day long,
           Singing their sweet, deceitful song.
           Mariners came sailing near,
           Heard that song so soft and clear—
           Answered the call that lured them all,
           And upon the reef, came straight to
               grief.

Refrain: "Come to us! We've waited so long
               for you!
           Every day we'll make a new song
               for you.
           Come, come to us; we love you so!
           Leave behind the world and its
               fretting,
           And we will teach (give) you rest and
               forgetting."
           So sang the Sirens ages and ages ago.

Bessie: Now long years have passed away,
           Sirens are a myth, they say.
           But you still find them, nonetheless,
           Singing today in modern dress.
           Just the same they set their snare,
           Sweetly smiling, false and fair—
           Turn a deaf ear when you are near,
           Or upon the reef you'll come to grief.

Refrain
Girls: "Come to us! We've waited so long
               for you!
           We'll make life one beautiful song
               for you.
           Come, come to us! We love you so!"
           That's the song the Sirens will sing
               you,
           And if you hark, to shipwreck they'll
               bring you,
           Just as they used to (did long) ages
               and ages ago.

THERE IT IS AGAIN

(When Your Favorite Girl's Not There)

(When the Orchestra's Playing Your Favorite Waltz)

(Billy and Girls)

Billy: Fiddlers are playing
           And dancers are swaying
           In close embrace.

Girls: Close embrace.

Billy: Bright eyes are yearning
           And soft fire is burning
           In each fair face—

Girls: Each fair face.

Billy: But though they're comely, you stand
               around glumly
           With gloom that is utter and stare
               at them dumbly—
           There it is again,

There it is again
It's the tune that you adore,
Which you've danced before on the
    ball-room floor—
There it is again.
Now it fills me with despair.
For the orchestra's playing my favorite
    tune (dance),
And my favorite girl's not there.

Girl/
Sally: You miss her sadly
For you love her madly—
But never mind

Girls: Never mind.

Sally: Seek consolation;
That recommendation
Is wise, you'll find.

Girls: Wise, you'll find.

Sally: As you can't get her, don't stop to
    regret her,
But take some one else—you'll find it
    much better—
There it is again,
There it is again—
She's not there whom you adore,
But there's plenty more on the
    ball-room floor,
There it is again,
There's no need for you to care;
For the orchestra's playing your
    favorite dance,
And a lot of nice girls are there.

Jane: For the orchestra's playing your
    favourite dance

Jane &
Billy: And (my) (your) favourite girl
    is here!

CLEOPATTERER

(Flora)

In days of old beside the Nile
A famous queen there dwelt;
Her clothes were few, but full of style;
Her figure slim and svelte;
On ev'ry man that wandered by
She pulled the Theda Bara eye;
And everyone observed with awe
That her work was swift, but never raw.

I'd be like Cleopatterer,
If I could have my way.
Each man she met she went and kissed.
And she'd dozens on her waiting list.
I wish that I had lived there
Beside the Pyramid;
For a girl today don't get the scope
That Cleopatterer did.

And when she tired as girls will do,
Of Bill or Jack or Jim,
The time had come, his friends all knew,
To say 'Goodbye' to him.
She couldn't stand by any means,
Reproachful, stormy farewell scenes;
To such coarse stuff she would not stoop;
So she just put poison in his soup.

When out with Cleopatterer,
Men always made their wills,
They knew there was no time to waste
When the gumbo had that funny taste
They'd take her hand and squeeze it;
They'd murmur: "Oh, you kid!"
But you bet they never started to feed (But they
    never liked to start feed)
Till Cleopatterer did.

She danced new dances now and then,
The sort that make you blush.
And when (each time) she did them, scores
    of men

Got injured in the crush (rush).
They'd stand there, gaping, in a line
And watch her agitate (agitated) her spine;
It simply used to knock (mow) them flat,
When she went like *this* and then like *that*.

At dancing, Cleopatterer
Was always on the spot.
She gave these poor Egyptian ginks
Something else to watch beside the Sphinx.
Mark Antony admitted
That what first (the thing that) made him
    skid
Was the wibbly, wabbly, wriggly dance
That Cleopatterer did.

She surely was a great success
When she wore two tea cups for a dress.

THE CRICKETS ARE CALLING

(Jane and Billy)

Billy: It's golden Summertime, and through
        the drowsy air
    Comes a well-known sound,
    Rising all around,
    It's the little crickets
    Chirping, chirping—
    Bidding you have done with gloom
        and care.
    Oh, days are gold and skies are
        blue,
    And merrily they sing to you:

    "The crickets are calling,
    Enjoy today,
    Never mind what comes after,
    For Youth was made for Love and
        Laughter.
    Time's always flying,
    Be glad while you may."
    That's what they are trying to say.

Jane: Oh, no! that's not the sound of
        crickets,
    No such thing.
    How can you (came you to) make
    Such an odd mistake?
    It's the little fairies dancing, dancing,
    Dancing in their magic fairy ring.
    They laugh and play the long day
        thru
    And this is what they sing to you:

    "The crickets are calling,
    Enjoy today,
    Never mind what comes after,
    For Youth was made for Love
        and Laughter.
    Time always flying,
    Be glad while you may."
    That's what they are trying to say.

An alternative version of the song—used in the 1959 revival:

Jane: If ever doubts or fears
    Are lurking in your mind,
    You can solve them all,
    When the crickets call.
    If you'll only listen, they will give you
    Very good advice, you'll always find,
    So never wonder what to do—
    Just hark to what they say to you—

Refrain: The crickets are calling—
    You must obey.
    There is naught gained by waiting,
    So what's the use of hesitating?
    "Danger defying have done with
        delay"
    That's what they are trying to say.

Billy: Yes, now you call it to my notice,
        I can hear
    Just that very thing
    When the crickets sing,

For they tell a fellow just to go
    ahead (and do his best) and
    have no fear
And if disasters should ensue,
Well—what's the odds?
Suppose they do?

Girls: Go on! Go on! Go on!

Jane &
Billy: The crickets are calling—
    "Enjoy today,
    Never mind what comes after,
    For Youth was made for love
       and laughter—
    Time's always flying,
    Be glad while you may"—
    That's what they are trying
       to say!

FOOTBALL SONG

Bessie &
Girls: With a Bevo, with a Bivo,
    With a Bevo-Bivo-Bum.
    Bum! Get a rat trap
    Bigger than a cat trap.
    Cannibal, Cannibal, Sis! Boom! Bah!
    Atwater! Atwater!
    Rah! Rah! Rah!

Bessie: I don't want to make a fuss;
    Still, it's pretty hard on us,
    Watching from a distant seat
    While they rush you off your feet.
    Oh, my goodness, it's a shame
    That we can't get in the game!
    I'd have bucked the line with joy,
    If I'd only been a boy!

Girls: If she'd only been a boy!

Boys: If she'd only been a boy!

All: If she'd only been a boy!

Bessie: Gee, a girl sure plucked a lemon in
    Being born so weak and feminine!
    She's no use,
    She's no excuse
    For living that I can see.
    She can never be a quarter-back,
    Wearing corsets to support her back!
    All that stuff
    Is mighty tough
    On girls like me!

SIR GALAHAD

(Flora, McGowan and Bub)

Flora: The days of chivalry are dead of
       which in stories we have read,

When knights were bold and acted
  kind o' scrappy.

McGowan: When guys would take a lot of
  pains and fight all day to please
  the Janes;
And if their dame was tickled, they
  was happy.

Bub: But now the men are mild and
  meek,
And seem to have a yellow streak:
They never wait (lay) for other
  gents to flatten 'em

Flora: They think they've done a darned
  fine thing, if they just buy the
  girl a ring
Of imitation diamonds and
  platinum.

Refrain
All: It makes me sort o' sad
To read about Sir Galahad,
Sir Launcelot and all of them
  today
(And all them knights of that
  romantic day.)
To amuse a girl and charm her
They would get into their armor,
And jump into the fray!
They called her 'lady-love'
They used to wear her little glove,
And ev'rything that *she* (the girl)
  said—*went*!
For them was the days when a lady
  was a lady
And a gent was a perfect gent.

Bub: Some night when they sat down to
  dine, Sir Claude would say:
"That girl of mine
Makes ev'ry woman jealous when
  she sees her!"

McGowan: Then someone else would yell
"Behave! thou malapert and scurvy
  knave!
Or I will smite thee one upon the
  beezer!"

Flora: And then next morning, if you
  please, they'd dress in iron
  B.V.D.'s
And mount a pair of chargers
  highly mettled,
And when Sir Claude, so fair and
  young, got punctured in the leg
  or lung,
They looked upon the argument
  as settled.

Refrain

THE SUN SHINES BRIGHTER

(I'm So Happy)

(Bessie and Stub)

Bessie: I'm so happy!
Life doesn't seem the same.
You can't see it,
But inside I'm all aflame!
I haven't felt this way since once I
  sunk a ten-foot putt,
Which I needed to win the game.

Refrain: Oh! The sun shines brighter than it
  used to,
And the world becomes worthwhile,
Little dicky-birdies sing the wedding
  march;
And Nature seems to smile.
The breeze in the trees brings a scent
  of orange blossom(s)
And the skies turn soft and blue,
When there's no one 'round except
  the man you love,
And the man you love, loves you.

Stub: I'm so happy!
I've simply got to sing!
I'll break records
When I run to buy the ring.
I don't know who the fellow was who
    first invented life,
But he started a darned good thing.

Oh! The sun shines brighter than it
    used to,
And the world becomes worthwhile,
Little dicky-birdies sing the wedding
    march;
All nature seems to smile.
The breeze in the trees brings a scent
    of orange blossom(s)
And the skies turn soft and blue,
When there's no one 'round except
    the girl you love,
And the girl you love, loves you.

I'M GOING TO FIND A GIRL

(Stub, Bub, Ollie and Girls)

Ollie: I want the sort of wife
Who'll lead a calm, domestic life.

Bub: For me that kind of dame
Would be a lot too tame.
I want to find a girl
Who'll help me buck the Social
    Whirl.

Stub: While I prefer the sort,
Who's fond of outdoor sport.

All: Our tastes, you see, do not agree,
But one thing you can take from me
That . . .

Refrain: . . . I am going to find a girl some
    day,

Stub: If I have to hunt till I am gray;
Yes, if you stick around a while
You'll see me walking down the
    aisle
With the little missus
She may be a blonde or a
    brunette;
I've not settled all the details yet.

This is all I want to say

Bub: Some fine day,

Ollie: Come what may

All: He is going to find a girl, you bet.

Ollie: The girl I have in mind
I know it will be hard to find.

Bub: And none that I can see
Have zip enough for me.
I'm pretty hard to suit
She must have style and be a
    beaut.

Stub: We'll track her down in time,
Then oh! That wedding chime.

All: Though cruel Fate may make us
    wait!
We're sure to find her soon or late.
Yes . . .

Refrain: . . . I am going to find a girl some
    day
If I have to hunt till I am gray;
Yes, if you stick around a while
You'll see me walking down the
    aisle
With the little missus
She may be a blonde or a brunette;
I've not settled all the details yet.

Stub: This is all I want to say.

Bub: Some fine day,

Ollie: Come what may,

All: I am going to find a girl,
               you bet.

Girls repeat refrain

The show toured for a month before opening on Broadway and at least five songs
were dropped, while two were added.
    Early in the first act was a number for
Flora, McGowan and the Boys . . .

Aline Chase and Oscar Shaw in *Leave It to Jane.*

WHY?

Flora: It's awful to have handed a good
               man the icy No,
           But I must tell you candid that
               you haven't got a show:
           The sort I like are dressy men,
               who look refined and swell,
           A well-pressed pair of pants
               affects me more than tongue
               can tell.

McGowan: I'm not the kind of specimen for
               which you've always fell,
           But

Refrain: Why judge a play by the poster
               on the wall?
           Why judge the goods by the
               label?
           Why judge a guy by his clothes?
               For, after all,
           He dresses just as well as he is able
           Treat with suspicion ginks who've
               got the soup and fish on
           For too often they play a villain's
               part,

           Oh, rags are royal raiment
               when they're worn for virtue's
               sake,
           And a sweater may conceal an
               honest heart.

Flora: I'm awful sentimental and I hate to
               have you say,
           Though you're a perfect gentleman,
               your face stands in the way.

I'd leave my home to follow boys,
    when they are long on looks,
I want a man like them Greek gods
    you read about in books.

McGowan: Forget it! Those Apollo boys are all
    a bunch of crooks,
Say!

Refrain: Why judge a play by the poster on
    the wall?
Why judge the goods by the label?
Why judge a guy by his looks?
    For, after all,
You bet he looks as pretty as he's able?
Don't go preferring ginks that ain't
    got nothing stirring,
For good looks are too often but
    a screen.
A handsome face my lie beneath
    a head that's made of bone,
And a homely mug may hide a
    clever bean.

In an early version of the show Jane and Billy had another duet just before the first act Finale, but presumably it was considered that one duet—"The Crickets Are Calling"—was enough. At one point the song was to have been "I've Never Found A Girl Like You"—which was replaced by . . .

WHAT I'M LONGING TO SAY

(This Is What I'm Longing [To Say])

(Jane and Billy)

Jane: Why can't you find
Words to make clear all that's lying
    behind,
Back in your mind?

Billy: I do not know
Why it is so
I must seem awfully stupid and slow.

Refrain: Somehow, whenever I'm with you
    I never
Can say what I'm longing to say.
When it's too late and
You are not near me,
I can finds words, but
You're not there to hear me.
That's why, when we're together
I just talk of the weather,
Simply because,
When I'm with you, I never
Can say what I'm longing to say.

Billy: There's not a doubt
I've lots of eloquence somewhere
    about!
Can't get it out.

Jane: If that is so,
I will soon show
It's just a question of trying, you know.

Refrain: Though I'm not clever, I can think
    of ever
So many nice things you can say.
Couldn't you pay me
Compliments charming?
Why be afraid? I am not so alarming;
So try, please, don't be downhearted.
It's not hard, once you have started.
Look in my eyes! Make your mind
    up and try
And I'm sure you'll find plenty to say.

The couple also lost a "getting to know you" number that was published, although it appears in no known version of the show.

IT'S A GREAT BIG LAND

(Billy and Jane)

Billy: Girls! Girls! This land is full of girls,
And I have met them all, I vow.

And most of the lot
I soon forgot:
Some I did not
Till now.
I've known girls who liked to flirt,
   and I've known girls
   who told their mothers,
Ah, but you're the only one who's
   really diff'rent from the others.

It's a great big land,
Full of Maries, Kates and Daisies.
It's a large, wide land
Simply stuffed with Mauds and
   Maisies,
As you travel from the Bronx to
   San Francisco,
Girls of ev'ry known variety you
   view:
But in all the population
Of this great and growing nation,
I have *never* found a girl like you.
From New York to Minnesota,
Ev'ry State supplied its quota,
But I never met a girl like you.

Jane: Men! Men! This land is full of men,
As all the census books agree:
But, try as I might,
I've never quite
Found one that's right
For me.

I have kept them at a distance, and
   I've treated them like brothers,
But I've always felt that each was just
   exactly like the others.

It's a great big land
Full of Toms and Dicks and Teddies;
It's a large, wide land
Cluttered up with Jacks and
   Freddies;

Even though you stay at home and
   never travel,
Men of ev'ry known variety you view:
I have seen them in their millions,
Soldiers, sailors and civilians,
But I never met a man like you.
I've seen big men, I've seen small
   ones,
I've seen short men, I've seen tall
   ones,
But I've *never* met a man like you!

They lost a second act duet called "I've Played For You."

I'VE PLAYED FOR YOU

(Billy and Jane)

Billy: I have never yet played
A game that made
Me so keen
To score.

Jane: Tell me why, then, today
You are keener, pray,
Than you've been
Before?

Billy: But surely you guess it?
You do! Come, confess it!
The reason you know very well.

Jane: Oh, no, I'm not clever,
And so I could never
Find out what you mean—till you
   tell.
Won't you kindly explain?
Hard work my brain
Wasn't made
To do.

Billy: Very well. Then I'll say
I played hard today.

For I played
For you.
And though 'twas mighty tough
    going,
I stood it, knowing
You were out there.
Though I was trampled and
    battered,
That never mattered:
I didn't care.
I simply thought of you:
And that's what pulled me through.

I've played for *you* today:
That's all that I can say,
I knew what you
Would have me do.
And so—
Did what I could:
If I made good,
You understood.
You know
I would not fail you now:
I'll see it through somehow!
But still, lose or win, come what
    may,
I've played for you today.

Jane: (You've played for me today.
What more is there to say?
I knew that you your best would do
And you
Did all you could, And you made
    good,
I understood.
I know
You would not fail me now,
You'll see it through somehow.
But still, lose or win, come what may,
You've played for me today)

Flora had to give up her second act comedy solo in which she laments the fact that Bub is the latest swain to leave her stranded.

POOR PRUNE

(Flora)

Mamah often used to tell me how imprudent
It is for girls to let their fancies roam
And go out walking evenings with a student,
Instead of washing dishes safe at home.
But I never thought my Percy (Harold) would
    deceive me;
He seemed as good and faithful as a lamb.
And now—dog-gone it, if he doesn't leave me,
The double-faced, horn-swoggling little
    clam!

"I will always love you, dearie!
Morning, night and afternoon;
And my heart will grow (be) so weary
If we don't get married soon!"
Oh, I fell for all that old time junk,
Them nights beneath the moon,
Poor Prune!

Now I can't enjoy my meals, my heart is
    broken
(I feel as if my trusting heart was broken)
I don't know when I've felt so awful wild.
Ah, since those crool remarks of his was
    spoken,
I've turned into a woman from a child.
It gets my goat for fair, when I remember
Them walks we used to take at close of day.
And how it used to fan Love's glowing (burning)
    ember,
When he to me these tender woids would
    say:

"I will always love you, dearie!
With a love that naught can kill;
And my heart will ne'er grow weary
Nor my passion get a chill!"
Yes, I fell for all the hot-air stuff
That Percy (Harold) used to spill,
Poor pill!

She was more than recompensed by being given "Cleopatterer" in the first act. Georgia O'Ramey (who had starred in *Miss Springtime*) invariably stopped the show with it. "Poor Prune" was restored for the 1959 revival.

In addition Billy and the Girls had a late second act number on the road called "I've Had My Share" ("I Don't Care").

I'VE HAD MY SHARE
(I DON'T CARE)

(Billy and Girls)

In this life there always come times,
When you're sick or else in love,
When you find that old man Trouble
sometimes
Packs a horseshoe in his glove.
When he rushes at you scowling
And he socks you on the chin,
There is nothing gained by howling:
It is best to try and grin.
I'm darned if I'm going to whine, now I am
getting mine!

I've always found when there was trouble
around,
That I've had my share;
But I don't squeal, when I've had my deal,
That it's not square.
Though life never seemed so bitter,
They shan't ever say that *I'm* a quitter!
What if the bottom has dropped out of
ev'rything?
I don't care!

Though bad luck is on you piling,
You're all right if you've got the stuff.
Look at Job! He always came up smiling,
Though, poor guy, he had it tough!
And we read that Samson bore his
Woes with resignation brave;

For he told no hard luck stories
When they clipped his marcelle wave.
According to the best report, he acted like
a sport!

The critics were generally kind, in fact perhaps overly well disposed in the glow of *Oh, Boy!*—"The musical has taken on a new lease of life," one of them wrote, although, in truth, there was nothing very novel about what was really a competent, conventional musical comedy. Its 167 performances could be marked up as a modest success but nothing more.

If there was a lesson to be learned—apart from the risk of taking on too many assignments at too short notice—it should have been to beware of adaptations of unsuitable original material. Unfortunately, it was not to be learned on this occasion, for Wodehouse turned straight to another one.

This time it was a twenty-year-old play by impresario David Belasco called *Sweet Kitty Bellairs*. Comstock & Gest wanted it for the Princess and Gest had held the rights to the piece for some time. Wodehouse and Bolton would write the book and lyrics and a rising young composer called Rudolph Friml (1879–1972) would provide the music.

It proved to be an unrewarding task and Wodehouse rarely talked about it, until in a letter to Ira Gershwin in 1946 he remembers the time:

> I helped to write *Kitty Darlin'*, the ghost of which rises before my eyes whenever people mention period pieces. *Sweet Kitty Bellairs*, on which the musical was based, was supposed to be the theatre's biggest cinch. Morrie Gest had been holding it for years until he could find someone worthy of having an easy fortune bestowed on them. He practically patted Guy's and my heads when he informed us that owing to our good work on *Oh, Boy!* etc., he had decided to let us do it. Of all the turkeys!

But Wodehouse is being a little economical with the truth here. There were two versions of the show. The first—the Wodehouse/Bolton version which played in Baltimore in September and the one that subsequently appeared (briefly) in New York—but not at the Princess—in November.

The logistics are explained by a contract offered by Comstock & Gest and accepted by Otto Harbach (1873–1963) on October 17th, 1917:

> Whereas the said Managers are the owners of the sole and exclusive right, license and privilege to produce and represent a certain dramatico-musical play, the book and lyrics of which were originated and written by Guy Bolton and P. G. Woodhouse (*sic*) . . . and the music of which has been originated and written by Rudolph Friml, the said book and lyrics in their present form are not satisfactory to said Managers, and they are desirous of engaging and employing said Author to reconstruct, revise and rewrite the aforesaid book and lyrics.

The "said Managers" further agreed to "produce and represent" the reconstructed show "on or before December 1st 1917." In fact, they did so on November 7th at New York's Casino theatre, where it lasted a mere 14 performances and then was heard no more.

In the program for the latter the "said Author" relinquished his given name of Hauerbach for the first time in his professional career and became "Otto Harbach." World War I was still raging and it was generally considered that "Hauerbach" was a "war casualty."

Friml may not have made his mark with *Kitty Darlin'*—it was, after all, no easy task for a Czech to write convincing Irish music—but he more than made up for it later with *Rose Marie* (1924)—also with Harbach—and *The Vagabond King* (1925).

KITTY DARLIN' (1917)

Presented by William Elliott, Ray Comstock, and Morris Gest at the Teck Theatre, Buffalo, on September 18, 1917.

BOOK   Guy Bolton and P. G. Wodehouse (Based on *Sweet Kitty Bellairs* by David Belasco)

LYRICS   P. G. Wodehouse

MUSIC   Rudolf Friml

At the Casino Theatre, New York on November 7, 1917 (14 performances).

BOOK

Otto Harbach

LYRICS

P. G. Wodehouse and Otto Harbach

MUSIC

Rudolph Friml

Alice Neilsen (*Mistress Kitty Bellairs*) and Juanita Fletcher (*Lady Julia Standish*) in *Kitty Darlin'*.

CAST

Prologue spoken by:
Miss RAY WELLESLEY

Sir Jasper Standish:
JACKSON HINES

Col. The Hon. Henry Villiers:
EDWIN STEVENS

Capt. Spicer:
FRANK WESTERTON

Lieut. Lord Verney:
JOHN PHILLIPS

Lieut. Tom Stafford:
JOHN HOPE

Candy:
H. JESS SMITH

Col. Kimby McFinton:
GEORGE CALLAHAN

Capt. Dennis O'Hara:
TEN EYCK CLAY

Major Owney McTeague:
C. TIEMAN

Lieut. Lanty McClusky:
WILLIAM REID

Mellow: FRANK BRADLEY

Lady Julia Standish:
JUANITA FLETCHER

Lady Maria Prideaux:
PAULINE HALL

Lady Bab Flyte:
SIDONIA ESPERO

Lydie: ELEANOR DANIELS

Mistress Kitty Bellairs:
ALICE NIELSEN

SYNOPSIS

Kitty, a flirtatious young lady from Bath, decided to flirt with Lord Verney. At the sound of a woman's approaching footsteps she hides under his bed. The new arrival is Lady Standish, who does precisely the same when she hears someone else coming. The room is about to be searched when Kitty gives herself up, thereby saving Lady Standish's reputation.

The critics considered the adaptation "violently faithful to the original" but uninspired.

A HEALTH TO NOAH

Baritone: I want to give a toast!

Tenor: He wants to give a toast at once
             while he is able!

Baritone: While I'm able! I'll drink a health,
             I vow!

Tenor: You'd better do it now!
             You'll soon be 'neath the table!

Bass: 'Neath the table!

Tenor: Och sure, you're soon beneath
             the table!
             'Tis right! 'Tis fitting, quite

Bass: The toast is fitting, quite

Tenor: 'Tis surely polite,
             His health to drink in bright red
             wine!

All: Drain your glasses! Drain your
             glasses!
             And I'll lead off with mine!

Bass: Come, before we wander home,
             Let's drink a toast to Noah!

All: For he was blessed with greater
             sense
             Than comes to most, was Noah!
             Hurrah for Noah!
             A cheer for Noah!
             Who planted the dear old vine.

Bass: So well he knew that by and by
             A time would come, did Noah,

All: When you and I would be so dry,
             We'd crave for rum, like Noah!

We'd die without it!
His health! Come, shout it!
For what he planted then is good
     for men,
Never doubt it!
So we'll make the glasses clink
     a little,
While we sit and drink a little
Wine, wine, wine!

DEAR OLD DUBLIN

1.

We're poor strayed lambs from over the sea,
Far away from where we would be;
It's an awful thing to be
Out of sight of old Ireland!
If we laugh, well, surely 'tis our style,
But though we try to smile,
Our poor hearts are aching,
Breaking all the while.

Refrain:
Dear old Dublin!
The thought of you has been troublin'
Our hearts while we've been frivolin'
Four hundred miles away.
And till I die, if ever I get back to Dublin
     Bay,
Hear my vow, boys, here and now, boys,
There I'll stay;
Dear old Dublin! 'Tis such a long road to
     Dublin!
And we're so tired of wandering across the
     water blue;
And oh! Lord save us! The things we're going
     to do,
Dear old Dublin, when we come home to you!

2.

The world has cities gorgeous and grand,
Far and near in every land;
Proud and haughty there we stand,

We've none like them in Ireland!
London's mighty fine, I have been told,
But though 'twere paved with gold,
Dear old dirty Dublin
Still my heart would hold.

Refrain

THE LAND WHERE
DREAMS COME TRUE

(Kitty and Lord Verney)

Verney: In the sky love's sun is high,
           I never thought dawn was near!

Kitty: Then there came that golden
                flame,
           To tell us that dawn was here!

Verney: Love was near; we did not know
           How soon its bright ray would
                shine,

Kitty: Till we found our hearts a-glow,
           Yours and mine, yours and mine!

Refrain
Both: We are standing in the land where
                dreams come true
           You and I
           And the black night and all its
                gloomy shadows fly,
           And the world is a-gleaming till it's
                seeming strange and new,
           Just because the dawn has come and
                brought me you, brought me you!
           Yes, I'm standing in the land where
                dreams come true, with you!

WHEN SHE GIVES HIM
A SHAMROCK BLOOM

Just three leaves,
Three wee leaves,
That's all a shamrock seems,
Yet it holds
And enfolds
All of Ireland's dream.

Many flowers there grow more fair to see
Than a shamrock in modest coat of green,
But no flower in all the world can be
Half so rare to an Irish lad's colleen.
When she gives him a rose or lily,
She but gives him a flower's perfume;
But believe me, she gives all the heart of her,
When she gives him a shamrock bloom!

Tiny leaves,
Shiny leaves,
Ah, if the world but knew,
All the tears,
Hopes and fears,
That you've listened to!

Refrain

Although this lyric is generally credited to
Otto Hauerbach, the lead sheet on the version published in 1918 by G. Schirmer, Inc.,
credits Wodehouse, and for this reason of possible collaboration I have included it here.

Even though it was yet another adaptation, *The
Riviera Girl* looked like a promising project.
The score was by the successful Hungarian composer Emmerich Kalman (1882–1953) with
additional material by Kern. Since Bolton and
Wodehouse had worked successfully with Kalman
on *Miss Springtime* a year or so earlier . . .

THE RIVIERA GIRL (1917)

(Originally THE CZARDAS PRINCESS)
(Also THE GYPSY PRINCESS)

Presented by Klaw & Erlanger at the New Amsterdam Theatre, New York, on September 24, 1917 (78 performances), after a tryout at the Forrest Theatre, Philadelphia.

BOOK
Guy Bolton and
P. G. Wodehouse
(Adapted from Kalman's
Czardasfürstin)

LYRICS
P. G. Wodehouse

MUSIC
Emmerich Kalman
and Jerome Kern

SCENERY
Joseph Urban

Wilda Bennett (*Sylva Vereska*) and Carl Gantvoort (*Victor de Berryl*) in *The Riviera Girl*.

CAST

(Note: A copy of the libretto contains handwritten original casting suggestions, which are added in parentheses.)

Sylva Vereska, a vaudeville singer:
WILDA BENNETT (D'Arte)

Baron Ferrier, an ex-Ambassador:
J. CLARENCE HARVEY
(George Houston)

Charles Lorenz:
ARTHUR BURCKLEY (Seeley)

Gustave, proprietor of the Côte d'Azur:
EUGENE LOCKHART

Anatole, (English) a waiter:
FRANK FARRINGTON
(Hugh Cameron)

Sam Springer of Fishburg, Ohio:
SAM HARDY
(Harry Morton)

Birdie Springer, his wife:
JULIETTE DAY (Hope Emerson)

Count Michael Lorenz:
LOUIS CASAVANT
(Goldsworthy)

Cleo:
BESSIE GROSS (Watson)

Julie:
FLORENCE DELMAR (Wilkins)

Lucile:
MAE CARMEN (ANNA WHEATON)

Babette:
ETHEL DELMAR (Christie)

Victor De Berryl:
CARL GANTVOORT (Guy Robertson)

Old Rigg, a broken-down lawyer:
WILLIAM SADLER
(Cosmore)

Claire Ferrier: VIOLA CAIN
(Barbara Newberry)

The Butterfly:
MARJORIE BENTLEY

Daisy:
MARJORIE BENTLEY

Paul:
J. LOWE MURPHY (Carl Randall)

The New Star:
LOUISE EVANS

SYNOPSIS

The Garden Theatre of the Côte d'Azur Theatre of Varieties, Monte Carlo, where Sylva Vereska, the star of the show, is singing her most famous song ("The Mountain Girl"). In the audience is her fiancé, Charles Lorenz. His father, Count Michael, wants him to marry Claire, the daughter of his friend, Baron Ferrier, instead. Also present are Sam and Birdie Springer. Given half a chance, Sam has an eye for the Girls and he explains his problem to them ("Sometimes I Feel Just Like Grandpa"). After the show Sylva and Charles celebrate their engagement ("The Fall of Man"). The Count and the Baron reminisce about the show girls they knew when they were young ("There'll Never Be Another Girl Like Daisy").

In the Casino Sylva meets Victor, a nobleman disguised as a waiter(!) and they are immediately attracted to one another. Sam devises a plan to help Charles. Sylva should marry the impoverished nobleman, then divorce him, having gained the aristocratic status that will make her acceptable to the Count. Unwillingly, she agrees to the plan ("Life's a Tale"). The marriage of convenience takes place ("Act 1—Finale") but later Sylva is troubled by the way she feels ("Just A Voice To Call Me Dear"). Victor is also less than happy with the situation ("Half A Married Man").

Now Claire Ferrier arrives, and to complicate matters further, she is in love with Charles. The two couples lament the complexities of life ("Man, Man, Man"). Sam and Birdie are no happier. They are homesick for their native land, where they could be "nestling in the poison ivy and watching the chickens rooting up our Spring radishes" ("Let's Build A Little Bungalow in Quogue"). Time for the divorce and Victor confesses he really loves his "wife" ("Will You Forget?") . Sam confesses to the Girls that his plan has backfired—but, then, that is the story of his life ("Why Can't They Hand It To Me?"). Visiting the Cabaret, a disconsolate Sylva hears one of her old favorites being played ("Gypsy, Bring Your Fiddle").

At the very last moment the loose ends are tied into the appropriate knots. Sylva stays married to Victor, who turns out to be Prince Victor, and Charles realizes that it is Claire he has loved all along ("Act 3—Finale").

THE MOUNTAIN GIRL

(Sylva)

Heia, heia, in the mountains I was born far away;
Heia, oh heia, in the mountains so forbidding
    and gray.
Where 'mid ice blooms the edelweiss
And around upon the frozen ground;
(Heia, oh heia) cheerless falls the sun's pale ray.
But those gray, forbidding mountains,
Towering far above,
They have secret charms and wonders,

Kept for those they love.
They seem icy from the distance,
As their snow-girt heights you view;
But, for all they frown so coldly,
If you're brave and storm them boldly,
They'll give up their hidden hearts to you.

That's the way with a mountain girl!
Learn this, pray, 'ere you start:
Crush her resistance,
For, if you tremble at a distance,
You'll not capture her heart.

Olala, with a mountain girl,
That's the way you should start:
Crush her resistance
For, if you tremble at a distance,
You'll not capture her heart.

SOMETIMES I FEEL
JUST LIKE GRANDPA

(Sam)

Grandpa was a Mormon, whose
Lifetime was devoted
To those quaint religious views
For which they are noted.
Wives were Grandpa's little fad;
Claimed his whole affection
All the tastes that Grandpa had
Lay in that direction.
Starting out when quite a lad,
He'd a large collection
Big or little, short or tall
Grandpa loved them all.

Sometimes I feel just like Grandpa;
Seems like there was something in my blood.
Kind of wish to act like Grandpa,
Though I try to nip it in the bud.
Grandpa always started winking,
Ev'ry time a girl came sailing by;
And sometimes I can't help thinking,
Grandpa was a pretty wise old guy.
When he'd married one or two
Wives in quick succession,
What was once a hobby grew
Into a profession.
Cautious friends would give advice
But he scorned their warning;
Every day you'd find some rice
Grandpa's coat adorning.
Often he'd get married twice
In a single morning.
And each time he took a wife
Said—"This IS the life!"

Sometimes I feel just like Grandpa;
Grandpa seemed to get on very well.
Kind of wish to act like Grandpa,
Grandpa had a heart like an hotel,
Knowing he could not resist her,
Ev'ry time a girlie caught his eye
Grandpa simply went and kissed her;
Grandpa was a pretty wise old guy.

But 'twas pretty tough for Grandpa
When the weekly bills he had to pay,
Oh, it gave a jolt to Grandpa
When his wives went shopping every day.
When he saw the Squad returning
With the things they'd purchased at the store
Grandpa felt a wistful—yearning,
Kind of wished he'd stayed a bachelor.

"THE FALL OF MAN"

(With burlesque intensity)

Sylva: Oh, hark, while I relate the most
      affecting story
    Of how poor Man one day set out in
      all his glory,
    And how his self-esteem was
      wholesomely corrected
    By finding he was far less great than
      he'd suspected.
    Oh, yes.
    His self-esteem was very soon
      corrected;
    He found that he was far less great
      than he'd suspected.

    Man went walking jauntily,
    Seeking admiration,
    Pompous and self-satisfied,
    Lord of all Creation.
    All the while, as on he went,
    Nature seemed to bellow;
    'Isn't he magnificent!
    What a splendid fellow!'

Then a little girl appeared, and
Man grew oh, so humble,
Gave a stagger, dropped his
    swagger:
Pride took quite a tumble.
One boon alone she heard him
    crave,—
Just to be her slave.

Yes, Man is lord of all:
He's great and big and tall:
He's strong and fierce and grim;
And all things bow to him.
Until there comes a girl,
A tiny girl, girl, girl, girl,
And round her finger this marvel she
    can twirl.

Charles: All that you have said is true,
With one reservation
That the girl must be like you;
There's the explanation.
Other girls my heart assailed;
Found it safely shielded;
Each attack upon it failed;
But to you I yielded.
For the moment that I saw you
Smiling there so sweetly
I surrendered, homage tendered
Wholly and completely.
For this was all I asked to do,—
Just to worship you.

THERE'LL NEVER BE ANOTHER GIRL LIKE DAISY

(Count Lorenz, Men and Baron Ferrier)

Count: Girls, I've noticed lately,
Have altered very greatly;
They aren't as pretty as they
    used to be.

Men: (Not as they used to be)

Baron
Ferrier: Odd that you should say that;
'Twas just the other day that,
The very same idea occurred to me

Men: (The same idea occurred to me)

Ferrier: Sad alas but true 'tis.
Today there are no beauties,
Like those we loved when we were
    twenty-three.

Men: (Oh, yes, they once were twenty-three)

Count: Oh! Those eyes as blue as Heaven!
Oh! Those lips! Those shining curls!

Ferrier: Back in eighteen-eighty-seven,
Girls were really girls.

Count: Do you remember Daisy,
Who drove us all so crazy?

Ferrier: I bought her jewels,
Fought twelve duels,
Four with princes, eight with
    dukes and earls.

Both: Oh, Daisy! Dear Daisy!
We loved her long ago,
Ere Life's merry Springtime
    had departed.
Our birthrights we sold, just to fill
    her lap with gold;
And if she was cold, we were
    broken-hearted.
We're apt, we regret, youth's glad
    moments to forget,
The years make our mem'ry rather
    hazy;
But search our hearts; you'll find
    her there,
Forever young and ever fair;
There'll never be another girl
    like Daisy.

Count: None to-day there are like
         That girl with eyes so
            starlike,
         And figure not too plump
            and not too thin.

Men: (And not a bit too thin)

Ferrier: Oh, her silv'ry laughter,
         When anybody chaffed
            her,
         And oh, that little dimple
            in her chin!

Men: (That little dimple in her
            chin)

Ferrier: We were always handy
         To buy her flow'rs and
            candy!
         For we'd have died a smile
            from her to win.

Men: (A little smile from her
            to win)

Sung by
JULIETTE DAY & SAM HARDY

THE BUNGALOW IN QUOGUE

Words by
P. G. WODEHOUSE
Music by
JEROME KERN

FROM
KLAW & ERLANGER'S
Successful Production
"THE RIVIERA GIRL"

Price 60 cents

T. B. HARMS
CO.
NEW YORK

Count: All the money in our purses,
         We would spend without regret.

Ferrier: Bless my soul, I wrote her verses!
         I have got these yet.

Count: She was our only idol,
         We felt quite suicidal . . .

Ferrier: If she deserted us and flirted
         With some other fellow in our set.

Both: Oh, Daisy, dear Daisy,
         We loved her long ago,
         When Life's pleasant paths lay all
            before us.
         When she used to sing that 'Youp!
            Tralalala' thing,

The rafters would ring, as we roared
   the chorus.
Past joys are inclined not to linger in
   the mind,
For time makes the mem'ry somewhat
   hazy.
But still a thrill will always stir
Our hearts as we remember her;
There'll never be another girl like
   Daisy.

LIFE'S A TALE

(Sylva and Victor)

Victor: Life's a thing of sweet (swift)
            surprises,
         Life is like those tales we've read,
         Baffling all our wild surmises

When we tried to guess ahead.
Life's a story which, when we
    began it,
Seemed a jumble, long drawn-out;
But you'll find the author, as you
    scan it,
Knows what he's about, not a doubt.

Sylva: But till the final page is turned,
That fact cannot be learned;

Victor: And so, the only way, you see,
Is just to read on patiently.

Both: For Life's a tale, unfolding slow;
What's coming next we never know.
Take Chapter Twenty,
Woes a-plenty
That may hold;
Later on you'll find things mending,
There will be a happy ending,
Wedding bells and gold,
Wait till the story's all been told.

Sylva: Life, howe'er you may surround it,
With a glamour of romance
Isn't like a book. I've found it
Far more like a game of chance.
Fortune, whether it be harsh or
    kindly,
Governs all the world I know,
Ev'ry thing just seems to happen
    blindly,
I found that was so, long ago.

Victor: But till the final die is cast,
Your luck may change at last
It's nothing if you lose or win,
The only rule is "Don't give in."

Both: For Life's a game that all must play,
If Fortune turns her face away,
Don't yield or falter,
Time may alter

Her disdain
Though today she gives you sorrow,
She may smile on you tomorrow,
Bringing joy for pain
Rattle the dice and throw again.

ACT 1—FINALE

Charles: Listen, my friends! I've news to
    impart
Of one who is dear to every heart.
On this spot you are treading
Witness a wedding.
Sylva, our pride
Now becomes a bride!

Sylva: *(Struggling to overcome her emotion)*
So full is my heart,
I cannot play my part,
You treat me so sweetly,
That my heart's overcome completely.

Chorus: A new life you start,
For love has conquered Art,
You go to a husband
From him never more to part.

Charles: Too full is her heart!
Now we, your loyal subjects, pray
That there may come to you joy
    today.

Chorus: It surely is not right to let a maiden
    marry
Without a bridal veil or bridal flowers
    to carry.
So take these gifts, and please
    remember as you do so,
Who weds in haste, must not expect
    a lavish trousseau.

*(At the end of Dance, Sam goes up and opens door
at back, enters, then emerges again while music is
still playing)*

Sam:	One moment, make way, here comes the groom!
Victor:	(*Enters*) Pardon my delay. I hope I have not kept you waiting long.
Sylva:	(*Astonished*) You!
Victor:	They tell me I am able to do you a trifling service, Mlle.
Sylva:	And I thought we would never meet again! (*She moves away slightly agitated*)
Charles:	Sylva, please do this for me— won't you?
Sylva:	Very well, I will. This is all like a dream!
Victor:	You see, now— Life's a tale I told you so. What's coming next we never know. But soon or late, if we but wait, The tale is told. Grief and joy you'll find it blending. Till there comes the happy ending— Wedding bells and gold That is how stories should unfold.

(*The wedding takes place*)

Victor:	There is one more trifling formality! Madame, my wife, Madame my wife, When folks embark on married life, They first, I think at times such as this Seal the contract with a kiss.
Chorus:	Yes, that is true! There's that to do. Enter on bliss Joined by a kiss.

Sylva:	You ask this, and I cannot refuse it. The boon is yours, if you choose it.
Victor:	So come now and kiss me! So come now and kiss me!
Chorus:	Oh, Man is lord of all, So great and strong and tall, So big and fierce and grim; And all things bow to him. Until there comes a girl, A tiny girl, girl, girl, girl, And round her finger and round her finger, round her finger, This great marvel she can twirl!

ACT 2—OPENING CHORUS

One, two, three, can you see, can you see,
Tie the knot there with care, peeping out
  isn't fair
Catch a man if you can, if you can
You must give him a kiss like this
One, two, three, can you see, can you see,
If you can't very well, if you can you must tell
Catch a man if you can, if you can
You must give him a kiss like this.

Love is blind so are you and therefore
Let us lend you what help we may
For a kiss is the sort of thing
We feel we'd care for
So we won't run away.
Oh, summer weather
And love together
They form a pleasant combination
Truth to say
For merry Maytime is Lover's playtime
And life's a jolly careless Carnival today.

JUST A VOICE TO CALL ME DEAR

(Sylva and Men)

Sylva:	I used to think it would be sweet, If at my feet,

The world in worship fell,
I thought that happiness and fame
Were just the same—
Success spelled Joy as well.
I thought that if loud plaudits
    rang
Whene'er I sang,
That that would be enough!
But now the shining fabric of my
    dreams,
It seems,
Was made of tinsel stuff.

Men: We are your slaves! Point out the way
        and we'll obey!
        Queen of song, our queen you are
        indeed.

Sylva: My gen'rous friends, your words
          I find
          Far too kind! (blind)
          But this is all I need:
          Just a voice to call me "Dear,"
          Just a hand in mine,
          Just a whisper in my ear
          "Darling, you're divine!"
          Rove the land and cross the sea
          In your search for bliss,
          You could never bring to me
          Greater joy than this.

Sylva: Oh, Joy's a bird that we pursue,
          with wings of blue,
          To each in turn revealed,
          And ever as we try to clutch
          It shuns our touch,
          And leads us far afield,
          So capture it before it goes,
          We all suppose
          A simple task enough;
          We follow where o'er valleys, hills
          and streams,

It gleams,
And oh, the road is rough.

Men: Oh, let us help you in that chase,
        from place to place.
        If we searched together, could we
        miss?

Sylva: But I could share it all alone,
          Long I've known,
          If Fate but gave me this;
          Just a voice to call me "Dear"
          Just a hand in mine,
          Jut a whisper in my ear—
          "Darling, you're divine!"
          Over roads that twist and wind,
          Howsoe'er you roam,
          Joy's blue bird you'll only find
          When you're safe at home.

HALF A MARRIED MAN

(Victor and Girls)

Victor: Mine's a sad and strange
           condition,
           Help me if you can:
           I am half a bachelor,
           Half a married man;
           Lend me, therefore, your assistance
           If you'll be so kind.
           Some solution, if we may,
           Let us try to find;
           For between ourselves, the thing's
           Preying on my poor mind
           I can't settle—that's a fact—
           How on earth I ought to act.

Refrain: For if I am single I'll embrace
            you—so:
            But if I'm married, well, I can't,
            you know:
            Just which I am, I can't decide

Tho' I have tried, tho' I have tried.
If I were single for a kiss I'd sue
But if I'm married, I must not
    kiss you:
So all the while I wait
And wonder and hesitate:
What else is a poor man to do?

Victor: Single men are careless creatures,
As no doubt you know:
Loving lightly here and there
Thru' the world they go;
But a husband has to be a
Sober man and grave;
To the strict proprieties
He must be a slave;
Most correctly all the time
He is bound to behave.
Which am I? A husband or
Just a giddy bachelor?

Refrain: If I am single I'll embrace you—thus,
But if I am married, that might cause
    a fuss.
That's how it stands and you'll agree
It's tough on me, it's tough on me.
If I were single, I could flirt with you
But, if I'm married, I must drop that,
    too:
This state of doubt, you see,
Must make me dull company,
But what is a poor man to do?

MAN, MAN, MAN

(Sylva, Claire, Victor and Charles)

Claire: I've found out, beyond a doubt,
What's wrong with this poor world.

Victor &
Charles: No more reproaches at random
Need be hurled

Claire: Woman might have set things
    right,
But man would spoil her game;

Sylva: He causes all of the mischief!
Man's to blame.

Refrain
All: Prove the facts are not as stated,
If you can.
Since the world was first created,
It began.
Hist'ry's pages through the ages,
If you scan,
You'll find that all the woes were
    caused by
Man, Man, Man.

Sylva: Jack and Jill went up the hill,
For water in a pail;
Somehow they had a bad fall so
Runs the tale.
P'raps they tripped or p'raps they
    slipped;
But still, it's all the same,
One thing is perfectly certain,
Jack's to blame!

Refrain

Sylva: Mister Spratt could eat no fat,
His wife could eat no lean.
This led to many a sad domestic
    scene,
When of course she sought
    divorce,
The Jury shouted "Shame!"
Give her whatever she asks for!
Spratt's to blame!

Once I'm told, a woman old,
Lived in a great big shoe.
She'd so many children

She knew not what to do.
Then folks said, 'twas wrong
To have so large a family.
She simply answered
"Don't put the blame on me."

Rip Van Winkle left his home
And slept for twenty years.
Mrs. Van Winkle, she—
Quickly dried her tears.
But just when she felt
That life was all her heart could
    wish
He spoilt it all by returning—
Home, poor Fish!

Refrain

(LET'S BUILD) A LITTLE BUNGALOW IN QUOGUE

(Sam and Birdie)

Oh, let us fly without delay
Into the country far away,
Let's leave this world of fevered strife,
    (Where, free from all this care and
        strife)
We'll go and live the Simple Life.
How clear the voice of Nature calls!
I'll go and buy some overalls,
And get a last year's Almanac
To read at night, when things are slack.

Let's build a little bungalow in Quogue.
In Yaphank, or in Hicksville or Patchogue
Where we can sniff the scented breeze,
And pluck tomatoes from the trees,
Where there is room to exercise the dog.
How pleasant it will be through life to jog
With Bill the Bull and Hildebrand the Hog:
Each morn we'll waken from our doze,
When Reginald the Rooster crows,

Down in our little bungalow in Quogue.

Each day, if you will show me how,
I'll go and milk Clarice the Cow;
Or for asparagus we'll dig,
Or slaughter Percival the Pig.
And if we find a snail or slug
Or weevil or potato-bug,
We'll track them down and wring their
    necks,
Regardless of their age or sex.

Let's build a little bungalow in Quogue,
In Yaphank or in Hicksville or Patchogue;
Where Hilda, our resourceful hen
Will lay us omelettes now and then
As easily as falling off a log,
The cheerful chirp of Frederick the Frog
Will greet our ears from some adjacent bog,
When we are sitting up at nights,
Comparing our mosquito-bites
Down in our little bungalow in Quogue.

Let's build a little bungalow in Quogue,
In Yaphank or in Hicksville or Patchogue;
If life should tend to be a bore,
We'll call on Farmer Brown next door,
And get an earful of his dialogue.
Then winter comes and brings the snow
    and fog,
We'll fortify our systems with hot grog;
And listen, when the nights are still,
To Wilberforce the Whip-poor-will
Down in our little bungalow in Quogue.

WILL YOU FORGET?

(Sylva and Victor)

Sylva: Now at last the farce is ended;
          (Now the comedy is ended,)
          With the tragic tho' 'twas blended

(If with tragedy 'twas blended,)
Still we found it worth our while.
(Still we find it worth our while)

Victor: Speak the tag and drop the
              curtain,
           Life is fickle and uncertain;
           We must take it with a smile.

Sylva: Fate steps in, our lives to sever;
           And so there's nothing more to
              say.
           And all that's been between us two
              will pass away,
           Fade forever.

Victor: Fate has come, our lives to sever;
           But is there nothing more to say?
           And will no mem'ry linger, to recall
              a day
           Gone forever?
           Will you forget?
           Or will there come times when you'll
              find me
           Near you again,
           Seen like some shape in a mist?
           I go and yet
           Shall I leave nothing behind me?

           Will there remain
           Naught to regret?
           These lips your own lips have
              kissed
           Will you forget?

Sylva: And will you remember me,
           When we've parted?
           You were careless, fancy-free,
           When we started:
           Wherefore, then, pretend to be
           Broken-hearted,
           Now we're parted,

Now we're parted.
Why recall what lies behind?
Life's before you.
Other maids you'll surely find,
Who'll adore you.

Victor: Though I found them, still I'd be
           Sad and lonely:
           You're the only
           Maid for me.
           Can I forget
           Ah no, through the years I shall
              find you
           Near me again.
           Phantom of joy I have missed.
           You go, and yet
           You will leave something behind
              you.
           There will remain
           Life-Long regret.
           My lips your own lips have kissed:
           Can I forget?

Victor: Hear me for an instant, pray.
           Little tho' I have to say.
           A foolish moth you should not
              blame
           For being attracted to the flame.
           I yielded to a swift temptation:
           Do you seek the reason why?
           I loved you! There's the explanation:
           As I shall love you till I die.

Sylva: You snared me—trapped me with
              a lie,
           And I'm your wife!
           Vowed you wished me happiness—
           Then wrecked my life.

Chorus: Love's a god who wields a pow'r that
                none may stay:
             He knows no law; but gives
                commands, and we obey.

Sylva: Her gifts our lady fortune
                scatters
                   carelessly:
              The good with bad she
                 blends.
              A short while since I
                 fancied she was kind
                   to me;
              But now that chapter
                 ends.

Victor: But wait! I'll make
                 amends.
              Take now what fortune
                 sends:
              My wife of two short
              months, behold, I set you
                 free:
              So let us part good
                 friends.

Sylva: Can you forgive me?
              Pardon I'm seeking.
              Unjustly, unkindly
              I have been speaking
              Harsh words I said. Ah!
              How I regret them:
              Gen'rous friend, can you
                 forget them?

Victor: You must not say that word;
                 for you
              Can do no wrong—
              The hearts of all your
                 subjects true
              To you belong.
              Let me serve my queen,
                 God save her!
              And I'll ask no other favor.
              (*Tears marriage certificate*)
              You are free!

Juliette Day (Birdie) and Sam Hardy (Sam)

Chorus: The word of a prince
              His bond must ever be.
              He promised her, promised her—
              Now he must set her free.

Victor: Goodbye, Sylva.

Sylva: Wait—please for a moment.

Victor: I have no further business here.
(*Spoken*)   May you be very happy together
                 as you bask in the sunshine of
                 Love's Golden Summertime.

Sylva: Love's Summertime!
(*Victor turns and exits slowly to melody of first four lines of refrain of "Will You Forget"*)
Gone! Gone! And yet
Will you leave nothing behind you?
Will there remain naught to regret?

Chorus: Years fly and memories die—
Will you forget?

ACT 3—OPENING CHORUS

'Tis night, sweet night, the world lies a
    dreaming,
The stars are all gleaming
The moon shines cool and white
'Tis night, dear night.
And trouble and sorrow must wait
Till tomorrow.
For now our hearts are light.
O'er night, o'er night,
Dull care can cast no blight
For love is King, of everything
In this world where all is right.
For love is King, of everything
On this fair night.

WHY CAN'T THEY HAND IT TO ME?

(Sam)

It makes me tired when I take a look around
    and see
All sorts of other men with more attractive jobs
    than me.
They all seem pretty satisfied as far as one can
    tell.

And I'm inclined to think that it would suit me
    very well
If I could take their places for a spell.

I want to do something that's different, you see.
Most any old job, don't care what it may be.
Build bridges for rivers, make pills for torpid
    livers,
Be a sailor or tailor or manufacture—Gum or
    Flivvers.
I don't care what it is I do.
I just want something that is new.
If that sort of job must be handed to someone,
Why can't they hand it to me?

I know the job I'd be wonderful at
Would be doing chores in a snug little flat:
I've a natural talent for
Bawling out a janitor:
I'd love to put an apron on
And wash the dishes till they shone;
Feed the goldfish and exercise the cat . . .
But what good is that—

I often thought I'd like, if it were not beyond
    my reach
To be policeman Mike, on duty at the bathing
    beach,
He's got the sort of job I'd greatly like to share,
I feel a lot of envy when I see him standing there.
So pleasant working in the open air.

He stands there all day by the Silvery Sea.
There's no one so zealous and active as he.
Performing his duties, by tracking down the
    Cuties
Who are wearing too daring
A brand of one piece bathing suits.
If they're too short by half an inch
He sees there's something he must pinch.
If that sort of job must be handed to someone,
Why can't they hand it to me!

It must give one a thrill to be a dancing teacher
    say—
If I had but the skill, I'd go and be one right
    away.
I'd slick my hair down straight in front
And wear a fancy vest.
I'd work from nine o'clock to six and never need
    a rest
With some sweet girlie nestled on my chest.

A dancer instructor I wish I could be
The man has a nerve to be charging a fee.
Each morning he fixes appointments
Then he mixes it with Celia and Delia
And other perfect thirty-sixes
And if they want to one-step right,
He says that they must hug him tight.
If that sort of job must be handed to
    someone,
Why can't they hand it to me?

My peace of mind it wrecks when I read in a
    magazine
Some lurid tale of sex, you know the sort of thing
    I mean.
Where Harold, who's an artist, pulls that tem-
    peramental stuff
With Grace his lovely model, till he gets a little
    rough.
And they print stars to show that that's
    enough.

I'd like being an artist, the life is so free
If I had my choice, that is what I would be.
My heart fairly races when reading about
    Grace's
Chats with Harold, appareled in something soft
    with frills and laces
Though I am not much good at Art
I could do all that other part.
If that sort of job must be handed to
    someone,
Why can't they hand it to me?

The song was originally intended for *Have a Heart* (1917) with the title "Why Can't It Happen to Me?"

GYPSY, BRING YOUR FIDDLE (or THE LILT OF A GYPSY STRAIN)

(Sylva and Ferrier)

Ferrier: Gypsy, Gypsy bring your fiddle,
    All your cunning show.
    Life's a mournful, mocking riddle,
    Solve it with your bow.
    Nothing matters much or long,
    That's the burden of the song!
    Laugh while you are young, while you
        are young and fair;
    Time enough when you are old for
        gloom and care!

Refrain: Whoop la! Be gay to-day! Be merry
        and sing!
    What though misfortune gray
        tomorrow may bring!
    Life will be glad
    If you but live it again,
    To the lilt of Gypsy strain!

Sylva: Grasp your bow with swarthy
        fingers:
    Speed it faster yet;
    Kill the pain that aches and
        lingers,
    Help me to forget!
    Youth cannot be crushed for long,
    That's the burden of the song!
    Youth's a cure for ev'ry ill that Fate
        can send;
    Hearts will heal if hearts are young,
        though love may end.

Refrain: Whoop la! Be gay to-day! Be merry
        and sing!

What though misfortune gray
    tomorrow may bring!
Life will be glad
If you but live it again,
To the lilt of Gypsy strain!

ACT 3—FINALE

Victor: Madame, my wife, Madame my wife,
    When folks embark on married life,
    They first, I think at times such as
        this
    Seal the contract with a kiss.

Chorus: Yes, that is true!
    There's that to do.
    Enter on bliss
    Joined by a kiss.

Sylva: You ask this, and I cannot refuse it.
    The boon is yours, if you choose it.

Victor: So come now and kiss me!
    So come now and kiss me!

Chorus: (*As Victor crushes Sylva in his arms*)
    Oh, Man is lord of all,
    So great and strong and tall,
    So big and fierce and grim;
    And all things bow to him.
    Until there comes a girl,
    A tiny girl, girl, girl, girl
    And round her finger and round her
        finger, round her finger,
    This great marvel she can twirl!

The show almost certainly suffered from the prevailing wartime disenchantment with all things Viennese, despite Bolton's attempt to adapt the story to contemporary American taste. Critics who had hitherto accepted the tradition on the nod now began to cavil. While praising "A Bungalow in Quogue," one of them wondered whether the European characters hearing the song had ever heard of Long Island, let alone Quogue!

Looking back on it, Wodehouse and Bolton were forced to conclude that perhaps they had been too ingenious with their revised plot. "It was one of those plots where somebody poses as somebody else and it turns out that he really was somebody else, they just think he is pretending to be somebody else. (It would be nice to make it a little clearer, but that is the best we can do.) . . . 'Boy,' Guy would say to Plum, his eyes sparkling, 'you could take that plot down to the bank and borrow money on it,' and Plum, his eyes sparkling, too, would agree that you 'certainly could.'"

Until the reviews came in . . .

While many enjoyed it for what it was, two of the more perceptive reviewers pinned down what was wrong with it. "There is no blinking the fact that (it) is by no means as funny as . . . other shows written by the venerable Chicken Wodehouse and the coruscating Guy Bolton. Every laugh carries with it the unfortunate suggestion of an oasis. . . . Perhaps we go to shows written by the v. C. Wodehouse and the c. G. Bolton expecting too much. They are being judged by their own standards."

Burton Mantle added: "The time will come, and sooner, I think, than most managers suspect, when this flimsy sort of song and clothes rack will no longer be acceptable. It is the very type of musical comedy plot that is dying fast."

1917 was a prolific year for the "trio of musical fame"—collectively and separately. Kern had no fewer than six musicals on Broadway, however briefly some of them rested there; Bolton had his hand on or in numerous dramatic projects and Wodehouse found time to publish two novels, *The Man With Two Left Feet* and *Uneasy Money*, and wrote a third, *Piccadilly Jim*, as well as having six New York openings of his own.

There was, however, one joint venture better left unattempted.

The Century Theatre was off the beaten Broadway track up on 62nd Street. Recollecting the place in anything but tranquility in *Bring On the Girls*, Wodehouse and Bolton remember it as being "the last word in theatres, its girders made of gold and $1,000 bills used instead of carpets." Most producers considered it a huge white elephant and gave it a wide berth. In late 1916, however, the unusual combination of competitors, Charles Dillingham (1868–1934) and Florenz Ziegfeld (1869–1932) had successfully staged a revue, *The Century Girl*, with music by Victor Herbert and Irving Berlin. For their 1917 offering they decided to replace Berlin with Kern and—in view of the runaway success of the Princess shows—signed Bolton & Wodehouse to provide the sketches and lyrics.

Wodehouse soon found to his dismay that writing lyrics for an American revue was not the occupation for a gentleman his London experience had accustomed him to. "A revue lyric of that period was a monstrous freak with one verse and twelve refrains, each introducing a separate girl in some distinctive costume. The lyric was written round the dresses. . . . One would represent a butterfly, another the Woolworth Building, a third a fish, a fourth a bird, a fifth a fruit salad and the others the Spirit of American Womanhood, Education Enlightening the Backward South, Venus Rising From the Sea, and so on." He was exaggerating—but not by much.

They then went on to prove that more can be less. Since the revue format does not suffer from the discipline of a formal plot—though the boys did try and provide comedian Lew Fields with a thread of one in which he searches for a girl with a strawberry mark, hoping to claim a reward from the police—anything and everything went but nothing added up . . . except the costs.

Kern rowed with Herbert, the cast lacked a sense of purpose and numbers came and went. It was a surefire recipe for the expensive disaster that inevitably resulted. Forty-eight performances and the company Dillingham & Ziegfeld had formed filed for bankruptcy.

Among the debris, however, were several vintage Kern-Wodehouse songs, one of which was to have long-term significance for Kern, at least. He felt that "The Land Where the Good Songs Go" was too good to lose and immediately inserted it into *Oh, Boy!* And when MGM came to make a film biography of his life in 1945 (*Till the Clouds Roll By*) at the composer's suggestion the song was used as the finale.

One of the more interesting aspects of the production was the fact that the rehearsal pianist (making $30 a week) was a nineteen-year-old young man called—George Gershwin. Determined to compose music, "the kind Jerome Kern was writing," Gershwin resigned immediately after the show closed and was taken on as a composer by song publisher T. B. Harms.

MISS 1917 (1917)

(a.k.a. THE SECOND CENTURY SHOW)

Presented by Charles Dillingham and Florenz Ziegfeld Jr. at the Century Theatre, New York, on November 5, 1917 (48 performances).

BOOK	Guy Bolton and P. G. Wodehouse
LYRICS	P. G. Wodehouse
MUSIC	Victor Herbert and Jerome Kern
SCENERY	Joseph Urban

CAST

Lew Fields, Vivienne Segal, Bessie McCoy Davis, Van & Schenck, Marion Davies, Elizabeth Brice, Charles King and Irene Castle

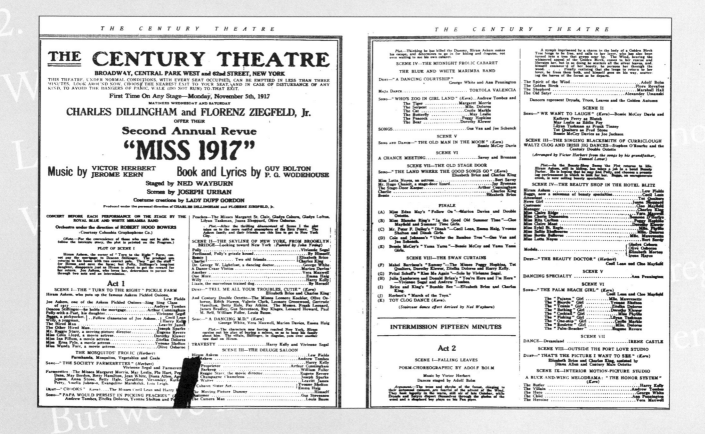

THE SOCIETY FARMERETTES

(Vivienne Segal and Farmerettes)

(Music by Victor Herbert)

Girls have found a way,
Today,
To do their bit:
They do not sit
At home any more
And shirk
Hard work,
For ev'rybody's doing it:
Uncle Sam they adore
Working for.

Refrain: Ev'ry girl, says Mister Hoover,
Finds that farm work will improve
    her;
From the city he'd remove her,
To become a farmerette.

Ev'ry morn they go
To hoe
Or drive a plow:
They soon learned how
To sow and to reap.
Each day,
They say,
They get more chummy with
    the cow,
And their love grows more deep
For the sheep.

Refrain: Mabel, Mamie, Maud, and
        Lizzie—
Watch the dear things getting busy!
Working never makes them dizzy,
Now that they are farmerettes.

Extra
Refrain: Ev'ry day there's something doing:
From the corn the hens they're
        shooing,

Or the pig requires shampooing,
Now that they are farmerettes.

Ever since they introduced her,
For the farm each girl's a booster:
And her closest friend's the rooster,
Now that she's a farmerette.

FOLLOW THE GIRL

(Brewster, Maimie, Stanton, Reggie and Olive)

Brewster: She's gone away, and there you are!
        She may be near; she may be far.

Mamie: We don't know if she went by car
        Or if she took a train.

Stanton: My check-book and my fountain pen!
        One million solid iron men
        I'll give to him who finds her, when
        He brings her back again!

        So follow the girl! Follow the girl!
        If you would earn the fee.
        Follow the girl! Follow the girl!
        Spot cash I'll guarantee!
        If you all start to chase her,
        Then surely you will trace her,
        And I shall then embrace her,
        You'll see.
        Oh, I've had troubles by the peck,
        And if they last I'll be a wreck.
        Follow the girl, follow the girl, follow
            the girl for me.

All: Follow the girl! Follow the girl!
        That is the plan, say we!
        Follow the girl! Follow the girl!
        No matter where she be.
        For if we start to chase her,
        Then some day we will trace her,
        And daddy will embrace her
        With glee:

And while he falls upon her neck,
We'll cash that million-dollar check,
So follow the girl, follow the girl,
follow the girl with me.

Reggie: I wonder if she left a clue?
Perhaps she dropped a glove or shoe.

Olive: 'Most any trifling thing would do
To set us on her track.

Stanton: My health will never stand these
shocks!
Get busy, please! Pull up your socks!
Again I say—one million rocks
To him who brings her back!

Refrain

WE'RE CROOKS

(Crooks)

(Willy and Bugs)

(Music by Jerome Kern)

Willy: When I was a baby with a rattle
and bib,
Dear old father taught me how to
crack a crib.

Buggs: When I was three, I learned at my
mother's knee
How to pick a person's pocket to
pinch a ring and hock it.

Refrain: We're crooks, crooks,
Like you read about in books.
We collar ev'rything on which we lay
our hooks
And our crimes at times are things to
shudder at,
But we've never been in Congress,
for we draw the line at that.

Willy: I owe all the skill that I possess to
dear old pop
He first taught me how to soak it to
a cop.

Buggs: And my first roll when I went out
and stole,
I remember dear old mother said,
"Go out and pinch another."

Refrain: We're crooks, crooks,
Like you read about in books.
We're strong on intellect, though
maybe not on looks.
All your silver spoons and jewels
we collect,
But we've never worked in Wall
Street, for we've got some
self-respect.

Extra
Refrains: We're crooks, crooks,
Like you read about in books.
We collar ev'rything on which we lay
our hooks.
If you leave your door unlocked, we
come inside
But we never could be lawyers, for
we've some proper pride.

We're crooks, crooks
Like you read about in books.
We're strong on intellect, though
maybe not on looks
We have done a lot of things which
we regret
But we've never sunk so low as to be
friends of La Follette.

Songs were revised up to and during the actual production. The version of "Peaches" as actually performed ran like this . . .

PEACHES

(Papa Would Persist in Picking Peaches)

(Andrew Tombes, Zitelka Dolores, Yvonne Shelton and The Peaches)

(Music by Jerome Kern)

Refrain: Papa would persist in picking
                    peaches
              Perhaps procuring peaches puffed
                    his pate
              Papa would persist in picking
                    peaches
              Platonic pride the prune presumed
                    to prate
              Prematurely pickled when he plucked
                    them
              Presenting pretty platinum pins for
                    luck
              They pinched his poke
              Now poor Pa's broke
              Because of the pickled peaches Papa
                    plucked.

              Mother sat at home preserving
                    peaches ev'ry day;
              Father said he'd like to help, if he
                    could find the way.
              Mother sent him out to pick some
                    peaches on the spot;
              And he picked an awful lot . . .
              Mother caught him picking them one
                    Summer afternoon
              Mother's gone to Reno, and the
                    case will come on soon.
              Lots of alimony poor Papa will
                    have to pay
              When the Judge hears mother
                    say:

The original must have given Wodehouse great pleasure to write but it was virtually unsingable . . .

Mother sat at home preserving
        peaches every day.
Father said he'd like to help, if he
        could find the way;
Mother sent him out to pick some
        peaches on the spot;
And he picked an awful lot.

Refrain: Father started picking peaches,
              He said he'd found the job he liked
                    the best.
              Father started picking peaches,
              He never seemed to need a rest.
              Every day he wandered in the
                    orchard
              And though the work was hard he
                    never kicked.
              He picked each peach that came
                    in reach,
              And here are a few of the peaches
                    father picked.

TELL ME ALL YOUR TROUBLES, CUTIE

(Anytime That You Have Troubles, Cutie)

(Elizabeth Brice and Charles King)

(Music by Jerome Kern)

King: I wonder why you look so sad?

Brice: I'm feeling blue.

King: Perhaps you'll find it not so bad,
          So cheer up, do!

Brice: My troubles make me gloomy,
          For life's gone wrong.

King: If you tell them to me,
          They won't last long.

Refrain: So won't you tell me all
                your troubles, Cutie?
            I'm waiting here to listen
                while you do:
            I hate to see you feel so
                blue,
            Come on and tell me,
                dearie,
            And I will comfort
                you.
            Oh, come along and tell me
                all about it.
            Some way to fix it we are
                sure to see.
            If you've a pal to help
                you out,
            You'll find there's nothing
                much for you to fuss
                about,
            You'll soon forget your
                troubles, Cutie,
            If you will tell 'em all
                to me.

Brice: I think you've something
                on your mind.

King: I'm worried, too.

Brice: To me you've been so nice
                and kind,
            I must help you.

King: Oh, no, I won't start
                whining,
            Please don't mind me.

Brice: Oh, yes, a silver lining
            We're sure to see.

Refrain: So won't you tell me all your troubles,
                Cutie?

Charles Dillingham

I'm waiting here to listen while
    you do.
Just tell me why you're feeling
    blue.
Come on, now, dearie;
And I will comfort you.
Ah, won't you tell a fellow all
    about it?
Some way to fix it we are sure to
    see . . .
If you've a pal to help you out,
You'll find there's nothing much for
    you to fuss about

You'll soon forget your troubles,
Cutie,
If you will tell them all to me.

King: Hello, there, kid; what's on your
mind?
You're looking blue.

Brice: The latest dancing-steps I find
So hard to do.

King: It's lucky that you met me,
Right here and now
I'll start in, if you'll let me,
And show you how.

Refrain: Just tell me all your dancing-troubles,
Cutie;
I've no one else to teach today but
you.
So I can spare an hour or two.
Come on, now, Cutie,
Let's see what we can do.
Ah, won't you tell a fellow what's
the matter?
Your dancing-doctor I would like
to be.
If you will let me watch your step,
I'll quickly teach you how to show
a bit of pep.
You'll soon get over all your troubles,
If only you will trust to me.

Brice: Oh dear, I'm feeling so depressed.

King: What's eating you?

Brice: I don't know what it will be best
For me to do.
My doggie had a spasm
Last night, poor dear.

King: Well, next time that he has 'em,
Just feed him beer.

Refrain: Oh, any time that you have troubles,
Cutie,
If only you will stick to me like glue,
I will be sure to pull you through.
Rely on me, dear,
I'll tell you what to do.
For I've a heart that's awful soft
and tender;
You don't know how consoling I
can be.
Yes, all the girls who know me say
That I have such a fascinating little
way;
You'll soon forget your troubles, Cutie,
If you will spill them all to me.

A song with a different title turns out to be essentially a variant, at least in its intro . . .

A DANCING M.D.

(Tell All Your Troubles to Me)

(Fancy Price and Willy)

Fancy: Oh dear, I'm feeling so depressed.

Willy: What's eating you?

Fancy: I don't know what it will be best
For me to do.
My doggie had a spasm
Last night, poor dear.

Willy: Well, next time that he has 'em
Just feed him beer.

Refrain: Oh, any time that you have troubles,
cutie,
If only you will stick to me like glue,
I will be sure to pull you through.

Rely on me, dear.
I'll tell you what to do.
For I've a heart that's awful soft
and tender:

You don't know how consoling I
    can be.
Yes, all the girls who know me say
That I have such a fascinating little
    way:
You'll soon forget your troubles,
    cutie,
If you will spill them all to me.

(After refrain, cue into dance)

Both: Now we dance, this is the way to
            dance

*(After dance of Fancy and Willy, enter Georgie
White, the dancing doctor and other characters)*

White: Just tell me all your dancing troubles,
            people
            Your dancing teacher I would like
            to be
            For I am the dancing M.D.
            Come on now, everybody just leave it
            all to me.

Davies: Oh, won't you tell me, doctor, what's
            the matter?

White: Your dancing doctor I would like
            to be.

Davies: What is this most peculiar dance
            attack?

White: That's a dancing germ makes you ball
            the jack.

Davies: Can you cure me of my troubles?

White: I can if you will follow me.

Davies: Do I dance?

White: Yes.

Davies: This is where we dance.

Maxwell: Doctor, something's wrong with me,
            I fear.

White: That's the latest dancing germ
            discovered this year
            It's the Schimi Schwabble

Maxwell: Can you tell me what's the matter
            with my step?

White: You do it just a bit too slow.
            You ought to show some pep.

Haig: The Spanish dance is very slow, that
            is why I lag.

White: Just follow me and I'll change that
            dance into a Spanish Rag.

(I'M) THE OLD MAN IN THE MOON

(Bessie McCoy Davis)

(Music by Jerome Kern)

Hello, ev'rybody, Hello ev'rybody,
I'm the sly old man in the moon.
Often I am thinking, you have seen me
    winking
When you've strolled outdoors to (for a)
    spoon.
It's not strange, now, is it? I should pay this visit,
Seeing that the earth was so near.
All the world is fighting, it looked so exciting,
Aren't you glad to see me down here?

Refrain: I'm the old man in the moon, boys,
            I'm all right.
            And I've come down to your town to
            Sit up all the night.
            I'm in love with the U.S.A.
            Though I've been living so far away,
            And so, when foe men attack her,

I won't be a slacker,
I mean to fight!

THE LAND WHERE THE GOOD SONGS GO

(Elizabeth Brice and Charles King)

(Music by Jerome Kern)

On the other side of the moon
Ever so far
Beyond the last little star,
There's a land, I know,
Where the good songs go
Where it's always afternoon;
And snug in a heaven of peace and rest,
Lie the dear old songs
That we love the best.

Refrain: It's a land of flowers
            And April showers
            With sunshine in between,
            With roses blowing
            And rivers flowing
            'Mid rushes growing green,
            Where no one hurries,
            And no one worries,
            And life runs calm and slow.
            And I wish some day
            I could find my way
            To the land where the good
                songs go.

Dear old songs forgotten too soon
They had their day,
And then we threw them away,
And without a sigh we would pass them by,
For some other, newer tune.
So off to a happier home they flew,
Where they're always loved,
And they're always new.

Refrain

WE WANT TO LAUGH

(Bessie McCoy Davis and Girls)

(Music by Jerome Kern)

Bessie: Long ago girls, you know, used to
               have a craze
           For romantic leading-men;
           But it's strange what a change there is
               nowadays,
           For their taste's improved since then.
           They pooh-pooh poor John Drew
               and the others who
           Used to give them such a thrill:
           When they go to a show and see
               Romeo,
           They just groan and say, "Poor Pill!"

Refrain
Girls: We want to laugh! We want to
               laugh!
           Of love-sick heroes weary we've
               grown.
           They give us chills. We like Nat
               Wills
           And love to see Fred Stone.
           We're tired of those strutting
               leading-men
           And posing juveniles,
           Their airs and graces, their handsome
               faces,
           Their lovely smiles.
           We want to laugh! We want to
               laugh!
           On sob-stuff we will not spend a
               dime.
           It's out of date. We've grown to hate
           Those heroes so sublime.
           Their fascinations we turn our
               backs on
           When there is a chance to see
               Joe Jackson;
           For we want to laugh and keep on
               laughing all the time.

WHO'S ZOO IN GIRL LAND

Girls—Girls—
The world is full of girls;
And I have met them all, I vow.
Some of the lot
I quite forgot;
Some I did not
Somehow.
I've met girls who liked to flirt, and
    I've met girls who told their
    mothers;
And I've found that what was true of
    one was true of all the others.

There's a bit of ev'rything in ev'ry little
    girlie;
That's a fact you're sure to discover late
    or early.
For you think a girl a kitten when you
    meet her,
But she's really just a cat, so people
    say:
And the lamb with whom you flirted
To a tiger is converted
When she's seeking for some human
    prey,
And kind words can never melt her,
So you'd better run for shelter;
That's a fact you find out ev'ry day.

There's a bit of everything in every little
    girlie;
That's a fact you're sure to discover late or
    early.
She's as vain, you soon will see, as any
    peacock:
And her charms, like his, are spread to catch
    the eye.
And until her beauties wither,
Flitting hither, flitting thither
She will skim just like a butterfly.
She will love you and deceive you

FLORENZ ZIEGFELD

She will fly away and leave you;
That's a fact you'll find out bye and bye.

There's a bit of ev'rything in ev'ry little girlie;
That's a fact you're sure to discover late or early.
When you see her in her sables at a distance,
You may find yourself exclaiming "She's a bear!"
But when she approaches nearer,
And you've time to know and fear her,
She'll turn out to be a snake—beware.
And she'll seize you when she's found you,
And she'll cast her coils around you,
And she'll crush you if you don't take care.

Sequence of "Animal" Number:

1	*Cat*	*Cecile Markle*
2	*Tiger*	*Margarite Morris*
3	*Peacock*	*Peggy Hopkins*
4	*Butterfly*	*May Leslie*
5	*Bear*	*Dorothy Klewer*
6	*Snake*	*Dolores Rose*

THE CLOG DANCE

(The Low-Back'd Car)

Chorus: Sing, sing, Music was given to
                brighten the gay,
            and kindle the loving
         Souls here like planets in heaven,
         By harmony's laws alone are kept
                moving.

Chorus: Repeat same chorus

Girls: The top of the morning to ye,
                Andy
         Won't you give us a song,
         Yes, give us a song
         Yes, give us the low back'd car.

LOW BACK'D CAR

Andy: When first I met sweet Peggy
         T'was on a market day
         A low back'd car
         She drove, and sat upon a truss
                of hay
         But when that hay was blooming
                grass
         And decked with flowers of spring
         No flower was there that could
                compare
         To the blooming girl I sing.

Chorus: As she sat upon her low back'd car
         The man at the Turnpike bar
         Never asked for his toll

But just rubbed his old pole
And looked after the Low Back'd Car

THE PALM BEACH GIRL

(Palm Beach Girl Song)

(Cecil Lean and Cleo Mayfield)

(Music by Jerome Kern)

When the winter has come with its snow and
      its ice
And there's always a blizzard or a storm,
Each sensible girlie will get away early
To where it is sunny and warm.
She knows that Palm Beach is a real Paradise,
Where existence of joy is a whirl:
Each hour, as it flies, some new pleasure supplies,
For the fortunate Palm Beach girl.

When she wakes up in the morning,
Of course there is mail to be read;
She skims lightly through it: there's just time to
      do it
While sipping her choc'late in bed.
But the sunshine outdoors there is calling,
And indoors it is wicked to stay;
So perhaps she'll decide on a bicycle ride
As the start of a Palm Beach day.

As the morning wears on, by eleven or so
She'll be needing some livelier sport:
She settles that then is the time to play tennis,
And goes to her favorite court.
When tennis is done and she's all in a glow,
To the beach she will go by and by;
And the sharks get a shock at about twelve
      o'clock
When her cute bathing-suit meets their eye.

When she comes out of the water,
The time for a cocktail is due;
So there she lingers, a glass in her fingers,
Till twenty-five minutes to two.
At a quarter to two there is luncheon,

With a few cigarettes by the way:
When it's over, 'twill be near a quarter to three,
And she's half through a Palm Beach day.

At a quarter past three she'll go out in a boat,
For to catch a big sail-fish she's planned:
Where others succeeded, it's quite time that
    she did,
Though said fish aren't easy to land.
To and fro, o'er the bay with her hook and
    her line
For an hour she's contented to rove;
But she comes back to shore at a quarter past
    four,
For a fox-trot in Coconut Grove.

Then she'll go off to the Beach House
To try out her luck at roulette;
And kind Mister Bradley will gather in gladly
Whatever she wishes to bet
When at last she is ready for slumber,
To her room she will then make her way;
And she'll pass out o' sight with a cheerful
    'Goodnight':
That's the end of a Palm Beach day.

(THAT'S) THE PICTURE
I WANT TO SEE

(A Picture I Want to See)

(Elizabeth Brice and Charles King)

(Music by Jerome Kern)

Brice: Do you like to watch a movie-show?
            So many men do not.

King: No, I never can
            Be a movie-fan
            Still, there's just one picture which,
                I know,
            Would please me quite a lot.

Brice: Won't you let me know
            The scenario?

King: The scene would be
            A church, you see.
            And you'd be standing there with me.
            I've got it planned, you understand:
            It's simply grand. I take your hand, -
            After that you leave the rest to me.
            First up the aisle we go in style:
            Your sunny smile makes life
                worthwhile,
            For my bride I know you're soon
                to be.
            A moment we linger,
            While the ring I put on your finger;
            Then, dear, we start, no more to part,
            That afternoon our honeymoon—
            That's the picture that I'd like to see.

Brice: I've a picture, too, inside my mind
            Which I would like to view.

King: Tell me, has it got
            An exciting plot?
            Is it the absorbing five-reel kind
            They're all so keen to do?

Brice: No, it isn't wild:
            It's quite tame and mild.
            The scene is at
            A little flat,
            And we are there. I've settled that.
            We sit and chat and nurse the cat
            Serenely at our little flat:
            Dearie, that is what appeals to me.
            When lights are lit, sometimes I knit,
            To do my bit, and as is fit,
            Then I sit upon your darling knee.
            In tones of deep affection
            You read me the sporting section:
            Then, oh! What bliss to steal a kiss
            And bill and coo—just I and you—
            That's the picture that I'd like to see.

Presumably feeling it had not been given the exposure it deserved, Kern and Wodehouse recycled the song the following year in *Oh, Lady! Lady!!* But even that wasn't the only Land to which the Good Songs went. In a 1917 production at London's Palace Theatre, the following variant was used:

THE PICTURE I WANT TO SEE

(Palace Theatre Version)

She: You work very fast just like the hero
In a Movie Show

He: Yes, I find there's need
Of a little speed

She: Heroes of the film all meet and
marry
In an hour or so—

He: Let's pretend that we
Are the he and she!

She: The scene would be—?

He: A church, you see
And you'll be standing there with me.

Refrain

He: I've got it planned—

She: I understand

He: I take your hand—

She: You have it—and—?

Both: After that you leave the rest to me.

He: Then up the aisle—

She: We go in style.

He: Your sunny smile

She: Makes life worth while.

Both: Because I know (your/my) bride
(I/you) soon will be.

She: One moment, we linger—

He: While the ring I put on your finger.
Then, dear, we start—

She: No more to part—

He: That afternoon—

She: Our honeymoon—

Both: That's the picture I'd like to see.

She: Shall we give our film a happy ending
Or the tragic kind?

He: Happy it shall be;
Leave it all to me.

She: But the wild and woolly Western sort
I really had in mind.

He: None of that for me—
This is what I see!
The lights are low—

She: The firelight glow—

He: We two are there, alone, and so—

Refrain

He: We sit and chat—

She: I nurse the cat—

He: Serenely at

She: Our little flat.

Both: What a scene of domesticity.

He: And as we sit,

She: Sometimes I knit—
            To do my bit.

He: The socks don't fit
            So you give them to others, not
                to me.

She: In tones of deep affection
            You read me the Sporting
                Section.

He: Then, dear, what bliss—

She: You steal a kiss!

He: Or three or four!

She: Or maybe more!

Both: That's the picture that I want to see!

Several other songs were written specifically for the show but don't appear in any of the programs, presumably because they were cut in rehearsal. Only one—"Go, Little Boat"—was subsequently published. The lyric was then revised to a tune by Louis A. Hirsch, re-titled and used in *Oh, My Dear!* (1918)

GO, LITTLE BOAT

(Assyrian Boat-Song)

Soft, softly as over the water we creep,
Winds seem to sigh.
Dark, dark is the night and the world is asleep:
Wakeful am I.
Slow, slow though the river may flow,

Soon, soon I shall be
Safe, safe in the harbor, where someone,
    I know,
Waits for me.

Refrain: Go, little boat, serenely gliding;
            Over the silver water riding.
            Nought but the stars I see,
            Shining above;
            Flow, river carry me
            To him I love.
            Go, little boat, serenely gliding;
            Love at the helm your course is
                guiding.
            Fair winds to hasten you may
                Fortune send,
            Till I come safe to Journey's End.

NURSE, NURSE, NURSE

(Miss Mayfield and Nurses)

In a hospital ward, where the sick are restored
To good health for a moderate fee,
All the patients write verses to one of the
    nurses;
So lovely and charming is she.
Her hair is as good as the sunshine, I'm told,
And her eyes are as bright as the moon;
And they all lose their heads in a bunch when
    their med'cine
She feeds them each in a spoon.

Refrain: (It's) "Nurse—nurse—nurse,
            I'm getting worse
            Come to me, nursey,
            You angel of mercy,
            Or I shall need a hearse.
            What's the trouble, I don't
                understand;
            But come along quick and hold
                my hand:
            Sit by my bed and stroke my head,
            Nurse—nurse—nurse."

Now young Percival Knox,
    who's as strong as an ox
And has always been
    perfectly well,
Chanced to meet her one
    morning and then
    without warning
Fell down in the street with
    a yell.
She knelt by his side, and
    he sobbed and he cried,
And she asked if he felt
    any pain:
And he answered "You
    betcher. So send for
    a stretcher.
I'll never get better again."

(It's) "Nurse—nurse—
    nurse,
I'm getting worse
Come to me, nursey,
You angel of mercy,
Or I shall need a hearse.
What's the trouble, I don't
    understand;
But come along quick and hold
    my hand:
Sit by my bed and stroke my
    head,
Nurse—nurse—nurse."

DEAR OLD STAGE DOOR

(At the Old Stage Door)

(At A Moving Picture Show)

(Betty and Matinée Girls)

Betty: In the days that seem so long
              departed
          On Wednesday afternoons from
              home we started,
          And for seats at every matinée
          Our money we would pay.

Ah!
At the stage-door, when the show was
    done,
Just to see our heroes,
We'd wait gladly, for we loved them
    madly;
But it's no use to wait there today.

Refrain
Matinée
Girls: Dear old stage door,
          You're not the same somehow.
          All the idols we used to worship
          Are in the movies now.
          On Wednesday afternoons
          We've nowhere to go;
          For there's no stage-door
          At the moving-picture show.

How we thrilled, when waiting on
   the corner,
To see Doug Fairbanks or dear
   Harry Warner:
We would watch them get into
   their car,
And worship from afar.
Ah!
We can't stand and wait outside
   the Strand
For our handsome heroes:
Life is gray today: they're miles
   away today;
And oh dear, how lonely we are!

Refrain: Dear old stage-door,
You're not the same somehow.
All the idols we used to worship
Are in the movies now.
On Wednesday afternoons
We've nowhere to go;
For there's no stage-door
At the moving-picture show.

THE NEW YORK GIRL

When Henry Hudson hit New York
Way back in sixteen-nine,
They asked him how he liked the place:
He answered: "Gee, it's fine:
This town," he said, "looks good to me
I shan't go home across the sea.
If you should ask what I like best,
The New York girl beats the rest."

Refrain: Time may fly and years go by
And fashions pass away
She was just the same when Hudson
Sailed along the bay.
But it's strange though my tastes
   may range,
The New York girl will never change.
She captured hearts then
As she does today.

When Washington came later on
To fight the foreign foe,
They asked him if he liked New York:
Quoth he: "You said it, bo:
This town," he cried, "for zip and style
Has got all others skinned a mile;
The New York girl, I'd like to say
I will mark Exhibit A."

ALL THE TIME FOR YOU

(You're the Little Girl I've Looked So Long For)

(Joe and Polly)

Joe: Hallo. Well, this is queer.
         Can it be you?

Polly: I must be dreaming, dear,
         For it just can't be true.
         It seems so long since I
         Last saw your face.

Joe: I tried to find you, but behind you
         You left not a trace.

Joe: Yes, you're the little girl I've looked
           so long for:
         Never thought I'd find you anywhere:
         Ev'rywhere I looked, but you weren't
           there;
         Till I started to get downhearted.
         Other little girls I was not strong for;
         Somehow there was none that
           seemed to do;
         So I had to go on hunting all the
           time for you.

Polly: I've missed you all the while,
         Day after day.

Joe: I haven't smiled a smile
         Since you wandered away.
         I've had an awful time:
         But that's all past.

Polly: I grew so weary, waiting, dearie:
Still, you're here at last.
Yes, you're the little boy for whom
   I've waited:
Ev'ry day I hoped to hear your call;
But you never seemed to come at all,
   at all;
Till I started to get downhearted.
Other men I found were over-rated;
Somehow there was none that
   seemed to do;
So I had to go on waiting all the
   time for you.

(Chorus of 24 Bathing Beauties and 8 One-piece Bathing Suit Girls)

The plot, having threaded its way through the maze of specialties and dancing acts, emerges triumphantly. The happy ending is almost spoiled by a rain storm.

The reviews were uniformly excellent. The *Times* called it "stupendous" and *Tribune* suggested that "if there are to be revues, let them be like the new one at the Century Theatre." Nonetheless, *Miss 1917* was doomed from the outset. Even if it had sold out every night, it would have lost between $3,000 and $4,000 a week.

The script had an innocently ironic ending with the hero saying to the heroine: "I've followed you through two acts and an intermission." To which she replies: "You've really followed me through all that maze of dancers and specialty people?"—and falls into his arms. On opening night the journey had taken him over four hours!

With their chores for other managements completed, it was time for the next Princess show. *Oh, Boy!* had come to the end of its time there and Comstock transferred it to the Casino. The trio sat down to contemplate what was to be the fifth—and, as it turned out, their last—musical as a team for that particular venue.

Kern made one more attempt to interest Comstock in *The Little Thing* but the producer would have none of it. Time was pressing . . . so out came the time-honored trunks.

OH, LADY! LADY!! (1918)

(Originally SAY WHEN)

Presented by the Comstock-Elliott Company at the Princess Theatre, New York, on February 1, 1918 (219 performances) after a tryout at the Harmarus Bleecker Hall, Albany, and Wilmington, Delaware.

BOOK   Guy Bolton and P. G. Wodehouse
LYRICS P. G. Wodehouse
MUSIC Jerome Kern

Vivienne Segal (*Molly*) and Carl Randall (*Bill Finch*) in *Oh, Lady! Lady!!*

CAST

Parker:
CONSTANCE BINNEY

Molly Farringdon:
VIVIENNE SEGAL

Mrs. Farringdon, (her mother):
MARGARET DALE

Willoughby ("Bill") Finch:
CARL RANDALL

Hale Underwood, a playwright:
HARRY C. BROWNE

Spike Hudgins, Finch's valet:
EDWARD ABELES

Fanny Welch ("Fainting Fanny"):
FLORENCE SHIRLEY

May Barber:
CARROLL MCCOMAS

Cyril Twombley:
REGINALD MASON

William Watty:
HARRY FISHER

Miss Lettuce Romayne:
LOIS WHITNEY

Miss Lotta Pommery:
BOBBY BREWSTER

Miss Della Catessen:
MAY ELSIE

Miss Hallie Butt:
ELSIE LEWIS

Miss Sal Munn:
DOROTHY ALLAN

Miss Marie Schino:
BILLIE BOOKER

Miss Mollie Gatawney:
MILDRED FISHER

Miss Marion Etta Herring:
EDNA HETTLER

Miss C. Ella Rhy:
GYPSEY MOONEY

Miss Barbara O'Rhum:
MILDRED ROLAND

Miss Clarette Cupp:
JEANNE SPARRY

Miss May Anne Ayes:
MABEL STANFORD

Miss Cassie Roll:
JANET VELIE

Miss Virginia Hamm:
BETTIE GEREAUX

Mr. Artie C. Hoke:
WILLIAM WALSH

Mr. B. Russell Sprout:
CHARLES HARTMAN

Mr. C. Ollie Flower:
CHARLES COLUMBUS

Mr. H. Ash-Brown:
J. RANDALL PHELAN

Mr. Stewart Prune:
JACK VINCENT

Mr. Con Kearney:
IRVING JACKSON

*(The names of the Girls and Boys
show Bolton's well known fondness
for punning—C. Ella Rhy, Celery, etc.)*

SYNOPSIS

Molly Farringdon is to marry Willoughby ("Bill") Finch and she is trying on her wedding dress for her Girl friends ("I'm To Be Married Today"). Her mother is a cynic when it comes to marriage. Molly tries to excuse her to Bill ("If men were dominoes, her last husband would have been a double blank"). It will be different for them ("Not Yet"). Hale, the best man, arrives, having met the world's most beautiful girl on the train. He now recognizes Bill's man servant, Hudgins, as an ex-jail-bird, specializing in burglary. Since Hudgins is also in love—with "Fainting Fanny"—the three of them celebrate "the gladness of love" ("Do It Now"). Fanny plans to steal the necklace Bill is to give Molly as her wedding present but Hudgins tries to change her mind. She should go straight and marry him ("Our Little Nest"). Molly and the Girls discuss Bill ("Do Look At Him"). Fanny steals the pearls but is caught by Hale, then returns them to Bill, who looks forward to the married state ("Oh, Lady! Lady!!"). May now enters. She is the Girl on the Train. May and Hale discuss the way they met ("I Found You and You Found Me"). The wedding rehearsal ("Act I—Finaletto"), during which Fanny steals the pearls again. It ends in shambles.

Greenwich Village and the adjacent studio apartments of Bill and Hale. The Boys and Girls sing "Moon Song." Hale arrives with the depressing news that Mrs. Farringdon has cancelled the wedding. May tries to cheer everyone up. You never know what's waiting round the corner ("Waiting Round the Corner"). Molly arrives to try and sort out the mess with Bill and confides to the Girls her conviction that things will turn out fine ("Little Ships Come Sailing Home"). Bill arrives and they are reconciled ("Before I Met You"). There are now so many different girls shuttling in and out of the two apartments that the place takes on the appearance of a French bedroom farce. But they are, after all, in Greenwich Village ("Greenwich Village"). Hale tells May how much he loves her ("Wheatless Days"). The Detective arrives in search of the missing pearls and refuses to let either Bill or Hale leave. The three of them lament the lot of man ("It's a Hard, Hard World"). All the misunderstandings are duly cleared up in time for the inevitable nuptials—Hudgins and Fanny, Bill and Molly, Hale and May. "Three weddings in one day. Oh, lady, lady!" ("Finale").

I'M TO BE MARRIED TODAY

(Wedding Day)

(Molly and Girls)

Molly: This is the day
That seemed so far away
That I thought it would never appear:
I can't conceal
That I somehow still feel
That it cannot be real, now it's here.
So queer—
Everything's seeming, it
Makes me fear
I may simply be dreaming it.
(Oh, dear, wouldn't that be dreadful!)
I can't believe
That I'm just on the eve
Of such bliss as no girl ever knew,
Soon I shall wake
And find my mistake;
For I know it's too good to be true.
Try my best to imagine it,
Though I may,
I just can't realize
I'm to be married today.

Girls: This is the day
That seemed so far away
That she thought it would never
    appear;
And she reveals
That she somehow still feels
That it cannot be real—now it's here,
So queer
Everything's seeming, it
Makes her fear
She may simply be dreaming it;
(Oh, dear, wouldn't that be dreadful!)
She can't believe
That she's just on the eve
Of such bliss as no girl ever knew;
Soon she may wake
And find out her mistake;

For it's really too good to be true.
Try her best to imagine it,
Though she may,
She just can't realize
She's to be married today

NOT YET

(Bill and Molly)

Bill: I cannot see
What need there can be
For any other people in the world but
    you and me.

Molly: Yes, go where we may,
They get in our way;

Bill: I wish we could contrive it
Now and then to get a word in
    private !

Refrain
Both: Oh, dear ! Won't it be just splendid
In the time that's coming soon,
When this weary waiting's ended,
We start our honeymoon !
None near us to see or hear us,
The whole wide world we will forget.

    Oh, what joy to stay in your arms
    all day—
But—not yet,not yet—not yet !

Molly: Each time I start
To pour out my heart
Some tactless person comes along and
    we are driven apart.

Bill: Life might be, my pet,
A lovely duet,
But all these folks who bore us,
Seem to think that we require a
    chorus.

Refrain

Cases of accidental lyrical "borrowing" abound in popular music, but is it fanciful to regard the line "no one near us to see or hear us" as a preemptive echo of Irving Caesar's "Nobody near us to see us or hear us" in *Tea For Two*, written in 1925?

On an earlier libretto there is a typed Wodehouse note: "Suggestion for business. Why not work this number on the same lines as that duet in *The Arcadians*, where the couple were constantly interrupted when trying to make love? It will be easy to bring on the maid with more wedding presents and bridesmaids wanting to look at the wedding dress, etc. P.G.W."

Vivienne Segal (*Molly Farrington*) and Girls in *Oh, Lady! Lady!*

DO IT NOW

(Bill, Hale and Hudgins)

Bill:	Oh, when I fell in love
	From earthly things I
	    turned:
	I kind of felt my soul
	    expand,
	I don't know if you understand.

Hale:	While I have felt all day I wanted to give things away, And stand a lot of drinks To impecunious ginks.
Hudgins:	Love makes you feel so full of pep, My kit I'd like to seize, And gaily round the corner step And burgle Tiffany's.

All:	Let three friendly natives tell you
	    this:
	Love's a thing you really shouldn't
	    miss,

It makes life wonderful and sweet;
So go and fall in love with the first
    girl you meet.
Grab your hat, and beat it for the
    street!
You'll get hold of some nice girl
    somehow
Make a note of what we say.
Try to fall in love today!
Take the tip from us and do
    it now.

Bill:	Oh, when I fell in love, My spirit sort of yearned. I wished that I could do, in fact, Some great, self-sacrificing act.

Hale: While all that I can wish
        Is that some wretched, hard-up fish
        Would suddenly arrive,
        And touch me for a five.

Hudgins: Love makes me feel so strong and
              grand,
           At nothing I would stop,
           I'd like to fill a bag with sand
           And swing it on a cop.

OUR LITTLE NEST

(Hudgins and Fanny)

Hudgins: Since first I was a burglar, I have
              saved in every way
           Against the time when some sweet girl
              would name the happy day.
           When I retired from active work and
              ceased at night to roam,
           I meant to own enough nice things to
              start a little home.
           And I achieved, as you will find,
           The object that I had in mind.

Chorus: Our home will look so bright and
             cheery
          That you will bless your burglar-boy.
          I got some nifty silver, dearie,
          When I cracked that crib in Troy.
          I lifted stuff enough at Yonkers
          To fill a fairly good-sized chest.
          And at a house in Mineola
          I got away with their victrola;
          So we'll have music in the evening
          When we are in our little nest.

Fanny: I've made a nice collection, too, to
            add, my love, to yours,
         Since I began professionally visiting
            the stores.
         I've been a prudent little girl and I
            have saved like you,

I never started squandering, as so
   many girlies do.
Each time I stole a brush and comb,
I said, "There's something for the
   home!"

Chorus: Our home will look so bright and
             cheery,
          With all the chintz I sneaked from
             Stern's
          And all the knick-knacks from
             McCreery
          And the silk I pinched at Hearn's.
          And we'll have stacks—from Saks
             and Macy's
          Of all the things that you'll like best.
          And, when at night we're roasting
             peanuts,
          Upon the stove I swiped from
             Greenhut's,
          Although it's humble, you won't
             grumble,
          You'll love our cozy little nest.

DO LOOK AT HIM

(Molly and Girls)

Molly: I have often dreamed that one fine
            day
         Somebody divine would come my
            way.
         One who'd be for grace and looks,
         Like the men in story books.
         There was I for years and years, it
            seems,
         Waiting for the hero of my dreams.
         And I kept on waiting till
         One fine day along came Bill.

Refrain: Oh, isn't he sweet, girls?
           Do look at his face
           Did you ever meet, girls,
           Such beauty and grace?

Oh, look at him
Do, look at him,
Just to be near him's a treat, girls,
I never can see
Why Bill loves me.

On the day we met
He looked so cute
In his new straw hat and flannel suit;
And I knew that he would be
Just the one, one man for me.
When his dreamy eyes gazed into
    mine,
Suddenly the sun began to shine,
And the birds began to trill,
Nature shouted: "Here comes Bill."

As it happened, the song that was destined to be Wodehouse's most famous was written for the show but never used in it. Molly was to have sung "Bill" at this point, but the lyric did not accurately describe the character as "Willoughby" emerged in the libretto or as debonair actor Carl Randall looked. "Do Look At Him" replaced it and "Bill"—in slightly altered form—had to wait for *Show Boat* in 1927. Never one to waste a note, Kern kept a substantial part of the melody in the first act Finale. Indeed, some copies of the libretti retain a fragment of the lyric.

OH, LADY! LADY!!

(Bill and Girls)

Bill: A lot of fellows I could name
Think marriage is a foolish game,
But I've discovered more and more
That being single is a bore.
For life's a pretty dull affair,
Chock full of trouble and of care
And nothing but a woman's smile
Can make the darned old thing
    worthwhile.

Oh, Lady, Lady,
When you come our way
You're like the sunshine
On a winter day.
Everything may have gone all wrong,
But when at last you come along,
You make the world seem wonderful
    and gay

Life seems to start again all strange
    and new,
Clouds roll away and skies are soft
    and blue,
Though we were sad and dull before,
Nothing can matter anymore
Lady, lady, after we've found you.

May: Fate's a funny thing, isn't it?

(YOU FOUND ME AND I FOUND YOU) I FOUND YOU AND YOU FOUND ME

(Hale and May)

May: I wonder whether
'Twas Fate brought us together?
I can't help thinking that it must
    have been.

Hale: So odd that you decided
To do the same as I did
And catch that "2:15."

May: I cannot doubt it,
There's something weird about it
I feel that we were meant to meet.

Hale: But, gee! We took an awful chance
For you came all the way from
    France,
While I was coming all the way
    from down near Bleecker
    Street?

Both:
There was I, and there were you
Three thousand miles apart!
Who'd have bet that we would ever
    have met
At the start?
But it's clear to me
'Twas meant to be.
In spite of every bar
For I found you and you found me,
You see, and here we are.

May:
When I was crossing
We got an awful tossing:
I never saw the sea in such a state.

Hale:
Oh, Gosh! It makes me shudder!
You might have smashed the rudder
And got in ten days late!

May:
I got a soaking—
Now, wasn't that provoking!
One day when it began to rain.

Hale:
You simply made my heart stand
    still
Just think! You might have caught
    a chill!
And if you'd caught the chill
You see, you'd not have caught the
    train.

Refrain

Note: It's interesting to notice Wodehouse using the phrase about a heart standing still in 1918. It would be 1927 before Lorenz Hart wrote "My Heart Stood Still" for *A Connecticut Yankee*.

FINALETTO

(Girls, Boys, Bridesmaids, Molly and Willoughby)

Bridesmaids
& Men:
Let's go through one more
    rehearsal:

Get ready for tomorrow
(Get ready!)
We'd feel sorrow
(It won't take long.)
If anything should go wrong.
(For tomorrow)
Smart papers will send reporters
Whom we must, of course,
    impress;
So we're working,
Never shirking
To bring success.
Some day the wedding
Which you're dreading
'S sure to come about.

Willoughby
& Molly:
Oh, dear! Won't it be just splendid
In the time that's coming soon?

Girls &
Men:
When this ceremony's ended,
They begin their honeymoon,
Off they'll fly, when they're united

Girls/
Men:
We'll not be invited
(To some spot)
For they've often shown,
(Where we're not—)
Lovers are delighted
(We'll not be invited)
Just to be alone.

Girls:
Just to have a man who loves you!
There can be no greater bliss—

Men:
Yes, you're right, just let us tell you
    this:
Love's a thing you really shouldn't
    miss.

Girls:
We'll get hold of husbands, too,
    somehow:

Everybody seems to do it now.
Smart papers will send reporters
Whom we must, of course,
    impress;
So we're working, never shirking,
To bring success.

Willoughby: Our life will be yet
A lovely duet,
But heartless people seem to want
    to keep me from my pet

All: All your troubles may
Disappear some day
But not yet.

Molly: Not yet
(*Spoken*)
Oh, I don't believe it!
I can't believe it
I can't explain it's surely not his
    brain,
That makes me thrill
I love him—because he's
    wonderful—
Because he's just my Bill.

MOON SONG

(Boys and Girls)

Oh, silvery, shimmering moon that I see shining
    above,
I've something to tell you: between you and me,
I'm in love!
Yes, there's no concealing, old friend,
I'm fairly knocked flat.
How, how in the world is it all going to end?
Tell me that!

Moon, in the silent heaven riding,
My painful secret, I'm confiding
Tho' you've heard many tales like mine
    before,

You won't mind listening to just one more.
Moon, not a thing from you I'm hiding.
This is the point that needs deciding
Tell me as man to man (Tell me, oh, silv'ry
    moon,)
How will it be?
Is there a chance that she'll love me?

You've seen quite a number of lovers,
No doubt, Moon, in your day.
True love is a thing that you know all about,
    people say,
But still I'm willing to bet,
Though love's in your line,
You never in all your existence have met love
    like mine!!
Moon in the silver heaven shining,
Though I look strong, I'm really pining;
At my emotions I hardly can hint;
I'd rather marry her
Than own the mint!

My health the thing is undermining;
I sit and mope instead of dining.
I'll go and throw myself into the sea
If I find out she won't love me!

An alternative version of the libretto has a
variant lyric sung by Bill . . .

Oh, moon, callous moon, cold and pale shining
    above,
How often before have I told you the tale of
    my love?
But now that she's thrown me aside and I'm
    in despair,
Heartbroken and hopeless but you don't care.
Moon in the silent heaven riding,
To you my story I'm confiding—(To you my
    love I've frequently confided)
When you are told a tragedy like mine
Can't you do anything but sit and shine?
I'm telling you my life is shattered, (Moon, you
    must know my life is shattered)

Do try and act as if it mattered, (But you don't
     act as if it mattered)
Have an eclipse or shed a tear or two,
That isn't asking much of you.

(SOME GIRLIE WILL BE) WAITING 'ROUND THE CORNER (SOME LITTLE GIRL)

(May and Boys)

May: Some men there are who say,
        They'll never wed
        They mean to keep their gay
        Single freedom instead,
        They'll never put their head
        They tell you so,
        Into the halter at the altar
        But—you never know!

Chorus: Some girlie may be waiting
             'round the corner,
           Quiet and demure till they
             come by:
           There will be a twinkle in
             her eye,
           And the victim
           Won't know she's picked
             him.
           He may make all sorts of
             resolutions,
           But he never will avoid his
             fate,
           And some little girl is sure
             to get him (you) soon
             or late.

May: Take care, you single men!
        Really, you ought;
        You never can tell when
        You are going to be caught.
        If you're not careful, then,
        There's not a doubt

Some day the wedding
Which you're dreading's
Sure to come about

Chorus: Some girlie may (will) be waiting
             'round the corner,
           Waiting 'round the corner just
             for you.
           And there's not a thing that you
             can do;
           If she's met you
           She's going to get you.
           You may try to sneer at orange
             blossoms
           Do it while you can—but just
             you wait!
           For some little girl is sure to get you
             soon or late.

LITTLE SHIPS COME SAILING HOME
(WHEN THE SHIPS COME HOME)
(SHIPS COME HOME)

(Molly and Girls)

(P. G. Wodehouse adapting
Herbert Reynolds's original lyric)

Molly: Life's an ocean grim
That has no charts;
And the ships that swim
On it are hearts;
O'er that lonely sea
Far, far they roam;
But they've Love at the helm and he
Will bring them home.

Girls: Yes, all the little ships come sailing
home
Across the sea.
The weary journey ended, their way
they've wended
Home where they would be.
They glide across the bar, where no
storms are,
All dangers past.
And, two by two, together come
sailing
Home at last.

Molly: Clouds may hide the skies
And gales may blow
Angry waves may rise
But on they go.
Filled each day, may be
With dangers new;
But they've Love at the helm, and he
Will guide them through.

BEFORE I MET YOU

(Bill and Molly)

Bill: Prepare yourself to hear the worst!
I'm sorry, but you're not the first
My heart to claim

I own with shame,
I'm thankful that I have confessed:
My conscience now will be at rest;
You may forgive me and love me just
the same
To force myself to say so;
(It's been) (Has been) I've had an
awful tussle
Yet still the fact I can't conceal
I once loved Lillian Russell

Chorus: But that was before I met you,
dearie, dear
That was before I met you.
Her image I've banished. All passion
has vanished
I think you're a million times sweeter
than Lillian
Don't scold me. You told me to tell
you the truth;
Just count it as one of the follies
of youth
I thought her a queen
When I was fourteen
But that was before I met you.

Molly: My pet, I know just how you feel;
I, too, have (for I have) something
to reveal:
For dear, I, too,
Once loved like you.
I shall be happier, no doubt
When I have let my secret out.
In days gone by, dear, I idolized
John Drew.
I used to hope that some day
We might become acquainted,
And when I got his autograph,
I thought I should have fainted.

Chorus: But that was before I met you,
dearie, dear
That was before I met you

His wonderful profile made all girls,
    you know, feel
That nothing could cheer them, if he
    wasn't near them.
Romances my fancies would weave
    about John!
But love seemed to wane as the long
    years went on:
I thought him divine,
But then I was nine,
And that was before I met you.

GREENWICH VILLAGE

(Something in the Air)

(Hudgins, Fanny, and Bill)

Hudgins: Oh, down in Greenwich Village
    There's something, 'twould appear,
    Demoralizing in the atmosphere.
    Quite ordinary people
    Who come and live down here,
    Get changed to perfect nuts within
        a year.

Fanny: They learn to eat spaghetti
    (That's hard enough, as you know!)

Bill: They leave off socks and wear
        Greek smocks
    And study Guido Bruno.

Refrain
All: For there's something in the air of
        (naughty) (little) Greenwich
        Village
    That makes a fellow feel he doesn't
        care.
    Directly he is in it, he
    Gets hold of an affinity
    Who's long on Modern Art, but short
        on hair,
    Though he may have been a model
    Youth from when (ever since) he
        learned to toddle

To his relatives and neighbors
        everywhere,
    When he hits our Latin Quarter
    He'll do what he didn't oughter:
    It's a sort of, sort of, a kind of,
    It's a sort of kind of something in
        the air.

Bill: My favorite Aunt Matilda
    Found Oshkosh rather slow.

Hudgins: It's going to be a painful tale, I know.

Bill: She came (so she moved) to
        Greenwich Village
    And took a studio
    When she was eighty-three years old
        or so

Fanny: She played (learned) the ukulele,
    She breakfasted at Polly's
    And, what is worse, she wrote free
        verse,

Hudgins: And now she's in the Follies!

Refrain
All: For there's something in the air of
        little (naughty) Greenwich Village
    That makes a fellow feel he doesn't
        care.
    All the (And) wops in Little Italy
    Have often muttered bitterly
    They'd rather live a million miles
        from there.
    For in bad MacDougal Alley,
    You'll discover generally,
    Life's a wicked and a desperate
        affair:
    When you live in dear old Greenwich,
    Your behavior gets quite Fren-wich
    It's sort of, sort of, kind of,
    It's sort of kind of something in
        the air.

WHEATLESS DAYS

(Simple Life)

(Hale and May)

Hale: If you will marry me, how happy we
        will be

May: Yes, life will seem so sweet.

Hale: If you should bid me, I
        Would pluck the stars from out
            the sky,
        And lay them at your feet.
        I'll give you all your heart can wish
        Except—that is to say—
        A mutton chop on Tuesday,
        For that's a meatless day.

May: What! Would you begrudge that
            favor
        To her whom you adore?

Hale: I could not love thee, dear, so much
        Loved I not Hoover more.

Chorus
May: When you are my hubby,

Hale: When you are my wife,

Both: We'll settle down somewhere in town,
        And live the simple life.
        But though economising
        In every kind of way
        With meatless days
        And wheatless days
        And heatless days
        And sweetless days
        We won't go through a bill-and-
            coo-less
        Bliss-less, kiss-less day.

May: We'll be so happy at our cozy
            little flat;
        When ends the honeymoon;

Hale: I'll think up dodges to
        Avoid the income tax, while you
        Prepare the evening prune.

May: And when our simple meal is done
        To keep from getting bored,

Hale: We'll talk about the sugar,
        Which once we could afford.
        Perhaps a little stranger
        Will come to us one day,

May: But, if the janitor objects,
        We'll give the child away.

IT'S A HARD, HARD WORLD FOR A MAN

(Cyril, Hale and Bill)

Cyril: No woman yet has understood
        We try our hardest to be good
        But something always seems to
            interfere

Bill: No gratitude our attitude
        Was ever known to win;
        But still we persevere,

Hale: We do our best, as we have said,
        The straight and narrow path to
            tread,
        Ignoring all temptations Fate
            may send.

Cyril: But of snares the world has plenty,
            meant
        To trap the man of sentiment,
        And one is sure to get us in the end.

Chorus
All: Oh, it's a hard, hard, hard, hard world
            for a man
        For he tries to be wise and remain
            aloof and chilly,

But along comes something feminine
   and frilly,
So what's the use?
He will run loose
Tho' he does the best he can
It's a hard, hard, hard, hard world for
   a man.

Cyril: The hist'ry books are full of tales
          Of fellows who were perfect whales
          At virtue when they started their career.

Bill: Sir Lancelot to glance a lot at girls
           was never known;
          Till he met Guinevere. Mark Antony,
           the records show,
          Was like a chunk of driven snow,
          But Cleopatra sent the poor man
           wrong.

Cyril: And King Henry was a paragon
          Till Catherine of Aragon
          And six or seven others came along.

Chorus
All: Oh, it's a hard, hard, hard, hard world
           for a man
          He'd be good if he could: but he can't
           and there's a reason:
          For the skirts are getting shorter
           every season
          So what's the use?
          There's no excuse (He will run loose)
          But we do the best we can (Tho' he
           does the best he can)
          It's a hard, hard, hard, hard world for
           a man.

FINALE

(Ensemble)

Yes, all the little ships come sailing home across
   the sea

The weary journey ended, their way they've
   wended
Home where they would be,
They glide across the bar
Where no storms are, all dangers past,
And two by two, together come sailing home
   at last.

There was I, and there were you,
Three thousand miles apart,
Who'd have bet that we would ever have met
At the start?
But it's clear to me,
'Twas meant to be,
In spite of every bar;
For I found you, and you found me,
You see, and here we are.

Once again, different libretti have alternative
numbers. In some versions part way
through Act 2 Molly and the Girls sing . . .

THE SUN STARTS TO SHINE AGAIN

(Molly and Girls)

Often on a bright summer day
When all the world's a golden dream of delight,
Angry clouds will hide the dear sun away
Till the sky grows dark as night.
The thunder will roar and the storm-clouds
   frown,
And we sit and sigh while the rain pours down.
But it's no use fretting, no use regretting
However dark the sky—just think how
   splendid—
When that's all ended and mended by and by.
Life may be dreary—and dull and weary—
When it brings clouds and rain.
But we'll all be gay when they pass away
And the sun starts to shine again.

Love is like the sun in the sky,
Warming our hearts here, as we bask in its glow.

But a time may come when its warmth will die
And the cold, cold winds may blow;
But wait! Soon or late when the storm is o'er,
It will beam and gleam through the clouds
    once more,
So it's no use fretting, no use regretting
Though love may seem to die—just think how
    splendid—
When that's all ended and mended by and by.
Once more together in golden weather,
You'll walk down lovers' lane,
For be sure some day clouds will pass away
And the sun will shine out again.

There is also a number—presumably from Act 1 in which Hudgins and Fanny recall the good old (criminal) days . . .

DEAR OLD PRISON DAYS

(Fanny and Hudgins)

Fanny: They are simply fascinating,
    The stories that you tell.
    You loved your course at Sing-Sing,
        did you not?

Hudgins: Why, today, when I hear someone
        give our dear old college yell,
    I feel like going back there on the spot.

Fanny: You played upon the football team:
    That must have been great fun,
    Though no doubt you found it
        something of a strain.

Hudgins: Well, of course, it's rather hard to
        make an eighty-five yard run
    When you've got to tote along a ball
        and chain.

Both: Oh, those . . .

Chorus: . . . dear old prison days!
    Life contained no jars or shocks

When I knew the joys of going with
    the boys
To break a pile of rocks.
Oh, they seem to gleam like a lovely
    dream
That is seen through a golden haze
And I weep, although it's silly,
When I think about the skilly
Of those dear old prison, dear old
    prison,
Dear old prison days.

Fanny: Then those jolly social evenings,
    What fun they must have been!
    You've told me all about them many
        a time.

Hudgins: When some jovial lifer,
    Beaming on the cozy, festive scene,
    Invited us to drink success to crime.

Fanny: Then there'd be music later on:
    You've not forgotten that?
    And when you performed the
        Warden cried: "Encore!"

Hudgins: Well, perhaps I shouldn't say it
    But I always knocked them flat
    When I imitated Ethel Barrymore.

Chorus
Both: In those dear old prison days!
    In those days we loved so well!
    When no storm and strife and stress
        of modern life
    Came near our peaceful cell.
    Oh, they seem to gleam
    Like a lovely dream
    That is seen through a golden
        haze:
    And it makes me glad I was born,
    When I think of Mister Osborne,
    And those dear old prison, dear old
        prison,
    Dear old prison days.

In *Sitting Pretty* (1924) the same idea would emerge as "Tulip Time in Sing-Sing."

Hudgins—called Mullet ("Finger Fred") in some versions of the libretto—has a love song (of sorts) to sing to Fanny . . .

YOU'RE HERE
AND I'M HERE

(Hudgins)

This way and that we've had a lot of troubles,
    sure enough
Coppers getting tough.
Judges doing their stuff.
We've had to buck some stormy weather—
But it's all right now we're together.

You're here and I'm here,
Just you and just me,
All alone in the night,
Which is how it should be.
Think of all that we'd have missed
If you and I were on the wanted list.
But you know and I know
We need have no fear,
We are nice honest people,
So we're in the clear.
And in the whole darned world
There's nothing that can matter
Now we're both here.

Old Man Luck has always been against us from
    the start
Keeping us apart—
Kind of broke my heart.
Things up to now were kind of gritty,
But now at last we're sitting pretty.

Refrain

There is a certain mystery here. Kern used a song with this title—with lyrics by Harry B. Smith—in *The Laughing Husband* (1914) and the tour of *The Marriage Market* (1913). However, it's unlikely that it would have been included in a pet Wodehouse/Bolton/Kern project without new Wodehouse lyrics and they are particularly appropriate to the character and plot.

"The Picture I Want To See"—another transposition from *Miss 1917*—was used at some point. But the most interesting number in the whole show is the song-that-almost-never-was—"Bill." We'll be looking at the more familiar published version in due course (*Show Boat*, 1927) and the controversy that surrounded it, but the original lyric Wodehouse wrote for *Oh, Lady! Lady!!* (to a tune Kern had written back in 1906) had an even simpler colloquial quality . . .

BILL
(MY BILL)

(Molly)

I used to dream that I would discover
The perfect lover
Some day:
I knew I'd recognize him
If ever he came round my way:
I always used to fancy then
He'd be one of the godlike kind of men,
With a giant brain and a noble head
    (He'd have hair of gold)
(And a noble head)
Like the heroes bold
In the books I read.

But along came Bill
Who's quite the opposite
Of all the men
In story books.
In grace and looks
I know that Apollo
Would beat him all hollow,
And I can't explain . . .
It's surely not his brain

That makes me thrill.
I love him because he's wonderful . . .
Because he's just old Bill

He can't play golf or tennis or polo
Or sing a solo
Or row.
He isn't half as handsome
As dozens of men that I know.
He isn't tall and straight and slim,
And he dresses far worse than Ted or Jim.
And I can't explain why he should be
Just the one, one man in the world for me.

He's just my Bill
He has no gifts at all:
A motor car
(He failed to win his college blue)
He cannot steer;
(And it is true)
And it seems clear
Whenever he dances
His partner takes chances,
Oh, I can't explain
It's surely not his brain
(Nor can it be his brain)
That makes me thrill
I love him
Because he's—I don't know—
Because he's just my Bill

The song was finally dropped. Apart from not describing the leading man, it was not felt to be suitable for Vivienne Segal's voice.

In the version Wodehouse claims singer Ethel Pettit subsequently sang to Ziegfeld—see *The Little Thing*—there were certain minor changes to the second verse . . .

Then along came Bill,
Who's not like that at all:
You'd pass him on the street and never notice
    him.
His form and face,

His manly grace,
Are not the sort that you
Would find in a statue:
I can't explain . . .
It's surely not his brain
That makes me thrill:
I love him because . . . oh, I don't know,
Because he's just my Bill.

In another version of the libretto a new character, Molly's uncle Tom Whitney, is introduced at the beginning of the plot. As he enters Molly's home, he hears familiar music playing . . .

THE MAGIC MELODY

(Tom and Chorus)

Tom: What's the name of that melody?
         Something hard to beat about it,
         Something mighty sweet about it,
         Oh, what's the name of that melody?
         What a pity not to know the name of
             such a pretty ditty,
         It always seems to interrupt you when
             you talk.
         It seems to lift you from your feet and
             start you walk-ing.
         When those cellos and fiddles start to
             fiddle that middle part
         Sighs, tears disappear as if by magic.

Chorus: The world goes around to the sound
             of a syncopated melody,
         Come on, take a chance and we'll
             dance to that syncopated melody.
         Beware, have a care when you're
             doing it.
         Keep moving or you'll ruin it . . .
         And just so you'll know, we'll show
             you
         All the late improvements
         In those syncopated movements.
         Oh, you start kind of slow

Till you know how to throw
Your shoulders in the air,
Then you slide and you glide in an
    attitude of I don't care.
You'll dance and you'll sway and
    you'll think and you'll talk to it,
You'll work and you'll play and you'll
    drink and you'll walk to it.
You can't get away from that Magic
    Mel-o-dy!

Later there is a trio for Fanny, Bill and
Hale . . .

WHEN A GENT WAS
A PERFECT GENT
(THOSE WERE THE DAYS)

Fanny: I like to read those tales of old
About the days when Knights were
    bold
And every kind of enemy defeated.

Bill: Wild dragons they would slay in
    droves

Fanny: And though they looked like kitchen
    stoves,
They knew just how a woman should
    be treated.

Hale: For chivalry was all the go,
And men would hasten (gallop) to
    and fro
To carry out a lady's lightest wishes

Bill: Each damsel then throughout
    the land
Was looked upon with reverence.

Fanny: And not just someone there (hired) to
    wash the dishes.

All: What the country needs today
Is somehow to find the way

To revive the gallant spirit of the
    knight;
For though lax in many small ways,
They could be relied on always
To treat a lady right.
They called her lady-love,
And they'd flaunt her little glove,
And everything that she said went,
For those were the days when a lady
    was a lady
And a gent was a perfect gent.

Fanny: Before we part I think it's time
To say how very grateful I'm;
There ought to be more guys like you.
We need 'em,
With you to help her it's a cinch
No cop can ever make a pinch
And rob a gentle lady of her freedom.
You both have spent your lives,
    I guess,
In rescuing damsels in distress

Bill: Why, yes, we love to do it when at
    leisure.

Hale: We're ready at the least excuse
To keep them from the calaboose,
Don't thank us. We assure you it's
    a pleasure.

Reprise
Fanny: A lot of tales we're told
About those gallant knights of old
And all the doughty deeds they
    uster do,
But for treating ladies proper
When in peril from a copper,
There was never one like you.
For when those words you spoke,
I sort of felt that I could choke
And all tingly down the spine I went.
It's swell for a gel
To discover that her lover
Is a first class Grade A gent.

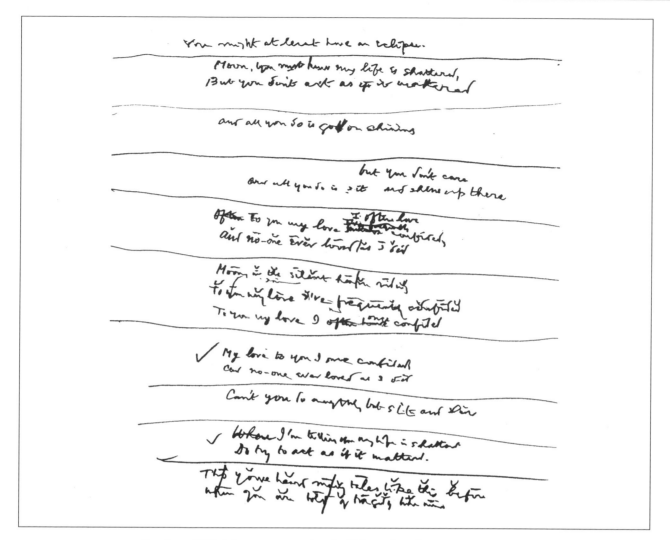

Section of Wodehouse manuscript for "Moon Song" in *Oh, Lady! Lady!!*

And in yet another later version of the script—when the characters are now Fanny, Jeff and Bill—there is still one more variant with the accompanying note: "This number, good as it is, might be best dropped. It is a case for consultation with the Choreographer—a question of what he feels he can do with it."

After the expected opening verse . . .

All: Oh, it makes you sort of sad
To think that good Sir Galahad
And all those gallant knights have passed away.
Any time, to please their sweeties,
They would bolt their breakfast wheaties
And jump into the fray.
They called her lady-love,
They used to wear her little glove,
And everything that she said went,
For those were the days when a lady was a lady
And a gent was a perfect gent.

Jeff: One knight would say "Compared with mine,
Your girl's a comic valentine"

Fanny: And that, of course, would cause a
           fine schemozzle!

Jeff: For the other guy would shout
           "Behave,
           Thou malapert and scurvy knave,
           Or I will smite thee soundly on the
           schnozzle."

Bill: Then after more unpleasant cracks
           Each grabbed his trusty battle-axe
           And stepped outside and started
           getting scrappy,

Fanny: And when they lost a limb or two,
           They didn't mind, because they knew
           It kept the little woman feeling happy.

All: Oh, it makes you sort of sad
           To think that good Sir Galahad
           And all his buddies aren't with us
           today.
           To amuse a girl and charm her
           They would put on suits of armor
           And jump into the fray.

           You never heard them beef
           If by bad luck they came to grief
           And finished with their spines all
           bent,
           For those were the days when a lady
           was a lady,
           And a gent was a perfect gent.

This number is clearly based on "Sir Galahad" from *Leave It To Jane* (1917) and was later adapted further into "The Days of the Knights" in *Betting On Bertie* (c. 1966). In one version of the libretto the trio sang that song with new verses. It was then used unchanged as a duet for Bertie and Pongo in *Betting On Bertie* with the title "Days of the Knights."

Uncle Tom is given another number which perfectly sums up the Wodehouse–Bolton philosophy of musical comedy, since it was the title of their later book of (sic) reminiscences . . .

BRING ON THE GIRLS

(Tom and Girls)

The other day, it so befell,
I wasn't feeling very well;
The world seemed grey and as I lay in bed
The doctor came and after he
Had thoroughly examined me,
He heaved a sigh and sadly shook his head.
He said, "I'll bet you ten to one
Your earthly course is nearly run;
Your chances of recovery are slim
Just try to linger on until
You've had the time to pay my bill."
And this is what I upped and said to him:

"Oh, doctor, bring on the girls and you'll soon
     see me revive.
Bring on the girls and I'll show that I'm still
     alive. (Bring on the girls and promptly/
     You'll know I'm alive)
We'll have a party and hale and hearty
I its life and soul will be.
Though I've got aches and I've got chills,
I don't need drugs, I don't need pills;
While there are girls, there's life and hope,
So put away your stethoscope
And simply bring on the girls and leave the rest
     to me."

'Twas in my very early youth
I first found out this simple truth
And now today of one thing I am sure;
If doctors for each invalid
Prescribed a blonde or redhead, she'd
With promptitude and speed effect a cure.
Their therapeutic properties,

As every thinking man agrees,
Are something quite amazing and unique;
No tonic anyone can mix
Can beat a perfect thirty-six
At bringing back the roses to the cheek.

So, bring on the girls, because without them
 what'll we do?
Bring on the girls and open a bottle or two;
I just need plenty
Aged one-and-twenty
And a change that's marked you'll see.
I really do not care a jot
If they are dark or fair or what
Or small or tall or dumb or bright,
Provided that the sex is right,
So simply bring on the girls and you can leave
 the rest to me.

Uncle Tom also has a duet with Parker, the
maid . . .

DANCING TIME

(Tom and Parker)

When the night has put to flight the day
And high up in the velvet sky the stars appear,
Cares and troubles gently fade away,
It means that dancing time, entrancing time,
 is here.

Dancing time is when there's a band that's
 playing
Sweet and low a tune we know so well.
Dancing time's the time when the music is
 saying—
"Magic's in the air!
Magic's everywhere!"
Dancing time is when violins, whispering clearer,
Tell you this is what life ought to be.
Every step brings Paradise near and nearer.
Dancing time is happiness time for me.

Another song with the same title and some
verbal similarities would appear in *The
Cabaret Girl*—1923.

In one of the many variant libretti for *Oh,
Lady! Lady!!* the heroine is not Molly but Kim.

Kim and Bill are also given a more romantic
version of—

YOU'RE HERE AND I'M HERE
(ALTERNATIVE)

Kim: Though everyone has been against us
 from the start,

Bill: Keeping us apart,

Kim: Trying to break my heart,

Both: Through all the storms we've had
 to weather
 We knew at last we'd come together.

Kim: You're here and I'm here,
 So what do we care?
 Just you and me and the moon
 That is shining up there.
 And it would spoil it all for us
 If people came around to stare and
 fuss and chatter:
 For you know and I know,
 As lovers all do,
 Because it is true,
 That summer nights were
 invented
 For me and for you.

Both: And in the whole darned world
 there's nothing that can matter
 But just we two.

Kim: I always knew that soon or late
 there'd come a day

Bill: When we'd see the gray
          Clouds all pass away.

Kim: Those wise old words I kept
               repeating—
          All journeys end in lovers meeting.

Bill: You're here and I'm here
          And everything's fine:
          Just let me gaze into your eyes
          As you gaze into mine;
          Each time you smile I start to glow,
          And all the while my heart is going
               pitter-patter.
          I seem in a dream,
          It's too good to be true
          That you are here, dear, with me
          And that I'm here with you.

Both: And in the whole wide world there's
               nothing that can matter
          But just we two.

The critics were divided, sensing perhaps, that the team was repeating itself.

The plot concerned a young couple who want to get married—as opposed to the young couple of *Oh, Boy!* who want to *stay* married. In both cases a matriarchal martinet gets in the way. Many of the supporting characters could easily step from one plot into the other—and as far as the songs were concerned . . . "Our Little Nest" was a clone of "Nesting Time In Flatbush," while "Before I Met You" bore more than a passing resemblance to "I Never Knew About You" and "The Sun Starts To Shine Again" is a clear sequel to "Till The Clouds Roll By."

Bolton & Wodehouse took their title from a minstrel show expression that was currently being revived by negro comedian Bert Williams—"Oh, lady, lady!" A couple of extra exclamation marks soon made it more commercial, and in adding those, they began to create an instant tradition

for the Princess shows in that each now ended with the title line. This one was advertised as "The Fifth New York Princess Theatre Musical Production." The *Times* considered it "virtually flawless" and the *Globe* found the lines "bright" and the lyrics "well written."

At one point there were two separate companies performing the piece—the second at the Casino—and it had the distinction of being staged in Sing-Sing with an all-convict cast. With his penchant for "prison" songs, Wodehouse must have savored that! Contracts were drawn up with Famous Players–Lasky for a film version in 1920 but there is no evidence it was ever made. The five-reel silent film released in November of that year (starring Bebe Daniels and Walter Hiers) was based on the libretto but obviously not the score.

But then, after the initial enthusiasm, audiences began to drop off dramatically and the run ended after only 219 performances—a far remove from the 475 of *Oh, Boy!*

It may have been disappointment with the Broadway run that brought the Kern-Wodehouse-Bolton collaboration to an unplanned temporary end, but there seem to have been other reasons—not significant in themselves—that brought this about.

Wodehouse, for instance, supposedly offered to exchange his interest in "Bill" to Kern for some other joint property—only to have Bolton (who can have had no hand in writing it) object. It was always difficult to determine exactly who had contributed what and perhaps the trio's time and temper had simply run out. They were to work together again in various combinations—but not for the Princess.

If *Have A Heart* and *Leave It To Jane* are counted, the Princess shows numbered just six and covered a mere three years. They did not break radical new ground but they did push the frontiers of musical theatre steadily forward in terms of intelligence, wit and style. Kern's melodies were insinuatingly accessible, while Bolton and Wodehouse wrote dialogue that was civilized and lyrics that sprang from colloquial speech. Above all, they achieved the unity of words and music which had been their common aim from the start. As Bolton said in an interview—"If the songs are going to count at all in any plot, the plot has to build more or less around, or at least, with them."

Ira Gershwin was to be called "The Jeweler" because of the meticulous way he fitted his words to brother George's music, but "the boys" deserved the title first for the way they created complete shows that emerged as polished little gems.

There was to be a residual benefit for Wodehouse, at least. He always said that *Oh, Lady! Lady!!* was his favorite of all the Princess shows and proved it by turning it into a novel— *The Small Bachelor* (1927).

In his April 1918 review for *Vanity Fair* he wrote . . . "Honestly, you ought to pawn the family jewels and go and see it, if only to reward Guy Bolton and myself for the work we put in on it on the road."

Anyone researching Wodehouse and Bolton will find themselves faced with libretti carrying the same titles but containing significantly altered material. As the years went by they nursed the ambition to revive their favorite shows and constantly tinkered with the books. After Wodehouse's death Bolton was particularly radical.

Soon after World War II they turned their attention to *Oh, Lady! Lady!!*, which they believed had the strongest plot line of any of their libretti. One possible way of strengthening it, they felt, was to import songs from other shows. The Equity Library Theatre, in fact, mounted a production from March 14th–31st, 1974, which incorporated songs from *Oh, Boy!* ("An Old-Fashioned Wife"), *Have A Heart* ("Napoleon"), *Sitting Pretty* ("Tulip Time in Sing-Sing"), and *Sally* ("The Church Round the Corner"). The first half finale included—

at the specific request of Wodehouse and Bolton—the original version of "Bill," which had been dropped from the show at the Princess.

Bolton and Wodehouse now took a project away from Kern. It was another adaptation—this time Pierre Veber's turn of the century farce, *The Girl From Rector's*.

Looking objectively at the team's record in any combination, it's hard not to conclude that, in racing parlance, they were inclined to "rush their fences." In the too little time they gave themselves—or allowed themselves to be given—between one project and the next, they too often took the easy option of reaching for an adaptation which all too often turned out to be unsuitable. In these cases—and *See You Later* was one such—a few catchy songs were not enough to save the whole venture. The team's best work invariably came when they were cutting from the whole cloth.

There are several unresolved questions about the next show—*See You Later* (1918). It was staged at the Baltimore Academy of Music and never made the transition to Broadway. In all seventeen numbers were eventually published, several of which do not appear in the first night program. In itself that would not be unusual, since numbers cut on the road or early in a show's run were frequently set aside. But what provides the first puzzle is that four of the pieces of sheet music attribute the music to "Joseph Szulc"—instead of the credited composers, Jean Schwartz and William F. Peters—and carry a copyright date of 1913. Were they interpolations, since two of the titles are in the program?

Then the Library of Congress turns up a libretto dated June 12th, 1918—two months after the show's abortive run—which is completely different in content and characters and appears to be a much closer adaptation of the original material. It also contains all the rest of the published numbers not accounted for.

The supposition must be that Wodehouse and Bolton prepared this version some time earlier, working with Szulc's existing music and then decided to "Americanize" it for Baltimore (presumably en route to Broadway), adapting a couple of the original songs in the process and changing everything else. (How many other songs from the "original" version were actually composed—and by whom—remains a matter for conjecture.)

The rest of the sheet music is dated 1919 and refers to "Elliott, Comstock and Gest present . . . ," suggesting the revised version was intended for a Broadway transfer, presumably to the Princess.

This was not to be. But, whatever the sequence of events, I have included the material from both versions as an interesting example of work in progress—even though the progress didn't take them far in this case . . .

SEE YOU LATER (1st Version?) (1918) (Unproduced)

BOOK   Guy Bolton and P. G. Wodehouse
LYRICS P. G. Wodehouse
MUSIC   Joseph Szulc

CAST

Vivoter (a.k.a. M. Castillon), President of The Moonlight Mixers	Renée, Her Daughter
	Captain Daburon
Richard Dupont ("Dicky Bird")	Monsieur Bru
Loute (a.k.a. Mme. Daburon)	Eugene, A Waiter
Professor Francollin, Cousin of Dupont	Gustave, The Head Waiter
Madame Castillon	Angélique, Maid to the Castillons

SYNOPSIS

The setting is a restaurant in the Bois de Boulogne. The guests, including the Society of Moonlight Mixers, are seated on the terrace. They call their orders to the waiter, Eugene ("Opening Chorus"). Vivoter, the President of the Mixers, arrives and reminds them of their pledge to remain celibate—love is their only enemy. Their motto is—"Marriage is the net in which the jade snares the jaded" ("Healthy Life"). Vivoter tells Gustave, the head waiter, he is worried that his friend "Dicky Bird" Dupont may be starting to slip in his convictions—he may be in love. The object of his affections is his childhood sweetheart, Renée Castillon—a situation complicated by the fact that Loute, the Lady Chieftain of the Midnight Mixers, is also attracted to Dupont. Loute arrives and tells them she is going away to the country. She suggests Dupont go too—it will take him out of temptation and away from the bad influence of Vivoter, whom she suspects may even be—horrors!—a married man! ("There Goes a

Married Man"). Loute tells Gustave she intends to marry Dupont but first she has to attend to a small matter—a divorce from her present husband, George.

Dupont's cousin, Francillon, arrives to borrow money for his wedding. Dupont tells him that he, too, intends to marry. They then discover they are both in love with the same girl—Renée. Francillon leaves and Renée appears in search of him, only to encounter Dupont. She tells him she only agreed to marry his cousin because she had heard he had sworn to remain a bachelor. Now Francillon returns with Mme. Castillon. Dupont has an inspiration. He will show them Paris ("Paris By Night"). They leave and Vivoter returns with a disturbing telegram. It becomes clear that he is an absentee husband to Mme. Castillon and Stepfather of Renée. The cable is to summon him back for the wedding. Loute learns his secret and sings of the joys of being single ("Happily Married? Bah!"). With a little prompting from Dupont, Mme. Castillon discovers that Francillon is simply a fortune hunter and sends him packing. But she has a wedding all arranged—perhaps Dupont could think of a solution. He certainly can. She leaves and the childhood lovers are reunited ("Years and Years Ago"). Meanwhile, Loute has arranged an intimate lunch on the terrace for herself and Dupont. She hints that she has a secret that involves him ("But Its Meaning Who Can Tell?"). She then tells him her plan to marry him, just as Vivoter and the Midnight Mixers arrive. Pandemonium ensues as Francillon tries to reveal the truth about Dupont's intentions ("Finale"). He is mistaken for an escaped lunatic and carted off by the police, as the principal characters set off—unknown to each other—for the same destination.

Act 2 is set in Mme. Castillon's home in Vire. We meet Captain Daburon, who is seated at an organ practicing the song he will play at the wedding. Mme. Castillon, Mme. Bru and the other guests join in ("Cantata"). It becomes clear that Daburon is the estranged husband of Loute (a.k.a. Léonie), whom he believes is in Paris engaged in charity work. Dupont and Renée arrive and Dupont is quizzed by the family. After all, they live by the most exacting standards ("Young Man"). The interview over, Renée and Dupont can relax ("You Whispered It").

Now Vivoter (a.k.a. M. Castillon) arrives, supposedly just back from raising silk worms in Cochin China. The party guests insist he tell them all about this exotic location ("Cochin China"). Daburon is telling the maid, Angélique, how he feels about his absent wife, when Loute enters and misinterprets the scene.

She tells him she wants a divorce and leaves. Vivoter now runs into Loute, who pretends he is mistaken. She is Léonie, a simple country girl, who likes nothing better than to sit outside her mother's cottage and listen to the old church bell ("Dear Old Church Bell").

The deceptions now begin to unravel, as Dupont meets Vivoter and all the Paris expatriates have their own reasons for keeping each other's secrets. Vivoter must maintain the illusion of his silk worms ("Annette"). Loute now discovers Dupont is to marry another. Despite her anger, she schemes to get him to return to Paris with her. There she will be on her own ground ("Mother Paris"). She tells Dupont she will unmask him unless he agrees to accompany her back to Paris for one last supper. Reluctantly, he agrees ("Act 2—Finale"). They leave but Daburon intends to follow them. For their own reasons, so do the rest of the principals . . .

Act 3. We are back in Paris at The Pink Cockatoo. The Moonlight Mixers are there, as usual ("Paris By Night"). Loute and a despondent Dupont enter. She goes off to greet her friends, and just then Daburon arrives in search of his wife. Dupont directs him elsewhere, just as Vivoter turns up, too. The Girls of the club are pleased to see Dupont but he tells them this is his swan song ("I'm Going To Settle Down"). Now the rest of the party arrives and Renée assumes the worst about Dupont and Loute. He tries to explain and they are reconciled ("Lovers' Quarrels"). Not surprisingly, all the other complications are rapidly resolved and everyone is agreed on one thing at least—the only place to live is Paris! ("Paris Song—Reprise").

OPENING CHORUS

All: Waiter, hi! Waiter hi! Waiter hi! Waiter hi!
Let us all take up the cry!
One . . . ! Two!
Waiter ha! Waiter ho! Waiter hey! Waiter hi!

(*Enter EUGENE, a waiter*)

Eugene: Don't shout and bang upon the table;
I'll come as quick as I am able;
So there you are!

All: Oh, there you are!
Shake the kinks from out your knees!

Eugene: Watch me hustle!

All: Come and take our orders, please!

Eugene: See me bustle.

All: One Vermouth . . . One Gin Fizz . . .
    Whiskey sour . . . Brandy
    punch . . . Clover-Club . . .
    Rock-and-rye . . . One Scotch
    High.

Eugene: Goodness! Who are these I see?

All: He doesn't know! He doesn't know!
    This will not do! Tell him who's who!
    We think
    You ought to know
    That we're the famous Moonlight
      Mixers;
    Who drink
    Quite *comme il faut*
    Champagne and other smart
      elixirs.

Clairette: We are
    A band that strives—
    In fact, this is our sole employment . . .
    To make our little fleeting lives
    A round of up-all-night enjoyment.

All: Oh, yes,
    You ought to know
    That we're the famous Moonlight
      Mixers,
    Who drink—quite *comme il faut*—
    Champagne and other smart elixirs.
    We are
    A band that strives—
    In fact, this is our sole employment—
    To make our little fleeting lives
    A round of up-all-night enjoyment.

A HEALTHY LIFE

(Vivoter)

Although physicians
With grave suspicions
Are apt to look upon the lives we've led;
Although our doctor
Is either shocked, or
Will not believe that we're not dead;
Despite their strictures,
Of health we're pictures,
And seem to thrive on never going to bed.
So that I somehow can't help thinking
That it is far the wisest plan
To cut out sleep and keep on drinking,
If you would be a healthy man!
Ah!

With what dread
The tales I've read
Of people who, it's said,
Have died in bed!
So take my warning!
Stay out till morning!
No danger then you'll run,
And you'll have lots of fun.

With your assistance,
I for existence
Have found the perfect recipe;
The lobster diet
That you and I ate
Is just as wholesome as can be.
Late suppers nightly
Make people sprightly;
At least it's always been that way with me.
So be a sport!
Have another quart!
For the waiter call.
If you are busy
With something fizzy,
No sort of harm can you befall,
And so a long and healthy life is
Within the reach of all!

THERE GOES A MARRIED MAN

(Loute, Vivoter and Dupont)

Loute: Very simply you can
    Detect a married man;

Though he tries to disguise
His shame from peoples' eyes.
Directly his sad face you scan,
You say "There goes a married man."

Vivoter: He wears a hunted look,
Which you read like a book.
His life devoid of joys is,
He starts at sudden noises.

Loute: With trouble he seems weighted,
Though he is twenty, he looks fifty.
His eye is weak and shifty,
His brow is corrugated.

Dupont: Poor miserable victim,
He slinks about the place,
As if someone has kicked him,
Or stepped upon his face.

Vivoter: He seems to wonder what,
Real happiness can be.
He knows he is a blot,
Upon the scenery.

All: There's a curse, there's a ban
On ev'ry married man,
Though he tries to disguise
His shame from peoples' eyes.
Directly his sad face you scan,
You say "There goes a married man."

Loute: We pity them and sigh,
When we see them slouching by
With that air that they wear
Of a hopeless despair,
And their dull and mournful eye.
We quake, we shake, dismayed,
As these poor lost souls parade:
It's a sight that well might
Give a hero a fright,
Is the Married Men's Brigade.

All: Very simply you can
Detect a married man,

Though he tries to disguise
His shame from peoples' eyes.
Directly his sad face you scan
You say "There goes a married man."

Dupont: You can see

Vivoter: Very plain

Loute: The effect

Dupont   Of the strain

Loute: Of the Ball

Vivoter: And Chain!

PARIS BY NIGHT

(Dupont, Francillon, Mme. Castillon and Renée)

Dupont: Paris—there's a place you ought
to see;

Francillon: Here's your chance to do the whole
thing free

Dupont: Do not wait,
And hesitate;
But come along with me.

Mme. C: We have only seen it in the day
In the night, it's quite a sight,
they say.

Renée: In the night,
When lights are bright,
Oh, then it's really gay.

Dupont: Come, then! Let us paint the
city red!
Day shall dawn before we go to bed
When we wake,
Our heads may ache;
But what's an aching head!

Mme. C: We're prepared for all you have
　　　　　to show,
　　　　Lead us where the morning
　　　　　headaches grow!
　　　　You'll always find
　　　　Us close behind,
　　　　Where 'er you go.

All: We'll set out hand in hand, a sturdy
　　　　little band,
　　　Prepared to do—to do or die!
　　　The revels we will lead: and, tho' we
　　　　mayn't succeed
　　　In waking Paris up,—we'll try!
　　　We'll leave, before we roam, our
　　　　consciences at home;
　　　And bid that home a long goodbye.
　　　For we won't go—home till
　　　　morning—
　　　Till daylight doth appear up in
　　　　the sky!

Ev'ry kind of taste the town can
　　please.
Strangers come from far across
　　the seas:
Ev'ry breed, from Jap to Swede,
From Finn to Portuguese.
Eskimosers fresh from off the ice,
Chinamen who ask the price of
　　rice:
All the horde, with one accord,
Call Paris Paradise.
Never mind where you were born
　　or bred,
If your folks were white or black
　　or red,
Cross the foam! A home from
　　home
Waits here for you instead.
Come where Paris greets you with
　　a smile!
Though you have to travel many
　　a mile,

Just pack your grip, and make
　　the trip;
For it's worth-while.

Just set out hand in hand, a sturdy
　　little band,
Prepared to do or die!
The revels you shall lead; and, tho'
　　you mayn't succeed
In waking Paris up—just try!
And leave, before you roam,
　　your consciences at home;
And bid that home a long goodbye;
For you won't go—home till
　　morning
Till daylight doth appear up in
　　the sky!

HAPPILY MARRIED? BAH!

(Loute)

Loute: Oh, but it's good to be
　　　　Alive on this lovely day,
　　　　And to know that we are free
　　　　From the chains which on others
　　　　　weigh.
　　　　If we were married, oh!
　　　　Life would be so sad and slow
　　　　With husbands interfering,
　　　　Prying and spying and peering.
　　　　Oh, shun them with persistence,
　　　　And gallop away in the distance.
　　　　Houp-la-la! Houp-la-la! Houp-la-la!
　　　　Happily married? Bah!

For, when you are single, you gallop,
　　you gallop through life.
You have to slow down to a hobble,
　　when you are a wife.
Your blood's in a tingle
All day when you're single,
And life is a race
At a break-neck pace.

Oh, when you are single, you merrily
    jingle along:
With jolly companions you mingle in
    frolic and song.
If men come to woo,
No matter how much they sue,
Let your heart from the start be
    of stone!
You must travel alone—alone!

Oh, men are sure to try
To snare you in ev'ry way:
They will yearn and burn and sigh;
But don't heed them, whate'er
    they say.
Don't let them take you in:
Be ready when they begin.
Be cold and calm and spurn all
Vows of devotion eternal.
They'll catch you, if you let them:
So gallop away and forget them!
Houp-la-la! Houp-la-la! Houp-la-la!
Happily married? Bah

Refrain

YEARS AND YEARS AGO

(Renée and Dupont)

Dupont: Years ago, when first we met—
                How I loved you—years ago!

Renée: Cruel fate our dreams upset,—
              Plunging me in depths of woe.

Dupont: That was years and years ago.

Dupont: I was then just eleven,
               And you a child of seven,
               Straight from Heaven!
               You were swinging on a gate:
               I knew at once you were my mate.
               Our eyes met! It was Fate!

Renée: You had a lollipop
             At the local candy-shop
             Years ago, dear.
             In the golden summer weather
             We passed it to and fro,
             Till it melted altogether—
             Years and years and years ago!

Dupont: I loved you, when
               Love seemed just a new game to
                play.

Renée: I loved you then,
             And I love you still today,—dear!

             Time may have flown:
             I'm still your own:
             I love you so,
             Just as I used to years ago.

Dupont: Time may have sped:
               Years may have fled;
             But still here you stand
             Beside me to guide me.

Renée: All journeys end. All troubles mend.

Dupont: (All journeys end)

Renee: Troth we have plighted, once more
               united

Dupont: (And our troth we have plighted,
               once more united)

Renee: Fate holds in store joys as of yore,

Dupont: (Fate holds in store joys once more)

Both: Joys that we used to know
             Years and years ago.

Renee: Golden haze and sunset glow

Dupont: Gild those days of long ago,

Both: Long ago—Years ago!

BUT ITS MEANING, WHO CAN TELL?

(Loute and Dupont)

Loute: Ha-ha-ha-ha-ha-ha-ha-ha!
If you could only read my mind!
Ha-ha-ha-ha-ha-ha-ha-ha!

Dupont: Ah, I wonder what I should find!

Loute: Ha-ha-ha-ha-ha-ha-ha-ha!

Dupont: For your laugh has just that sound.
There is something that's mischievous
in it:
Very plainly
You reveal it.
I shall guess the whole thing in a
minute;
And you'll try vainly
To conceal it.

Loute: Though, my friend, you are second
to few men
In acumen,
In acumen.
If you guessed till we both were quite
old, you
Couldn't find out the truth till I
told you.
Ha-ha-ha-ha-ha-ha-ha-ha!
If my laugh you could only read!
Ha-ha-ha-ha-ha-ha-ha-ha!

Dupont: Ah! I would that I could, indeed!

Loute: Ha-ha-ha-ha-ha-ha-ha-ha!

Dupont: It is like a silver bell.

Loute: Ha-ha-ha-ha-ha-ha-ha-ha!
But its meaning—who can tell?

Dupont: But its meaning—who can tell?

ACT 1—FINALE

Ensemble: Is this really true
What we've heard say?
Is it a fact you
Must go away?
Paris will be dull without you,
All our fun revolves about you.

Dupont: Yes, my friends, it
Is sad, but true;
There's nothing else that I can do.
I have an Auntie dear,
And she, I fear,
Needs me near, for she's feeling
queer.

Loute: But when at length
Your mournful task is ended
And you come back to me once
more,
With all the strength
Which my ardent nature's justly
noted for
You and I will adore—
Just you—no more!

Dupont: That would be
Very nice,
But, my dear,
Do think twice!
Someone else
Has a claim
To the love
Which you name.
Hardly fair
It would be
If you left
Him for me.

Is it right?
Are you quite
Free?

Loute:
Upon my word!
That's quite absurd
The facts you have
Heard.
I am yours,
As you know,
Didn't I
Tell you so
Just a short while ago?

Ensemble:
Yes, if some man
Has a claim
To the love
Which you name,
Hardly fair
It would be
If you left
Him, you see,
Are you sure your
   heart is free?

(While Loute and Ensemble are singing as above, Dupont sings . . .)

Dupont: Someone else
           Has a claim . . .
           . . . for me
           That is right, you must agree

(Francillon enters ready to denounce Dupont but Loute pretends he is an escaped lunatic and tells Gustave to call for the Police. The crowd begins to panic . . .)

Dupont: *(To women)*
           Stay! Don't faint or run away!
           We'll see that you're not harmed,
              so please don't be alarmed.
           Don't fear. We're here!

Men of
Ensemble: Stay! Stay! Please, ladies, do not
              run away!
           For we'll protect you, come what
              may!

Women of
Ensemble: That's true! You know exactly what
              to do!

We feel so safe, so nice and safe,
   when we're with you!

(Women run to Men, who embrace them)

Loute: *(Flings herself into Dupont's arms)*
            Yes, you'll protect
            With your life,
            Your timid little, shrinking little
               future wife!
            I am safe from all alarms
            Here, nestled in your arms,
            Your dear, strong, loving arms!

(Enter the Park Police)

Police: We're the police who guard the
               Park, Park, Park!
            Without our consent no dog may
               bark, bark, bark!
            We are here to keep the peace,
            All troubles cease when you call
               upon the vigilant police!

Ensemble: Saved! Saved! Saved!
            Dangers cease!
            When handled by the Park
               Police!

Police: We hate to boast,
            But we are wonders!
            The Force, of course,
            Never blunders.
            Here at our post
            We keep the peace
            We're the Park Police.

Ensemble: They hate to boast,
            But they are wonders!
            The Force, of course,
            Never blunders.
            Here at their post
            They keep the peace,
            Three cheers for our Park
               Police!

(During the above singing by the Ensemble, the Police have gone to the porch. They now emerge, dragging Francillon. The party resumes as the curtain falls.)

CANTATA

(Daburon and Ensemble)

We're gathered here
In Vire
From far and near:
Upon this happy day
We've come from all directions.
It is our plan
To greet the lucky man,
Upon whom our dear Renée
Has bestowed her young affections.

All Hail
To Renée and Charles we sing!
It is a splendid thing
That they are marrying.
May they
Be free from all grief and care!
So let us welc-
Joyfully welc-
Welcome the happy pair.

Repeat from "All Hail"

YOUNG MAN!

(Dupont and Family)

Dupont: I know just what it means to be
Made one of such a family.
It is an honor rare and great,
Which I, of course, appreciate.
And I shall try my very hardest
To be quite worthy, too.
And I am hoping that I'm
    welcome,
Now I am one of you.

Family: Young man, do you smoke or chew?
Young man, some men drink—
    do you?
Now you're our relation,
We want information.
Young man, are your morals weak?
Young man, now's the time to speak!
Young man, if you can,
Answer these, if you please.

Dupont: Though it's not easy to reply,
To give an answer I will try.
It is Yes—and No!

Family: Oh!

Dupont: I was a bad boy not long ago—

Family: Oh!

Dupont: Yes, it's true, I own with grief now—
But I've turned a brand new leaf now,
As you'll find quite soon I shall
    show.

Family: Young man, if you intend to be
A credit to your family;
Young man, if you will recollect,
To do what's fitting and correct,
If to the path that's straight and
    narrow
You will but stick like glue—
If you have cast off your bad habits—
Why then, young man, you'll do!

YOU WHISPERED IT

(You—You—You!)

(Dupont and Renée)

Renée: There's a word, one small word—
When it's heard, hearts are stirred,
    eyes are blurred—
You—you—you!

Dupont: All agree it should be, as you know,
Spoken so—soft and low—
You—you—you!

Renée: Doubt and fear disappear,
When I hear, sweet and clear, in
my ear—
You—you—you!

Dupont: For it tells of wedding bells,
And the bliss of your kiss hides
in this—
You—you—you!

In my heart that word is ringing,
Like a bird sweetly singing,
Ever strange and ever new—
That one word YOU.
Let Time steal whate'er it may,
It cannot take this away.
The music of that dear YOU
Will echo my whole life through.

Renée: Whisper, dear! Whisper, dear!
Just once more, as before, I implore—
You—you—you!

Ev'ry breeze in the trees,
Passing by, seems to sigh, soft
and shy—
You—you—you!

Dupont: Sorrow gray flees away,
Life's a gay holiday, when you say—
You—you—you!

Both: For it tells of wedding bells,
And the bliss of your kiss hides
in this—
You—you—you!

COCHIN CHINA

(Vivoter and Girls)

There is a place called Cochin Chin-ah;
You've heard about it quite a lot.

Maybe to visit it you pine-ha,
Because it's such a lovely spot.
Thousands of miles across the brine-ah,
Down where the tropic sun is hot
It's a Paradise on the Gulf of Siam—
You'd be as fond of it as I am.

In lovely Cochin Chin-ah
Far over the sea.
The weather's always fine-ah,
And life's one long spree.
The girls are quite divine-ah,
So experts agree,
In dear old Cochin Chin-ah,
And that just suits me.
Every day,
Every day,
'Neath the jub-jub tree,
They sit upon your knee,
They're never shy,
And I know
When I go,
They'll be good to me.
So back to Cochin China I shall fly.

Ladies out there in Cochin Chin-ah
Dress in a simple sort of style,
Beauty with frankness they combine-ah,
That's why a visit is worth while.
They put on a piece of twine-ah,
That's all they wear, except a smile.
On a summer night it is quite entrancing,
Just to sit and look at them dancing.

For out in Cochin Chin-ah
The dancing is quite gay.
They twist about their spine-ah
In this sort of way.
They never draw the line-ah,
The guide books all say,
In distant Cochin Chin-ah
At a cabaret.
With their peace
The police

Never interfere.
Although it's very clear
They really should.
That's the stuff;
Long enough
I've been waiting here.
A trip out there would do me lots of good.

DEAR OLD CHURCH BELL

(Loute and Vivoter)

Loute: I was born, born and bred in these
          parts, as I said.

Vivoter: And you've not been away?

Loute: Not so much as a day.

Vivoter: I will not swallow that. I will not—
          I tell you flat.
          I tell you flat.

Loute: I'd grieve—pray believe—to deceive.
          Do you then, doubt my word?

Vivoter: It's all too damned absurd.

Loute: I've never wished to roam from my
          dear village home.

Vivoter: Come now, please don't make me
          laugh.

Loute: For my love is too deep for the cows
          and the sheep
          And the hen and the pig and the calf.
          Country sounds, country sights are
          my simple delights.

Vivoter: You are Loute, I know you well.

Loute: And beyond and above all things that
          I love

Is the sound of our church bell.
That dear old church bell. I love our
dear church bell.

That old church bell that calls so
sweetly
Across the dell and o'er the lea;
I cannot tell you how completely
Its gentle spell takes hold of me.
If it should ring when I'm depressed,
It seems to bring me peace and rest.
No tongue can tell, no tongue can tell
How much I love our dear church bell.

Vivoter: Ah, a fool, I can see, you would make
          out of me.

Loute: No, for nature got there first.
          I would not give you pain, but I think
          you're insane.

Vivoter: If you keep this up, I'll burst.
          Come now, cease to pretend that I'm
          not your old friend
          And admit you know me well.

Loute: You are mad, I'm afraid. I am just
          what I said
          And I love our dear church bell.

Vivoter: Oh, darn that church bell. Don't drag
          in that church bell.

That old church bell that calls so
sweetly,
Across the dell and o'er the lea.
I cannot tell you how completely
Its so-called spell is lost on me.
If it should ring, I feel depressed;
It shatters—bing!—my peace
and rest.
No tongue can tell, no tongue can tell
How much I hate that darned
church bell.

ANNETTE

(Vivoter, Loute and Mme. Castillon)

I have a silk worm, named Annette,
    Named Annette
    Named Annette
She's the most virtuous thing I've met
    Ever met,
    Ever met.
She doesn't spend her nights and days,
    Nights and days,
    Nights and days
Whooping it up in cabarets.
    Never strays,
    Never strays.
Imitate her if you can,
She's a vegetarian.
And she never, never flirts,
She's too busy spinning shirts.

Oh, Annette,
Sweet Annette,
She's my pet,
Don't forget.
You can bet
That I'd regret
If we'd not
Met.

She will ever leave behind her all that's shady,
And you never need remind her she's a lady.
By coarse remarks she's quite upset,
And she's a slave to etiquette.
Ev'ry day she grows more virtuous and sweeter,
Till it makes a man feel better just to meet her.

Oh, Annette,
Sweet Annette,
She's my pet,
Don't forget.
You can bet
That I'd regret
If we'd not
Met.

Most of the silk worm younger set,
    Younger set
    Younger set,
Come and make love to sweet Annette
    Sweet Annette,
    Sweet Annette.
They are a wicked, sporty bunch, sporty bunch,
    sporty bunch
Trying to date her up for lunch,
    Come to lunch, come to lunch.
But she'll never go alone,
Always takes a chaperone
She knows what young silk worms are
If you let them go too far.

Refrain

MOTHER PARIS

(Loute)

Loute: Whenever life has hurt us,
    Whenever friends desert us,
    One comforter remains
    To heal us of our pains.
    When we're in desperation,
    She is our one salvation.
    To her we always fly
    When we need consolation.
    She gives us her protection,
    Her care and her affection;
    She softens our distress,
    And brings us happiness.
    Whatever may occur,
    We've a mother in her.
    All our woes she is banishing,
    Till we find them vanishing.

    Oh, Paris, Paris, Paris,
    Our own dear mother Paris,
    Whatever we may do,
    You're always true,
    You're always true.
    Though sorrow may assail us,

Though friends may grow fickle and
    fail us,
We've still a friend in you.
We can come back to you.

(Enter Chorus)

All: We stray, but you don't lose us;
                For still your voice pursues us;
                Though we are far away,
                We hear it night and day.
                No mother could be fonder,
                You sit and beckon yonder,
                And call your children home.
                Though far, far they may wander,
                Dear Paris, never sleeping,
                Your vigil you are keeping
                With myriad lamps that burn
                A-glow for my return.
                Your distant blaze of light
                Seems to call and invite;
                Many leagues us are sundering,
                But I hear your thundering.

Refrain

Note: This song was tried in Version 2 but dropped, probably because it was a stretch to integrate it into the new American plot, whereas here it is integral to the story and characters.

ACT 2—FINALE

Renée: Oh dear, what's this you say?

Dupont: I fear I cannot stay.

Vivoter: The lucky dog!

Renée: You cannot go away
           Just before our wedding day.

Dupont: The call I must obey.

Loute: And now let us not delay.
           Say goodbye while we may.
           Don't waste time in conversation.

Renée: If you must go away,
           There's nothing more to say;
           But, oh my darling, when we part
           It will nearly break my heart.
           Ev'ry hour will be a year,
           While you're gone from here,
              my dear,
           I'll be plunged in gloom and
              sorrow
           Till you come back tomorrow.

Dupont: There's no need to shed a tear;
           Though I go from here, don't
              fear,
           Just reflect, to soothe your sorrow,
           That I'll be back tomorrow.

(Enter Ensemble)
(Renée and Dupont embrace lovingly)

Loute: *(eyes them angrily)*
           I would not be abrupt,
           But I must interrupt.
           If longer we remain,
           We're sure to miss the train.

Ensemble: We know just what you mean;
           It is a touching scene,
           But if they don't refrain,
           You're bound to miss that train.

Loute: For engine-drivers hate
           To sit around and wait
           While lovers kiss each other,
           For they have no heart,
           So—

Cut short that last embrace;
We've simply got to race;
I'm sorry, but the time has come
    to part.

Dupont: Goodbye, dear!
Goodbye. Now, please do not cry!
Be brave, dear heart,
I have got to start.

Ensemble: For engine-drivers hate
Etc.

Exit Dupont and Loute
Enter Daburon
Dialogue through music

Daburon: Where is my wife?

Mme. Castillon:
She has just this moment left.

Daburon: Left? What do you mean?

Renée: (*Crying*)
And Charles has left, too.

Down from heav'n I've been
    hurled
To a drear, empty world;
And my heart's like a stone,
For he's left me all alone.
Oh! how sad I shall be
Till he comes back to me;
For I'll pine till I see
His dear smile;
And his kiss I shall miss
All the while.

Ensemble: Down from heav'n she's been hurled
To a drear, empty world;

And her heart's like a stone,
For he's left her all alone.

Renée: Oh, how sad I shall be
Till he comes back to me;
For I'll pine till I see
His dear smile;
And his kiss I shall miss
All the while.

Ensemble: For she'll pine just to see
His dear smile.
And his kiss she will miss
All the while!

Daburon: (*Impatiently*)
Yes, yes, yes! I'm very sorry for you,
    but I'm worried about my wife !
    Where has she gone?

Vivoter: To Paris! Lovely Paris!
She took the train to Paris.
At duty's call she fled;
That's what she said!
That's what she said!

Ensemble: Self-sacrificing always,
Not only in great but in small ways.
She went where Duty led;
When duty called, she sped

I'M GOING TO SETTLE DOWN

(Dupont and Girls)

Dupont: I've had enough
Of dancing and dining
Of revelling and wining
Ev'ry night with you.
That sort of stuff
Is fun when you begin it;
But now there's nothing in it,
And I'm through—through—
    through.

And I'm going to settle down,
Though my friends may frown:
To some peaceful spot I'll go,
And I'll sit and watch the daisies
    grow.
I'll wander there with a straw
    between my teeth,
Till the sun has baked me brown:
I don't care a hang what anybody
    says—
I am going to settle down.

It's not a joke,
I give you fair warning:
At five o'clock each morning
I'll be out of bed.
Then I shall stoke
The furnace till I'm dropping,
Or do a bit of chopping
In the old wood-shed.

For I'm going to settle down
Miles away from town,
There a man may sit and think
Where there's only new-laid milk
    to drink.
So speak up, girls, if you want another
    brooch
Or a ring or hat or gown;
For this is the last time I shall
    settle up,
For I'm going to settle down.

LOVERS' QUARRELS

(Renée and Dupont)

Renée: As long as I shall live, your sins I'll
not forgive.

Dupont: Will nothing turn you from this stern
resolve at all?

Renée: On second thoughts, I may—when
years have rolled away—

Dupont: Ah, well, some scope is left for hope,
however small.

Renée: If pardon you should seek, I might
forgive—next week:

Dupont: That's better still. If you but will, ah,
how I'll sue.

Renée: Yet all the while somehow, a voice
says "Do it now,"
And so I do—and so I do—and so
I do.
For lovers' quarrels are like a
show'r
Which comes and goes in an hour
And leaves the air still more sweet
and fair,
When it's ended and all is
mended.
A short, sad moment of rain,—
And then the sky's clear again.

Let me look into your dear eyes.
Let me peep for a short, short while
into Paradise.
Let me look in your eyes and see
Your dear heart, where it waits
for me.

I thought I could be strong. I see now
I was wrong.

Dupont: But still you made me all afraid for
quite a while.

Renée: My anger so severe was just a mere
veneer.

Dupont: I'd but to wait, for soon or late I knew
        you'd smile.

Renée: My acting was too thin. It didn't take
        you in.

Dupont: I was aware your love was there, tho'
        it was hid.

Renée: For all the time I know I'd soon be
        kissing you,
        And so I did—and so I did—and so
        I did.

For lovers' quarrels are like the snow,
So soon, so quickly they go.
We freeze and frown till the sun
    shines down,
Then it's ended and all is mended.

For love shines gallant and gay,
And melts the quarrel away.

Let me look into your dear eyes.
Let me peep for a short, short while
    into Paradise.
Let me look in your eyes, and see
Your dear heart where it waits for me.

SEE YOU LATER
(2nd Version) (1918)

Presented by Alfred H. Woods at the Academy of Music, Baltimore, Maryland, on April 15, 1918.

BOOK	Guy Bolton and P. G. Wodehouse
	(Based on *The Girl From Rector's* by Pierre Veber)
LYRICS	P. G. Wodehouse
MUSIC	Jean Schwartz and William F. Peters

Even now the problems persist. The location has now been moved from Paris to The Chateau on the north shore of Long Island. The opening night program had the following cast list.

Although the entire score was published, this show never made it past out-of-town tryouts . . .

. . . It is debatable which changed more often: the cast or the script.

CAST

Sam, waiter at The Chateau: JAMES E. SULLIVAN	Lord Glenochtie: ERNEST TORRENCE
Commodore "Johnny" Walker: HERBERT CORTHELL	Mrs. Wellington Green: CHARLOTTE GRANVILLE
Jane Packard: TOT QUALTERS	Bettina Weston, her daughter: MARIE FLYNN
Polly Andrews: BETTY ALDEN	Horace Blossom, her cousin: JOHN DALY MURPHY
Dickson Paige: CHARLES RUGGLES (courtesy of Oliver Morosco)	George Potter, another cousin: JED PROUTY
Jo Romaine: MABEL MCCANE	Mrs. Honora Blossom: ISABEL O'MADIGAN
Sheriff Sims: WILLIAM SELLERY	Angélique, maid: ZITELKA DOLORES

These were the musical numbers listed:

ACT 1

1. Opening number
   Ensemble
2. "I'm Going to Settle Down'"
   Dicky & Ensemble
3. "If You Could Read My Mind"
   Jo, Commodore & Dicky
4. "Keep Out of the Moon"
   Betty & Ensemble
5. "No One Ever Loved Like Me"
   Betty & Dicky
6. "The Finest Thing In the Country"
   Jo & Ensemble
7. Finale
   Company & Ensemble

ACT 2

8. Opening Cantata
   Potter, Mrs. Green, Mr. Blossom,
   Mrs. Blossom & Ensemble

9. "Young Man"
   Dicky, Mrs. Green,
   Mr. Potter, Mrs. Blossom,
   Mr. Blossom
10. "Honeymoon Island"
    Betty & Ensemble
11. "That Old Church Bell"
    Jo & Commodore
12. "I Never Knew"
    Jo & Ensemble
13. "Nerves"
    Dicky, Commodore & Potter
14. Finale
    Company & Ensemble

ACT 3

15. "Rally Around"
    Mr. Potter & Ensemble
16. "Run Away"
    Jo & Ensemble

17. "Our Little Desert Isle"
Mr. Potter, Commodore &
Lord Glenochtie

18. "If You Could Read My Mind"
Jo & Potter

Finale

However, the only extant libretto—which contains Guy Bolton's handwritten annotations—differs significantly. In and of itself, this would not be unusual, since Bolton was forever chopping and changing different versions of a basic property. What makes this one unusual is that it contains specific and quite different casting. Does this simply reflect their original "wish list" cast—or suggest the possibility of yet another version? What does seem clear is that the basic plot point of characters masquerading as other people was retained throughout.

"Bolton's Version" reads as follows:

CAST

Ivy Prospect, a cutie:
MISS EVELYN MCVAY
Sam, head waiter at the Chateau:
MR. JULES EPAILLY
Tot and Ollie, Patrons at the Chateau:
MISS JOSEPHINE HARRIMAN
MISS LEONORA HUGHES
Dickson (Dicky) Paige, an
ex-cabaret-hound reformed
by true love:
MR. T. ROY BARNES
"Commodore Walker," in reality
Mr. Greene, supposed to be in China:
MR. VICTOR MOORE
Mrs. George Potter, of Utica,
President of the Young Men's Rescue
League in New York as
Jo Romaine:
MISS FRANCES CAMERON
Lord Glenochtie, one look and
you know who and what he is:
MR. GEORGE GRAHAM

Mrs. Greene, wife of the Commodore:
MISS KATHARINE STEWART
Betty Weston, her daughter by a
former marriage, in love with Dick:
MISS WINONA WINTER
Uncle Horace, out of the family album:
MR. RALPH NAIRN
George Potter, a tea taster, with a warm
heart that is misunderstood:
MR. ROBERT O'CONNOR
Angelique, maid at
Mrs. Greene's home:
MISS IRMA IRVING
Jack R. Abbott, a dancer:
MR. ALLEN H. FAGAN
The Little Dears:
Grace Fall
Kitty Knight
Bee Haive
Arline Honey
Beema Darling
Ann May

June White	May Queen
April Folly	Ella Trick
Iva Paine	Wedding Guests:
Wanda Holme	Pagc Carle
Grace Stone	Irving Gay
Caroline Fenway	Chick Henry
Jan Rush	Knight Leigh

MUSICAL NUMBERS

ACT 1

1. Opening
   Sam and Ensemble
2. "I'm Going to Settle Down"
   Dicky & Ensemble
3. Dance
   Miss MackVay
4. "Josephine"
   Jo and Ensemble
5. "Keep Out of the Moon"
   Betty and Ensemble
6. "Paradise in Mo"
   Dicky and Betty
7. "Country Life"
   Jo and Ensemble
8. "Rooster Dance"
   Miss Cameron & Mr. Fagan
9. Finale ("See You Later, Girls")
   Ensemble

ACT 2

10. "Happy Pair"
    Ensemble
11. "I Never Knew"
    Betty and Ensemble

12. "Young Man"
    Dicky, Mrs. Greene, Horace and Potter
13. "That Old Church Bell"
    Jo and Commodore
14. "I Want to Dance"
    Jo and Ensemble
15. "See You Later" (trot)
    Miss Cameron and Mr. Fagan
16. "Isn't It Wonderful?"
    Betty and Dicky
17. "Nerves"
    Dicky, Commodore & Potter
18. Finale
    Ensemble

ACT 3

19. Opening ("Trip Along")
    Ensemble
20. Duet Dance
    Miss Harriman and Mr. Fagan
21. "Make the Best of Tonight"
    Jo, Dicky & Commodore
22. "Desert Island"
    Dicky, Sam, Allen and Commodore, Tot, Tiny, Lulu and Ollie
23. Finale
    Ensemble

What follows is an aggregation of the extant numbers from both American "versions," as well as some songs that appear on neither list.

ACT 1

OPENING CHORUS

(Sam and Boys & Girls)

Past ten o'clock, and there's no one about.
Waiter, Waiter, Waiter.
Let's give a shout and we'll soon fetch him out.
Waiter, Waiter, Waiter.
Make all the noise you are able to make
If he's asleep he will soon be awake
We would like to mention
We want some attention

Refrain   Sam, Sam, Oh Dear, he's nowhere to
           be seen

(*Sam enters*)

Sam: Here I am, Here I am, I'm hurrying

(*Flock around and shake Sam*)

Sam: That's enough, don't be rough
           It's so worrying

Chorus: When you come to life
           Produce the menu
           For we would like to remark
           That we're waiting to see
           Omelettes and coffee are all that
           we need.

Sam: Hush, Hush, I'll take the order then
           I'll rush
           It's some speed that you need
           Watch me scurrying

Chorus: Be quick nothing seems to matter
           Till we hear the breakfast gong
           Please make the quickest time
           you're able
           Don't take an hour to set the table
           For we can't, for we can't, for we can't
           wait long.

I'M GOING TO SETTLE DOWN

(Dicky and Ensemble)

1.

Dicky: I've had enough of this all night
           party stuff
           And the life that's swift and gay:
           I want to creep out of sight and get
           some sleep,
           And I mean to start today.
           It's no use asking me why.
           Please understand that this means
           goodbye,
           For I'm . . .

Refrain 1: . . . Going to settle down
            Just about a million miles out of
            town
            To some quiet peaceful spot I'll go,
            Where I can sit up upon a fence and
            watch the daisies grow.

2.

Never more I'll pine
For those nights of lights and wine;
I mean to chuck it just as quick as
can be.
That old oak bucket seems to beckon
to me;
Yes, it's sad but true
That I've done with you all. I'm
through,
For I'm . . .

Refrain 2

Girls: . . . Going to settle down
            Just about a million miles out of town,
            In some place where I can sit and
            think,
            Where I'll have nice fresh air to
            breath and new laid milk to drink.

3.

Dicky: Never more I'll pine
            For those nights of lights and wine.

I've played the dickens,
But that's finished, you see,
Those pigs and chickens seem to
    whisper to me;
Yes, it's sad but true
I've done with you all. I'm through.

While this song is close to the lyric sung by Dupont in Version 1, there are enough significant differences to justify including both versions.

KEEP OUT OF THE MOON
(I NEVER KNEW)

(Betty and Girls)

Betty: When I was little in the days gone by,
And summer had begun,
My nurse used to tell me I must
    always try
To keep out of the sun.
But since then I've discovered to
    my surprise
It's in the moon that danger
    really lies.

Refrain
(Enter Girls)

Chorus: You can walk as much as you like in
    the sunshine,
But Oh! Keep out of the moon
When it's shining, be wise
Just stay indoors and shut your eyes
For if you go for strolls when it's high
    in the skies,
You're sure to be sorry soon.

Betty: If the sun should burn you, your poor
    face will smart,
But the moon's much worse, for it will
    break your heart.
You can walk as much as you like in
    the sunshine,
But oh! Keep out of the moon.

THE FINEST THING
IN THE COUNTRY

(The Train That Leaves for Town)

(Jo, Commodore & Ensemble)

1.

Jo: The farmer leads a happy life
At five a.m. he wakes his wife.

Comm.:   Then hand in hand they go and dig,
Or, as a treat, they kill the pig.

Jo: They love the cow just like a son
They take the turkey for a run.

Comm.:   Then, pausing from their labors,
They sit around and knock the
    neighbors

Refrain: Country life's a happy life:
That's what I've heard. Have you?
Some say chickens
Grow upon one like the dickens:
Roosters, too, have a few boosters.
It's such fun to let the sun
Bake you until you're brown,
But to me quite the nicest thing in
    the country
Is the train that leaves for town.

2.

Jo: The farmer's is a lively lot:
All sorts of int'rests he has got

Comm.:   Each morning to the field he'll go
To watch (help) the dandelions
    grow.

Jo: And when he's tired of that, he'll lie
(Or else, with an indulgent eye)
And watch (he'll watch) the snails go
    racing by:

Comm.:   And then he takes his vittles
And sits upon a fence and whittles.

Refrain: Country life's a happy life,
           Cheery and gay and bright,
           For New Yorkers know the joy of
               feeding porkers:
           Farming really is quite charming.
           Life out there, so some declare,
           Cures you when you're down:
           But to me quite the nicest thing in
               the country
           Is the train that leaves for town.

ACT 1—FINALE

SEE YOU LATER, GIRLS

(Dick, Jo, Commodore and Girls)

Dick: I'd like to stay, but I must rush away
               to my train

Girls: Hurry! Hurry! Hurry!

Comm.:   Girls, don't you cry, for we'll all by
               and by meet again

Girls: Hurry! Hurry! Hurry!

Jo: Tell all the bunch to cheer up and
               to smile!
           I have a hunch we'll be back in a
               while.
           Tell old Sam the waiter
           Goodbye! See you later.

Girls: Goodbye! we wish you didn't have
               to go.

Refrain
Dick,
Comm.
and Jo: Never mind! Never mind!
           See you later, Girls!

Girls: We know that life without you will
               be slow.

Dick,
Comm.
and Jo: We'll be back! We'll be back!
           See you later, Girls!

Girls: Yearning, we will wait for your
               returning.
           We won't know how in the world we
               can get through the day,
           Things will be dreary while you
               are away.
           Do try to come and see us by and by!

Dick,
Comm.
and Jo: Don't fret! It's a bet!
           See you later, Girls!

Girls: Come back! You will find us waiting.
           Celebrating as before:
           Goodbye!
           And though life may be dreary,
           We'll try to keep alive and cheery,
           Till we meet, till we meet, till we
               meet once more.

YOUNG MAN!

(Dick and Family)

Dick: Don't think I don't understand just
               what it means to be
           Made one of such a blameless and
               respected family:
           It is a bit of luck for me, an honor
               rare and great,
           And one which, let me tell you, I of
               course appreciate.

Refrain
Family: Young Man. Young Man!
           Do you drink?
           Is your language ever blue?
           Do you ever bet, smoke or chew?
           When you meet girls, do you wink?
           Are you ever tempted to

Utter such remarks as "Oo-oo?"
Come! Come! Come!
Do you shun the bad Demon Rum?
Are you sure
You are really quite good and pure?
Young Man, these are
Just a few
Simple little questions we're asking
    of you.

Dick: I'm glad you've brought the subject up.
I want you all to know
My morals are so pure,
I'm like a chunk of driven snow;
I keep the straight and narrow path,
And never, never stray:
I couldn't drink or flirt or bet
I shouldn't know the way.

Refrain
Family: Young Man. Young Man!
If that's true,
If you really blush with shame
When you see a small poker game,
If, when fast, bad Girls you view,
You are sure you pass them by
With a modest shy, down-cast eye.
If, of course,
You would scorn to bet on a horse,
If you say
You have never been near Broadway,
Then, young man, there's
Hope for you,
And upon the whole, we think maybe
    you'll do.

HONEYMOON ISLAND

(Betty and Ensemble)

(Music by William Frederick Peters)

(Sheet music says Joseph Szulc)

Betty: Honeymoon Island lies over the sea,
Millions of miles, they say:

Further by far than the last little star
That shines in the Milky Way:
And the noise of the world with its
    trouble and care
Cannot reach you, when once you're
    there.

Refrain: It's a neat little, sweet little paradise
    for two;
And there it lies under skies always
    smiling and blue:
A scented breeze stirs the trees: birds
    are twittering:
Gaily the bay 'neath the sunbeams
    is glittering.

It's hard to find; no explorers ever
    stray to it:
But some folks, I'm sure, must have
    found out the way to it:
And some day I shall go there, too,
When my dreams come true.

Honeymoon Island lies over the sea,
Nobody quite knows where:
No one I've met has discovered it yet,
But everyone knows it's there:
And it's strange how familiar and
    friendly it seems,
When you find yourself there in
    dreams.

I NEVER KNEW!

(Jo and Ensemble)

Jo: I used to think the world was dull
    and gray.
The days went by each in the same
    old way.
And nothing seemed to matter,
And life kept getting flatter:
But ev'rything seems changed and
    strange today.

Refrain
Ensemble: I never knew the sunshine could be
half so bright,
Or the world so fair to view,
I never knew the stars could shine so
clear at night,
Or that the sky was so tender and
blue.
Oh! The wind seems to whisper a
message divine,
Just because there are two eyes that
look into mine:
I never knew how wonderful the
world could be,
Until I knew that my love loved me.

Jo: I never saw the sunset on the sea,
I never heard the wind's soft
melody . . .
When thrushes homeward
winging,
Their ev'ning song were singing,
I never knew they sang it just
for me.

NERVES!

(Dick, Potter and Commodore)

1.

Dick: Let's pull ourselves together for
there's not a thing to be . . .

All: . . . frightened at!
What was that?

Comm.: It must have been a bird we heard
a-roosting in a tree.

Potter: Or the cat,
On the mat.

Dick: I'll have to take a tonic or a cocktail
on a tray

All: For I'm not myself today
Oh! I . . .

Refrain
All: Feel so nervous,
That I don't know what to do,
For my heart is going bump,
My pulse is going thump,
At ev'ry sound I leap and bound,
And jer-jer-jer-jer-jump!
Every word I'm uttering,
I'm stuttering
And my legs move 'round in curves,
Do not thut-thut-thut-thut-think
This is due to der-der-drink,
It is simply ner-ner-nerves!

2.

Dick: Let's pull ourselves together, we'll
regard this by and by

All: As a joke!
Holy smoke!

Comm.: Keep cool for there's no danger, it just
happens that a fly,
On my coat,
Cleared its throat

Dick: I though it was a dynamite explosion
'cross the way

All: For I'm not myself today.

DESERT ISLAND

(Our Little Desert Isle)

(Potter, Commodore and Lord Glenochtie)

1.

I'd like to fly some distance,
As quickly as I can,
From civilized existence,
And try another plan.

I'd like if I could do so:
To be another Caruso
Upon some Island in the sea,
Yes, that is what would just suit me.

Refrain
All: Let's go and live upon a Desert Island
Where there isn't any worry, fuss
    or care.
We'd build some little wooden huts,
And feed on yams and cocoanuts:
Oh! We'd be happy there.
We would listen with elation
To the parrots' conversation
When they've anything of interest
    to say.
And at nights we'd lie at rest
With a scorpion on our chest
In our little Desert Island far away.

2.

Each morning on awaking
I'd go and light the fire,
And bread-fruit I'd start baking
As much as we'd require.
I'd chase a goat and catch it,
And bean it with my hatchet.
And if you let it get away,
Why, that would be our meatless day.

Refrain
All: Let's go and live upon a Desert Island
Where there isn't any worry, fuss
    or care.
We'd loaf around and dress in beads,
And learn to love the centipedes,
And they would all love us.
With the snake that goes a-wriggling
On its tummy we'd be chummy.
We'd grow fonder of the monkeys
    ev'ry day
And some local shark we'd get
For a nice domestic pet
In our little Desert Island far away.

IT DOESN'T MATTER

(Music by Jean Schwartz)

1.

When I was little in the days gone by,
And used to break my toys,
My nurse would tell me it's no use to cry
And fret and make a noise;
Tears, she'd explain won't bring back dolls again,
When they've been thrown away,
It's no use fretting and regretting,
It's much better to say:

Refrain: It doesn't matter! It doesn't matter!
So hide your tears away!
When things are ended,
They can't be mended,
That's all there is to say.
It's no use sighing,
It's no use crying,
You'll soon forget somehow;
Though fate your toys may shatter,
It doesn't matter now.

2.

And now I'm older than I used to be,
One thing I've understood.
It's no use crying for the moon, I see;
For that will do no good.
For tears, it seems, will never bring back dreams,
Or make a dream come true:
Forget about them, do without them,
That is all you can do.

Refrain: It doesn't matter! It doesn't matter!
So hide your tears away
When things are ended,
They can't be mended,
That's all there is to say.
It's no use sighing,
It's no use crying.
The time will pass somehow;
Though fate your dreams may shatter,
It doesn't matter now.

LOVE'S A VERY FUNNY THING

(Jo, Commodore and Sam)

1.

Jo: Oh, love's a strange condition:
          Deny it if you can
          'Twill change the disposition of nearly
             every man.

Comm.:   The grouch gets gay and sunny:
          The hard-boiled egg spends money.

Sam: The man who painted Broadway red
          Will stay at home and read in bed.
             It's . . .

Refrain
All: . . . Strange how love will act on
             diff'rent people:
          Why, you can't tell how a fellow will
             behave
          The tramp will start in buying hats
          And canes and lemon colored spats:
          The dude forgets to shave.

Sam: Traffic cops, so proud and haughty,
          Will just murmur:
          "Naughty! Naughty!"
          When you break the regulations in
             your car.
          And they'll add: "Now, don't be hurt
          If my manner seems too curt."

All: Love's a very funny thing and there
             you are!

Sam: Oh, love's a sort of frenzy
          That works in ev'ry clime
          Like Spanish influenzy,
          It gets us all in time.

Jo: New Englanders with mittens,
          And Esquimaux and Britons,

Comm.:   And even men in far Peru
          Will have it just like me and you.
             It's . . .

Refrain
All: . . . Strange how love will act on
             diff'rent people,
          And you can't tell what a fellow's
             going to do:
          Because he feels that love is sweet
          The janitor will send up heat
          If you request him to.

Sam: Hatcheck boys, when love has
             gripped 'em
          Often thank you
          When you've tipped 'em,
          And declare that you're too generous
             by far.
          And your waiter will unbend and will
             treat you as a friend.

All: Love's a very funny thing, and there
             you are!

"SEE YOU LATER" SHIMMY

Come on,
It isn't hard to do,
It's just a shake,
And then a quake,
And then a crawl and a whirl and a twist or two,
Oh! Boy,
Come on, and let it go:
You simply give a little wiggle,
Then a little jiggle, so,
That's right
I knew you'd find it easy,
That's right,
I knew you weren't a dunce:
Each chance you get just grab it
This dance becomes a habit
Nobody is timid,
After they have shimmied once, only once.

ANYTIME IS DANCING TIME
(I WANT TO DANCE)

(Jane)

Jane: Gee, I want to dance,
Just every time I get a chance:
How ever late it be,
It's never late for me.
That's the way I feel

I don't care if I miss a meal.
Don't want to go to bed
I dance instead,
I'm getting thinner,
I dance through dinner
And tea and luncheon, too
And, though I'm dropping,
I'm never stopping
Until the band gets through.

Refrain: *(In a snappy tempo)*
Any time is dancing time!
I'd dance all night and day, night
    and day:
Any time is dancing time!
You can't keep me away, me away.
All the while I'm aching to begin,
    begin it.
Gee, I simply hate to waste a single
    minute!
When the music starts, I want to be
    right in it,
Any time those jazz-bands play.

IN OUR LITTLE PARADISE
(PARADISE IN MO)

(Dick and Betty)

Dick: I'm tired of noisy Broadway life;
I'm absolutely through,
For all I want's a home and a wife

Betty: And all I want is you.

Dick: How nice 'twould be to go and
    dwell
In some far state, say, Nev. or Del.
I've heard folks say, who ought to
    know,
It's jolly in the state of Mo.

Refrain   Let us build a home in Mo.
Way out there, you know,
Life is never slow:

Dick: I was told so long ago
By my aunt in Cleveland, Oh.
And you don't need lots of
    dough.

Both: For in dear old Mo.
There's no fuss and show.

Dick: And I've got a hunch

I'd be a perfect ray of sunsh.

Both: In our little paradise in Mo.

2.
Dick: Or would it not be, more judish
If we our life began
In some desirable posish.

Betty: Near Kansas City, Kan.

Dick: To Oklahoma let us roam
And build a little oklahome;
Why, yes! I've heard a lot of folk
Speak very well of life in Ok.

Refrain   Let us build a home in Ok.
Where we needn't choke
In the city smoke;

Dick: Ev'ry morn, when I awoke
The old furnace I would stoke;
I would shovel on the coke!

Both:	For to folk in Ok. Heavy work's a joke: And, though short of cash, We'd love each other with a pash. In our little paradise in Ok.
Dick:	In winter, dear, if it should snow As though 'twould never stop, We'd leave our country home, and go . . .
Betty:	To live in the metrop.
Dick:	For in the snug metropolis, Our rustic joys we'd never miss: New York suits many folks, but still I much prefer Chicago, Ill.
Refrain:	Oh, in fair Chicago, Ill. We could coo and bill At our own sweet will.
Dick:	Would your love, dear, e'er grow chill? No! The chance of that is nil! Then no tears I'd ever spill,
Both:	For my heart would thrill If you loved me still; And we'd both endeav. To keep away from Reno, Nev. And remain a happy pair in Ill.

Note: Though Ira Gershwin generally receives the credit for introducing abbreviated English into the lyric with his song "Sunny Disposish" in the 1926 revue *Americana*, here was Wodehouse using it eight years earlier! He had also had the character of Jim Marvin use the trick in *Oh, Boy!* (1917).

ISN'T IT WONDERFUL!

(Betty and Dick)

Betty:	Now that you are here, I'm so happy dear,

	How can such happiness be? Why should it come just to me? That is what I cannot see, dear!
Dick:	I've been thinking, too, Much the same as you, And I must say I agree: Why should life be divine for you and me?
Refrain Both:	Isn't it wonderful! Isn't it wonderful! Just like dreaming a dream, I'm afraid I may wake Find there's been some mistake, Much too good things seem.
Dick:	Fancy the bliss of being here with you!
Betty:	Having you kiss me as you used to do!
Dick:	Isn't it wonderful!
Betty:	Isn't it beautiful!
Dick:	Isn't it marvelous! (glorious!)
Betty:	Isn't it heavenly!
Both:	I can't believe that it's true.
Betty:	Just suppose, my pet, We had never met! We'd have been lonely and sad: Might both have moped and gone mad, What an escape we have had, dear!
Dick:	If I had not got you, I know what I'd do, Put Paris Green in my tea! Yes, things have happened just right for you and me.

Refrain

Both: Isn't it wonderful!
    Isn't it wonderful!
    Just like dreaming a dream,
    I'm afraid I may wake
    Find there's been some mistake,
    Much too good things seem.

Betty: I want to creep and nestle close to you

Dick: If I'm asleep, just let me sleep on, do!

Betty: Isn't it wonderful!

Dick: Isn't it glorious!

Betty: Isn't it heavenly!

Dick: This is the life all right!

Both: I can't believe that it's true.

It was at this point that Klaw & Erlanger made another entrance. Clearly choosing to remember *Miss Springtime* and forget *The Riviera Girl*, they signed Bolton & Wodehouse to do the book and lyrics for their next show—yet another adaptation, this time a French farce called *Madam and Her Godson*. Kern was not to be part of this collaboration, since the producers had already secured the services of Ivan Caryll (1860–1921), a composer equally successful on both sides of the Atlantic with twenty-nine musicals to his name already, many of them for the late George Edwardes at the Gaiety.

Taking advantage of the chauvinistic spirit abroad in the land, the show was entitled *The Girl Behind the Gun* and to ensure patriotic authenticity, George M. Cohan (of "Yankee Doodle Dandy" fame) was brought in to help with the staging of the set pieces.

THE GIRL BEHIND THE GUN (1918)

Presented by Klaw & Erlanger at the New Amsterdam Theatre, New York, on September 16, 1918 (160 performances), after a tryout in Atlantic City.

BOOK
Guy Bolton and
P. G. Wodehouse
(Based on *Madam and Her Godson* by Maurice Henniquin and Pierre Veber)

LYRICS
P. G. Wodehouse

MUSIC
Ivan Caryll

CAST

Robert Lambrissac: DONALD BRIAN	Harper Wentworth: BERT GARDNER
Pierre Breval: JOHN E. HAZZARD	Eileen Moore: EVA FRANCIS
Georgette Breval: ADA MEADE	Brichoux: JOHN E. YOUNG
Colonel Servan: FRANK DOANE	
Lucienne Lambrissac: WILDA BENNETT	Zellie: VIRGINIA O'BRIEN

Note: There appear to be no extant copies of the libretto of *The Girl Behind the Gun*; consequently, it is not possible to fit the songs into the context of the plot. Since *Kissing Time* (1919) was closely based on it, the numbers that were common to both shows are to be found in the chapter on the latter show, where they can be placed. Variations are bracketed.

OPENING CHORUS—

GODSONS AND GODMOTHERS

(Georgette and Chorus)

A HAPPY FAMILY

(Colonel, Georgette and Lambrissac)

SOME DAY WAITING WILL END

(Lucienne and Girls)

As he hears the voice of Lucienne approaching, singing "Some Day," the Colonel himself sings...

Over the top through shot and shell,
Thro fire and hell
I'll lead my herd,
The fighting Forty-third,
Smashing our way along

Over the top where bullets soar,
Where cannons roar,
Where heroes fall,
Yet off in the distance through it all,
I'll hear this wondrous song . . .

I LIKE IT, I LIKE IT

(Breval, Lambrissac, Colonel and Georgette)

OH, HOW WARM IT IS TODAY

(Lambrissac, Colonel and Georgette)

THE GIRL BEHIND (THE MAN BEHIND) THE GUN

(Lambrissac and Girls)

Lambrissac: Everyday new tales we read,
Telling of some gallant deed
Wrought by soldiers fighting to
defend their native land.
But there's someone I could name,
Who, tho' all unknown to Fame,
Ought to be considered just as
wonderful and grand.
Yes, there's one who's doing, too,
All it's in her power to do.
Trying hard and working,
Never shirking night and day,
One who's weathered ev'ry test,

One who always does her best,
Who's fighting, although safe at
    home she has to stay
Far away from the battle whirl.
There is work to be done

And that's there you will find
    the girl
Behind the man behind the gun.
Brave and gay, there she toils away,
Tho' her heart's torn in two.
For tho' the heart may ache,
Her nerve will never break,
While there is work she can do.

Lambrissac
& Girls: Far away from the battle whirl
There is work to be done,
And that's where you will find
    the girl
Behind the man behind the gun;
Brave and gay, there she toils away,
Tho' her heart's torn in two.
For tho' the heart may ache,
Her nerve will never break,
While there is work she can do.

In those far off days before France
    sent out her sons to war,
Girls like lovely butterflies through
    life would idly flit.
Who'd have guessed that such as
    these, shelter'd, petted, fond
    of ease,
Soon would give up everything
    and come to do their bit?
See them working hand in hand,
Sturdy gallant little band,
All their pleasures laid aside for
    toil that's hard and rough.
But butterflies of yesterday,
    frivolous and spoil'd and gay,
They know that their France needs
    them now, and that's enough.

WOMEN HAVEN'T ANY MERCY ON A MAN!

(Breval)

Breval: Gosh! Women are the hardest
    propositions!
You plead with them for hours and
    they don't care,
They listen to the silv'ry voice of
    reason
With nothing stirring underneath
    the hair.
I flirted with the smallest girl in Paris
But now at home we suffer grief
    and pain
As if I'd been and gone and
    overdone it,
And flirted with a Violet Loraine.

Alternative
lyric: (I flirted with the littlest girl in
    Paris
But still my wife gets sore with me
    and kicks,
As if you'd been and gone and
    overdone it,
And flirted with a perfect thirty-six.)

Refrain: For women haven't any sense of
    justice,
They never make allowances at all;
They never think it makes it any
    better
If the girl they catch their husband
    with is small.
When we dined, I had to sit her on
    a cushion!
(She only weighed one hundred
    pounds—one hundred!)
But my wife is making all the fuss
    she can,
I could hardly do her homage,
This petit piece of fromage;
(It's that unjust view that rankles,

You could hardly see her ankles—)
Women haven't any mercy on a man!

You've been sitting with a maiden in
the moonlight
Amid the scent of jasmine and of
rose,
And suddenly you get that clammy
feeling
That tells you you are going to
propose!
You try your best to keep yourself
from speaking,
You know that you'll be happy if
you don't.
Your guardian angel whispers:
"Don't you do it!"
And you reply: "All right, old man,
I won't!"

Refrain: But women haven't any sense of
fairness
Their sporting instinct always has
been blurred:
They never throw small fish back in
the water.
They always like to shoot a sitting
bird.
You want to ask her if she'll come
to dinner
And you hesitate, you poor
flat-footed can,
You say: "Will you?" She says:
"Rather!
Oh! You darling, why, there's Father!"
Women haven't any mercy on a man!
(The moment you start edging off
the hammock
She will snuggle up as closely as
she can,
And she'll whisper to you—'Willie,
Hold my hands. They are so
chilly.')
Women haven't any mercy on a man!

I've often gone to see a fellow married
And watched him stagger dumbly up
the aisle;
His eyes are kind of glassy and he's
gulping;
He looks as if he's never learned
to smile.
You'd think the bride would feel a
pang of pity:
She knows that he's been cut off in
his prime;
You'd think that she would whisper to
him gently:
"You chump! Why don't you beat it
while there's time?"

Refrain: But women haven't any sense of pity
For, if they had, the bride would stop
and think,
She'd say: "Why should I marry this
poor fathead?
What have I got against the wretched
gink?"
But no! She fills the church with her
relations,
Who would grab him by the coat tails
if he ran;
All his pals have been soft-soaped,
(And although she sees him falter,
She still leads him to the altar)
And his best man he's been doped.
Women haven't any mercy on a man!

THERE'S LIFE IN THE OLD DOG YET

(Lambrissac and Lucienne)

Lambrissac: I've not danced for ages, but still . . .

Lucienne: When you start you mustn't lose
heart!

Lambrissac: Although no doubt I've grown
stiffer . . .

Lucienne: If at first it quite strange is . . .

Lambrissac: If you think I've quite lost my skill . . .

Lucienne: You'll find dancing quite a new art . . .

Lambrissac: You must permit me to differ . . .

Lucienne: For there have been lots of changes.

Lambrissac: Try one and I soon will show . . .

Lucienne: All the steps you used to know . . .

Lambrissac: All the steps I used to know . . .

Lucienne: Grew old-fashioned long ago . . .

Lambrissac: Although the fact is . . .

Lucienne: You'll find that lately . . .

Lambrissac: For some years . . .

Lucienne: All the styles . . .

Lambrissac: I've had no practice . . .

Lucienne: Have altered greatly . . .

Lambrissac: If I once begin it . . .

Lucienne: We've made great improvements . . .

Lambrissac: Smoother every minute . . .

Lucienne: In our dancing movements . . .

Lambrissac: I shall grow . . .

Lucienne: As I'll show . . .

Lambrissac: Did you know how to show . . .

Lucienne: Is that so? Must I go! . . .

Lambrissac: Lots of skill long ago?

Lucienne: And forget all I know?

Lambrissac: I've been out of it quite long.

Lucienne: You've been out of it so long,

Lambrissac: There's not a doubt of it.

Lucienne: There's not a doubt of it.

Lambrissac: But still I vow . . .

Lucienne: 'Twill all seem strange
Why don't you try, just to prove to me you've not forgotten how?
Yes, I confess that at first the thing is likely to be strange.

Lambrissac: I'd come back again, and soon pick up the knack again,
If I danced now.

Lucienne: When you're back again, and try to get the knack again,
You'll see the change.
Some day, you know, you must start again, so why not do it now?

Lambrissac: Quite out of date I am sure to feel when I behold change.
If at first I made some stupid blunder,
Would you recall the handicap I'm under?

Lucienne: But still I doubt if you make a blunder,

Tho' such a handicap you say
   you're under?

Lambrissac: Should I awkward be,
   Would you laugh at me?

Lucienne: Tho' our steps are new,
   Will that wrong you?

Lambrissac: I wonder!

Lucienne: I wonder!

Lambrissac: I was told that I had great ability
   and lightness and agility.

Lucienne: Times have moved but you will
   find in just one small respect
   we've not changed at all

Lambrissac: In days gone by . . .

Lucienne: And that I'll name:
   I don't know why you don't start
     again:
   I'm sure you can't be shy . . .

Lambrissac: Do tell me, please, for
   I want to find out all about
     the game.
   Girls were sweet about the way
   I threw my feet about, I don't
     know why.

Lucienne: Tho' our steps are new,
   We flirt just as we used to do:
   That's still the same:
   You'd make them praise you today,
     if you would try.

Lambrissac: Just think of that:
   There is something still the same,
   And so I must start to train
     once more.

Lucienne: So you will feel quite at home,
   you see.
   You can't resist it,

Lambrissac: Now, what's she hinting?
   I'll try that ball-room floor.
   That's how it looks to me
   I'm a veteran, I regret,
   But there's life in the old dog yet!

Lucienne: You will certainly show our set
   We must have missed it;
   Be a regular social pet
   If there's life in the old dog yet.

Lambrissac: Her eyes are glinting!
   What she's driving at is,
   I'll bet,
   That there's life in the old dog yet.

BACK TO THE DEAR OLD TRENCHES

(Lambrissac, Breval and Brichoux)

Lambrissac: I've a yearning for returning
   To my dug out, truth to tell,
   When I'm there I'll never roam.

Brichoux: Oh, to wander over yonder
   To the trench I love so well,
   It is a perfect home from home.

Breval: As for me, too, I agree to
   Every word you fellows say:
   The right idea I know you've got,
   There are millions of civilians
   Who would like to step that way,
   And I'm the keenest of the lot.

All: Let's begin the journey:
   Each will help the others:
   Like a little band of brothers
   We will be, we three.

Lambrissac &
Breval: We're going back to the dear old
                trenches!
            Cozy trenches, good old trenches.
            Life's getting too exciting,
            Trouble's on our track,
            That is why you and I must go
                back, back, back.
            Never mind tho' our wives may be
                broken-hearted
            When we've parted. Let's get
                started!
            Words of farewell are always
                difficult to say,
            So we'll write them tonight,
            When we're far away.

Brichoux: Far more pleasant than at present
            Things out there are sure to be.
            Give me the trenches!
            That's the life!

Lambrissac: Foemen's rifles are but trifles
            I would charge a battery,
            But I'm afraid to meet my wife!

Breval: Tho' a stranger to the danger
            And the perils of the Front,
            I've always been, you know as yet,
            I own sadly I'd more gladly
            Bear the battles' deadly brunt
            Than have to face my dear
            Georgette.

All: Let's be off at once, then,
            Each will help the others
            Like a little band of brothers
            We will be, we three.

THERE'S A LIGHT IN YOUR EYES

(Lambrissac and Lucienne)

An additional song was published, though
where it fits into the sequence is not clear.

I'VE A SYSTEM

(Lambrissac and Girls)

Lambrissac: When but a child with golden
                curls,
            I always used to love the girls,
            And every year I older grew,
            I love them as I used to do.

            And when to man's estate I came,
            I found I loved them just the same,
            And somehow I've discovered that,
                wherever I may be,
            I am sure to find a girl around, or
                two, or even three.
            They run away from other men,
                but snuggle up to me.

Refrain: I've a system. A simple little system.
            And it gets good results,
            It's never missed them
            It's not hard to learn

            For the secret's this:
            Never waste your time in talking,
            When you've got a chance to kiss.
            That's the system, my little system.
            As a rule girls get friendly
            When you've kissed 'em
            But if they do not, well, then it's
                plain
            That the best way's to kiss them
                once again.

Girls: He's a system, a simple little
                system:
            And it gets good results
            It's never missed 'em
            It's not hard to learn,
            For the secret's this:
            Never waste your time in talking
            When you've got a chance to kiss.
            That's his system, his simple little
                system

For he finds girls get friendly
when he's kissed 'em.
And, if they do not, he's made
    it plain
That the best way's to kiss them
    once again.

Lambrissac: I've tried out the haughty girls,
    and pious girls and naughty
    girls,
In every variety of feminine society
And every time I must confess,
    It's been a wonderful success
For when it comes to flirting,
    all the experts are agreed
That looks are simply nothing
    when compared with zip
    and speed.
And I have always found that I
    have all the zip I need.

FINALE

There's a light in your eyes
On your lips there's a smile,
And you seem all the while
To be yielding, in tender surrender,
And love dreams arise
Ever sweet, ever new,
Till my heart to you flies
Till my soul for you sighs.
And I would pluck the stars from the skies
For one kiss from you.

All: You'll like it! You'll likc it!
    He'll cook you something good
    Until you've tried his cooking,
    You've never tasted food.

Colonel: You'll like it,
    Pray have no doubt of that!
    We hear his cooking is a thing to
        wonder at!
    You'll like it!

He'll cook you something good.
Until you've tried his cooking
You've never tasted food
You'll like it!
You'll likc it!

THAT TICKING TAXI'S WAITING AT THE DOOR

(Wentworth and Girls)

It was a common practice for writers of musical theatre libretti to indicate the presence of a song in the text—sometimes by a title but often by a descriptive tag. The song was often not actually composed by that point and sometimes it never was composed—leaving the poor historian to search high and low for items that may or may not actually exist. Bolton's notes of revisions to the script contain several such references.

For instance, before "Some Day" he refers to the "Rin-Tin-Tin" song sung by Lambrissac and the Girls. Later he specifies "You're Me and I'm You" for Lambrissac and Brichoux, a reference to the plot situation, common to most farces, whereby two characters change identities. At one point Breval, bemoaning the increasing hopelessness of his situation, is given the "When a Fellow Needs a Friend" song, another standby of farcical plots.

Two other numbers appear in the program which deserve a mention. "True to Me" (Brichoux and the Girls) was written by George M. Cohan, and it would be hard to believe that the Act I Finale ("Flags of the Allies") was not his work, too, since a feature of any Cohan show was a certain amount of jingoistic flag waving. The man, after all, did write "Over There" (1917).

"A merry wartime show" (*Sun*) just about summed up the critics' reaction. Few could make head or tail of the plot and even fewer cared. Wodehouse's lyrics, as usual, were well received, particularly the by-now-typically mysogynistic comic song, "Women Haven't Any Mercy On

A Man," but the critics couldn't summon up much enthusiasm for Ivan Caryll's score.

When it took to the road after 160 performances, it was not lack of audience interest but a previous booking for the New Amsterdam that prompted the move.

George Grossmith Jr. was in New York immediately after the war and saw the show. He took the manuscript away to read on the boat, changed the title and sought a theatre in London. He discovered the run-down New Middlesex (formerly the Old Mogul) Music Hall, bought it, rebuilt it and re-named it the Winter Garden, where he opened with a modified version of this show, now called *Kissing Time*, which would run for 430 performances from May 20th, 1919.

The show clearly remained a favorite of Wodehouse's. When he died there were notes on his bedside table that indicated he was even then revising some of the lyrics—more than fifty years later!

The New York Public Library contains a puzzling undated libretto of an unproduced show called *Ladies, Please!* credited solely to Wodehouse. In suggesting a date of 1917/1918 we are following such clues as there are.

The manuscript has the pencilled comment "F. Ray Comstock," suggesting that Wodehouse had a Princess production in mind. Since the last show that he, Bolton and Kern were involved in at the Princess was late 1918, this is likely to have been somewhere in that vicinity.

There is also the suggestion of casting Oscar Shaw as Wally. Shaw had starred in their 1917 *Leave It To Jane*.

The libretto also contains a version of "Church 'Round the Corner," which was intended for the trio's *The Little Thing* back in 1916 but did not finally see the light until *Sally* (1920). This would seem to be an intermediate version.

LADIES, PLEASE! (?1917/1918)

"A Musical Comedy" (Unproduced)

BOOK AND LYRICS   P. G. Wodehouse

CAST	
Lord Reggie Meopham	Zoë Shelton
(pronounced "Moom" to rhyme with "Bluffinghame")	Bobbie Roberts
Dear Old Squiffy	Wally Henderson
	(?OSCAR SHAW) actor
Mrs. Waddesleigh Clayton, a society hostess	Hortense
	Jane Usher
Spink, the butler	Watson, the maid

2.

The Girls are setting up a charity bazaar and exhorting all their friends to . . .

BUY! BUY! BUY!

(Girls and Boys)

Girls: Won't you buy? Won't you buy?
           Now is the time to start.

Boys: Well, how much are the roses?

Girls: One dollar fifty, please

Boys: Rather high! Rather high!
           Couldn't you have a heart?

Girls: We've also sofa-pillows
           We're asking ten for these.

Boys: Oh, surely not? That seems a lot!
           The price looks big to me.

Girls: But then, you know, the proceeds go
           To help a charity.

Girls: Buy! Buy! Buy!
           Won't you buy? Do try!
           Just to help the Starving Swedes.
           We must raise in a few short days
           All the cash that nation needs.
           Don't you think us grasping, pray:
           You will find we are fair.
           For when you go away,
           We will leave you carfare.
           Do please buy
           Just a knitted tie
           Or a fifty-cent cigar:
           Don't feel shy if the price is high,
           For you know what these things are.
           Though you're no millionaire,
           You can buy a teddy-bear
           For he's not wise who tries
           To economise

At a Charity Bazaar.

A version of this song was later included in *Pat* (1924).

Mrs. Clayton enters with Lord Moom, a penniless and chinless wonder, eking out a living as "Bertie Brighteye," the society columnist for the *New York Chronicle*, and here to cover the event. Moom has come with his pal Squiffy ("we went together through Eton, Oxford and the Bankruptcy Court"). Mrs. Clayton's niece, Zoë, now arrives to tell fortunes at the bazaar. She has just been saved from a nasty road accident by a brave young man who didn't give his name. Moom hopes to interview the famous Wally Henderson, the Speed Kid, but his mind is not really on the job, because he is in love—something the Girls, who know him of old, find highly amusing.

LADIES, PLEASE!

(Moom and Girls)

Moom: Please regard me, if you can,
           As quite a different sort of man
           From the chap I was a month or
                two ago!
           You've really not a notion
           How love—that is, devotion—
           Makes a feller change completely,
                don't you know?

Girls: All your fun and all your flirting
           You're deserting—what a shame!
           We've had some times together that
                were splendid.

Moom: Rather! Yes, I quite agree;
           But no more of that for me
           That sort of thing is absolutely
                ended

Girls: It's ended!

Moom: It's ended! It's positively ended.
    So, I beg you, keep your distance,
    Ladies, please! Ladies, please!
    And be careful not to cluster or
       to coo.
    You'll forgive my seeming frigid
    But my code is rather rigid,
    And, by Jove, you really scare me—
       yes, you do.
    For if girls, you know, start winking
       at me nowadays,
    Why, I feel like running off and
       climbing trees:
    Recollect I love another,
    So just treat me like a brother,
    Ladies, Please! Ladies, Please,
       Please, Please!

Bobbie enters. She is Mrs. Clayton's companion who is meant to be running the Lucky Tub and it soon becomes clear that she is the love of Moom's life. Bobbie has just come into a legacy and asks Moom to invest it for her. Now they can finally get married.

THE CHURCH 'ROUND
THE CORNER

(Bobbie and Girls)

There's a church round the corner that sightseers
    miss;
It's just above Madison Square.
And it's simply a gateway that opens a straight
    way
That leads to a Paradise rare.
And the joy-waves that flow from this centre
    of bliss
Are felt for a radius of miles:
Till if anyone sad is on Fifth or on Madison
Quickly he cheers up and smiles.

Dear little Church 'Round The Corner
Where so many lives have begun:
Where folks without money see nothing that's
    funny
In two living cheaper than one.
She's a girl, so it's useless to warn her;
He's a boy, so of course he don't care:
But their hearts start to beat as they turn down
    the street,
For the Church 'Round The Corner—
It's just round the corner—
The Church 'Round The Corner is there.

To that wonderful church on a magic green bus
You go for ten cents all the way
And there's naught to be fearing, for Cupid is
    steering
And he wouldn't lead you astray.
He will take you right there without worry or
    fuss:
Anxiety no one need feel.
With a smile that's seraphic he steers through
    the traffic
Disguised as the man at the wheel.

Dear little Church 'Round The Corner,
Where couples run off to be wed:
They know it is rash, for they haven't much
    cash,
So they mean to make love do instead.
Of dull prudence, of course, she's a scorner:
They are happy, so what do they care?
Twenty-ninth is a glad street for those not in
    Bradstreet:
The Church 'Round The Corner—
It's just round the corner—
The Church 'Round The Corner is there.

Wodehouse had a particular fondness for the song, since it had been inspired by the actual church—the Little Church Around the Corner off Madison Avenue on 29th Street—in which he and his wife, Ethel, had been married on

September 30th, 1914. It was originally intended for *The Little Thing*, the show that Comstock rejected at the trio's first meeting with him. Wodehouse then found a temporary home for it in this other unproduced piece. Kern then played it for Ziegfeld on a 1920 boat trip when they were pitching a version of *The Little Thing* as a vehicle for Ziegfeld's favorite, Marilyn Miller. Audiences finally heard the song in the 1920 extravaganza *Sally*, which starred Miss Miller—who had now added a second 'n' and become Marilynn—and was loosely based on *The Little Thing*.

Although Kern wanted to involve him, *Sally* was in no real sense a "Wodehouse show," since he was too occupied in the UK when their early idea finally became a reality. Wodehouse was, in fact, more than a little miffed when Kern—never lauded for his tact—curtly asked for two Wodehouse lyrics for the show. Finally, after a family counsel, "I answered in the affir." But even as his permission was winging its way westward, he received from Kern "the sort of cable that the Kaiser might have sent to an underling." Relations between the two men would never again be as easy, although they did continue working together for another five years.

The lyric for *The Little Thing* differed in some respects from the one included in *Ladies, Please!* . . .

Girl: There's a church 'round the corner
        that's waiting for us:
        It's just above Madison Square.

Boy: I'll borrow a dollar and buy a clean
        collar,
        And then I'll be meeting you there.

Girl: There'll be crowds in the pews and
        excitement and fuss,
        For I mean to be married in style,
        And the girls will go dizzy and
        whisper "Who is he?"
        When I start to step up the aisle

Both: Dear little, dear little Church 'Round
        the Corner,
        Where so many lives have begun,
        Where folks without money see
        nothing that's funny
        In two living cheaper than one.
        Our hearts to each other we've
        trusted:
        We're busted, but what do we
        care?
        For a moderate price
        You can start dodging rice
        At the Church 'Round the Corner,
        It's just 'round the corner,
        The corner of Madison Square.

. . . while the version that was used in *Sally* differed even more. It was sung as a duet by the comic leads, Otis and Rosie . . .

THE CHURCH 'ROUND THE CORNER

Rosie: There's a church round the corner
        that's waiting for us
        It's just above Madison Square.

Otis: Very soon to the altar like sheep
        to the slaughter, (my neck in
        a halter)
        My love, you'll be leading me there.

Rosie: All the bells will be ringing, so don't
        make a fuss
        Just fancy how happy we'll be;

Otis: I'm sure I am plucky and you're
        very lucky
        To cop such a bridegroom as me.

Refrain
Both: Dear little, dear little Church 'Round
        the Corner,
        Where so many lives have begun.

Rosie: Where folks without money

Otis: See nothing that's funny
In two living cheaper than one.

Rosie: Of dull care, of course, I'm a
scorner.

Otis: We're busted but what do we care?

Rosie: I'll be dressed all in white

Otis: I'll be dying of fright

Both: At the Church 'Round the Corner,
It's just 'round the corner,
The corner of Madison Square.

Rosie: To that wonderful church we will go
you and I.
We'll be quite the happiest pair;

Otis: My fate I must meet it there's no time
to beat it
Besides it's my duty—so there.

Rosie: I feel so excited I just want to die,
I'll never get left on the shelf

Otis: I'll look so seraphic, I'll stop all the
traffic
They'll think I am Cupid himself.

Refrain
Both: Dear little, dear little Church 'Round
the Corner
Where couples run off to be wed

Rosie: I'll swear to be tender

Otis: And if I surrender
Will you bring my breakfast to bed?

Rosie: You'll look fine in your new Turly
Warner

(Otis):   Let a smart 'Maison Lewis' adorn her

Otis: Your Mouslin-de-soir you must wear;

(Rosie):   My Mouslin-de-soir I must wear

Rosie: All the people will think

Otis: Here's another poor gink

Both: At the Church 'Round the Corner.
It's just 'round the corner,
The corner of Madison Square.

Refrain
Both: Dear little, dear little Church 'Round
the Corner
Where soon I shall make you my own.

Rosie: The cars will be parking.

Otis: The dogs will be barking,
They'll doubtless take me for a
bone,

Rosie: Fine ribbons the bride will adorn her

Otis: And I shall look sweet, I declare

Rosie: Twenty-ninth is a glad street

Otis: For those not in Bradstreet

Both: At the Church 'Round the Corner
It's just 'round the corner
The corner of Madison Square.

FINALE—ACT 2

Both: Dear little, dear little Church 'Round
the Corner;
We'll slip off one day on the sly
We don't want a fuss
Nothing gaudy for us,
We have quite settled that,
You and I.

Otis: She's a girl
            So it's useless to warn her!

Rosie: He's a boy
            So, of course, he doesn't care

Both: In out hearts we shall sing,
            And the joy bells will ring
            At the Church 'Round the Corner
            It's just round the corner
            It's just round the corner
            The corner of Madison Square

One of the many variant libretti for *Oh, Lady! Lady!!* contains yet another version. This time there is a double wedding, since Jeff (Hale) is also marrying Jane (May), while Kim (Molly) is marrying Bill. The two couples sing . . .

Kim: As we pass through the door, there'll
               be sunshine above
            And a carpet of flowers at our feet;
            And the bells will be ringing
            And crowds will be singing
            The Mendelssohn March in the
               street.

Jane: I've a new Paris hat the spectators
               will love;
            It's the kind you can never forget;

Bill: And my custom-made trousers
            Are real rabble-rousers;
            They'll make me a popular pet.

Kim: Dear little, dear little Church 'Round
               the Corner,
            I feel it was built for us.

Bill: Our friends and supporters
            Will come from all quarters
            To wish us prosperity plus.

Jane: Policemen directing the traffic
            Seraphic expressions will wear,

Jeff: And the parson will whoop
            As we jump through the hoop
            At the Church 'Round the Corner
            It's just 'round the corner,
            The corner of Madison Square.

Kim: Dear,
            The vows uttered here, you can bet,

Bill: Are more binding than promises
            Made at St. Thomas's
            By the Park Avenue set.

Jane: Though we may not be leaders of
               fashion,
            Of passion we've more than our share;

Jeff: And true love is enough
            When you're doing your stuff
            At the Church 'Round the Corner,
            It's just 'round the corner,
            The corner of Madison Square

Wally enters with Watson the maid, having hurt his wrist in a car accident. As she goes off to fetch him a bandage, Bobbie arrives. They are old friends and have a lot in common—including being broke. There's no alternative for it, he will have to get a job. They look through the directory together to see what might suit him.

THERE'S LOTS OF ROOM FOR YOU

(There's Lots of Chance For You)

(Bobbie and Wally)

Bobbie: I'm very glad, I must confess, you've
               quit your life of idleness:

Wally: Well, yes, of course, but though I hate
               to shirk,
            It turns a mere beginner pale to have
               to buy a dinner-pail
            And sally out to find a job of work.

Bobbie: Well, work's a thing that others do,
    so why should it be hard on you?

Wally: It's very hard to choose a job, you
    know!
The only person I recall was Sister
    Susie
Who sewed those socks for soldiers
    long ago.

Bobbie: A score who toil as hard as she
You'll find in this Directory

Ambrose Ash makes aeroplanes for
    actors:

Wally: Bernard Boole builds bungalows
    for bees:

Bobbie: Cootes & Cohan sell collars for
    commuters:

Wally: Dave Davinsky deals in BVDs.

Bobbie: Francis Fane sells furniture and
    frat pins:

Wally: Gooch & Gould have always stuck
    to glue:

Bobbie: Henry Higgins has a yard where he
    sells humidors and hardware.
So there's lots of chance for you.

Imagine for a moment, do, what fame
    may have in store for you,
And what a thrill of pleasure it
    would bring
If people, as you came along, in
    whispers passed your name along,
And said, "There goes the Sock-
    Suspender King!"

Wally: Well, yes, I see just what you mean,
    but still, I own, I'm far from keen
On working every day from eight a.m.

Bobbie: You mustn't be fainthearted.
You'll enjoy it once you've started
A lot of men work hard and look
    at them!
Just think of all that they go through:
What they've accomplished, you
    can do.

Wally: Peter Park packs pickles for policemen:

Bobbie: Percy Pink makes pumpkin pies
    for Poles:

Wally: Smith & Son sells sausages and soda:

Bobbie: Clarke & Co. can corn and carry
    coals.

Wally: Thomas Todd makes toys and ties
    and toothpicks

Bobbie: Teddy Taylor trades in tar and tea:

Wally: Martin, Morrison & Miller sell soft
    soap and sarsparilla,
So there's lots of room for me.

Wally persuades Moom to invest Bobbie's inheritance on Battling Bodger in the forthcoming heavyweight fight. (Bobbie has told him she will never marry him if he ever gambles again.) As they leave, Bobbie and Zoë enter, Zoë enthusing about her unknown savior. Moom returns and the three of them turn lyrical on the subject of love.

IT'S ABSOLUTELY GRAND (ISN'T IT WONDERFUL?)

(Moom, Bobbie and Zoë)

Zoë: Oh, love's a thing some people shun:
By others, too, it's overdone.

Bobbie: King Solomon, the tales admit,
Made quite an indoor sport of it.

Moom: And so it's clearly to be seen,
          We ought to hit the happy mean

Zoë: In earth below or heaven above
         There's nothing half so fine as love.

All: It's wonderful! It's marvellous!
         It's absolutely grand!
         It makes you go all shivery
         And curious and quivery.
         When you're feeling livery,
         It makes your soul expand.
         It's wonderful! It's marvellous!
         It's absolutely grand!

Moom: Love's microbe's working overtime
          In every land, in every clime

Bobbie: And Leagues of Nations by degrees
            Go in for freedom of the Squeeze.

Zoë: It works in France. It works in Spain.
         It works on Russia's icy plain.

Bobbie: And when it bites a Bolshevik,
            Three simple words you'll hear him
               speak . . .

All: It's wonderful! It's wonderful!
         It's absolutely grand!
         He murmurs, "Oh, you kid-o-vitch,
         I'm fairly off my lid-o-vitch!
         I feel I'm going to skid-o-vitch,
         In fact, you understand
         It's wonderful! It's wonderful!
         It's absolutely grand!

News arrives that Battling Bodger has lost—and so have Wally and Moom! Wally determines to win the money back. He will raffle himself off to the women of America.

I ONLY WANT ONE GIRL

(Wally and Girls)

I'm told a guy named Bernard Shaw
Has said that it's a natural law
For women to pursue a man
And hunt a man and woo a man:
And now I know that that is true:
That's just what all you women do.
From dewy eve till early dawn
I feel just like a hunted fawn.

Hundred of Hildas
And thousands of Janes
Are camping all day on my track:
Scores of Matildas
And Mauds and Elaines
Are making my future look black.
I dream ev'ry night of confetti and rice:
I feel like Eliza when crossing the ice.
I only want one girl—I'm modest, you see:
But there's five hundred thousand want me.

If I go out to take the air,
A million girls flock round and stare
It simply means, if this goes on,
I'll have to put false whiskers on.
I simply dare not wander out
While there is anyone about
I always thought this land was free
It's nothing but a gaol for me.

Hundreds of Tessies
And thousands of Sues
Are camping all day on my track
Reg'ments of Bessies
And Jessies and Lous
Are making my future look black.
I feel like a possum that's up in a tree
I smell orange-blossom whe'er I may be.
I want one girl, but what can you do
When there's five hundred thousand want you?

Zoë enters, masked for her fortune telling stint. She realizes that Wally is her mysterious savior and reads his hand. They realize their mutual attraction and he tells her he will work to earn her love and be back to claim her . . .

A YEAR FROM TODAY

(Wally and Zoë)

Wally: There are millions of men in the
world, dear,
Though I hate to believe that it's
true:
There are millions of men in the
world, dear,
Simply waiting to rob me of you:
They will have you around them—
confound them!
While goodness knows where I
shall be:
And cold reason suggests that each
one of those pests
Will endeavour to take you from me.

Zoë: No, dear, I'll meet you a year from
today:
I shan't be changed, dear, a year
from today.
I'll still remember through snows of
December
The roses and sunshine of May.
We'll be together, though far you
may stray:
What is a year, dear? 'Twill soon
pass away:
And Oh! What a lot, dear, we'll both
have to say
When I meet you a year from today.

There are millions of girls in the
world, dear,
And they're all of them nicer than me.
Do you think you will wish you'd not
met me,
When those wonderful beauties
you see?
They will love you the moment they
meet you:
They are bound to unless they
are blind:

So I won't think it strange if your
feelings should change
And you tell me you've altered
your mind.

A revised version of the song would turn up in the 1924 *Sitting Pretty*.

Bobbie and Moom meet. Is she really going to marry Wally, if she wins? Certainly. She tells him she can hardly believe the two of them were engaged only two short months before.

(The script indicates a duet between Bobbie and Moom at this point, followed by another number—"Easter Parade"—in which Bobbie and the Boys and Girls celebrate the fact that Bobbie mistakenly believes she has drawn the winning number. Neither lyric appears to have been written.)

Wally and Moom lament the fact that love's web appears to have become hopelessly tangled for both of them . . .

I MEAN TO SAY— WHAT! WHAT! WHAT!

(Moom and Wally)

Moom: The world's on the loose and has
gone to the deuce,
That's a fact now, when all's said
and done:

Wally: The world is a spot that's decidedly
not
The right place for a minister's son.

Moom: Take magazine-writers. Today all
the blighters
Write tales about women who slip.

Wally: Yes, the yarns in St. Nicholas once
used to tickle us,
Now we want something with zip.

Moom: Well, I mean to say. What? Don't
            you know?
        It's just a bit thick.

Wally: Oh, *très chaud*!
        They're all of them whales on the girl
            with a past.

Moom: Did you read *Snappy Tales* of the
            week before last?
        There's a story called 'Purer Than
            Snow,'
        Where the heroine's lured on a
            yacht.

Wally: Did she—well, so to speak?

Moom: I shan't know till next week
        But I mean to say, What! What!
            What!

        Take some of the plays they put on
            nowadays:
        Why, my goodness, they make a chap
            blush

Wally: My aunt tried to go to one passionate
            show
        And was nearly destroyed in the
            crush.

Moom: There's always a scene in a bedroom,
            I mean
        And at nothing, by Jove, will they
            stop.

Wally: The procedure, in fact, is to see the
            first act
        And then rush out and call for a cop.

Moom: Well, I mean to say, What? Don't
            you know?
        I've frequently gone to a show

Where a couple were shown late at
    night in retreat
Absolutely alone in a snug private
    suite:
Well, of course, someone enters
    de trop
Just in time to—er—alter the plot

Wally: But suppose he was late
        And they had a stage-wait!

Both: Well, I mean to say, What! What!
            What!

Moom: I think that the new kind of dances
            they do
        Are most frightfully bad on the whole.

Wally: The Galatine Quiver is good for
            the liver,
        But cannot be good for the soul.

Moom: All round one detects the most fearful
            effects:
        You can see them wherever you go.

Wally: Why, my young brother Jim taught
            poor Granny to shim
        And she now speaks of Ziegfeld
            as Flo.

Moom: Well, I mean to say, What? Don't
            you know?
        That must be a terrible blow?

Wally: Well, it gave us a chill when we heard
            Granny speak
        About topping the bill at the Palace
            next week
        And she talks about stopping the show
        With the up-to-date act she has got:
        And she's taken a flat
        And become a White Rat.

Both: Well, I mean to say, What! What!
What!

Moom: It's not my affair, but the suits the
girls wear
When they go in to swim are
unique.

Wally: My poor cousin Sammy saw some
at Miami
That shattered his nerves for a week.

Moom: It's silly to storm and to talk of
bad form,
Though you'd think that they might
draw the line:

Wally: No, however you preach at the girl on
the beach,
It's agreed that her form is divine.

Moom: Well, I mean to say, What? Don't
you know?
Each year to the seashore you go,
And it's worse than before, for the
suits, I declare,
Are a little bit more—so to speak,
as it were:
And I murmur, 'Gadzooks!' or
'What ho!'
Or 'Good Heavens!' or that sort
of rot:

Wally: For it just makes you think—
"Now, suppose they should
shrink!"

Both: Well, I mean to say, What! What!
What!

Bobbie enters and teases Wally about their
forthcoming marriage, but he is not amused.

As she leaves, Zoë enters. (In the ms. a duet is
indicated.)

When Wally has gone, Bobbie returns and
confides in Zoë that she really has no intention
of marrying her man. She still loves Moom but
she hasn't finished exacting her revenge on him
yet. In fact, when she sees him, she invites him to
her wedding. ("It wouldn't seem complete without you.")

CHURCH 'ROUND THE CORNER

(Reprise)

(Bobbie)

To the Dear Little Church 'Round the
Corner
We'll slip off one day on the sly:
We don't want a fuss. Nothing gaudy for us.
We have quite settled that—he and I.
We will purchase a new Turly Warner,
And my best winter frock I will wear.
For I've got to look neat down in Twenty-Ninth
Street,
For the church round the corner,
It's just round the corner,
The Church 'Round The Corner is there.

Unaware of the true situation, Wally and
Moom devise various stratagems to
unscramble the "wrong" relationships, all of
which misfire. They blame each other for the
mess and Bobbie has to separate them, remind-
ing them in song that "Ladies Are Present"
(another lost or unwritten number).

In the final plot twist Wally's old nurse
arrives. She was the real owner of the winning
lottery ticket and she feels obliged to marry
Master Wally. The day is saved when it is discovered that she is already married to the butler,
Spinks. The two young couples are left free to
plan a double wedding.

The Canary (1918)

Presented by Charles Dillingham at the Globe Theatre, New York, on November 4, 1918 (152 performances).

BOOK
adapted from the French
by Georges Barr and
Louis Verneuil

LYRICS
Anne Caldwell and
P. G. Wodehouse

MUSIC
Ivan Caryll, Irving Berlin,
and others

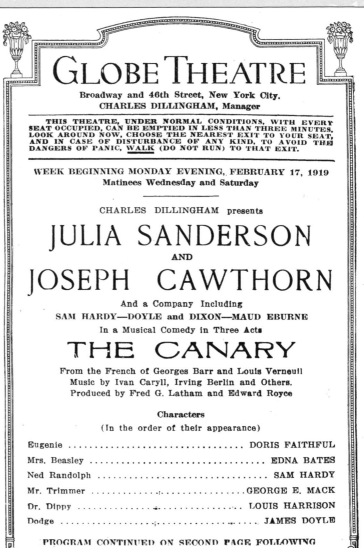

GLOBE THEATRE

Broadway and 46th Street, New York City.
CHARLES DILLINGHAM, Manager

THIS THEATRE, UNDER NORMAL CONDITIONS, WITH EVERY SEAT OCCUPIED, CAN BE EMPTIED IN LESS THAN THREE MINUTES. LOOK AROUND NOW, CHOOSE THE NEAREST EXIT TO YOUR SEAT, AND IN CASE OF DISTURBANCE OF ANY KIND, TO AVOID THE DANGERS OF PANIC, <u>WALK</u> (DO NOT RUN) TO THAT EXIT.

WEEK BEGINNING MONDAY EVENING, FEBRUARY 17, 1919
Matinees Wednesday and Saturday

CHARLES DILLINGHAM presents

JULIA SANDERSON
AND
JOSEPH CAWTHORN

And a Company Including
SAM HARDY—DOYLE and DIXON—MAUD EBURNE
In a Musical Comedy in Three Acts

THE CANARY

From the French of Georges Barr and Louis Verneuil
Music by Ivan Caryll, Irving Berlin and Others.
Produced by Fred G. Latham and Edward Royce

Characters
(In the order of their appearance)

Eugenie .... DORIS FAITHFUL
Mrs. Beasley .... EDNA BATES
Ned Randolph .... SAM HARDY
Mr. Trimmer .... GEORGE E. MACK
Dr. Dippy .... LOUIS HARRISON
Dodge .... JAMES DOYLE

PROGRAM CONTINUED ON SECOND PAGE FOLLOWING

CAST

Eugenie: DORIS FAITHFUL	Fleece: HARLAND DIXON
Mrs. Beasley: EDNA BATES	Timothy: JOSEPH CAWTHORNE
Ned Randolph: SAM HARDY	Julie: JULIA SANDERSON
Mr. Trimmer: GEORGE E. MACK	Rico: WILMER BENTLEY
Dr. Dippy: LOUIS HARRISON	Mary Ellen: MAUDE EBURNE
Dodge: JAMES DOYLE	A Minister: GEORGE EGAN

SYNOPSIS

The story concerned a character who accidentally swallowed a diamond, and was then pursued in an attempt to recover the jewel. The inevitable pair of crooks (Dodge and Fleece) emerged, but the number of composers whose work was included in the score—Ivan Caryll, Irving Berlin, Jerome Kern, and Harry Tierney—suggest that it was not a particularly well integrated show.

THOUSANDS OF YEARS AGO

(Julie)

(Music by Ivan Caryll)

Julie: Mummy standing there with that
                cold, calm stare,
           It's no wonder you look so wise;
           For the laughter and tears of six
                thousand years,
           You have watched with those
                painted eyes,
           Oh, the sights you've seen when the
                world was green,
           I can guess by the way you smile,

           Could you speak as well,
           What a tale you'd tell
           Of those days on the banks of
                the Nile.

Refrain: Have you a someone you were
                meeting just like me?
           Someone it sets your heart a-beating
                just to see?
           Did you stand waiting by the River
           Down where the rushes quiver,
           Love's old tale repeating?
           Were there two tender eyes that
                glistened long ago?

Was there a voice to which you
    listened whispering low?
Were there two arms to hold you,
Two lips to pet and scold you,
Thousands of years ago?

Julie: I was born, you know,
Twenty years ago,
So you're older, you see, than me;
You were once a king, yes, or some
    such thing,
But I count on your sympathy;
You're so calm and grand, but you'll
    understand,
And you'll listen to what I say,
For I know that you once loved
    someone, too.
Yes, I'm sure you did in your day.

Refrain

JULIE AND HER JOHNNIES

(Julie and Girls)

(Music by Ivan Caryll)

Julie: Excuse me but really I should like
    to say
It's foolish to follow me around all day.
Though I'm in love, it's true,
I'm not in love with you.
But don't get down-hearted
There's no need to be:
You'll find there are lots of nicer girls
    than me,
Yes, scores of girls far prettier and
    hundreds toittier,
You're sure to see.

Girls: Come with me! Come with me!

Julie: So, go away! Run along! Run
    along!
Trot off and play! Run along! Run
    along!

Please don't come closer
Oh, sir, let go, Sir!
Don't touch me, pray!
For it's wrong, for it's wrong.
You heard me say
Run along! Run along! You're all
    quite nice, I dare say,
But today you're in the way:
Run along, little boys! Run along
    and play.

Girls: We heard you say: "Run along! Run
    along!
Trot off and ah . . . please don't
    come closer
Oh, sir, let go, Sir!
You're all quite nice I dare say
But today,
Run along, little boys,
Run along and play."

Julie: My heart is another's, as I said before,
I'll treat you as brothers,
But I can't do more,
So that's what I will do;
Won't that be nice for you . . .
To be your good sister I will always
    try,
At Christmas for each of you I'll knit
    a tie;
But if you start pursuing me or go on
    wooing me,
I'll say goodbye

Girls: Not goodbye! Not goodbye!

Julie: So go away! Run along! Etc...

THAT'S WHAT MEN ARE FOR

(Julie)

(Music by Ivan Caryll)

When I was a child of three
Mother used to say to me:

"Don't look down on men, my darling;
Don't dismiss them with a sneer
Ev'rything however low,
Has its uses, you must know:
Even your poor father's useful,
You will be surprised to hear.
Nature knew her bus'ness when
She stocked up the world with men,
Though they are an aggravating,
Irritating, stupid sex;
For, if they did not exist,
They would certainly be missed.
For in spite of all their faults,
They're very good at signing checks."
I still re . . .

Refrain: . . . call what mother told me,
            Though she filled me then with
                great surprise,
            And I can see how true her
                words were,
            Time has shown that her advice
                was wise.
            We can't dispense with men
                entirely,
            For there's just one point we
                can't ignore,
            Somebody has got to pay the bills,
                and
            That's what men are for!

Later on dear mother said:
"Now it's time that you were wed;
Every girl should have a husband,
But it doesn't matter which,
Men are all about the same.
Some are wild and some are tame,
All that really matters is to
Pick out one that's nice and rich.
Never mind about his face
Or his lack of style and grace;
You can always keep him hidden
Snugly stowed away indoors.
Don't care if his mind's a blank.

Has he money in the bank?
That's the point; and will he give
You charge accounts at all the stores?"

Refrain: So I recalled what mother told
                me
            Ruled by her, I made my choice
                with care;
            I kept refusing all proposals,
            Till I found a multi-millionaire.
            I might have picked one better
                looking
            Still I'm not complaining on that
                score;
            All I want's a man to pay the bills,
                and
            That's what men are for!

Oh, My Dear! was to be the last of the Princess musicals and bore many of the marks of scissors and paste. Wodehouse was to refer to it later as the team's equivalent of Gilbert & Sullivan's *Ruddigore*—a dying fall.

For one thing the "team" was no longer the team. Kern was not happy with Comstock and stood aside, forcing his old partners to work with Louis Hirsch, a former resident songwriter for the Shuberts. The professional chemistry was not there and both Bolton and Wodehouse had too many other commitments to give the piece their full attention. The result was mostly a cold collation of leftovers from the still unproduced *The Little Thing* and the barely tasted *Miss 1917*.

OH, MY DEAR! (1918)

(Originally ASK DAD)
A Musical Farce in Two Acts

Presented by Ray Comstock and William Elliott at the Princess Theatre, New York, on November 27, 1918 (189 performances) after a tryout at the Alexandra Theatre, Toronto, under the title *Ask Dad*.

BOOK   Guy Bolton and P. G. Wodehouse
LYRICS   P. G. Wodehouse
MUSIC   Louis A. Hirsch

(Wodehouse used the *Ask Dad* title as early as June 1918 in a Jeeves/Wooster story, "A Letter of Introduction" in *The Inimitable Jeeves*. It was the production in which Cyril Bassington-Bassington manages to obtain a part.)

CAST

Hazel: EVELYN DORN	Georgie Van Alstyne: HELEN BARNES
Dr. Rockett: FREDERICK GRAHAM	Pickles: MIRIAM COLLINS
Broadway Willie Burbank: ROY ATWELL	Babe: HELEN CLARKE
Grace Spelvin: MARJORIE BENTLEY	Mrs. Rockett: GEORGIA CAINE
Bagshott: JOSEPH ALLEN	Jennie Wren: JULIETTE DAY
Bruce Allenby: JOSEPH SANTLEY	Joe Plummer: FRANCIS X. CONLAN
Hilda Rockett: IVY SAWYER	Nan Hatton: FLORENCE MCGUIRE

SYNOPSIS

Dr. "Pop" Rockett runs a health farm and is almost as eccentric as his "guests." He meets Broadway Willie, a dipsomaniac on the run from his alimony-seeking wife, Jennie Wren. He bemoans his lot to the Girls ("I Shall Be All Right Now"). Bruce Allenby, heir to the Allenby Umbrella fortune, crashes his plane on the asylum and meets Pop's daughter, Hilda. They realize they have met before and been mutually attracted ("I Wonder Whether I've Loved You All My Life"). Willie is joined by three out of work chorus girls he knows, who hope to touch him for their fare home to New York. He doesn't have the money, but perhaps Pop will have the answer ("Ask Dad"). The girls tell Willie Jennie is on her way and he leaves. Mrs. Rockett finds her husband carousing with assorted females, but Pop pretends Bruce is really Willie. He doesn't care, as long as he can stay around Hilda ("City of Dreams").

Mrs. Rockett signs Bruce up for the famed "Rockett treatment" ("Come Where Nature Calls"). Jennie arrives and finds her "husband" has suddenly grown more attractive. The Girls feel the same, especially Pickles. The other girls warn Bruce her nickname is Phoebe Snow, after the train that runs between

New York and Buffalo ("Phoebe Snow"). The local Sheriff arrives to arrest Willie (Bruce). To save him, Jennie pretends to be his wife. When she hears this, Hilda believes her.

A sad Hilda is serenaded by the Boys and Girls ("Go, Little Boat"). The Rocketts are giving a "Cobweb Party." Every man is given a string and when he winds it up, which partner will be at the end of it? ("You Never Know"). Bruce tries to explain the misunderstanding to Hilda—this time with Jennie's help ("Try Again"). Willie has seen how Jennie behaves around Bruce and it makes him jealous ("It Sort of Makes a Fellow Stop and Think"). The complications of mistaken identity are now making everyone wish for the simpler days of childhood ("Childhood Days"). Bruce tells Hilda of the legal problems his family face that may part them after all ("City of Dreams—Reprise"). Left alone, Hilda and Jennie reflect on the nature of true love ("I'd Ask No More"). Willie is reunited with Jennie ("If They Ever Parted Me From You"). With all the misunderstandings cleared up and all the problems solved . . . ("Finale").

I SHALL BE ALL RIGHT NOW

(Willie and Girls)

Willie:
I don't mind telling you,
Since you have asked me to,
I've had the deuce of a time:
I got it in the neck,
I'm a most awful wreck,
Nearly cut off in my prime.
I painted Broadway red:
I never went to bed
While there were drinks to be sold;
But while I'm here to stay
For a brief holiday,
I mean to be good as gold.

Refrain
That's why I want you, girls
If you don't mind,
To be extremely kind
And sweet, you see, to me:

(And sweet to me)
Just pat my hands awhile
And stroke my hair:
I need a lot of care
And sympathy:
Please don't be harsh or cross,
A single frown
Would simply break me down
And do for me.

You can help cure me, girls, and I'll
    tell you how:
Just print (an occasional kiss) on
    my brow, (a soft kiss or two
    right here)
Continue the treatment—say—
A few hundred times a day,
And I shall be all right now.

Many's the night I've seen
Spiders, both pink and green,
Fox-trotting over the floor

Also in twos and threes
Lizards and chimpanzees

Sometimes a dozen or more;
Often my head would ache,
Watching a crimson snake
Waltz with a mauve kangaroo:
After a while, you know,
Life used to seem to grow
Rather like life in a Zoo.

I WONDER WHETHER I'VE
LOVED YOU ALL MY LIFE

(Bruce and Hilda)

Bruce: Just as soon as I came inside that door,
Something told me that we had met
    before;
I'm sincere, though it may sound
    queer,
And you'll laugh, I fear, when I say;
"I love you—yes, indeed I do,
Though I only met you today."

Alternative:
Just as soon as we met that day last
    spring,
I felt sure—it's a most peculiar thing
Sure I'd met you before: and yet
I had never seen you, I know,
That is why I'm convinced that I
Must have known you ages ago.

I wonder whether
We were together
In some existence
Lost in the distance,
At different stages
Right through the ages.
Why, Julius Caesar or his father
Or his mother
May have introduced us to each
    other!

Ah! Could but we see
That time that's B.C.
You'd know you'd met me,
Though you forget me.
And now, you see, we've simply
    met again
If that's not so, I can't explain
Why I should feel I've loved you all
    my life

Hilda: I'm not laughing, for I felt just
    the same
Long before I had ever learned
    your name:
My heart stirred like a waking bird;
For it seems absurd but it's true,
I'd known some day that you would
    come,
So I simply said "Why, it's you."

You and I may have known each
    other well
In the days when in caves men used
    to dwell.
Then maybe you protected me
And you fought wild beasts, while
    I hid.

Bruce: Though I find it has slipped my mind,
I will bet that's just what I did.

Hilda: I wonder whether
We were together
At different stages
Right through the ages.

Bruce: For all we know, I may with ecstasy
    have fainted
When Cleopatra bade us "Get
    Acquainted!"

Hilda: Time draws a curtain. One can't
    be certain.

But some have stated these
   things are fated:
We only met this afternoon
   (the other day) you see,
And yet you say that you love
   me (and yet you feel this
   way to me)
While I just feel I've loved
   (known) you all my life.

ASK DAD

(Georgie, Pop, Willie, Pickles and Babe)

Georgie: What shall we do? That's the
            question!
           Say! Haven't you a suggestion?

Willie: I've no inspiration:

Pop: What a situation!

Willie: These three are in dutch!
           They're completely stranded:
           Haven't a cent between them.

Girls: Who shall we touch? We had
            best be candid.

Pop: Wish I had never seen them!

Willie: You will agree they cannot
            touch me:
           Think of another plan, sir!

Georgie: We'll make a dash at raising the cash
           From someone—what's the answer?

All
(except
Pop):   When you're in doubt, ask daddy!
           He'll help us out, will daddy!
           When you're in bad:
           Leave it to dad
           Lucky we had a

Juliette Day (*Jennie Wren*) and Roy Atwell (*Broadway Willie Burbank*) in *Oh, My Dear!*

           Pal like dadda!
           He is our best adviser:
           Nobody would be wiser.
           If there's a way to end our woes,

Willie: Then dad is the lad—Ask dad!
            He knows.
           So cheer up and don't be sad or mad:
           It's all right—Ask Dad!!!

           I've got a scheme that's a pippin!
           Girls, it's a dream! Simply rippin'!
           Come here for a visit!

Girls: Oh, that's just corking!

Pop: Is it?

Pickles: We told you before,

Babe: It's an awful problem,

Georgie: We have no dough, we've spent it.

Willie: Wolf's at the door. He'll get in and
           gobble 'em

Girls: If you do not prevent it.

Willie: Have them to stay. That's far the
           best way,
           It solves the problem neatly.

Georgie: You'll be a most acceptable host.

Pop: I disagree completely!

All
(except
Pop):   Let's give a cheer for daddy!
           He is a dear, is daddy!
           When you're in bad,
           Leave it to dad:
           Lucky we had a
           Pal like dadda!
           He's such a kind old buster
           When a girl's woes have fussed her
           What a relief! It simply shows

Willie: That dad is the lad . . . etc.
           Ask dad, he knows . . .

CITY OF DREAMS

(Hilda and Girls)

Hilda: Down in the valley where sunbeams
           (rainbows) grow

And stars go to rest (live) when
     they're old,
Stands, ever covered in sunset glow
A wonderful City of Gold.
Often I hoped I should see some
     day
That city which others have known;
It's easy to find if you know the way:
But no one can find it alone.

Refrain
Girls: Dear golden city!
           Life is happy and serene there,
           Where lovers go
           When its spell they can't resist
           And how I pity
           All the folks who've never been there:
           They'll never know
           All the wonders they have missed
           And soon I'll (I'm going to) stray
                there;
           I've some one now to show the
                way there;
           We'll go and stay there,
           It's much more simple than it
                seems.
           No one will find us
           For we'll leave the world behind us
           In our dear city
           Our city of dreams, dear golden
                dreams.

Hilda: Many are going there every day
           And though some have sought it
                in vain,
           No one who ever has found the way
           Can ever forget it again.
           Close to a river whose wavelets
                leap (creep)
           And splash on the silvery sand,
           It's not very far from the Hills
                of Sleep,
           And they are in Fairy Land

COME WHERE NATURE CALLS

(Mrs. Rockett, Pop, Hilda and Bruce)

Mrs. R.: I think of New York with a sigh and
a frown,
For it's full of worldly snares;

Bruce: Which you try to duck, but you don't
have luck,
And they sneak on you unawares;

Hilda: I've read of their crimes in the paper
sometimes,
And there's always something new.

Pop: The women's frocks give people
shocks—
At least, I'm told they do.

All: So, come where Nature calls!
Oh, come where Nature calls,
With all its sheeps and Lovers'
Leaps
And waterfalls;
Oh, get a spade and hoe
And let your whiskers grow,
And go and get, in case it's wet,
Some overalls. (A suit of overalls)
The guinea-hen will coo
Its morning hymn to you
As sweetly as the bands that jazz
In gilded halls.
And see! Beyond the gates
The poison ivy waits!
So come, come, come where
Nature calls!
So come, come, come where
Nature calls!

Mrs. R: What wonderful moral examples
we find
In the beasts on ev'ry hand.

Pop: Yes, I've known our cow for a long
time now,
And her morals are simply grand.

Hilda: No rooster I've met ever gambled
or bet,
Or went in too late to bed.

Bruce: And no one ever saw a pig
That had a morning head.

All: So, come where Nature calls!
Oh, come where Nature calls!
With all its sheeps and Lovers
Leaps and waterfalls
Oh, get a spade and hoe
And let your whiskers grow,
And go and get, in case it's wet,
Some overalls. (A suit of overalls)

Observe the gentle slug,
The mild potato bug;
Their life is tame, but all the same
It never palls;
They rise at five a.m.
Oh, let us be like them,
And list, list, listen when Nature calls!
And list, list, listen when Nature calls!

PHOEBE SNOW

(Jennie and Girls)

Jennie: You've heard of Phoebe Snow
Who makes those trips to Buffalo:
She travels, dressed in white
Upon the Road of Anthracite:
And somehow, though she looks
demure,
Though calm and saint-like she be,
You never know; you can't be sure:
And I've my doubts of Phoebe.
It's strange she always rides alone
And never has a chaperone.

Girls: Oh! Phoebe Snow! Oh, Phoebe Snow!
Who buys your ticket to Buffalo?
That point, my pet, we can't forget,
Has not been properly cleared up yet:
Some millionaire bought the dress
    you wear,
That fact is easy to see.
Oh, Phoebe Snow! Phoebe Snow!
You're too good to be true, you
    know,
Oho, oho!
It looks funny to me

Jennie: Should Phoebe hungry grow
Near Water Gap or Pocono,
She'll go and take a bite
Upon the road of Anthracite;
The pictures show her lunching there
Alone—but ask the waiter:
You'll find some mystic millionaire
Is going to join her later:
The artist who that picture drew
Knew Phoebe's lunch was lunch
    for two.

Girls: Oh, Phoebe Snow! Oh, Phoebe Snow!
Who travels with you to Buffalo?
I know you are too wise by far
To sit alone in a dining-car:
Who pays your check for your
    extra sec?
Someone, I'm sure, there must be
Oh, Phoebe Snow, Phoebe Snow,
Tell us frankly who is your beau:
Oho! Oho!
It looks funny to me
Oho! Oho!
It looks funny to me

Extra
Refrain: Oh, Phoebe Snow! Oh, Phoebe Snow!
What happens when you reach
    Buffalo?
Do you alight to spend the night

Or just stick around with the
    Anthracite?
I'm quite aware it's not my affair:
But I am puzzled, you see,
Oh, Phoebe Snow, Phoebe Snow
I just thought I would ask, you know.

Encore
Chorus: Oh, Phoebe Snow, Oh, Phoebe Snow.
What is the story that grips you so?
If we'd a chance to take a glance,
I think we'd find that it came
    from France.
It does not look like an Elsie Book,
To judge by what we can see.
Oh, Phoebe Snow, Phoebe Snow,
Tell us why you are blushing so,
Oh, oho!
It looks funny to me.

Hilda: No one will find me
For I'll leave the world behind me,
In my dear city,
My city of dreams.

GO, LITTLE BOAT

(Boat Song)

(Hilda and Boys & Girls)

Hilda: Softly my boat o'er the water creeps:
Winds, passing by, seem to sigh;
I am alone in a world that sleeps;
Wakeful and watchful am I.
Gentle and slow though the stream
    may flow,
Night time will end, and I'll be
Safe in the harbor, where one I know
Watches for me, only me.
Yes, there's someone who waits
    for me,
Where the river winds to the sea.

Go little boat, serenely glide and seek
    the sea;

Boys &
Girls: Over the silver water ride to where
        I'd be.

Hilda: Only the stars can behold us now,
        Shining high in the sky

Boys &
Girls: Glittering ripples before our prow
        Softly flow, to and fro.

Hilda: Go, little boat, serenely glide down
        to the sea

Boys &
Girls: Love at the helm,
        Your course will glide so smooth
        and free

All: Starshine above will light us down
        the river.
        Breezes of love have set your sails
        aquiver;
        Carry me down to him (her) I love,
        who waits for me.

YOU NEVER KNOW

(Bruce and Ensemble)

Bruce: Life is a kind of a gamble:
        Life is a leap in the dark:
        And things more or less have been in
        a mess
        Since Noah came out of the Ark.

        Fate puts a string in our fingers;
        Says to us, "Cheer up! Don't fret!"
        So just shut both your eyes and you'll
        get a surprise!
        And, by Jove! That is just what we get.

Chorus: You never know
(Boys): Never know

Bruce: Do you,
        What today Fortune may bring:
        We only know it's up to us
        To try our luck and make no fuss:
        So—right or wrong—come along,
        No use waiting,

Boys: Hesitating

Bruce: Fate, you'll find, may be kind to you.
        Fate may hold any old thing.
        We don't know what it is we've got.

Boys: It may be good

Bruce: It may be not:
        You'll know when you wind up
        your string.
        Maybe you think you'll get married!:
        Maybe you've furnished the flat:
        But don't be too sure. You can't feel
        secure,
        There may be a string tied to that.
        You mayn't have picked out the
        right one,
        May have been wrong all the while:
        For there's none can see, who his
        bride's going to be
        Till they walk arm in arm up the aisle.

Chorus
Bruce: You never know, never know, do you,
        What today fortune may bring:
        You think you'll marry Kate or Jane,
        But cruel fate says "Guess again!
        That's not the one, not the one:
        Come on, brother, pick another!"

        Fate, you'll find, may be kind to you:
        Fate may hold any old thing:
        And Fate's the fellow who'll decide
        Which girl is going to be your bride:
        You'll know when you wind up your
        string.

Some versions of the song have additional verses . . .

Hilda: Never mind I'll be kind to you
           It is clear luck's a queer thing
           And, wrong or right, it's settled quite
           That I'm your partner for tonight!
           You chose me by winding my string.

Pop: You never know, never know, do you
           What today fortune may bring
           So, if you're not quite satisfied,
           Your disappointment you must hide
           You mustn't show that you know:
           If you feel it, please conceal it.

Bruce: Never mind she'll be kind to you
           It is clear, luck's a queer thing.
           And, wrong or right, it's settled quite
           That she's your partner for tonight!
           And I chose her by winding my
               string.

           Fate, you'll find, may be kind to you
           Fate may hold any old thing
           And Fate's the fellow who'll decide
           Which girl is going to be your bride
           You'll know when you wind up your
               string.

TRY AGAIN

(Hilda, Bruce and Jennie)

Hilda: I really cannot understand
           Why quarrels should occur.

Jennie: A loving life as man and wife
           Is what I should prefer.

Bruce: To me there's nothing half so grand
           As true domestic bliss.

Hilda: Well, you'd obtain it once again
           If you'd remember this:

           Ev'ry morning try to say
           Something sweeter
           When you meet her.

Jennie: Say "I love your hair today,
           Or your dimple!"
           It's so simple.

Hilda: Praise the hats and frocks she's
               wearing,
           Don't be cross or overbearing,
           It's so easy to be happy,
           If you only know the way.

Reprise
Bruce: Ev'ry morning I must say
           "Hello, dearie," bright and cheery;

Jennie: Fix my breakfast on a tray;
           Toast and oolong
           Won't take you long

Hilda: Kiss her softly on the forehead,
           Never be unkind or horrid;
           It's so easy to be happy
           If you only know the way.

COUNTRY LIFE

(The Train That Leaves For Town)

(Jennie and Girls)

Another recycled song from *See You Later*, where it was sung by Jo and the Commodore.

IT SORT OF MAKES A FELLOW STOP AND THINK

(Willie)

Willie: It's awfully good of you to rally
               'round me
           And give me so much sympathy,
               because

Between ourselves, though you may
not suspect it,
You know, I'm really not the man
I was,
I've thought about the thing a whole
lot lately:
I may be wrong; but on the other
hand,
It might be wise to try a course of
Zoolak
That's only what I think, you
understand.
But . . .

Refrain: When you find you're scared by
sudden noises,
When you bite your tongue and jump
eleven feet
Just because, some lovely afternoon
in Summer
A birdie in the tree top says: "Tweet,
tweet";
Well, you've simply got to pull
yourself together.
Of course, the thing may not be due
to drink,
It may just be nerves or liver,
Not Bacardi and Green River.
Still—it sort of makes a fellow stop
and think!

And yet sometimes I've got quite
sentimental,
And thought that there could be no
happier life
Than just to settle down in some
nice suburb,
With half a dozen kiddies and a
wife.
I've met a lot of fellows who have
done it,
They tell you it is fine—and try
to grin,

You see, they've all been stung
themselves, poor devils,
So they want to let some other
fellow in.

I've visited these earthly Paradises
But it somehow happens, every time
I come,
Little Percy's having fits upon the
hearthrug,
And little Willie aches inside the
tum;
Then you're told that little Rollo has
the measles
And little George has drunk up all
the ink;
P'raps they're right who say no bliss is
Half so wonderful as this is;
Still—it sort of makes a fellow stop
and think!

My old Pal, Reggie Banks, is pretty
careful,
But still one moonlit night last June
he fell:
He lost his head, poor chump, and
got engaged to
A girl he met at some seashore
hotel.
He trotted off to break the news to
mother,
And ask her leave to name the happy
day;
He asked the fam'ly: "May I steal
your Mabel?"
The family said: "You bet your life
you may!"

Now Reggie's got an unsuspicious
nature,
But he did begin to think it rather
odd
When her father gripped his hand
and shook it warmly

And muttered in a broken voice:
    "Thank God!"
Then her mother said: "At last" and
    started singing.
Her brother smiled and Reggie saw
    him wink.
Well, as Reggie said, poor chappie,
It was nice to see them happy,
Still—it sort of makes a fellow stop
    and think.

Alternative Version:

You sometimes get a wedding
    invitation
That asks you to (if you'd) care to
    come along
And take a seat next Thursday at the
    ringside
To watch one more good fellow going
    wrong:
The message reads: "Alonzo Frederick
    Simpson
Next week is going to wed our
    daughter May,
So rally round and help us guard
    the exits,
In case he tries to make a getaway."

You see the execution squad
    assemble;
While the organ plays a sad and
    mournful strain;
And you watch the victim shuffle to
    the altar,
Where willing hands adjust the
    ball-and-chain.
For one moment, he's a happy living
    creature:
Ah, the next, they've gone and
    shoved him off the brink;
And your legs get all unsteady

When the Judge says: "Wilt thou,
    Freddy?"
For it sort of makes a fellow stop
    and think.

CHILDHOOD DAYS

**(Bruce, Pop, Bagshott,
Georgie, Babe and Pickles)**

Bruce: I have often felt quite sad, you know,
    Thinking of those days of long ago
    I'm aware I've gone from bad to worse
    Since I parted from my nurse.

Pop: I was my parents' joy when I was a boy,
    For I never lied.

Bagshott: And at the age of three, they never
      found me
    Starting homicide

Bruce: People loved me ev'rywhere I went,
    Mother thought I'd be President
    Ev'rybody said my way was clear
    To a wonderful Career.

Pop: And I was gay all day, when but a
      child of four:
    Then, you see, I was a bachelor.

Bagshott: In days gone by I wouldn't have killed
      a fly

Refrain
All: Oh, those happy days of childhood!
    Happy, happy days of childhood!
    Days I wish I could restore once more
      somehow.
    No one nowadays is under the
      delusion I'm a wonder,
    Though I'd feel lots of gratitude for
      that attitude now;
    People then thought we'd be famous.
    No one knew just how or when;
    Thought America would name us
    Her most celebrated men.

That was when we used to prattle
With our teddy bear and rattle;
Oh, we were far more wonderful
Much more wonderful then.

Bruce: When I was a child of nine or ten
All my tastes were much more
　　simple then;
Pleasures somehow never seemed
　　to cloy
When I was a little boy.

Pop: When I was five or six
I'd soldiers and bricks,
And a duck with wings

Bagshott: I had a top, (and) a hoop
And mumps and the croup
And all sorts of things.

Bruce: I'd go dancing every chance I got,
When it started, I was on the spot
Everywhere I went my golden curls
Used to paralyze the girls.

Pop: I used to feel that I could never get
　　enough
Hide and seek and tag and
Blindman's Bluff.

Bagshott: And I would go
And stand 'neath the mistletoe.

Refrain
All: Oh, those happy days of childhood!
Happy, happy days of childhood!
Days I wish I could restore
Once more somehow
We were always willing workers
At the polkas and mazurkas,
But we have less facility and ability
　　now.
Once the girls would flock around us,

All the while we'd nine or ten:
They would search until they found us.
Now they look for other men.
How they petted us and kissed us,
And were wretched when they
　　missed us;
And we were much, much happier
Far, far happier then

CITY OF DREAMS (Reprise)

(Bruce and Hilda)

Bruce: Oh, my dear, have no fear,
Though we two must part
　　awhile:

Hilda: Only wait. Soon or late
Fortune once again will smile.
Troubles mend. Journeys end.

Bruce: Sunshine follows after rain.
Joy comes tomorrow, drives out
　　our sorrow!

Hilda: Some day we shall meet again.
　　　Yes, wait—
And by and by.
Some day—some day.

Bruce
& Hilda: We'll meet, dear (again), you and I.

Hilda: Some day—some day.

Bruce
& Hilda: In our dear city: We'll be happy and
　　serene there,
Where lovers go, when it's a spell
　　they can't resist:
And how we pity all the folks who've
　　never been there,
They'll never know all the wonders
　　they have missed.

Hilda: And soon I'll stray there:
I've someone now to show the way
    there:
We'll go and stay there
It's much more simple than it seems.
No one will find us, for we'll leave
    the world
Behind us.

Bruce: In our dear city,
Our City of Dreams.

I'D ASK NO MORE

(Hilda, Jennie and Boys)

Hilda: Many girls you meet are sordid,
And would only
Wed a man
If a fortune he had hoarded,
But that seems a foolish plan:
For I have a motto which is this,
That love counts more than riches;
And I think the highest bliss is
Just a life of bread and cheese and
    kisses.

Refrain: I'd give up everything to marry
    some one
I could adore
For if you've love,
Wealth you ignore:
The latter doesn't matter.
Love in a cottage is the only thing
    that
I'm pining for;
I could be absolutely happy and
    content,
If we had only got enough to pay
    the rent:
If I could simply sit on someone's
    knee,
And have him make a fuss of me,
Why, I'd ask no more.

Jennie: I am just the same. I'm longing for a
    cottage built for two;
If we couldn't get a cottage, why, the
    Ritz would have to do.
Yes, though life was small and
    humble,
I'd be brave and never grumble,
Well, I mean, of course, provided:
That he liked the same champagne
    that I did.

Refrain: I'd give up ev'rything to marry
    someone I could adore
Love is the thing:
Wealth's just a bore:
Some prize it, I despise it.
All I would want would be a charge
    account at
Every store.
If I only had a Packard and a yacht,
I should be perfectly contented with
    my lot:
But I should need, of course, some
    hats and things
And furs and pearls and diamond
    rings,
But I'd ask no more.

IF THEY EVER PARTED
ME FROM YOU

(Willie and Jennie)

Willie: Life is lived by two and two.
You want me and I want you,

Jennie: Nothing counts but you and I,
If we parted, I should die

Refrain
Willie: For even a cabbage is lonesome
When there's no cornbeef around;
Shad roe finds life full of woe
If there's no bacon to be found.

| Jennie: | And a poor fried egg will nearly pass away; If it sees no ham upon the breakfast tray. |

| Both: | That is why, dear, I should feel awfully blue; If they ever parted me from you. |

| Jennie: | Two by two is nature's plan, Ricker sticks to Hegerman, |

| Willie: | Furthermore I would remark, Every Tilford has his Park. |

Refrain

| Jennie: | And even a cracker is lonesome When the cheese is nowhere near; Baked beans make terrible scenes, If ever pork does not appear. |

| Willie: | And the seltzer always feels its future's vague, When it's parted from its loving Haig and Haig. |

| Jennie: | That is why there'd be |

| Willie: | A most awful fuss, If they ever started parting us. |

Encore Refrain

| Jennie: | Even a pickle is lonesome; When the Heinz is not around. Life's dull and flat for a hat, If Truly Warner can't be found. |

| Willie: | And a cough drop finds that joy's an empty myth; If one day it fails to see the Brothers Smith. That is why, dear, I should feel awfully blue, If they ever parted me from you. |

FINALE

| All: | You never know, never know, do you, What today fortune may bring We only know it's up to us, To try our luck and make no fuss So—right or wrong come along No use waiting, hesitating. Fate you'll find may be kind to you Fate may hold any old thing We don't know what it is we've got, It may be good, it may be not! You'll know when you wind up your string. |
| | In our dear city, Life is happy and screne there: Where lovers go, When its spell they can't resist; No one will find us: For we'll leave the world behind us: In our dear city Our City of Dreams. |

Several other songs turn up in different versions of the book. When Bruce and Hilda confess their attraction for each other, they sing . . .

ISN'T IT WONDERFUL!

(Bruce and Hilda)

This was previously used as a duet for Betty and Dick in *See You Later* in April 1918, but since the show didn't reach Broadway . . .

Then, when misunderstandings drive them apart . . .

THE LAND WHERE JOURNEYS END (AND DREAMS COME TRUE)

(Bruce and Hilda)

| Bruce: | What can I say? I am going away, |

But a happier day, there will be:
Things have gone wrong,
But there's nothing so strong
That can part us for long, you and me
No need to be sad: It's not worth
    a tear:
Let's say goodbye with a smile.
It isn't so bad, for I'll still be here,
Here in my dreams all the while.

Chorus: Yes, just the same
You'll know I'm near you
Whisper my name, and I shall
    hear you;
Journeys end, they say, in lovers
    meeting.
Troubles mend some day and griefs
    are fleeting.
Life will start again, all wonderful
    and new.

Hilda: For me and you.

Bruce: Wait! And one day
We'll be together
Storms will give way,
To golden weather
Clouds will break and sunshine
    follow after:
Soon we'll live a life of love and
    laughter
In the land where journeys end and
    dreams come true.

Hilda: What can I say?
You are going away,
Yes, but still, though we may be apart,
Don't ever fear,
I'll be lonely, my dear,
For you'll always be here in my heart:
The birds in the trees, will all sing
    of you,
Just as they did when we met:
And every breeze,

Will be whisp'ring, too,
Two little words: "Don't forget!"

Chorus: Yes, just the same
I'll know you're near me.
I'll breathe your name,
And you'll hear me:
Journeys end, I know, in lovers
    meeting:
Troubles end, and woe and grief
    are fleeting:
Life will start again all wonderful
    and new:

Bruce: For me and you.

Hilda: Wait! And one day
We'll be together:
Storms will give way
To golden weather:
Clouds will break and sunshine
    follow after:
Soon, we'll live a life of love and
    laughter,
In the land where journeys end and
    dreams come true.

In Act I Bruce, Bagshott and Pop lament their lack of luck with the ladies.

WHAT'S THE USE?

(Bruce, Bagshott and Pop)

All: What's the use?
We never seem to have a bit of luck.
So, what's the use?
It doesn't (seem to) matter how we try
    to duck;
For twist and turn and wriggle as
    we may,
We are sure to stray from the narrow
    way
(When tempted)

What's the use?
If they'd not interfere, we might
    be good!
But what's the use?
They'll never let us do the things
    we should.
They come round camping on our
    trail and start in vamping;
Oh, the deuce!
What's the darned use?

Bruce: Hist'ry's pages through the ages
             Show a sad and mournful group
             Of men who women led astray;

Pop: Poor old Adam, thanks to madam
             Was as deeply in the soup
             As any husband of today.
             Cleopatra was a shatt'rer of each
             happy home she found;

Bagshott: For all her ways were deep and dark
             And her popper couldn't stop her,
             She was always hunting round
             To try and find an easy mark.

Bruce: When they put their hair up

Pop: Then it's hard to bear up;

Bagshott: Now and then
             For men.

The *Times* critic caught the general feeling about the show when he observed that it suffered by comparison with *Oh, Boy!* And *Oh, Lady! Lady!!*—"It has two exclamation points fewer than the latter and ever so much less comedy. . . . Mr. Wodehouse's lyrics, as always, are workmanlike, although somewhat less intricately rhymed than usual, and accordingly not quite the customary treat."

In *Vanity Fair*, Wodehouse's successor, Dorothy Parker, disagreed—"Mr. Wodehouse's lyrics would make anything go."

With its closing—after a respectable 189 performances—the "Princess shows" were over. The principals would go on to other things and work together in varying combinations for years to come. The theatre itself stayed open but the glory days were over and it passed through various incarnations and changes of name before the wrecker's ball finally claimed it in 1955. But for as long as there remained people who had actually seen a "Princess show," the jewel box continued to glitter in memory.

When *The Girl Behind the Gun* was staged in London in 1919, it was felt that the title would have to be changed. Producer George Grossmith advised that no one in England wanted to hear the word "gun" after the horrific war that had just ended with the loss of so many British lives. "Who anymore wanted girls behind guns?" he wrote. "We wanted them on our knees—and so the play was re-christened *Kissing Time . . .*"

When he heard the new title Guy Bolton was appalled and was only placated when Wodehouse pointed out that a song of that name had been the hit of *Chu Chin Chow* (1916)—a show that would run for more than 2,200 performances in London.

Suddenly, it seemed a *very* good title . . . and Ivan Caryll presumably thought so, too, as he composed the music for an American show of the same title but with a completely different book, which opened at the Lyric Theatre on October 11th, 1920.

KISSING TIME (1919)

(English version of *The Girl Behind the Gun*)

Presented by George Grossmith Jr. and Edward Laurillard at the Winter Garden theatre, London, on May 20, 1919 (430 performances). Wodehouse anglicized the book and Clifford Grey produced lyrics for new Ivan Caryll songs. The original three acts were reduced to two.

George Grossmith (*Max Touquet*) and Phyllis Dare (*Lucienne Touquet*) in *Kissing Time*

CAST

Captain Wentworth: STANLEY HOLLOWAY	Max Touquet: GEORGE GROSSMITH JR.
Georgette St. Pol: YVONNE ARNAUD	Lucienne Touquet: PHYLLIS DARE
Lady Mercia Merivale: ISABEL JEANS	Col. Bolinger, Georgette's Guardian: TOM WALLS
Zélie: AVICE KELHAM	
St. Pol (Bi-Bi): LESLIE HENSON	Lili, Bi-Bi, Maude, Claude, Violette, Nanette, Yvette, Nichette: DANCERS
Brichoux: GEORGE BARRETT JR.	

SYNOPSIS

The report of the reviewer to the Lord Chamberlain's Office provides the most succinct summary of the complex plot as it is possible to provide.

"The heroine, Georgette St. Pol, a popular actress, has taken as her war-time 'godson' a military cook, whom she has never seen and who has been induced to change places with an author anxious to dispose of a piece to the lady. With him she flirts outrageously in order to punish her equally flirtatious husband (Bi-Bi St. Pol), for whom he is mistaken by her newly-arrived guardian (Col. Bolinger) who has never seen any of them.

Further complications are due to this guardian's attempted love-affair with the supposed 'godson's' wife, when she turns up in search of her husband but fails to recognise him because he has shaved off his beard. There are many other flirtations and misunderstandings, all due to this French 'godmothering' system, and all leading up to a general 'kissing time.' Though husbands are temporarily left out in the cold while 'godsons' are petted, nothing more serious than this comes, or ever seems likely to come, out of it: and the compromising situations and misapprehensions are handled with dexterous propriety if not with perfect lucidity."

OPENING CHORUS—
HERE'S ANOTHER GODSON, GIRLS

(Wentworth and Girls)

Girls: Here's another godson, girls
We found him in the street
He belongs to us.

Wentworth: I won't make a fuss

Girls: We are going to share him
Don't you think he's rather
    sweet?

Wentworth: Ladies, kindly hush!
Or you'll make me blush!
Very happy I shall be now you
    have all adopted me
What a stroke of luck!

Girls: Isn't he a duck?

Wentworth: I will do the best I
    may, your
    kindness, ladies,
    to repay!
I'm so glad I'm here.

Girls: Isn't he a dear!

GODMOTHERS
AND GODSONS

(Georgette and Girls)

Georgette: Godmothers who are as
    young and fair as you
Must be circumspect!
For now and then will
    try to act like men
If they are not checked;
Be kind and sweet, when
    your godson dear
    you meet,

But take my advice,
And treat the man just as nicely as
    you can;
But don't be *too* nice.

Refrain
Georgette: You will find
There are lots of things to bear
    in mind!
In each respect, recollect!
You must be careful and correct
Turn away (Never stray)
If he tries to steal a kiss one day
(From the straight and narrow way)
Be severe
If he says that you're a perfect dear
If you mean to be a good
    godmother.

2nd refrain

Girls: Never stray
From the safe and straight and
narrow way,
If you mean to be a good
godmother
We will find
There are lots of things to bear
in mind;
In each respect, recollect!
You must be careful and correct.
Never roam
In the moonlight far from home,
If you mean to be a good
godmother

Georgette: If Godson sighs and begins to
praise your eyes
Firm measures adopt;
And understand, if he starts to
stroke your hand
It's time he was stopped;
If round your waist he a loving arm
has placed
And giv'n you a squeeze,
You'll be aware that there's danger
in the air;
Take care, if you please
You will find
There are lots of things to bear
in mind,
In each respect—recollect!
You must be careful and correct!
Never stray from the safe and
straight and narrow way
If you mean to be a real Godmother

Girls: Never stray, etc.

A HAPPY FAMILY

(Georgette, Bi-Bi and Max)

Georgette: When far from the din of the battle
Our heroes come home for a rest,

It's well understood that there's
nothing too good
For the boys who've been doing
their best.

Bi-Bi: When far from the roar and
the rattle
Of cannon they're able to roam,
We just love to get 'em,
We spoil 'em and pet 'em
We want them to feel quite
at home.

Max: I quite understand it shall be as
you've planned
I'll make myself really at home.

Georgette: My husband's cigars are worth
smoking.

Max: All right, I'll regard them as mine.

Georgette: I'll lend you a box of his favourite
socks.

Bi-Bi: Now dash it all, do draw the line.
Don't listen to her, she is joking.

Georgette: I'll lend you his brush and his comb,
His shirts I'll be airing for you to
be wearing,
(And then you will feel quite at
home)

Bi-Bi: I'm willing as Cupid to roam!

Max: Now all I need, mama's his silken
pajamas
And I shall feel really at home.
(Lend me your pyjamas)

Bi-Bi: (From Huntley and Palmer's
And then you will feel quite
at home.)

All: A happy family,
            I'm sure we're going to be.
            We'll do our best to please the guest,
            Who's come to test our little nest
            In perfect harmony
            We'll pass the time, we three.

Bi-Bi: Papa—papa!

Georgette: Mama—mama!

Max: And the baby boy—that's me!

SOME DAY WAITING WILL END

(Lucienne)

Lucienne: Tho' weary and dreary life seems
                today,
            Although the man I love is far
                away,
            Still near me to cheer me he seems
                to be
            And all the while I hear him call
                to me:
            I hear him still whispering soft
                and clear
            His message of hope and cheer,
            He says that:

Refrain: Some day waiting will end,
            Some day trouble will mend.
            We'll forget our sorrow,
            Clouds are breaking
            Will it be tomorrow?
            Hopes are waking.

Lucienne: Some day hating (sorrow) will
                cease,
            Some day there will be peace.
            (Someday—now there is peace)
            And with laughter and singing,
            And with wedding bells ringing,
            We'll drive all our cares (tears) away.

I'll only be lonely a short time
    (while) more,
For golden days I know life
    (the future) holds in store;
Though aching and breaking my
    heart may be,
I know a day of joy will come to me.
The shadows will vanish,
The sun will shine,
And his eyes will gaze in mine.
I know that:

Refrain: Some day waiting will end,
            Some day trouble will mend.
            We'll forget our sorrow
            Clouds are breaking (Life will
                be gay)
            Will it be tomorrow?
            Hope is waking. (No one can say)

            Some day now there is peace,
            Some day sorrow will cease.
            (Some day hating will cease,
            Some day there will be peace)
            And with laughter and singing
            And with wedding bells ringing
            We'll drive all our tears away.

I LIKE IT, I LIKE IT

Colonel: So many, who have married
             Unhappily, you meet,
             That when you see a couple
             So devoted, it's a treat.

Georgette: I love my darling hubby!

Lambrissac: I love my little wife!

Bi-Bi: I never felt so vicious in my life.

Colonel: No joy so great as this is
             To see a man who kisses
             His lawful wedded missus.

Bi-Bi: Where's a knife?

Colonel: I like it! I like it!
             It's charming, I maintain,
             You're like a pair of
                 sweethearts
             Who walk in Lover's
                 Lane.
             I like it! I like it!
             Go on and don't refrain
             And after you have
                 finished,
             You can start again.

Max: I like it! I like it!
             It's charming, as you say,
             No method would be
                 sweeter
             For passing time away!
             I like it! I like it!
             Your orders I'll obey
             I'll make the thing a
                 perfect hobby
                 from today.

Colonel: In days when real
                 domestic
             Felicity is rare,
             It does a fellow good to
             See a truly happy pair.

Bibi St. Pol (MR. LESLIE HENSON).   Georgette St. Pol (MISS YVONNE ARNAUD).

Max: I love my little wiffie.

Georgette: My hubby I adore!

Bi-Bi: I'm hanged if I can stand this
                 any more!

Colonel: This cooing and this billing
             Is positively thrilling
             Proceed, if you are willing,
             As before.

Georgette: I like it! I like it!
             It's charming, I agree:

             I'll hug him and embrace him,
             I'll sit upon his knee.
             I like it! I like it!
             It's just as it should be!
             This sort of thing is just the very
                 thing for me.

Bi-Bi: Don't like it! Don't like it!
             That fellow should be shot:
             Beneath my fourteen collar
             My neck is getting hot
             Don't like it!

Colonel: What!

Bi-Bi: I like it
            Oh! Yes an awful lot!
            (*Aside*) I'd like to kill them both,
            I would, upon the spot!

FINALE—
I'VE JUST COME BACK FROM PARIS

(Colonel, Max, Georgette and Bi-Bi)

Max: I've just come back from Paris,
            To spend a week at home
            I wish I could arrange it
            Never, never more to roam—
            We're like two little love-birds
            That sit and bill and coo.

Georgette: I only wish we'd nothing else to do!

Colonel: That's right my boy! You pet her!
            She wants to kiss you—let her!
            You make the world seem better

All: Oh, they do!

Max: I could go through this business ten
                times daily.

Georgette: And so could I, my pet, I'll do it
                gladly!
            Oh, Heavens! There's Zélie!
                We're lost! The game is up.

Enter Zélie in tears, because she has been refused the evening off to see her soldier boyfriend. She may enlighten the Colonel about the true situation.

Max: What shall we do? She'll give the
                game away.
            Tell her to go. Just think what she
                may say!

Colonel: Hello, hello, there! Crying?
                What's amiss?

Georgette: It's nothing, uncle, nothing

Colonel: Nothing? What's all this?

Zélie: I've a soldier boy
            Home on leave today,
            I would like to meet him
            But I cannot get away

Chorus: Isn't that a shame? Here she has
                to stay
            For Georgette won't let her have
                a holiday.

Zélie: I haven't seen my soldier boy
            Since we parted last July.
            I've sent him cakes and things
                to eat,
            And big cigars for a special treat.

Chorus: But what good is that if they
                can't meet?
            It's no wonder that you cry.
            (It's enough to make you cry)
            Won't you let her off to go today
            To her boy from the trenches
                far away?

Colonel: Come, come, Georgette my dear!
            Have you no heart?
            How can you keep these poor young
                things apart?

Georgette: It's all right, uncle dear, (Guardian)
                I have changed my mind,
            She may go now, I wouldn't be
                unkind.

Chorus: She hasn't seen her soldier boy
            Since they parted last July—
            She's sent him cakes and things
                to eat

And big cigars for a special treat.
But what good is that if they
    can't meet?
It's no wonder that they cry
    (It's enough to make you cry)
Won't they let her off to go today
    (So they're going to let her off
    today)
To her boy from the trenches
    far away!

Colonel: But wait before you go!
One thing I want to know:
There's just one point we must
    discuss;
Who's going to cook the lunch for us?
As far as I can see,
There's only just we three.

Max: Papa, papa!

Georgette: Mamma, mamma!

Colonel: And the handsome guest—
    that's me!

All: But wait before we go:
One thing he wants to know:
I'm sure he's going to make a fuss,
If no one cooks the lunch for us.
It's easy as can be,
There's only just we three
Papa, mamma,
And the handsome guest that's he.

(Zélie indicates Bi-Bi)

Colonel: Come here, my lad. No slacking!
We've got a job for you
Get busy in the kitchen,
And let's see what you can do.
You've got to cook the luncheon,
And serve it on a tray—

Bi-Bi: Oh, Gosh! I think my hair is
    turning grey!

Max: The kitchen's there. Get in it,
Don't waste a single minute,
We're waiting to begin it.

Bi-Bi: What a day!

Max: You'll like it.

Georgette: You'll like it.

Max: He'll cook you something good.
He's certain to do wonders.

Bi-Bi: I only wish I could!

Colonel: I'll like it! I'll like it!
I have no doubt of that.

Bi-Bi: I don't know how to cook enough
    to feed a cat!

Chorus: You'll like it! You'll like it!
He'll cook you something good.
Until you've tried his cooking
You've never tasted food
You'll like it!
You'll like it
Pray have no doubt of that.
We hear his cooking is a thing to
    wonder at!

(Everyone looks expectantly at Bi-Bi as the curtain falls)

ACT 2—Opening Chorus

WOULDN'T YOU LIKE US ALL TO HELP YOU?

(Bi-Bi and Girls)

1st Girl: Wouldn't you like us all to help you?

Girls: What is he reading? Oh, look here!

Bi-Bi: Somebody took my cookery book!
            Please give it me back, my dear.

2nd Girl: Wouldn't you like us all to help you?

Girls: If you entreat us, we will stay.

Bi-Bi: Really you know, I wish you would go,
            You're very much in the way.

1st Girl: He seems in quite a state!

Girls: Poor dear! he's losing weight!

Bi-Bi: Oh! it's too bad! you'll drive me mad!
            I want to concentrate!
            So run away girls! I've got no time
            To stand and talk to you,
            I've got to collect by hook or crook
            Some hints from this darned
                cookery-book.
            I started a stew that tasted like glue,
            I'll have to change it . . . Say!
            Run away!

Girls: Oh, isn't he rude to say such things
            And talk like that to us!
            That isn't the way to speak or look!
            I never saw a surlier cook!
            I cannot see why he makes such a fuss;
            What right has he to say:
            "Run away!"

1st Girl: How many plates have you been
                breaking?

Girls: Did you clean all the knives today?

Bi-Bi: Speaking of knives, you're risking
                your lives
            By hanging around this way!

2nd Girl: There is no need to get excited!

Girls: If I were you, I'd be polite!

Bi-Bi: If I were you, with nothing to do
            And nothing to cook, I *might!*

1st Girl: How rude some men can be!

Girls: The same thought just struck *me!*

Bi-Bi: Stewed prunes with fish—a dainty
                dish—
            Consult page twenty-three.
            Oh, run away, girls! I've got no time
            To stand and talk to you!
            Do give me a chance to take a look
            At this confounded cookery book.
            I might have got through a page
                or two,
            If you'd not come here . . . Say!
            Run away!

Girls: I'm sorry we came to try to help
            This most ungrateful man!
            Our kindly intentions he mistook,
            I never saw a sillier cook,
            We'll let him get on as best as he can!
            What right has he to say:
            "Run away!"

(Girls exit)

OH, HOW WARM IT IS TODAY

(Colonel, Georgette, Max and Bi-Bi)

Colonel: Oh, how wonderful 'twould be, you
                must agree,
            If when next I pay a visit, I should
                see
            Half a dozen kiddies playing round
                your knees.

Georgette: Just a moment, uncle! (Guardie)
            Won't you have some cheese?

Colonel: Yes, how splendid it would be, as
            I just said!

Lambrissac: May I offer you another slice of
            bread?

Colonel: Let me finish, please, what I was
            going to say.

Georgette &
Max: Oh, how warm, how very warm it
            is today!

Colonel: Were . . .
            I in your position, I'd have one
            ambition:
            Just to found a family.
            You would find me daily cultivating
            gaily
            Branches on the family tree.

(*To Max*)
            Damme! it's your duty! You're a
            pretty beauty
            Shirking in this idle way!
            Come along—get action! Give me
            satisfaction. . . .

Georgette &
Max: Oh, how warm it is today!

Georgette: This is a nice position:
            His only ambition
            Is to see a family

Max: Did you hear him stating
            That he was awaiting
            Branches on a family tree!

Georgette: Jumping to conclusions
            Leads to these confusions,
            But there's nothing we can say.

Max: Don't try explanation,
            Get him at the station.

Georgette &
Max: Oh, how warm it is today.

Colonel: Yes, I seem to see that sturdy
            little band,
            Playing round here in the garden
            hand in hand!
            I can hear them prattle round the
            nurs'ry fire.

Max: You can *what*? Ring off? You're on
            a busy wire!
            (Please ring off: I think you're on
            a busy wire!)

Colonel: Won't you try to have some news
            for me next year?

Georgette: Won't you try another radish,
            Guardie dear?

Colonel: Very soon, no doubt, I'll hear they're
            on their way.

Georgette &
Max: Oh, how warm, how very warm it
            is today!

Colonel: I'm . . .
            . . . Just a plain old buffer, you may
            think me rougher
            Than I've any need to be,
            When I feel sincerely, I speak
            pretty clearly,
            Call a spade a spade—that's me!
            Don't believe in screening, wrapping
            up my meaning
            What I have to say, I *say!*
            Come now, time is flying, there's no
            harm *trying*

Georgette &
Max: Oh, how warm it is today!

Max:	Each moment it gets tougher.

Georgette:	I know how you suffer!

Max:	Yes, it's awful I agree,	(Bi-Bi: Why not pity little me?
	Risk his indignation	I don't want a stranger
	Change the conversation	Trying to arrange a
	Other subjects there must be	Future for my family tree)

Georgette:	Couldn't we together Talk about the weather?

Max:	That might burn his thoughts away. Any topic, go on! Politics or so on. (Bi-Bi: If he doesn't chuck it, Hit him with a bucket!)

Georgette & Max:	Oh, how warm it is today!

SOME DAY, NEVER FORGET

(Colonel and Lucienne)

Lucienne:	Some day, never forget I may marry you; yet, I've not quite decided To surrender. But I will, provided You are tender; Someday wait just a while I may walk down the aisle; To your arm I'll be clinging, And with wedding bells ringing, It might happen.

Colonel:	When?

Lucienne:	Some day.

(An Officer enters)

Officer:	Sir, important message from the War Office.

Colonel:	By Jove! What luck, I have just been demobilized. There's no need for me to hurry away, I can stop here for A month with my dear children.

Georgette & Max:	Oh! Heavens!

Bi-Bi:	Oh! Hell. . . .

Colonel:	There's not a doubt of it, I'm happy to be out of it! Of course you've just heard,

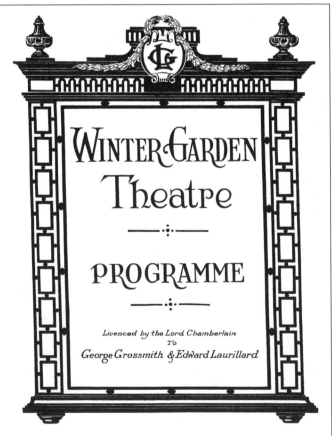

I'll command again a lot of
Splendid fighting men,
The "Forty -Third."

Georgette: I dread to think the danger
   you're under,
   Right in the midst of battle's
   awful thunder.

Lucienne: Should you fearful be.
   Will you think of me,
   I wonder?
   I am sure that you have great
   ability
   And courage and stability
   When you command.

Max: Girls go mad about the way he
   throws the Huns about.

Bi-Bi: Give me your hand.

Colonel: So my luck I will try once more:
   Just you I'm fighting for
   I'm a veteran. Don't forget
   That there's fight in the old
   dog yet.

Alternative:

Colonel: There's no doubt of it,
   I'm happy to be out of it!
   Of course you've heard
   I've just been advised today
   They have been demobilized—
   The Forty-Third!

Georgette: I'm glad to think no danger you
   are under,
   No more you'll hear the battle's
   awful thunder.

Colonel: Now that you are free,
   Will you think of me,
   I wonder!

Winter Garden Theatre,
DRURY LANE, W.C. 2.
Licensed by the Lord Chamberlain to
GEORGE GROSSMITH AND EDWARD LAURILLARD.
Telephone : Gerrard 416 (3 lines).

OPENING PERFORMANCE
By GEORGE GROSSMITH and EDWARD LAURILLARD
On TUESDAY, the 20th of May, 1919, at 8 o'clock.

(Alterations and Decorations by Messrs. WHITE, ALLOM & Co., 15, George Street, Hanover, Square, W.)

Messrs. GEORGE GROSSMITH and EDWARD LAURILLARD
PRESENT
"KISSING TIME"
A NEW MUSICAL PLAY, IN TWO ACTS,
By GUY BOLTON and P. G. WODEHOUSE.
Founded on the French Play "Madame et son Filleul," by HENNEQUIN and WEBER.
Additional Lyrics by CLIFFORD GREY.   Music by IVAN CARYLL.
At this first performance Mr. IVAN CARYLL will conduct.

THE CAST.

Captain Wentworth ..				Mr. STANLEY HOLLOWAY
Georgette St. Pol ..				Miss YVONNE ARNAUD
Lady Mercia Merivale				Miss ISOBEL JEANS
Zelie ..				Miss AVICE KELHAM
Bibi St. Pol ..				Mr. LESLIE HENSON
Brichoux				Mr. GEORGE BARRETT
Max Touquet	of the 33rd Regiment			Mr. GEORGE GROSSMITH
Lucienne Touquet ..				Miss PHYLLIS DARE
Colonel Bolinger ..				Mr. TOM WALLS

Police Officer	.. Mr. M. Edmond		Rastaquouere	..Mr. Harold Bedford
Military Police	{ Mr. Stanley Brightman		Cabotin ..	.. Mr. Frank Iverson
	Mr. Frank Lester		Flaneur ..	.. Mr. Austin Camp
Vieux Marcheur	..Mr. Campbell Keith		Violette ..	.. Miss Lila Wood
Chef d'Orchestre	Mr. James Whigham		Yvette ..	.. Miss Eileen Darton
Maitre d'Hotel	Mr. Charles Buckmaster		Babette ..	Miss Gladys Ponsonby
Lord Bill ..	.. Mr. Ralph Coram		Nanette ..	.. Miss Eileen Joyce
Apache ..	.. Mr. George Stevens		Michette ..	.. Miss Dux Davies
Officers ..	{ Mr. Lyn Perring		Lillie ..	Miss Liza Varvara
	{ Mr. Pat Carnarvon		Bibi ..	Miss Marie Sewell
	{ Mr. Hugh Lyndhurst	Dancers	Maudie ..	Miss Sybil Furley
Walters ..	{ Mr. Harold Ritch		Claudie ..	Miss Dorie Pickton-Phillip
	Mr. Tim O'Connor		Vestiare ..	.. Miss Joan Emney
Porter ..	..Mr. Peter Shannon		Little Paul ..	.. Miss Yvonne Bose
Chasseur ..	.. Mr. Gerald Knott		Little Marie ..	.. Miss May Wilcox

and Full Chorus.

The names of the Artistes are placed in the order in which they appear in the play.

Lucienne: All I ask is pardon my simplicity,
   I trust you most implicitly
   Now you are here.

All: We'll all meet in town,
   We'll simply turn it upside down!
   I want to cheer,
   So my luck I will try once more,
   For you're worth waiting for.
   Get together and show them how
   And we'll all have a good time now!

THERE'S A LIGHT IN YOUR EYES

(Max and Lucienne)

Max: Since first, my dear, I met you
   The shrine wherein I set you

Has sacred to me grown;
That shrine that's all your own
I never shall forget you.
I'll live for you alone
And carry in my heart my whole life
   through,
This picture of you.

Refrain: There's a light in your eyes,
On your lips there's a smile,
And you seem all the while
To be yielding in tender surrender,
And love dreams arise, ever sweet,
   ever new,
Till my heart to you flies,
Till my soul for you sighs.
And I would pluck the stars from
   the skies
For one kiss from you.

Each night I lie a-dreaming,
False dreams in which you're
   seeming
My own, my very own;
I awake—and I'm alone!
I see your dear eyes gleaming:
I wake—and you have flown!
The mocking dawn proclaims my
   dreams untrue,
And robs me of you!

Refrain
Lucienne: There's a light in your eyes, etc.

Some versions of the libretto have another
number for Wentworth . . .

THAT TICKING TAXI'S WAITING AT THE DOOR

(Wentworth and Girl)

Wentworth: Modern times are trying times for
   lovers, you'll agree,
Don't you wish the world
   contained only you and me?

All my burning thoughts, my own,
I'd love with you to share,
But I can't afford to, for I'm no
   millionaire.

Girl: Everything is such a rush, it's hard
   to bill and coo
Don't you wish the world
   contained only me and you
Just to say: "I love you!" would be
   comforting and nice?
But the taxi's at the door. Is it
   worth the price?

Wentworth: I would gladly sit on here
With you, dear, for a year!
But it can't be done, I fear,
Altho' the fact I much deplore

If I had more time, you know,
I would show, I'm not slow,
Like a second Romeo. I'd sing you
    love songs by the score.

Girl: Yes, my darling angel pet,
          Do not let us forget
          We've a taxi, I regret,
          That's waiting, waiting at the door.
          Singing love songs is an art,
          But, dear heart, do not start!
          I could never play my part
          While there's a taxi at the door.

Wentworth: At the door!

Girl: What a bore!

Wentworth: Here a tick!

Girl: Quick, quick, quick.

Both: Oh!
          How aggravating

The taxi's waiting
It goes on tick, tick, tick, tick,
    ticking all the time;
And my devotion, and my
    emotion
I can't express for that would cost
    another dime.
It cramps my style, dear,
I try to smile, dear,
But still the bill, I feel,
Is growing more and more,
I can't forget, dear,
That all the while, dear,
The ticking taxi's waiting at
    the door.

While the British were busy kissing *The Girl Behind the Gun*, Wodehouse and Bolton took a trip to China—and regretted it ever after. It was the China of musical comedy and their by-now-annual offering to Comstock, although this was not to be staged at the Princess but New York's Lyric Theatre.

THE ROSE OF CHINA (1919)

A Romantic Musical Comedy
(Working Title: *The Rose of Cathay*)

Presented by Ray Comstock and Morris Gest at the Lyric Theatre, New York, on November 25, 1919 (47 performances).

BOOK Guy Bolton
(Based on *East Is West* by Samuel Shipman)
LYRICS P. G. Wodehouse
MUSIC Armand Vecsey

CAST

Dum Tong, gardener:
PAUL IRVING

Ton Ka, a Chinese dancer:
LOUISE BROWNEL

Ling Tao: JANE RICHARDSON

Ting-Fang-Lee:
STANLEY RIDGES

Tsao Ling:
WILLIAM H. PRINGLE

Tommy Tilford:
OSCAR SHAW

Wilson Peters:
FRANK MCINTYRE

Polly Baldwin:
CECIL CUNNINGHAM

Priest: LEO DWYER

Chung, Tommy's servant:
THOS. E. JACKSON

Grace Hobson:
CYNTHIA PEROT

Mrs. Hobson, her mother:
EDNA MAY OLIVER

SYNOPSIS

The Garden of the Mandarin's Palace ("Opening Chorus—Sunrise Intermezzo"). Lee enters and tells the Girls about his happy years at Yale ("Yale"). Ling Tao, the Mandarin's daughter, tells them she hopes to find a husband—with her lucky rabbit's foot to help her ("Bunny, Dear"). At that moment Tommy Tilford climbs over the wall. He has just saved an American girl from the mob and is on the run. He tells Ling girls make him shy and she tells him the legend of the Tea Tree ("A Chinese Adam and Eve"). Tommy's friend, Wilson Peters, arrives with the news that Tommy's guardian, Henry Hobson, is arriving to arrange the wedding to his daughter, Grace. Tommy, Wilson and Lee invoke the old college spirit ("College Spirit"). Polly Baldwin— the American girl Tommy saved—now arrives. She is in China to find the "mail order" husband who jilted her, and Wilson looks a likely candidate. He, however, is flirting with Ling, who tells him his feelings are caused by the Rose of China. Its scent makes people fall in love. Wilson kisses her, much to Ling's horror. Such an act destroys her caste. Now she may only marry the man who kissed her. When her father demands the man's name, she names Tommy, the man she loves.

Ling prepares for her marriage to Tommy ("Little Bride"). Tommy—now two small steps from bigamy!—has signed Wilson's name on the wedding

certificate but he is now falling in love with Ling ("Our Chinese Bungalow").
Polly searches for Wilson, who, naturally, now pretends to be Tommy but is by
now finding her attractive ("Proposals"). Meanwhile, the Hobsons are preparing
for the wedding. They want the Chinese Bridesmaids to dance like Americans
("American Jazz"). Tommy and Ling reflect on how quickly things have happened ("Yesterday"). Ling's father has found out about Tommy's engagement
to Grace. This disgraces his daughter and he drags her away ("Ling Tao's
Farewell").

The girls sing of their sadness ("The Land of the White Poppy").
Wilson and Polly plan their future ("Down on the Banks of the Subway").
Grace releases Tommy from his engagement, so that he can marry Ling
("Love Is A Wonderful Feeling"), but Ling has vanished. As her loved ones
search for her, she tells her friend, the Gardener, she is going away for ever
("Broken Blossoms"). But, of course, when Tommy finds her, they are
reunited.

OPENING CHORUS— SUNRISE INTERMEZZO

Shadows fly from valley and plain
Look, Lord, the Sun is risen again.
His throne he's ascended.
Glowing and splendid:
Darkness and night are ended
Humbly our knees are bended:
Homage we bring to the King:
We sing to greet our King.
Hark to our cry,
Oh, Sun, enthroned on high.
Sun be kind to us, we pray:
Bring happiness today.

Wake him up: for, while he dozes,
Caterpillars creep
And eat the tender blossoms of the roses.
He must work, not sleep.

Hullo, there,
Shirker, wake and
Take your rake and
Start your labors
Like your neighbours.
They are working.
They're not shirking.
Start your labors
Like your neighbours.

Sacred rose-trees, mystical rose,
With respect we bow and we pray:
May no slug or bug with shameless
    appetite
Eat your petals today.
May no bad greenfly disturb your repose,
Nor too fiercely shine the sun:
May you rest in peace until the shadows
    close
And the long, long day is done.

YALE

(Lee and Girls)

Lee: Though from fair New Haven
I have had to part,
Have I forgot?
I'll say I've not.
Still that name's engraven
Neatly upon my heart:
Though far away,
Still I am dreaming of it night
  and day.
After every meal I
Cheer for dear old Eli:
In my tub I never fail
While I scrub, to think of Yale.

Girls: Oh, won't you tell us, please,
All about wonderful Yale?

Refrain
Lee: Yale!
Some day you must make a trip to it.
Yale!
There's nothing else on the map.
Why, it was just the thought of
  finding room for Yale
Made Columbus sail for America

Girls: Yes, that made it worth his trouble.

Lee: Yale!
The very name has a zip to it.
Yale!
It's full of ginger and snap.
Though I am modest by nature, gee,
  I feel a whale
When I think that I once went
  to Yale.

Go to fair New Haven:
That's the only way
To get your name
In Halls of Fame.

Poe, who wrote *The Raven*,
Might have made writing pay
And got some kale
If he had only had a course at Yale.
Though Napoleon's fighting
Made things quite exciting,
He'd have turned the foemen pale
If he'd learned his job at Yale.

BUNNY, DEAR

(Ling Tao and Girls)

Ling Tao: There's a genie that inhabits,
So Amellican wise men say,
August foot of hon'rable rabbits
When the bunny has passed away.
If you pray to him polite
And take the foot like this in your
  right hand,
He will welly kindly do, all that you
  ask him to.
Bunny show me how;
Make a magic now!

Refrain: Bunny dear, hear me,
This is quite private:
Bring me a nice young man!
Bring him to cheer me:
You can contrive it
Oh yes, I know you can!
I would not dream of bothering you,
Bunny dear, only I am so lonely.
Do what you can, please,
Bring me a man, please,
Bunny dear, bring him here, Oh do!
Now Ling Tao want you to send her
Someone tall just about like this.
Someone nice and plitty and slender,
Not want any one short and fat.
Let his hair be dark and curly,
Please make haste!
Deliver him early!
It is all the same to you,

Let his eyes be blue.
Bring him, Bunny dear,
I'll be waiting here.

TAO LOVED HIS LI
(A CHINESE ADAM AND EVE/
THE LEGEND OF THE TEA-TREE)

(Tommy, Ling Tao and Girls)

Ling: Down in a garden, fair and scented
        Li and Tao, quite contented,
        Spent their life man and wife—
        No one but just they two.

Tommy: Ev'rywhere enchanted trees were
          planted,
        Flowers too, of every hue.

Ling: Oh! But it was gay, and so they say.

Both: That's where the tea-tree grew.

Girls: The tea-tree grew.

Tommy: When the sun was in the West
        And birds and flowers had gone
          to rest,
        They'd sit beneath the tree, just he
          and she
        And drink their tea.

Ling: While the little tree swayed to and fro
        And whisp'ring low, shed its white
          blossom light
        On the head of Li and Tao.

Tommy: Tao loved his Li.

Ling: Li loved Tao, too.

Both: They were happy there in that garden
          fair,
        Trouble, sorrow and care they never
          knew.

Girls: They never knew.

Both: Tao and his Li sipped their magic tea,
        And their hearts were gay as they
          went their way,
        All alone in the garden there
          together.

Ling: But the great Joss his heart did
          harden,
        Drove those lovers from the garden.

Tommy: Sadly they went away into a world
          all new

Ling: Sorrowfully weeping, softly creeping,
        Went those two the garden through,
        Slowly till at last the spot they passed.

Both: Down where the tea-tree grew.

Girls: The tea-tree grew.

Tommy: Tao tore a branch away
        And bore it in his hand, they say
        "'Twill grow into a tree," said he to Li,
        "For you and me."

Ling: That is why all Chinamen today are
          taught to pray
        And to think, while they drink
          grateful thoughts
        Of Li and Tao

Tommy: Tao loved his Li,

Ling: Li loved Tao more

Both: Though their hopes were dim,
        And the future grim,
        She was happy with him just as
          before.

Girls: Just as before

Both: Tao and his Li
Sipped their magic tea,
And their hearts were light
And the world seemed bright,
Just so long as they knew
They were together

COLLEGE SPIRIT

(Tommy, Wilson and Lee)

Tommy: Oh, how sweet it is, you really must
acknowledge,
When you come on a College chum.

Wilson: When I meet a man from Yonkers
Business College,
I admit that I weep a bit.

Lee: If I can help a college man,
There is nothing that I wouldn't do.

Wilson: If he should make a touch,
Would you lend him much?

Lee: All he asked me to.

Tommy &
Wilson: Now you've said it, it does you credit.

Refrain   College spirit! The great uniter,
It seems to make life brighter
And hearts grow lighter.
Once you get it,
You won't regret it
It's always fair weather,
When good fellows get together.

Lee: Oh! When I think of Yale
That I loved so well.

Wilson: Oh! When I hear that dear old
Business College Yell!
Oh! Baby!

All: O'er me stealing,
I'm not concealing
There comes a feeling more sweet
than words can tell.

Second Verse

Lee: Collegemen who've not forgot their
Alma Mater,
You will find, yes, of ev'ry kind.

Tommy: Now and then while lunching
You will see your waiter give the grip
And refuse a tip.

Wilson: What is more, my old janitor,
When he found I belonged to his Frat.
Said he would send up heat
As a special treat.

Lee: When I took the flat.

Tommy &
Lee: If he said it, it does him credit.

Refrain

WHAT! WHAT! WHAT!

(Polly and Tommy)

This would appear to be a variant of the song of the same name in *Ladies, Please!*

LITTLE BRIDE

(Ling Tao and Girls)
(Lyric Missing)

IN OUR BUNGALOW
(OUR CHINESE BUNGALOW)

(Ling Tao and Tommy)

Ling Tao: Let's find a little nest
Where we'll have peace and rest
With none to interfere;

Tommy: Yes, that idea's the best.
          To some far spot we'll go away,
          Out in the jungle,
          And build a little bungalow,
          For oh! I love to bungle.

Both: In our . . .

Refrain: . . . Tiny, six by nine-y bungalow
          In our Chinee, yours and mine-y
              bungalow.

Tommy: We will live on love and kisses,
          And how quick the time will go.

Both: In our breeze-y free and easy,
          Hug and squeeze-y will you please-y,
          Come and sit up on my knees-y
              Bungalow.

Ling Tao: There in our cozy nook,
          I'll have to learn to cook,
          And know the price of rice,
          And keep a market book.

Tommy: Hard work you'll leave to me,
          If you respect my wishes.
          So I'll go out and feed the bee,
          While you wash up the dishes.

Both: In our . . .

Refrain: . . . Cozy, dream and dozy bungalow,
          In our cozy peach and rosy bungalow.

Tommy: Ev'ry night I'll put the cat out,
          Then to bye-bye we will go.

Both: In our dewy bill and coo-ey
          Just we two-ey
          I and you-ey
          Ev'ry thing quite "*entre nous*-ey"
              bungalow.

PROPOSALS

(Polly, Wilson and Lee)
(Lyric Missing)

AMERICAN JAZZ

(Grace and Bridesmaids)
(Lyric Missing)

YESTERDAY

(Ling Tao and Tommy)

Ling: Great big Joss who lives in the sky,
          Always answer prayers by and by,
          Makes his magic oh, welly quick.

Tommy: Yes, just like a conjuring trick!
          He's a sudden kind of Joss,
          Moves with a spring;
          When he puts a job across,
          He does it, bing!
          Oh, yes, I'll say he takes your breath
              away!
          Yesterday our paths were still divided
          Yesterday you knew no more than
              I did,
          That fate was wond'ring whether
          To bring us two together.
          Fate never mentions its kind
              intentions.

Ling: Yesterday Ling Tao tired of
              hoping,
          Went her way all miserable and
              moping,
          And oh! Her heart was aching!
          Though smiling face she making,
          How strange to think that was only
              yesterday

Tommy: Lightning's slow compared to your
              Joss
          He's a lad who gathers no moss.
          He is a hustler, I will allow
          Quite a whale on doing it now!

Ling: Joss has great big heart right there.
        Send me my mate
        Heard Ling Tao make her prayer,
        He didn't wait.

Tommy: I know! Agreed! He shows some flash
            of speed!
        Yesterday I never even knew you,
        Yesterday my name meant nothing
            to you.
        We lived at quite a distance
        A separate existence,
        Until this morning
        We had no warning.

Ling: Yesterday the world had nothing in it,
        Sad and gray Ling Tao found each
            minute;
        When birds above were winging,
        She never heard their singing.
        How strange to think that was only
            yesterday.

LING TAO'S FAREWELL

(Ling Tao)
(Lyric Missing)

THE LAND OF THE WHITE POPPY

(Girls)
(Lyric Missing)

DOWN ON THE BANKS
OF THE SUBWAY

(Wilson and Polly)

Polly: Although it is the fashion,
         I'm given to understand,
         I've never had a passion
         To live in Dixieland.

Wilson: And I could never see the charm
         Of what they call the dear old farm.

There's only one locality
That makes a hit with me.

Refrain   Down by the banks of the
              Subway
          Where the motorbuses wait,
          Where all around
          There is not a sound,
          Except the janitor
          Calling to his mate,
          We will live and we'll love there
              together,
          And our life will be *couleur de rose.*
          Yes, we'll dwell there quite
              content,
          Till the landlord wants the rent,
          Down where the subway flows.

Polly: Upon the Rapid Transit
         We'll travel hand in hand.

Wilson: There's nowhere where you *can* sit,
         And so we'll have to stand!

Polly: But mostly we shall have to hike,
         Because there's been a traffic
             strike.

Wilson: The men have all walked out,
             so you
         And . . .

Polly: I must walk out too.

         Although it brought depression,
         And misery to some,
         When Congress met in session
         And soaked the Demon Rum,

Wilson: Resourceful folk like you and me
         A way to beat the game can see
         We'll keep our courage up and try
         To brew our own supply.

LOVE IS A WONDERFUL FEELING

(Tommy and Girls)

I used to think that I was smart
In never having lost my heart:
And, every time a girl would smile,
I'd climb a tree or run a mile;
But now I find that I was wrong:
For love, I'll tell the world I'm strong
Just paste these words inside your hat,
"True love's all right!" And more than that

It's wonderful! It's wonderful!
It's absolutely grand!
It makes you go all quivery,
All-overish and shivery!
When you are feeling livery,
It makes your soul expand;
It's wonderful! It's wonderful!
It's absolutely grand!

Love's microbe's working all the
    time,
In every land, in every clime;
Till leagues of nations, by degrees
Go in for freedom of the squeeze,
It works in France, it works in
    Spain,
It works on Russia's icy plain
And when it bites a Bolshevik,
These simple words you'll hear
    him speak!

"It's wonderful!
It's wonderful!"
He murmurs, "Oh, you kid-o-
    vitch,
I'm fairly off my lid-o-vitch!
In short, you understand
It's wonderful! It's wonderful!
It's absolutely grand.

(See *Ladies, Please!*)

BROKEN BLOSSOMS

(Ling)

The Joss has spoken.
My dream has broken;
My vision splendid,
Is done and ended,
For dreams, alas, when they are broken
Can't be mended;
The dawn is breaking
And hope forsaking;
Alone, alone I'm waking
With a heart all sad and aching
To meet the cruel day.

Different versions of the libretto and program raise a number of questions about certain songs.

In Washington—immediately prior to Broadway—there was a song in Act 1 called "Romeo and Juliet." This was replaced by "What! What! What!" which would seem to be from the unproduced *Ladies, Please*. The same show also provided the song Tommy sings in Act 3—"Love Is A Wonderful Feeling" ("It's Absolutely Grand"). The program indicates a song in that same position for Tommy and the Girls called "My China Rose," which suggests a totally different lyric.

Again, according to the program, Act 2 has a song for Ling, Tommy, Grace and Mrs. Hobson called "When You Are In China," whereas the libretto has "American Jazz." Although the habit of giving a song several different titles was prevalent, this also seems to suggest different content.

Also in Act 2—and apparently lost—are "Little Bride" (Ling & Ensemble), "Finale/Ling's Farewell"; while Act 3 has "Spirit of the Drum" (Ton Ka & Girls)—replaced in the libretto by "The Land of the White Poppy," a number for the Girls.

If there was any chance of too much success going to the collective heads of Bolton & Wodehouse, then *The Rose of China* provided a valuable antidote. Being wise after the event, Wodehouse considered it "a musical version of a lousy—in my opinion—but very successful play . . . done in 1918. . . . I think it's frightful." In *Bring On The Girls* he added—

"The writing of this blot on the New York theatrical scene was due entirely to too much rich food, too much potent liquor and the heady effect of Oriental music on top of these . . . the music was that of Armand Vecsey, rendered by himself in the Oval Room of the Ritz-Carlton Hotel, where he was *chef d'orchestre*. . . .

"The advice that should be given to all aspiring young authors is: have nothing to do with a title like *The Rose of China* or *The Willow Pattern Plate* or *The Siren of Shanghai* or *Me Velly Solly* . . . in fact, avoid Chinese plays altogether. Much misery may thus be averted.

"What happens when you write a Chinese play is that before you know where you are your heroine has gone cute on you, adding just that touch of glucose to the part which renders it unsuitable for human consumption. She twitters through the evening saying, 'Me Plum Blossom. Me good girl. Me love Chlistian god velly much' and things of that sort."

In retrospect he would claim that without referring back to the script—something he was squeamish about doing—he could not recall whether or not the heroine "turned out in the end to be the daughter of an American missionary, kidnapped by Chinese bandits in her infancy, but it would seem virtually certain that she did. All heroines of Chinese plays turn out in the end to be the daughters of American missionaries, kidnapped by Chinese bandits in their infancy. There is no reason to suppose that in this instance there should have been any deviation from the straight party line." In point of fact, Ling Tao was all too Chinese.

For all the jokes, the scar clearly went deep.

What the Broadway run of 47 performances obscured was the fact that the show had been popular in tryout and would be equally popular on tour. Perhaps the verdict that would please Wodehouse most, however, was the *Times*'s verdict that his rhyming of "Los Angeles" and "man jealous" was "probably the greatest single achievement of its kind this season." Sadly, the lyric that contained it must be one of those that have disappeared.

There was to be a rather bizarre postscript nearly a decade later. Ziegfeld suddenly felt he must have a musical version of *East Is West*—

presumably he had been out of town when *The Rose of China* was briefly in. Or perhaps, being Ziegfeld, he felt only he could do it properly.

The book was to be by his favorite librettist, William Anthony McGuire, the lyrics (again) by Wodehouse and the music by Vincent Youmans ("if he ever gets around to doing any," Wodehouse wrote to a friend).

In the same account he persists in the story that the heroine turns out to be the daughter of an American missionary after all and goes on . . .

"I am collaborating on the lyrics with a very pleasant lad named Billy Rose, who broke into the Hall of Fame with a song entitled 'Does the Chewing-Gum Lose Its Flavour On the Bedpost Overnight?' As far as I can make out, Billy and I are the only members of the gang who are doing a stroke of work. I go round to his hotel every morning and we hammer out a lyric together and turn it in to Youmans, after which nothing more is heard of it." (Sadly, the results of the collaboration are not to be found in either the Wodehouse or the Billy Rose archives.)

THE LITTLE THING
(1916–1920)

(Unproduced)

BOOK Guy Bolton and P. G. Wodehouse
LYRICS P. G. Wodehouse
MUSIC Jerome Kern

A show with the working title of *The Little Thing* was to be a *leitmotiv* in the combined careers of Bolton and Wodehouse and Kern. It was one of their first two submissions to producer Ray Comstock—a story about a poor girl who works as a dishwasher but who dreams of becoming a star on the musical stage. In early 1916 Comstock turned the idea down in synopsis form.

Then came the Princess shows and steadily the balance in the relationship changed. After *Oh, Lady! Lady!!* (1918), when the team were looking for the next subject, Bolton suggested it again, and again Comstock vetoed the idea. Undeterred, the trio revised the piece in June of that year, taking advantage of the current World War I jingoism that was in the air. Few Broadway shows lacked a flag-waving scene in the patriotic tradition George M. Cohan had done so much to establish.

Although he could no longer afford to turn their submissions down out of hand, Comstock found it hard to warm to what was now an unashamedly anti-war satire. Having mulled it over politely, he rejected *The Little Thing* for the third and last time.

SYNOPSIS

Only the second act of this version has survived and it makes bizarre reading indeed. Sally, the heroine, dreams she is involved with German spies, mysterious gypsy women, a secret formula for explosives and . . . Sherlock Holmes!

Sally eventually captures the spies, saves the world and is commended by President Wilson.

Back in the real world all the characters turn out to be versions of people she actually knows—rather like *The Wizard of Oz*. She is now in England with the war going on around her and a mission to show people that they must look for life's silver linings and be content to do the "little things" that will help win the war. She herself ends up taking a temporary job as a dishwasher as her own contribution to the war effort.

The main love interest is provided by her friends, Jack and Sally. Jack decides to volunteer to fight and the two girls speed him on his way . . .

WHEN YOU COME BACK

(Claire, Sally and Jack)

Claire: You're going away;
But still I know
You're sure to come back safe;

Sally: Well, I should say!
Yea, bo!

Claire: And on that day
When war is over,

Sally: Step round this way!
You'll find yourself in clover.

Claire: When you come back, dear, nothing
will be too good for you;

Sally: We'll pet you when we get you—
yes, that's what we'll do

Claire: I'll put your slippers on for you and
light your cigar, pet.

Sally: And let you drop your ashes on the
parlour carpet;

Both: Nothing will be too good for you
When you come back.

Claire: While you're away
I'll write to you;
I'll send you twenty pages every
day;

Sally: Me, too!

Jack: And from the start
I'll keep each letter
Close to my heart

Sally: Tucked underneath his sweater.

Jack: When I come back, dear, nothing will
be too good for you;
You bet I shan't forget how brave
you've been and true;
Each morning I will prove afresh how
much I adore you;

Sally: He means that he'll get up and light
the furnace for you.

Jack: Nothing will be too good for you
When I get back.

There was another trio for them that anticipated "Nerves" in *See You Later* (1918) . . .

EVERYTHING LOOKS DIFFERENT IN THE DARK

(Sally, Claire and Jack)

Jack: Oh, when the sun is beaming
         With courage I am teeming;
         No lion, however brave it be,
         Has anything on me.

Claire: And I am never nervous
         Or frightened in the day;
         I don't think twice of ghosts or mice;
         And that's a lot to say.

Sally: In the morning
         If burglars call,
         Danger scorning,
         I'd stab them all;
         Yes, I'd tackle them in dozens, if
            they'd only come my way
         In the bright, white light of day.

Refrain
All: But oh! Oh! Oh! When the night
            time comes
         And the shadows fall
         And crawl
         Along the wall,
         When the lights are dim and it's dark
            and grim,
         Oh, it's not the same at all.
         Though you may have lots of pluck
            by day,
         In the night you've not a spark;
         Hark!
         What was that?
         It must have been the cat.
         Everything looks different in the dark.

Jack: Oh, when the sun is shining,
         You never find me pining;
         I'm always cheerful as can be
         And nothing bothers me.

Claire: You feel so optimistic
         And happy in the day;

         If troubles come, you don't get glum,
         You drive them all away.

Sally: And though maybe
         You're short of cash
         Or the baby
         Has got a rash,
         You just murmur, "I should worry!"
         It's the only thing to say
         In the bright, white light of day.

Refrain

Claire: Look!

Jack: Look?

Sally: Where?

Claire: What's that thing over there?

All: Everything looks different in the
            dark.

Now the American Army arrives and a Capt. Parker reminisces about Wilbur, the most efficient soldier under his command.

WHAT'LL I DO AFTER THAT?

(Parker and Girls)

When Wilbur joined the Army, he made up his
   mind to work;
He wished to do his duty, and he vowed he'd
   never shirk;
He toiled away from break of day till he was
   nearly dead;
And every time his tasks were done he stood
   right up and said—
"What comes after that?
What comes after that?
I want to do, I want to do
Whatever I'm expected to;
This Army stuff is good enough,

I've got the thing down pat;
I've drilled and recruited
And hiked and saluted,
So what comes after that?"

When Wilbur got to France he found the girls
    were fair and slim
And every girl in every town made quite a fuss
    of him;
And when he found them flock around, young
    Wilbur did not quit;
He said, "I'm not complaining, for I want to do
    my bit!"
"What comes after that?
What comes after that?
I want to do, I want to do
Whatever I'm expected to;
At Duty's call I've kissed them all;
Upon my knees they've sat;
I've hugged 'em and squeezed 'em
And petted and teased 'em
And what'll I do after that?"

When Wilbur started in to fight, he gained ten
    miles a day;
He didn't care for shot or shell, for that was
    Wilbur's way;
And when they heard that he was near, the
    Prussian Guard would sob;
For Wilbur used to say each time he finished
    any job—
"What comes after that?
What comes after that?
I want to do, I want to do
Whatever I'm expected to;
I capture guns and slaughter Huns
Each time I come to bat;
Tomorrow I'll try, sir
To capture the Kaiser—
But what'll I do after that?"

The fragment of script also indicates a song called "Mr. Lincoln" but no lyrics appear to remain.

At one point the exotic German lady spy (Mareska von Papevich)—a dream vision of her landlady—sings a song about her ideal man.

"Nero" is in the "historical hero" genre Wodehouse was so fond of—"Napoleon" (*Have A Heart*—1917), "Cleopatterer" (*Leave It To Jane*—1917), "Julius Caesar" (*Pat* 1924).

NERO

The Emperor Nero lived, you know,
In the palmy days of Rome;
And things were never, never slow
When *he* was round the home;
The widow and the orphan, too,
He persecuted always;
And by degrees had 'em climbing trees
And ducking into hall-ways.

I want a man like Nero;
His kind appeals to me,
I want a guy who's fierce and tough,
Who's got no heart and treats 'em rough;
Yes, that's my kind of hero,
Who's got some pep and vim;
I want a man like Nero;
I'd leave my home for him.

At poker Nero used to play,
And he never found it tame;
He cleaned the bunch out every day
When he sat in a game;
For soon or late a startled groan
Would the other players' throats leave,
When Nero shook with a guileless look
Five aces from his coat-sleeve.

Refrain

Comstock's rejection, however, was not the end of the story. It may, indeed, have simply served to make the trio even more stubborn.

Producer Florenz Ziegfeld summoned them to join him on a yacht down in Palm Beach. He and a few famous friends were taking a short cruise while he considered the next vehicle in which he would star his legendary Marilynn Miller (*née* Mary Ellen).

On the trip the boys once more proposed *The Little Thing*, now the story of Sally, the waif who dreams of being—a ballerina. Gone were the jingoistic touches. Instead Kern played another piece of pseudo-history, "Joan of Arc," and, for the big finish, "The Church 'Round the Corner," throwing in the *Oh, Lady! Lady!!* reject, "Bill," for good measure.

Ziegfeld seemed to like it—providing the heroine changed her dream. None of this ballerina stuff. The kid would want to dance in the *Follies!* They even left with a draft agreement. A few weeks later they heard that the impresario was, as usual, considering other options and *The Little Thing* was returned to what must by now have been a bulging file.

Then, in May of the same year, Marilynn Miller's husband was killed in a car accident. Ziegfeld determined that his star must be kept busy and that the script he had heard on the yacht was the nearest suitable thing to hand.

Work began on *Sally Of the Alley* or *Sally In Our Alley* . . . which eventually begat *Sally*. . . .

Although the conversation on Ziegfeld's yacht finally resulted in a commission to do the Marilynn Miller show, by the time it took shape other events had overtaken the trio and Wodehouse in particular. A number of commitments—most particularly the adaptation of *The Girl Behind the Gun* into *Kissing Time* for the West End—had taken him to London and he could not get away to collaborate on the libretto of *Sally* with Bolton in the usual way. Bolton went it alone and Wodehouse sent his suggestions over in a form of long distance collaboration.

The problems arose over the lyrics. Clifford Grey and Anne Caldwell were called in as lyricists and, although Wodehouse had collaborated with both of them more than once in the past, on this occasion for some reason his nose was put out of joint. In the end—after the rather bitter altercation with Kern related earlier—he contributed just two songs. Both of them—"Joan of Arc" and the finale, "Church 'Round the Corner"—were taken bodily from *The Little Thing*. He urged Bolton and Kern to use "Bill" but Miss Miller decided it did not suit her voice and was not sufficiently "glamorous" and that was that—for now.

SALLY (1920)

Presented by Florenz Ziegfeld Jr. at the New Amsterdam Theatre, New York, on December 21, 1920 (570 performances).

BOOK	Guy Bolton
LYRICS	Clifford Grey (and Anne Caldwell)
	(Additional lyrics by P. G. Wodehouse)
MUSIC	Jerome Kern
SCENERY	Joseph Urban

"The Little Church 'Round the Corner" in the London production of *Sally*: Leslie Henson, Dorothy Dickson, George Grossmith and Heather Thatcher.

CAST

'Pops' prop. of the Alley Inn:
ALFRED P. JAMES

Rosalind Raffery, a manicurist:
MARY HAY

Sasha, violinist at the Alley Inn:
JACQUES RABIROFF

Otis Hooper, a theatrical agent:
WALTER CATLETT

Mrs. Ten Brock, a settlement worker:
DOLORES

Sally of the Alley, a foundling:
MARILYNN MILLER

Connie, a waiter:
LEON ERROL

Miss New York, a niece:
AGATHA DEBUSSY

The Admiral Travers, a gay one:
PHIL RYLEY

Blair Farquar, an only son:
IRVING FISHER

Jimmie Spelvin:
STANLEY RIDGES

Richard Farquar:
FRANK KINGDON

Billy Porter:
CARL ROSE

Harry Burton:
JACK BARKER

SYNOPSIS

For a synopsis of the plot one can do no better than quote from Gerald Bordman's definitive *Jerome Kern* (1980):

"Bolton's story opens at the Elm Tree Alley Inn, a chic Greenwich Village bistro. Wealthy Mrs. Ten Brock brings a group of orphan girls to tour the place just when a dishwasher is needed. One of the young girls, Sally, is selected. A fellow employee is 'Connie,' the exiled Duke Constantine of Czechogovinia. He soon befriends the new girl. Blair Farquar, scion of the Long Island Farquars, arrives to book a party. He is momentarily captivated by Sally, but quickly moves on to other business. Connie, as Duke, is to attend a gala at the Farquars'. A theatrical agent, Otis Hooper notices little Sally dancing and decides to pass her off as his leading lady. At the gala Sally is nervous and, when Blair fails to recognize her, she is crestfallen. She has an argument with Blair, he berates her, and nonplussed, she drops her disguise. Connie quietly offers to take the humiliated little girl home. Otis, however, soon discloses that he has arranged for Sally to dance in the *Ziegfeld Follies*. She triumphs there in a 'Butterfly Ballet.' Hooper and his girl friend, Connie and Mrs. Ten Brock, and Sally and Blair head for a triple nuptial at the Little Church 'Round the Corner."

YOU CAN'T KEEP A GOOD GIRL DOWN (JOAN OF ARC)

(Sally and Girls)

(Lyrics by P. G. Wodehouse and Clifford Grey)

Sally: Joan of Arc was on her own
          When she was quite a child;
          They thought her head was made
              of bone,
          But she just calmly smiled.
          They had their troubles at the time,
          And everybody knew it,
          When Kings and Dukes kept making
              flukes,
          She said: "Here, let me do it."

Refrain: I wish I could be like Joan of Arc,
          You bet that girl won through;
          They joshed her when she
              started,
          But she never got down-hearted,
          And it shows what a kid can do.
          She wrote her name on the
              nation's roll of fame,
          And it gained her great renown.
          Though her Pa and Ma, poor
              fishes,
          Tried to keep her washing
              dishes,
          But you can't keep a good girl
              down.

Sally: She had no stairs to wash
          With soap suds and a pail.
          She just cut out domestic bosh
          And bought a suit of mail.
          They handed her the icy mitt,
          But still she was unshaken.
          She showed the foe some
              tricks—yea bo!
          And soon brought home the
              bacon.

Refrain: I wish I could be like Joan of Arc,
          She was "it" right from the start.
          When the hired girl was busy,
          Well, it used to make her dizzy
          So she said: "Here's where we part."
          She loved to fight, and when foemen
              came in sight
          She would toast them good and
              brown,
          She would hand them Dempsey
              punches
          Where they used to keep their
              lunches,
          For you can't keep a good girl down.

Wodehouse contributed one more song to the show in collaboration with Clifford Grey, though he was not credited in the U.S. program. Considering the number of strictly

British allusions it contains, it is most likely that this was intended for the London production.

THE SCHNITZA-KOMMISSKI (WHERE THE SCHNITZA FLOWS DOWN TO THE SEA)

On the banks of the Schnitza-Kommisski,
Lord Northcliffe's expected out there,
He will speak by the day or the week,
And at banquets preside in the chair.
He alone they will offer the throne,
So the country quite firm it will be,
He will make it, they say, just like England
    today,
Where the Schnitza flows down to the sea.

On the banks of the Schnitza-Kommisski,
No animals act on the stage.
Little dogs do not hop over logs
And canaries aren't smashed in the cage.
Elephants dressed in comical pants
Are not goaded to climb up a tree,
And no flea ever will bite the top of the
    bill
Where the Schnitza flows down to the sea.

On the banks of the Schnitza-Kommisski,
We're all simply hopeless at sports.
Every team thinks we're simply a scream,
Our results a succession of noughts.
All the world simply puts us to bed,
We are dubbed with a capital 'D'.
So the English, I hear, we will challenge
    next year,
Where the Schnitza flows down to the sea.

Marilyn Miller (*Sally*) and Leon Errol (*Connie*) in the Broadway production of *Sally*.

As it turned out, the story of *Sally* had much in common with two other Broadway shows of the same season—*Irene* and *Mary*. All three were rags-to-riches tear-jerkers and for the next few years established a popular Cinderella *genre*. Bolton, however, could legitimately claim to have invented it, since *The Little Thing* pre-dated the other two by at least four years!

The critics welcomed the show as "the most imposing musical comedy of the year" (*Graphic*) and "nothing less than idealised musical comedy" (*World*). The young Noël Coward, seeing the show the following year on his first trip to the U.S., "came away cheerfully enchanted" and ambitious to work with Kern himself.

When Ziegfeld finally closed the show late in the 1923–24 season, it had made him over $5 million.

There has always been a controversy about one additional song in *Sally*. The lyric for "Look For the Silver Lining" is usually credited to Buddy DeSylva, and certainly a song of that name was included in *Zip Goes A Million*, a collaboration with Kern that took place earlier in 1920 but closed out of town. When it was subsequently used in *Sally*—a typical piece of Kern recycling—there is no hint of Wodehouse participation, even though both in theme and in tone it is highly reminiscent of "Till the Clouds Roll By." However, when the film version came along, the sheet music gives the lyric credit to Wodehouse alone.

LOOK FOR THE SILVER LINING

Blair: Please don't be offended if I
                preach you a while,
            Tears are out of place in eyes
                that were meant to smile.
            There's a way to make your best
                biggest troubles small,
            There's the happy secret of it all:

            Look for the silver lining,
            When e'er a cloud appears in
                the blue,
            Remember somewhere the sun
                is shining,
            And so the right thing to do
            Is make it shine for you.
            A heart full of joy and gladness,
            Will always banish sadness and
                strife.
            So always look for the silver lining,
            And try to find the sunny side of life.

Sally: As I wash my dishes, I'll be following
                your plan,
            Till I see the brightness in ev'ry pot
                and pan.
            I am sure your point of view will ease
                the daily grind,
            So I'll keep repeating in my mind:

            Look for the silver lining,
            When e'er a cloud appears in the blue,

Dorothy Dickson (Sally) and Leslie Henson (Connie) in the London production.

Remember somewhere the sun is
    shining,
And so the right thing to do
Is make it shine for you.
A heart full of joy and gladness,
Will always banish sadness and strife.
So always look for the silver lining,
And try to find the sunny side of life.

There was inevitably a London production. By now a profitable working relationship had been established with the George Grossmith–Edward Laurillard management. 1919 had seen the staging of both *Oh, Joy!* and *Kissing Time*, so *Sally* was an obvious successor. The English production was presented by George Grossmith at the Winter Garden Theatre, London, on September 10th, 1921 (383 performances), with the following cast:

CAST

Sascha: HERBERT FIREMAN

Jimmie Spelvin:
SEYMOUR BEARD

Otis Hooper:
GEORGE GROSSMITH JR.

Rosalind Rafferty:
HEATHER THATCHER

Sally of the Alley:
DOROTHY DICKSON

Mrs. Ten Brock:
MOLLY RAMSDEN

"Pops" Shendorff:
ALARIC ARNEF

Constantine:
LESLIE HENSON

Blair Farquar:
GREGORY STROUD

Admiral Travers:
LEIGH ELLIS

Richard Farquar:
ERNEST GRAHAM

Billy Porter:
JACK BRADLEY

Harry Barton:
DERICK GLYNNE

The year 1921 was a busy one for Wodehouse. He and Bolton started work on a show called *The Blue Mazurka* for Colonel Savage. Wodehouse got as far as writing two dummy lyrics—"The Hickey Doo" and "If You've Nothing Else To Do"—before they moved on to other projects.

He was also engaged in a particularly intensive period of fiction writing. In quick succession he had produced the novels *The Coming of Bill* and *Jill the Reckless* (both 1921), while *The Girl On the Boat* and *The Adventures of Sally* were in the works for publication in 1922.

He also managed to write 35 short stories for the magazines in the four years 1919–1922, some of which were collected and published in book form as *Indiscretions of Archie* (1921), *The Clicking of Cuthbert* (1922) and *The Inimitable Jeeves* (1923).

It was at this time, too, that he was beginning to develop the character of Jeeves. "Stumped," as he put it, for a name of the archetypal valet, "I remembered a cricketer, in the years before the war, called Jeeves. . . . Calling a character after a county cricketer is lucky. Sherlock and Holmes were both county cricketers. . . . Jeeves seemed to me just right for the sort of bloke I wanted."

"Just to keep his hand in"—as he put it—he also wrote the lyrics for *The Golden Moth*.

THE GOLDEN MOTH (1921)

A Musical Play of Adventure

Presented by Austen Hurgon and Thomas F. Dawe at the Adelphi Theatre, London, on October 5, 1921 (281 performances).

BOOK
Fred Thompson and
P. G. Wodehouse
(Adapted from *L'Auberge des Adrets*, a play by B. Autier; previously adapted as *The Roadside Inn*)

LYRICS
P. G. Wodehouse
(Additional lyrics by
Adrian Ross)

MUSIC
Ivor Novello

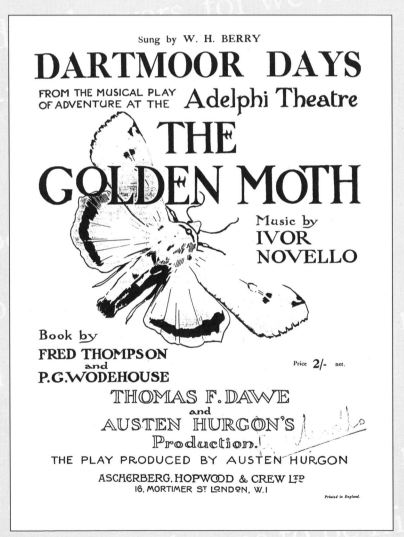

CAST

Pierre Caravan
(alias The Blackbird):
ROBERT MICHAELIS
Dipper Tigg (alias The Marquis):
W. H. BERRY
Captain Paul D'Artois:
THORPE BATES
Armand Bercy
(Asst. Commissioner
Of Police):
FRED MAGUIRE
Gallipaux (Prop. Of "The Estaminet"):
MARSTON GARSIA
Major Podoritza (A Montenegrin):
MOSTYN GODFREY
Dupont (Prop. of "The Golden Moth"):
BOBBIE COMBER
Waiter
(at "The Golden Moth"):
HENRY CHANNON
Sergeant:
W. E. STEPHENS
Corporal:
LIONEL BROOKE
Henri (An Apache):
AUSTIN CAMP
Guiseppe Palata (ex-Opera Singer):
ELLIS WILLIAMS
The Gambetta Gang
Butcher Bertrand:
DENHAM CHARLES
Stranger of Marseilles:
PARKER SCOTT

Horrible Harry: M. NOEL
Alonzo the Assassin:
HERBERT FENWICK
The Gasper King/
Cocaine Charlie:
ANDREW JONES
Aline:
NANCY LOVAT
Rose (her Maid):
CICELY DEBENHAM
Zozo (an *habituée* of
"The Golden Moth"):
SYLVIA LESLIE
Simone:
BARBARA ROBERTS
Madame de Crillon
(Aline's Mother):
MAY CLARKE
Madame Dupont
(Prop. of "The Golden Moth"):
MARY EWIN
Yvonne:
KITTY HOLD
Marie:
MARJORIE MARS
Nini (Alice):
AUDREY BENTHAM
Angele:
KATE ZOLLER
Fifi (Melie):
MARGERY WOLLASTON
Nicolette:
BERYL HARRISON

SYNOPSIS

At the de Crillon Estate the Girls are preparing for Aline de Crillon's 21st birthday ("We've Had a Busy Day"). Aline is to be the subject of an arranged marriage with Captain Paul d'Artois, whom she has never met, but she yearns to meet the man of her dreams ("Prince Charming"). She now runs into d'Artois by accident. They are mutually attracted but he refuses to identify himself—something Aline considers quite romantic ("Romance is Calling"). Paul meets Bercy, an old friend, and now a senior policeman sent to trap the notorious criminal "The Blackbird" at the local café, the Golden Moth. He invites Paul to meet him there later. Rose (Aline's maid) and the Girls prepare a meal for the arriving soldiers ("Lonely Soldier"). The Blackbird and his side-kick, "The Marquis," arrive and wonder if there are pickings among the birth-day presents. An encounter with Rose and Aline (who is posing as her own maid) leads to an invitation to meet later at—the Golden Moth. For The Marquis, at least, a life of crime is beginning to pall ("Dartmoor Days").

The Blackbird realizes that his confederate has already stolen a valuable miniature with Aline's likeness on it. Paul sees it and persuades them to sell it to him ("Dear Eyes That Shine"). Now the party begins but, as the attraction between Paul and Aline is developing, the miniature comes to light and Paul is accused of stealing it. He leaves in distress.

At the Golden Moth—a haunt of low repute—The Blackbird arrives and toasts all the girls at the bar ("My Girl"). Rose arrives and soon the Apache dancers are ready to fight over her ("Nuts in May") but The Marquis now enters and it is clear that he is the preferred object of her affections ("If I Ever Lost You"). Aline arrives and Rose reveals the identity of the two criminals—just before The Blackbird, still believing Aline to be the maid, tries to enlist her in a plot to rob herself at the ball the next evening.

The night of the ball and both ladies are in compromising positions, since neither is who she claims to be. To complicate matters further, The Blackbird and The Marquis arrive in heavy disguise. The Marquis is meant to be a society lady from Montenegro, who tells the Girls about her "native" land ("The Island of Never-Mind-Where"). Aline discovers that Paul, the man she *now* loves, is the man she was intended to marry all along ("Dear Eyes That Shine—Reprise"). The Blackbird reveals himself to the lovers and tells them that, although he had intended to rob them, love has softened his heart. Rose and The Marquis are also united as everyone joins the party ("Finale").

OPENING CHORUS—
WE'VE HAD A BUSY DAY

(Girls and Men)

Girls: We've had a busy day
What a crush and riot,
It's nice to get away,
Where there's peace and quiet.

This must be where we meet tonight!
Not so bad,
Looks all right,
We ought to have, before we've done,
A lot of fun.

Men: It's a fact,
We are not in the best of humours.
We've just back'd a long, long list
  of stumers.
Still at this frolic,
We'll try to rollick,
And endeavour to be quite a cheery
  crowd tonight.

FAIRY PRINCE
(PRINCE CHARMING)

(Aline)

I once read, I remember,
A story of a fair princess
Whose suitors, though they wooed her
  boldly,
All were treated coldly,
Much to their distress;
She somehow knew 'twas fated
A gallant prince would claim her hand;
So always wistfully she waited,
Hoping he would seek her
Straight from Fairyland.

Oh, Fairy Prince!
(Softly she'd cry)
My Fairy Prince,
Time's passing (slipping) by!
For you I sigh!

Come to me, do!
Hurry, Prince Charming,
I'm waiting for you.

Bold knights came on their chargers,
And gallant (haughty) monarchs from the
  East;
But could not, spite of their orations
And fond protestations,
Move her in the least
Rich jewels by the fistful
They'd gladly give to her, they said;
She simply went on looking wistful,
And with great decision
Shook her little head.

Oh, Fairy Prince!
(Softly she'd cry)
My Fairy Prince,

Time's passing (slipping) by!
For you I sigh!
Come to me, do!
Hurry, Prince Charming
I'm waiting for you

ROMANCE IS CALLING

(Aline and d'Artois)

D'Artois: If you listen, if you listen,
There's a voice that's softly
  calling
Rising, falling, rising, falling.
If you listen, if you listen,
And are brave and do not hear it;
You can hear it, you can hear it.
Like the whisper of the breeze
Sighing through the trees.

Romance is calling
Will it call in vain to you?
The spell enthralling
Will you not obey?
To a world it welcomes you

Of joy and laughter
Where life is gallant and gay
No care for after.

Aline   Romance is calling
Will it call in vain to me?
Its spell enthralling
How can I obey?

D'Artois: To a world it welcomes you
Of joy and laughter,
If you will follow
I will show the way.

Aline: As I listen, as I listen,
Louder, like a bugle blowing,
It is growing, it is growing
As I listen, as I listen.

First it seems all faint and
    distant.
Then imperious and insistent
Tearing fiercely at my heart
Bidding me to start.

Romance is calling
Will it call in vain to me?
Its spell enthralling
How can I obey.

D'Artois: To a world it welcomes you
Of joy and laughter
Where life is gallant and gay
No care for after.

Both: Romance is calling
Will it call in vain to you/me
Its spell enthralling
Will you not/How can I obey
To a world it welcomes you/me
Of joy and laughter
If you/I will follow
I'll/you'll show the way.

SOLDIERS' ENTRANCE

Over the hills all day they've had us tramping,
And from our homes we've all journeyed far
And it is time, we feel, to think of camping
Tho' we do not know just where we are:
Still we're not particular,
Just dump us anywhere,
Any old place will do to rest our feet in
If there's a nice girl there.

What tho' our quarters may be somewhat humble?
What tho' our wives are waiting afar?
We'll make the best of that without a grumble,
Like the courageous soldiers we are:

No we're not particular
Just dump us anywhere,
Any old place will do to rest our feet in
If there's a nice girl there!

LONELY SOLDIER

(Rose and Soldiers)

Rose: A soldier's is the sort of lot,
That few would willingly face;
They live in barracks where
    there's not
A girl in the place
They march and drill for years
    and years,
It's not too much fun, you'll agree;
I often pity them, poor dears,
How dull they must be.

Refrain: So never allow a soldier to be lonely,
Cheer up his life as much as you can;
Rapid results you're sure to get, if only
You go and make a fuss of the man;
They do so appreciate
A kindly word or two.
And every time you (if you will only)
    treat a soldier kindly
He will be kind to you

Rose: Be nice to soldiers everyday,
   Whatever else you may do,
   Neglect just makes them pine
    away.

Soldiers: That's perfectly true.

Rose: You only need a loving heart
   With room for two or three,
   It's easy then to make a start

Soldiers: So start on me.

Rose: Now when I meet mere privates,
    they
   Just smile politely at me,
   But when I meet a corporal

Soldier: She sits on his knee.

Rose: By sergeants I am always kissed,
   So I am wondering . . . when
   I meet a sergeant-major what

Soldiers: *Will* happen then?
   Never allow a soldier to be lonely,
   Sit in the twilight, holding his
    hand.
   Give him a kiss that's sisterly,
    and only,
   That he may know you quite
    understand.
   He will so reciprocate
   Your kindly action too,
   And every time you love a lonely
    soldier,
   He will make love to you

Refrain

Ivor Novello

ROUND THE CORNER

(Blackbird and Aline)

Blackbird: When a maid half afraid,
   In the doorway lingers,

   And you see how the key
   Trembles in her fingers.

Aline: Something's hiding in the hall,
   Waiting there for her to call.
   Something's never met before.

Both: Behind the door!

Refrain: Just round the corner
   (What will she find) A girl will
    go,
   Her friends may warn her
   (She does not mind) What can
    they know?

Aline: Ah no! You never know what there
             may be,
          You never know until you see,
          You never know
          You want to know
          Like me—

Blackbird
& Aline: Just round the corner,
          A girl will stray,
          Her friends (the wise) may warn her,
          She goes her way!
          For if you never dare to give a glance,
          (For though you never knew what
             may be there,)
          You'll never meet your life's romance,
          (You'll never know unless you dare,)
          There's something strange and new
          For you!

Blackbird: When she's pass'd round at last
           What will she discover?
           Dragons (dire) breathing fire,
           Or a gallant lover?

Aline: She may find before she's done,
          Knight and Dragon both in one;
          Will he kiss or will he kill?

Both: It's as you will.

DARTMOOR DAYS (DEAR OLD-FASHIONED PRISON OF MINE)

(Marquis)

(Lyric by P.G. Wodehouse and Adrian Ross)

There's a spot in dear old Devon
Like a little bit of Heaven,
Where happy years of idleness I've spent
All among the moorland heather
Just my pals and I together
And the landlord never troubled for his rent.

And when they ask'd you in to stay
You couldn't get away.

It's a long, long way to Dartmoor by the sea,
But it's there that I want to be;
So tell the old head warder
To expect another boarder,
And to put the cell in order for me!
We had great, great times at Dartmoor,
   you'll agree,
Up at six and to bed at nine,
Just a happy band of sinners,
Picking oakum and the winners
In that dear old-fashioned prison of mine!

Not a fear of unemployment
Interfered with our enjoyment,
We were happy and contented all the day.
And on Sundays regularly
Came a Chaplain, not a Charlie,
Tho' we found him quite amusing in his way.
And if we'd nothing else to do
We'd break a stone or two.

When did I go on the downward path?
I'll tell you, I've time to spare;
A woman it was, sir, who brought me to rags,
With a bone and a hank of hair.
Mottle-faced Maggie they called her,
And her heart was as black as your hat.
But her face—well, you've seen Pauline
   Frederick,
Well, she wasn't a bit like that.
There was something about her face, though,
Something I can't explain,
It seemed to remind me of something
I think 'twas the back of a train.
Well, she dragged me down till I took to drugs,
And it makes me mad to think
Of the money I spent on patent pills
That I might have spent on drink.

Then I started stealing trifles—post office
   pencils and string

Lamp-posts, nosebags, cab-shelters—any
    old thing!
Then the crash came, they caught me at last, sir,
I was nabbed for a Government ramp;
For I sent a postcard with fourteen words
And only a penny stamp.
I remember the scene in court, sir,
The Counsel with wigs and bags,
And the Judge sitting there so solemn
Cracking his moth-eaten gags.

But the 'Ayes' had it and guilty was the verdict
    they brought in for me
So I said to the Judge, "When you put me away,
Make it Dartmoor, the place by the sea."

It's a long, long way to Dartmoor by the sea,
And it's there that I want to be!
If the afternoon was chilly I could ask the
    warder, Willy
To put whiskey in the skilly for me,
For I've had enough by this time you'll agree,
Of the world and its women and wine.
So bob my hair and shove me
Where I know the warders love me,
In that dear old-fashioned prison of mine.

It's a long, long way to Dartmoor by the sea,
But it's there that I want to be;
(Take me back, on the track, to the shack)
And I'll trundle garden barrows
Full of vegetable marrows,
With a lot of big broad arrows on me,
(When it's chilly, serve the skilly, Warder Willy)
And I'll never try from Dartmoor to be free,
For the warders would all resign
(On the level, I'm a devil, when I revel)
If I bolt—perhaps they'd miss me,
And when I go back they'll kiss me,
At that dear old-fashioned prison of mine!

It's a long, long way to Dartmoor by the sea,
But it's there that I want to be;
(Take me back, on the track, to the shack)

And I'll trundle garden barrows
Full of vegetable marrows,
With a lot of big broad arrows on me!
(Or a lorry, in the quarry, very sorry)
And I won't, won't try from Dartmoor to be free,
For the warders would all resign!
(Or they'd pot me if they got me when they
    shot me)
For when I come they'll kiss me
If I bolt—perhaps they'll miss me—
At the dear old-fashioned prison of mine!

It's a long, long way to Dartmoor by the sea,
But it's there that I want to be—
(Call the van, for a man, when you can)
You needn't fear a riot,
For I'm going very quiet,
It's the good old prison diet for me!
(When it's chilly, serve the skilly, Warder
    Willy)
Just a good, good rest at Dartmoor, you'll agree
For I'm weary of women and wine—
(On the level, I'm a devil—when I revel)
I won't indulge in orgies
As a guest of good King George's
In that dear old-fashioned prison of mine!

DEAR EYES THAT SHINE (THE MINIATURE)

(d'Artois)

Picture a (pictured) face,
So full of tender
Girlish grace
And queenly splendour,
Hinting at a soft surrender.

Am I he
For whom you seek, dear?
If to me
You could but speak, dear,
Would you make me sad?
Would you make me glad?

Dear eyes that shine at me so brightly,
Sweet lips that smile without a care;
If I could read your message rightly,
Would it bring rapture or despair?
Those lips would they dismiss me lightly?
Or bid me hope that I and you
Together hand in hand
Might find some day that land
Where journeys end and dreams come true.
    (love is there)

Lady mine,
Behold me kneeling
At your shrine
For aid appealing,
All my hidden hopes revealing.
To my mind
Grim doubts are flocking;
Shall I find
You cold and mocking?
If I could but guess!
If you'd but confess!

MY GIRL

(Blackbird and Chorus)

Blackbird: I have a way
        With the ladies, so they say!
        I can't deny it;
        It's true.
        None I have met
        Have resisted me as yet,
        No use to try it,
        They knew.
        I prefer a courtship brief,
        I just throw the handkerchief,
        For I've no time to woo.

Refrain: I do not wait
        When I meet my chosen mate,
        I claim her,
        My girl.
        Fierce she may be
        To the rest, but not to me,

I tame her
My girl.
She is my bride
And she shares with me my throne,
Reigns by my side
In a kingdom of our own.
Her subjects court her,
For who would dare to thwart her
Whom I've named my girl!

But I regret
That no queen has held as yet
Her proud position
For long.
I own with grief
That her reigns are rather brief,
For competition
Is strong.
Charms like mine so highly prized,
Must not be monopolized,
That would be very wrong

Refrain: Fair tho' she be,
        And tho' passionately she
        Adores me,
        My girl
        Yet, sure as Fate
        I discover, soon or late
        She bores me,
        My girl.

*Then I inform her
Politely she's dismissed,
And in due course
Choose another from the list,
And then forget her as tho' I'd
    never met her!
She's no more my girl. (She's just
    one more girl.)

Alternative: Then I inform her
        That she has had her day
        Bid her goodbye,
        Pass lightly on my way.

Extra
Chorus:
(*addressed to*
his current
lady love)

Stray tho' I may
Always I come back to you;
You own me,
My girl.
I will repay
All the love so brave and true
You've shown me,
My girl.
You shine apart
Like the starlight and the sun,
You hold my heart
When light loves are dead and
     done,
And nothing ever my life
From you shall sever
You're my girl—my girl.

(GATHERING) NUTS IN MAY

(Rose and Men)

Rose:

When I was little I used to play
A rather jolly
Game known as "Gathering Nuts
     in May."
Now I am older, still
I have not quite lost my skill.
See the Nuts I have gathered
     today.

Refrain:

I do like gathering Nuts in May
If you've a dimple
It's very simple;
All you need is a smile that's sweet
     and shy,
And a sort of twinkle in your eye.
Here I come gathering Nuts in May:
When I detect them,
I soon collect them.
They stand all round me, simply
     waiting to be pick'd,
I catch their eye and something tells
     me I have click'd.

I go like *that* and in a minute and
     a half,
They're on my staff.

Rose:

Experts agree that there seem to be
In my collection
Nuts of each kind and variety.
Shows what a girl can do
If she takes the trouble to;
And no trouble is too much for me.

Refrain:

I do like gathering Nuts in May,
On strings I lead 'em,
You see I need 'em,
Ted for tennis and golf, and Ned
     to swim,
When I'm ready to Jazz, I call for Jim.
I do like gathering Nuts in May,
They come in handy
To buy me candy,
If I'm inclined to flirt I simply call
     for Tom;
Jack's rather useful, I get *him* to hold
     my Pom.
Billy is silly but because he makes
     me laugh
He's on my staff.

Extra
Refrain:

I do like gathering Nuts in May,
On strings I lead 'em,
You see I need 'em.
To the races I like to go with Joe,
George can drive the old car—and
     not too slow.
I do like gathering Nuts in May.
They come in handy
To buy me candy.
Rupert is serious, and talks about
     my soul,
Peter is mushy, but quite nice upon
     the whole,
Billy is silly, but because he makes
     me laugh,
He's on my staff.

IF I EVER LOST YOU

(Rose and Marquis)

Rose: I have not known you long,
            and yet
           It's plain that this was meant
            to be,
           For something told me when
            we met
           That you were my affinity
           I cannot tell you all you mean
            to me.

Refrain: Think how sad the flowers
            would be
           If sunshine went away,
           Think how sad the bees
            would feel
           Without a Summer Day.
           Think how a couple of lovers
            would swoon
           If they walked out one night
            and found no moon;
           Then you'll understand—I hope
            that you do—
           How I'd feel if I ever lost you.

Marquis: You have inflicted on my heart
           A wound that Time can never
            heal;
           You woke in me right from the
            start,
           Emotions I cannot conceal,
           Just let me sketch for you the way
            I feel:

Refrain: Think how sad a carrot would be
            (feel)
           If no boil'd beef was near.
           Think how sad an egg would feel
           If ham should disappear.
           Think how a sausage's hope would
            be dash'd

"The Golden Moth"

           If one day it awoke and miss'd its
            mash'd.
           And what grief a steak would feel if
            it found—

Rose: Yes!

Marquis: That there wasn't an onion around.

THE ISLAND OF NEVER-MIND-WHERE

(Marquis and Girls)

Marquis: There's a little island which is simply
           terrific,

Somewhere in a corner of the
Southern Pacific,
Where there is nothing to do—
Oh, the lagoon is so blue!

Refrain
Chorus: In the Island of Never-Mind-Where
Never-mind-where,

Marquis: I know it's there—
Nobody worries (frets) or fusses
They have no taxis or buses,
In the Island of Never-Mind-Where
Life is as free as the air—
It's a happy release
From the horrors of Peace—
In the Island of Never-Mind-Where.

Chorus: In the Island of Never-Mind-Where
Life is a simple affair.

Marquis: If you call for a drink
Well, it's not Stephen's Ink—

Chorus: In the Island of Never-Mind-Where.

Marquis: It's a Paradise, where no sorrow or
sin come;
Income Tax is nothing, for they
haven't any income!
No one pays milliners' bills,
Girls don't put on any frills!
In the Island of Never-Mind-Where.

Chorus: Never-Mind-Where—I know it's
there
They have such flowing tresses
Why should they bother with dresses.
In the Island of Never-Mind-Where
Clothes are a simple affair,
Some mustard and cress is a full
evening dress,
In the Island of Never-Mind-Where.

In the Island of Never-Mind-Where
Life is a simple affair,
If a girl is a prude,
She has undies tattooed
In the Island of Never-Mind-Where.

Encore
Refrain   In the Island of Never-Mind-Where,
Never-Mind-Where, I know it's there.
There are no funny transactions,
Bottomley doesn't bring actions,
In the Island of Never-Mind-Where
No one subscribes for a share,
For they're not very fond of a Victory
Bond
In the Island of Never-Mind-Where.

2nd
Encore: And in fact, they don't know who
is Horatio
In the Island of Never-Mind-Where.

In the Island of Never-Mind-Where,
Never-Mind-Where—I know it's
there,
Nothing could ever be dreamier,
What a nice spot for the Premier,
In the Island of Never-Mind-Where
Life is as free as the air
In some tropical gorge, he'd be
unemployed George
In the Island of Never-Mind-Where.
And I ought to explain, there is
Sinn but no Feign
In the Island of Never-Mind-Where.

Note: The structure of the song would be repeated in "Bongo On the Congo" in *Sitting Pretty* (1924).

DEAR EYES THAT SHINE (Reprise)

(Aline & d'Artois)

D'Artois: Dear eyes that shine on me so brightly,
Sweet lips that smile my cares away

Aline:	Now I can read your message rightly And know the words that you may say

Both:	We'll meet what comes without a care
	(We two will face the future lightly,
	We'll greet what comes without a
	  care)
	And wandering hand in hand
	Together find that land
	Where journey(ing)s end, for love
	  is there.

FINALE—ACT 3

Blackbird:	Put care away Let us be gay
Aline:	Laughter and song
D'Artois:	All the night long
Marquis:	Food to be gained Drinks to be won
Chorus:	Start up the music And let's carry . . .

(GONG heard off)

Marquis:	Supper is served.

So never allow a soldier to be lonely,
Cheer up his life as much as you can.
Rapid results you're sure to get,
  (find) if only
You try (go) and make a fuss of
  the man.
They do so appreciate
A kindly word or two;
And if you will only (every time you)
  treat a soldier kindly,
He will be kind to you.

Curtain

Although it does not feature in the script submitted to The Lord Chamberlain's office, another duet exists for Aline and d'Artois. It seems likely that it was considered as an alternative "getting to know and being attracted to" number, which invariably preceded the out and out "love declared" love song in musical comedy. As such it may have been replaced by "Romance Is Calling" in Act 1.

GIVE ME A THOUGHT NOW AND THEN

(Aline and d'Artois)

Aline:	I wonder whether You'll forget me altogether As the days go marching by? I don't expect that You will ever recollect that There was such a girl as I. Absence breaks friendships But tho' very few survive it; Think of me sometimes, If somehow you can contrive it.

Refrain:	When you've gone your way and
	  I have gone mine,
	Try to give me a thought now
	  and then.
	Nothing important and serious. It'll
	Do if you just say "I liked her just
	  a little!"
	Tho' my face may have passed from
	  your mind, I'm aware
	You may not remember my eyes or
	  my hair,
	Still tho' you forget where you met
	  me and when,
	Try to give me a thought now
	  and then.

D'Artois:	Don't be upset You needn't fear that I'll forget you;

But will you remember me?
Men in their millions,
Dashing soldiers, smart civilians,
You are sure to meet, you see,
How can I hope that,
When poor me you've said goodbye to,
You will recall me
Still, I hope you'll sometimes try to.

Refrain   *(First 2 lines same)*
If you are feeling kind-hearted and
     mellow
Say "Well after all, I rather liked
     the fellow!"
Tho' you not remember a detail
     or two,
My face may have slipped from your
     mind it's true;
Still, tho' you forget where you met
     me and when,
Try to give me a thought now
     and then.

The Lord Chamberlain's Office appointed G. S. Street to be the reader of the libretto for licensing purposes. On November 8th, 1921, there is a note that the "play had been revised. The alterations were chiefly that the second act had been pulled together and shortened and that in Act 3 there is a Servants' Ball song (lyric by Adrian Ross) introduced and the comedian is dressed up as a woman. There is nothing oppressive in this and the alterations generally are immaterial from the point of view of the department."

Strangely, Wodehouse makes no mention in any of his writings of the experience of working with Ivor Novello on *The Golden Moth*. Although it would be another decade or so before he became London's favorite composer of romantic scores—a position he would maintain until his early death in 1951—Novello was already reasonably well known for his revue material. It appears to have been a mutually satis-

fying collaboration and it's slightly surprising that there was never an encore.

But then, even as he was handing in his contribution, Wodehouse was deeply involved in his next project—a collaboration with George Grossmith Jr. on what they hoped would be the successor to *Sally*.

Grossmith (1874–1935) was a dominant character in London theatre by this time. Son of the George Grossmith of D'Oyly Carte fame, he was a combination of actor, librettist, lyricist, director and producer. As an actor he had introduced the character of the "dude"—not far removed at all from the Wodehousean universe—to London musicals and was usually to be seen on stage complete with top hat and monocle or uniform and monocle. ("The trouble with George," Wodehouse wrote, "is that, if there's a prince in the show, you can't keep him away from it with an injunction. Show him a white uniform with gold frogs across the chest and a lot of medals, and he starts making mewing noises.") Grossmith had also been closely associated with Kern shows since 1906.

With *Oh, Joy!*, *Kissing Time* and *Sally* his contribution had been largely to adapt and anglicize American successes but now he was determined to participate in something original with the team—or, at least, part of it—that he admired so much. He penciled himself in to co-write the book and contribute to the lyrics with Wodehouse. Kern would write the music and the show would be put on at the Winter Garden, a theatre on which Grossmith had taken a long lease.

Nothing could have been more of a contrast to the petite Princess. Built in Drury Lane as the New Middlesex Theatre of Varieties, it was acquired by Grossmith and his partner at the end of the decade and became a home for musicals—usually starring Grossmith himself. For many theatre-goers it continued the tradition of George Edwardes's sadly defunct Gaiety.

Fittingly, *Kissing Time* had been the opening production. With a seating capacity of 1,800, it also had the widest seating area of any West End theatre.

Never one to look a successful gift formula in the mouth, Grossmith and Wodehouse set about creating a sort of *Sally* sequel. It was another showgirl rags-to-riches story, exchanging the American setting for a British one, and it had all the signs of Wodehouse making up the ground he felt he had lost by not being as closely involved in the original as he would have wished.

A typical "in" reference was to call the heroine Marilynn Morgan—the double "n" being a reference to the way *Sally* star Marilynn Miller chose to spell her name. Coincidentally or not, Miss Miller went "single" that very year!

Grossmith recalled the way he and Wodehouse would work with "dummy" lyrics—a method widely employed by lyricists working to music already written. It was a way of fixing the metre and remembering where the accents should fall.

Ira Gershwin's famous dummy lyric for "I Got Rhythm," for instance, began . . .

Roly poly,
Eating solely,
Ravioli,
Better watch your diet or bust.

Grossmith quoted one of their own . . .

Today is our holiday, it is our holiday
We merrily sing, we merrily sing:
This is our hol-i-day (*three long notes*)
In the chirrupy, syrupy month of May.

By March 1922 Grossmith and Wodehouse had enough of a draft script to sail to America and persuade Jerry Kern to sign on . . .

As a dedication to his new novel related to the musical theatre—*The Adventures of Sally* (1922)—Wodehouse was to write to Grossmith . . .

"Dear George,

The production of our mutual effort, *The Cabaret Girl,* is a week distant as I write this; and who shall say what the harvest will be? But whether a week from now we are slapping each other on the back or shivering in the frost, nothing can alter the fact that we had a lot of fun writing the thing together. Not a reproach or a nasty look from start to finish. Because of this, and because you and I were side by side through the Adventure of the Ship's Bore, the Episode of the Concert in Aid of the Seamen's Orphans and Widows, and the Sinister Affair of the Rose of Stamboul, I dedicate this book to you.

P. G. Wodehouse,
The Garrick Club"

The title of the show, incidentally, was Grossmith's idea. As he wrote—"Cabarets were started everywhere (in England) and soon spread to the provinces. While the word 'cabaret' was still new, I wanted to make the most of it . . ."

THE CABARET GIRL (1922)

Presented by George Grossmith Jr. and J. A. E. Malone at the Winter Garden Theatre, London, on September 10, 1922 (462 performances).

BOOK George Grossmith Jr. and P. G. Wodehouse
LYRICS George Grossmith Jr., P. G. Wodehouse and Anne Caldwell
MUSIC Jerome Kern

The *Cabaret Girl* herself, Dorothy Dickson (*Marilynn Morgan*).

CAST

Marchioness of Harrogate:
MISS FORTESCUE

Marquis of Harrogate (her son):
FRED LESLIE

Effie Dix:
VERA LENNOX

Commissionaire:
JACK GLYNN

A Customer:
DOROTHY BENTHAM

Mr. Gripps:
GEORGE GROSSMITH JR.

Mr. Gravvins:
NORMAN GRIFFIN

James Paradene:
GEOFFREY GWYTHER

Harry Zona:
THOMAS WEGUELIN

March:
SEYMOUR BEARD

April:
ENID TAYLOR

Little Ada:
HEATHER THATCHER

Lily de Jigger:
MOLLY RAMSDEN

Marilynn Morgan ("Flick"):
DOROTHY DICKSON

Feloosi (an agent):
JOSEPH SPREE

Quibb (a piano tuner):
LEIGH ELLIS

Mrs. Drawbridge (Housekeeper):
MURIEL BARNBY

The Mayor of Woollam Chersey:
CLAUDE HORTON

Laburnum Brown:
MOLLY VERE

Lilac Smith:
VERA KIRKWOOD

Poppu Robinson:
DOROTHY DEANE

Hyacinth Green:
MONICA NOYES

Tulip Williams:
BETTY SHIELDS

The Vicar at Woollam Chersey:
ERNEST GRAHAM

Box Office Keeper:
FRED WHITLOCK

Cabaret Dancer:
JINOS

SYNOPSIS

Gripps and Gravvins, song publishers, Bond Street, London. To their staff even the best composers can become a bore ("Chopin Ad Lib"). Effie, the efficient but overworked secretary, is always ready to sell the company product ("You Want the Best Seats, We Have 'Em"). Gripps is clearly the brains of a fairly brainless enterprise, while Gravvins is of a more eccentric disposition. Effie, who has her eye on Gripps, acts as referee. When the two men converse, they tend to converse in verse ("Mr. Gravvins—Mr. Gripps").

The hero, Jim, arrives in search of a song to sing at the village concert—but it must be about love and roses. Effie explains that *all* G&G songs are about love and roses ("First Rose of Summer"). Jim stands to inherit a fortune when he marries—if his trustees (Lord and Lady Hastings) approve of his choice. Since he wants to marry Marilynn, a chorus girl, they most certainly don't. Marilynn arrives to audition for the cabaret G&G are staging. She turns down Jim's offer to give it all up. She wants to succeed in her own right. Maybe they should go their separate ways ("Journey's End"). The sextette already hired for the show rehearse the Grand Opening ("Whoop-De-Oodle-Do!").

Jim has a brainwave. If he and Marilynn pretend to be married already, the Hastings will *have* to give their blessing. Gravvins offers to lend them his country retreat for the vital meeting ("Our Little Place in the Country").

The Pergola at Woollam Chersey. (In the play *Good Morning, Bill* [1928] Wodehouse placed the hero, Bill Paradene, at his country house at Woollam Chersey. It was also named as the location of Bertie Wooster's Aunt Agatha's country estate in "Jeeves and the Impending Doom" [1926].) An assortment of locals praise their unique environment in song . . . ("The Pergola Patrol").

All the characters we have met start to arrive ("Entrance Scene"). Marilynn finds that the locals are rather starved for entertainment and she has a suggestion for them ("Shimmy With Me").

Gravvins now has a problem. He had promised to pack the place with notables to impress the Hastingses. The problem is—he doesn't *know* any notables. Ah, well, his cabaret friends will have to impersonate them. He recalls the days of his mis-spent youth ("Those Days Are Gone Forever"). Jim and Marilynn speculate on what being *really* married would be like ("Looking All Over For You"). The prospect of the play-acting they are about to undertake makes the leading actors more than a little nervous ("Nerves"). Not surprisingly, the deception is discovered and the tentative approval the Hastingses had by now given to Jim and Marilynn's wedding is withdrawn ("Act 2—Finale").

The Cabaret. Jim arrives, looking for Marilynn, who has disappeared. He has seen the light. He can't expect her to bury herself in the country. The city is where they both belong ("London, Dear Old London"). Lord Hastings has also had a change of heart and arrives ready to give his consent. Meanwhile, the show continues and Marilynn appears for the big number ("Oriental Dreams" / "Dancing Time").

OPENING CHORUS—
CHOPIN AD LIB

First
Chorus: Love's song is ended;
  Fires which we tended
  Have left not a single ember.
  Love's flow'rs once cherished
  Long since have perished
  In snows of December.
  Yet love though it die,
  Leaves echoes sighing.
  Remember
  Though fate may sever
  We'll hear them forever,
  You and I.

Girls: Chopin at one, Chopin at two.
  Chopin at half past three,
  Oh! Can't you give the man a rest?
  We wish he could disappear,
  Nobody wants him here!
  We find that kind
  Of tune too slow;
  We're sick of Nevin, Debussy and
    Chaminade,
  And for a change we want that lively,
    rough
  Irving Berlin stuff
  That's got some zip and go!

YOU WANT THE BEST SEATS,
WE HAVE 'EM

(Effie and Girls)

Effie: Just now the season's at its height,
  With new productions ev'ry night.
  Each theatre's crammed from stalls
    to pit,
  For every show's a hit
  And you can get a perfect view, no
    matter where you sit.

1st
Refrain: You want the best seats?

Girls: We have 'em.
  For all the shows in town.
  Tickets here we've got for you
  For any play you want to view,
  Sad or funny.

Girls: Take your pick and pay your money!

Effie: Plays with a bed scene; French farces
  That made the censor frown.
  Plays by Barrie, plays by Milne; and
    all extremely good;
  Plays where people stab themselves,
    or where you wish they would.

  You want the best seats.

Girls: We have 'em

All: For all the shows in town.

2nd Verse
Effie: We've plays about romantic crooks;
  We've plays made out of well-known
    books;
  We've Eastern dramas where they
    dress
  In strings of beads, or (and) less.
  And every play upon our list's a
    genuine success.

Girls: There's His Majesty's, the Queens,
    the Globe and Strand,
  And the Aldwych and the Palace,
    Wyndham's
  And the Ambassadors, the Playhouse
    and the New
  And the Gaiety and Winter Garden,
    too.

2nd Refrain

Effie: You want the best seats?

Girls: We have 'em

Effie: For all the shows in town.
           On our list we've ev'ry kind,
               (We have plays of ev'ry kind,
           But still in all the lot you'll find
               (But upon all our lists you'll find)
           Not a (one) bad 'un
           All were praised by Archie Haddon;
           Plays with a bed scene, French farces
           That made the censor frown.
           Plays where wives behave as wives
               should never, never do;
           Also plays nice-minded girls take
               their mothers to.
           You want the best seats. We have 'em!
           For all the shows in town.

MR. GRAVVINS—MR. GRIPPS

(Gravvins and Gripps)

Gripps: Forgive me if I speak a little
               weightily:
           We two should strive our hardest
               to agree.

Gravvins: We ought to strive to get along as
               matily
           As any pair of love birds on a tree.

Gripps: Misunderstandings, we should try to
               clear away,
           We're partners, let us, therefore, act
               as such.

Gravvins: One moment, while I wipe a silent
               tear away:
           These few kind words that you have
               said have moved me very much.

Gravvins: Mister Gripps, I've just been
               thinking—

Gripps: Mr. Gravvins, that is strange!

Gravvins: That if you could spare a moment,
           We might possibly arrange
           To proceed (adjourn) around the
               corner.

Gripps: For a moistening of the lips
           Are you with me, Mister Gravvins?

Gravvins: Absolutely, Mr. Gripps!

Gripps: I never have encountered your
               superior
           In dignity, ability and grace.

Gravvins: Your gifts are not confined to your
               exterior,
           Your soul is just as lovely as your
               face,

Gripps: You raise the moral tone of the
               community,
           Your nature is so pure and undefiled.

Gravvins: Your parents missed a golden
               opportunity;
           They should, of course, have drowned
               you in a bucket as a child.

Gravvins: Mister Gripps, I'd like to mention
           That your gifts are wasted here.

Gripps: Mr. Gravvins, I don't take you:
           Kindly make your meaning clear!

Gravvins: Well, a job you'd do much better
           Would be selling fish and chips.

Gripps: You're a blighter, Mister Gravvins!

Gravvins: You're a blister, Mister Gripps!
Mister Gripps, you are a blot upon
The so-called human race:

Gripps: Mister Gravvins, I'm revolted
Ev'ry time I see your face:
And next time you're eating peas, I
Hope the knife will cut your lips!
You're *impayable*, Mr. Gravvins

Gravvins: You're another, Mister Gripps!

The song was a pastiche of a song introduced by comedians Gallagher & Shean in the recent *Ziegfeld Follies*. There are further exchanges of conversation in verse between the two which appear intermittently throughout the libretto.

FIRST ROSE OF SUMMER

(Jim and Brown)

(Words by P. G. Wodehouse and Anne Caldwell)

(New lyrics for a song of the same name from *She's A Good Fellow*—[1919])

Refrain
Brown: There she stood in a world of roses;
Eyes a-dreaming and sweet cheeks
a-glow;
Breezes playing went astraying
Through her tresses with soft
caresses.
All around, with their petals gleaming
Shone the roses in a brave array;
But the first rose that blooms in
Summer
Was not so lovely as her face that day.

Jim: It was golden Summer weather,
The skies were ablaze,

As we wandered there together,
In the sunlit garden ways.
Merrily their songs of welcome
Birds trilled in each tree;
The roses knew their queen was nigh:
They bowed their heads as she passed
them by,
On that day when first she came
to me.

Jim: When the burning day was over,
Like some sweet refrain
Came a fragrant scent of clover
From the meadows down the lane.
Shadows o'er the lawn went creeping
And dark grew the sky.
The roses slept with their petals
furled
We seemed alone in a magic world,
All alone together, she and I

Brown: There we stood in a world of roses
'Neath the shy light of the sickle
moon,
Birds were sleeping—stars were
peeping
In the gloaming the bats were
roaming
Far and near (All around)—in the
dewy twilight,
All the roses hid their heads away,
But the first rose that blooms in
Summer
Was not as lovely as her face that day.

JOURNEY'S END

(Jim and Marilynn)

Jim: Once a wise old poet
Wrote a line for me and you,
Because some day we'd read it
(Someday we both would read it)
And would need it, he knew.

"Though long," he said, "and hard
    the way
That lovers have to wend,
Upon some far off, happy day
They'll meet at Journey's End."
However black the clouds may
    lower, still
Each Jill will find her Jack,
Each Jack his Jill

Journeys end in lovers meeting,
Journeys end in dreams come true.
There's a haven blest of peace and
    rest
At Journey's End for you.
Cheer up, for trouble's fleeting,
And sorrows soon will mend,
And there's laughter and song
The whole day long,
When you come to the Journey's End!

Marilynn   (*Spoken*)
It may happen sometimes, but
    personally . . .
(*Sings*)
Don't think much of poets;
Never read a poem yet
But I'll give this one credit,
For he said it!
You bet!
He means "Cheer up, though things
    look bad,"
That's what he's driving at,
I never knew that poets had
The sense to write like that!
We won't turn back, we'll just plod
    on until
Poor Jill has found her Jack, and Jack
    his Jill.

2nd
Refrain: Journeys end in lovers finding
All the dreams they dream'd
    (they've dreamt) come true;

If you just take heart and make
    a start,
That's all there is to do:—
The road is rough and winding
But soon you'll find it mend

Jim: And there's laughter and song
The whole day long.

Both: When you come to the Journey's End.

A version of the same song was also used in *The City Chap* which opened at New York's Liberty Theatre on October 26th, 1925. In this version the first verse is carried by the girl, while the man responds with "Don't think much of poets. . . ." Later there is an alternative ending to the lyrics, as he sings . . .

I'll do my very best to carry out
    your plan;
And very soon I'll be a married man.

Journeys end in lover's mating;
Somewhere, some sweet girl must be
Unsuspectingly awaiting my arrival
    C.O.D.
The road is rough and winding
You've planned for me, my friend;
But I'll do up the job,
So help me Bob!
When I come to the Journey's End!

WHOOP-DE-OODLE-DO!

(Gravvins and Cabaret Troupe)

Lily: If you've the blues and you wish you
      were dead,
If you've a tear that you're starting
      to shed,
Dry it!

All: Dry it! Dry it!

March: I have a simple, infallible rule,
And I am sure it will cure you,
    if you'll
Try it!

All: Try it!

Harry: If you'll just warble "Whoop-de-
    oodle-do!"
Life will at once seem bright and fair
    to you.

Gravvins: Ev'ry time you're in the soup
Put the accent on the *Whoop!*

Little
Ada: If you do, you are sure to find
(If you follow my tip, you'll find)
Troubles vanish away
Ev'ry cloud will be silver-lined;

All: Just begin it today! (Start and do
    it today!)

One-Two-Three!
Fill up your lungs and shout it!
"Whoop-de-oodle-doo! Whoop-de-
    oodle-doo!"
You'll soon see
Life is a blank without it,
"Whoop-de-oodle-doo! Whoop-de-
    oodle-doo!"
Sing it down the garden path,
Try it over in your bath:
Let it rip, for there's a zip about it.
One-Two-Three!
Pull up your socks and shout it!
"Whoop-de-oo-dle, Whoop-de-oodle,
    Whoop-de-oodle do!"

Lily: When all your bills and your taxes
    are due,
And to the workhouse you're feeling
    that you

May go,

All: May go! May go!

Gravvins: When you are caught in the rain with
    no um-
Brella and think you are sure to
    get lum-
Bago

All: Bago! Bago!

Harry: Buck up and yodel "Whoop-de-
    oo-dle-do!"
That's the only thing that's left
    to do.

March: If the baby has the croup
Start right in and whoop the
    whoop.

Little
Ada: If you do, you are sure to find
Troubles vanish away;
Ev'ry cloud will be silver-lined.

All: Just begin it today
One-Two-Three! etc.

Marilynn asks to see Gravvins about a role in the show. Gripps warns him to behave appropriately.

Gripps: Mister Gravvins, here's a lady,
Be as courtly as you can.

Gravvins: Mister Gripps, I will receive her
Like an English gentleman.

Gripps: When conversing please refrain
    from
Any questionable quips.
Can I trust you, Mr. Gravvins?

Gravvins: Positively, Mister Gripps.

ACT 1—FINALETTO
MY LITTLE PLACE IN THE COUNTRY
(Gravvins and Gripps)

Gravvins: My little place in the country,
You cannot imagine its charms;
Just (It's) two steps (doors) down
    from the Rose and Crown,
And close to the Waggoners' Arms,
Come then and pay us a visit!
    (give it a trial)
Why go to foreign parts
Before, I mean, you've been and seen
"The Pergola," Woollam Chersey, in
The County of Herts.

Gripps: Have no fear,
For I'm sure quite perfect,
You'll declare her
When you chance to meet,
Slim and slender
Sweet and tender,
Unaffected,
Though well connected;
All in all,
One might well compare her
To a rose bud
In the month of May,
But the first rose that blooms in
Summer
Is not as lovely
By a dashed long way!

Gripps: Mister Gravvins, it's one-thirty,
And I feel the need for lunch.

Gravvins: We have had a busy morning,
We've got rid of all the bunch.

Gripps: From a bottle of Pol Roger
We'll take long and frequent nips.
    (sips)
Are you with me, Mister Gravvins?

Gravvins: I precede you, Mister Gripps!

THE PERGOLA PATROL
(Company)

Dorothy: Oh, bright his fate and glad his lot
Who settles in this model spot.
It's just the very place to take your
    wife and daughter to.
No cook would ever leave you here,
    if you besought her to.
Each house has got its telephone and
    gas and water, too,
Oh, happy spot! Oh, happy spot!

Tradesman: Good morning, mum,
For your custom we have come,
So kindly say:
Any orders for today?
We'll rush to execute commissions
    with agility,
For we endeavour to the best of
    our ability
To serve our customers with
    promptness and civility.

All: Oh, is this not
A model spot?

The "Outdoor
Girls": The air has so much ozone,
It gives a wonderful tone
To our lungs and muscles.
We're out all day.
No other air anywhere
Is half so good as a food
For the red corpuscles,
So the doctors say.

The Young
Men: Our local girls, we maintain,
Have a charm it's rather hard to
    explain;
But once you've kiss'd 'em,
You'll understand,

And nowhere else will
     you meet
Others half as dainty and
     sweet.
And our drainage system
Is simply grand!

The Businessmen:
     We've just come back
          from town,
     And beg to state
     The trains—both up
          and down—
     Are never late.
     In short, life's full of bliss,
     (In fact, there's only
          bliss)
     For those who've got
     The sense to dwell in this
     Delightful spot.

All (*fortissimo*):
     Can you wonder that the
          place is dear
     To our grateful hearts?
     Oh, if a fellow once comes here,
     He never departs;
     Can you picture a keener bliss,
     Or a happier lot
     Than to settle down for life in this
     Delightful spot?

The Young Men:
     Let's go and golf, we suggest
     It is awf'ly jolly
     We've lots of fun.
     We've got a wonderful "pro,"
     And he'll have us playing, we know,
     Like Cyril Tolly before he's done.

     You'll find us out on the links
     Which, I'm told, Jock Hutchinson
          thinks
     The finest course in

SHIMMY WITH ME

GEORGE GROSSMITH & J.A.E. MALONE
PRESENT

THE CABARET GIRL

MUSICAL COMEDY

Vocal Score (complete)
Selection
Dancing Time
Journey's End
Ka-lu-a
First Rose of Summer
Looking all over for You
Shimmy with Me
Oriental Dreams

Book & Lyrics by
GEORGE GROSSMITH
& P. G. WODEHOUSE

Music by
JEROME KERN

CHAPPELL & CO. LTD.
50, NEW BOND STREET, LONDON. W. I.
& SYDNEY.

HARMS INCORPORATED.
62.-64. WEST 45TH STREET
NEW YORK

The world today—
Not only that, but the air
Is so pure and bracing out there
It ensures enjoyment
Each time we play.

(*Exeunt*)

The "Outdoor Girls":
     We'll come and caddy for you
     And if good shots you should do
     With your cleek and putter,
     We'll give three cheers.
     But if you do foozle or slice,
     Why, then, by mother's advice,
     To the words you utter, we'll shut
          our ears.

     We'll come and caddy for you,
     If you encourage us to;

For a nice long tramp we
Have long desired;
Don't fear that we shall suggest
We want to sit down and rest,
For in Woollam Chersey
One's never tired.

(Exeunt)

All:
Oh, bright his fate
And glad his lot,
Who settles in
This model spot.
With thankful hearts each day we go
    to sleep and wake in it.
Words simply can't express the pride
    and joy we take in it,
For Woollam Chersey's just an Eden
    with no snake in it.
Oh! happy spot!
Oh, happy spot.

Dorothy &
Walter:
Let's hasten to the clergyman who
Will swiftly tie the knot.
And then we'll bill and coo,
Just I and you
In this delightful spot!!

ENTRANCE—ACT 2

*(Two porters come in with bags, then Jim
and Marilynn)*

The
Porters:
Praise for our zeal and love of work
    we have from many won.
We carry any luggage anywhere
    for anyone.
And smile quite nicely, even when
    the tip's a penny one.

Marilynn
& Jim:
Oh, is this not a lovely spot?

Marilynn:
The road is rough and winding,
But soon you'll find it mend

Jim &
Marilynn:
And there's laughter and song the
    whole day long,
When you come to the journey's
    end.

Marilynn:
All around with their petals
    gleaming
Shine the roses in a proud array.

Jim:
But the first rose that blooms in
    summer
Is not as lovely as your face today.

SHIMMY WITH ME

(Marilynn)

Marilynn:
If you find you're getting the hump,
If you are feeling blue,
If your nerves are all on the jump,
I'll tell you what to do;
Just get up and shimmy a while,
That's the thing for you.
You'll find you can dig up a smile,
After a shake or two!
Shimmy with Me and I will shimmy
    with you;
You'll find it's easy to do
I'll see you through—you'll need
    a lesson or two
Just at the start when it's new.
If you've never shimmied, start
    learning now,
Don't be shy or timid; I'll show
    you how
It's just a knack; wiggle your back,
Give a sort of shiver, then a kind
    of quiver,
Sway, if you please, just like the trees
    in a breeze,

You'll pick it up by degrees
Once you begin, you'll shake right
    out of your skin.
Go in and win!
Shimmy from your shoulders down
    to your knee,
Give the dazed beholders something
    to see;
Pull up your socks
    (start up the music) and just
    come out and shimmy with me.

Additional
Refrain
Ensemble: Shimmy with me, and I will shimmy
    with you,
You'll find it easy to do,
Shimmy with me, come on and
    shake up your spine,
For it will make you feel fine.
Don't be shy or timid; I'll show
    you how.
If you've never shimmied, start
    learning now.
It's just a knack, wiggle your back,
Give a sort of shiver, then a kind
    of quiver.
Just try to feel as if you'd swallowed
    an eel;
You'll find that helps a good deal!
Once you begin, you'll shake right
    out of your skin;
Go in and win.
Shimmy from your shoulders, down
    to your knee,
Give the dazed beholders, something
    to see!
Pull up your socks and just (Start up
    the music and)
Come out and shimmy with me!

This show introduced British audiences to the new American dance craze—"The Shimmy"—which Mae West claimed to have been the first to spot in a black Chicago café back in 1918. *The Oxford English Dictionary* defines it as "a kind of lively ragtime dance involving much shaking of the body."

Gripps: Mister Gravvins, you're the limit!

Gravvins: Mister Gripps, you're even worse.

Gripps: You offend my finer feelings
    You're the nation's leading curse.

Gravvins: If I started to describe you,
    Every word would scorch my lips.

Gripps: Let me thank you, Mr. Gravvins

Gravvins: You are welcome, Mr. Gripps.

THOSE DAYS ARE GONE FOREVER (LONG YEARS AGO)

(Gravvins)

Gravvins: Long years ago girls used to have
    For me a perfect craving,
    They used to wait outside my gate,
    To try to watch me shaving.
    I used to write romantic verse
    My nickname was "The Flapper's
       Curse."

    Oh! Dear days of long ago!
    We cannot bring them back, ah no!
    However we endeavour
    It sometimes makes me rather sad
    To think of all the times I've had.
    I was so handsome as a lad:
    Those days are gone for ever!

    Today the price of ev'ry thing
    Is rising like a rocket,
    And bandits dash to pinch your
       cash

Before it's in your pocket.
When you've saved up to buy
    some coal,
They sneak the lot for someone's
    dole.

Oh! Dear days of long ago!
We cannot bring them back, ah, no!
However, we endeavour.
My father used to say to me
That, back in eighteen-eighty-three,
He often had an egg for tea:
Those days are gone for ever!

Have you observed the modern girl?
I have, with consternation!
For what Dean Inge would call
    a "binge"
Is her pet recreation.
She dresses at her dancing club
Like Venus rising from the tub.

Oh, dear days of long ago!
We cannot bring them back, ah, no!
However we endeavour.
When you took out a girl to dine
In ninety-eight or ninety-nine,
You never knew she *had* a spine;
Her stays are gone for ever!

LOOKING ALL OVER FOR YOU

(Jim and Marilynn)

Jim: For years I hunted high and low
                Just trying to discover you.

Marilynn: Did you get tired?

Jim: For somehow, dear, I seemed to
                  know
                That I was just the lover you
                Indeed required
                And if I kissed a girl or two,

I simply thought that they were you
It's easy you'll agree, to make
That sort of innocent mistake:
For I was looking all over,
All over, all over
Just searching all over for you;
Sometimes I'd think I had found
    you—and then, (but no!)
I'd see that I hadn't and start once
    again (—then off I would go)
Looking over,
And over,
All over and over,
A regular rover I grew,
Buzzing around like a bee in the
    clover,
And looking (searching) all over—
For you!

Marilynn: It's odd, but I did just the same;
              For five long years or thereabouts;
              I tried my best
              Although I didn't know your name,
              To ascertain your whereabouts.

Jim: Now you can rest,

Marilynn: And if I listen'd now and then
              To compliments from other men,
              'Twas just because, as girls will do,
              I thought those other men were you.
              For I was looking all over . . . (etc.)

NERVES

(Gravvins, Gripps and Ada)

Note: This lyric is very comparable to the lyric bearing the same title in *See You Later* (1918). And it is interesting to note that Wodehouse was able to adapt practically the same text to two different musical scores. For purposes of comparison, in this case we have included both versions in their relevant context.

He was also to suggest a version of it to Ira Gershwin when *Oh, Kay!* was revised in 1960, but it was not used.

Gripps: Let's pull ourselves together!
For there's not a thing to be
frightened at.

All: What was that!

Gravvins: It must have been the bird you heard
A-roosting on the trees,

Gripps &
Gravvins: Or the cat
On the mat.

Ada: We'll have to take a tonic or a cocktail
on a tray.

All: For we're not ourselves today!
Oh, I feel so ner-ner-ner-vous,
I der-don't know what to do!
For my heart is going b-bump,
My pulse is going th-thump;
At ev'ry sound I leap and bound
And jump!
Oh, I feel so ner-ner-nervous
And my legs go 'round in cur-cur-
curves,
Please don't ther-ther-think
It's due to der-der-drink,
It is due-do-do-do-do to ner-ner-
nerves!

Gripps: Let's pull ourselves together!
We'll regard this by-and-by
As a joke.

All: Holy smoke!

Gravvins: Don't let that noise alarm you:
It just happened that a fly
On my coat
Cleared his throat:

Ada: I thought it was a dynamite explosion
'cross the way,

All: For we're not ourselves today!

FINALE—ACT 2

(Effie, Rev. Hugo Pebblewhite, Master Pebblewhite, Miss Pebblewhite; Gravvins comes in dressed as a Vicar)

Chorus A: Who d'you think that this is?

Chorus B: Doubtless someone who
Used to teach the bridegroom when
a lad,
To seek the good and shun the bad.
I think so, don't you?

Gravvins: *(Speaks)*
"My friends" "My *dear* friends" . . .

(Sings)
I was working in my study
On a sermon for next Sunday
On some foolish superstitions
Which have lately been revived.

Chorus A: Observe with what a genial air,
He beams upon the happy pair.

Gravvins: When old George, our worthy
sexton,
Brought the welcome information
That the young and happy couple
Had arrived.

Chorus B: This speech no doubt is kindly
meant
He's cordial and benevolent.
But on the whole we must confess
We wish he'd talk a little less!

Gravvins: Permit me, if you'll pardon my
audacity,

To state that I consider you have
    shown
The utmost taste and sense and
    perspicacity
In choosing Woollam Chersey for
    your own.
The guide books call our village
    paradisical,
And we who live here know that this
    is true,
And so I hasten'd hither on my
    tricycle,
To say I hope 'twill prove to be
    a paradise for you.

Chorus A: And so he hasten'd hither on his
    tricycle,
To say he hopes 'twill prove to be a
    paradise for you!

Gripps: *(Aside)*
Mister Gravvins, just a moment!

Gravvins: *(Aside—with a haughty gesture)*
Mister Gripps, (Fellow, do not)
    don't interfere!

Gripps: *(Aside)*
I must beg that you be careful
    (Pray be careful of your conduct)
Of your conduct while you're here.
    (While you're masquerading
    here!)

Gravvins: *(Aloud to villagers)*
Oh, my brethren, I'm as joyful
As a lamb that leaps and skips.

Gripps: *(Aside)*
Have an éclair, Mister Gravvins!
(You're a liar, Mister Gravvins)

Gravvins: *(Aside)*
Go to blazes, Mister Gripps!

Chorus: We'd like to say that we
With no dissent,
Endorse most heartily
His sentiment:
Like him we hope that bliss
Will be your lot;
That you'll find in this
Delightful spot. (Model spot!
    Model spot!)

(Exit Gravvins. The real vicar, Mr. Pebblewhite, steps in)

Pebblewhite: *(Spoken)*
I am the Vicar of Woollam Chersey

Chorus: Yes! This is our Vicar
What he says is true. (That, of
    course, is true.)
Why, the other man must be
    a crook!
He had a nasty shifty look,
He's bad through and through!

Jim: Most towns, I own
Have one vicar—one alone.

Gripps: But in this place
They engage them by the brace.
It may seem odd I know at first,
But there, well, there it is.

Jim: Two vicars tend our little flock,
But in their care it is.

Gripps: Sin thus becomes the very rarest of
    all rarities.

Chorus: Oh! Is this not a model spot?

Marilynn: All my rainbow visions are over
    and ended.

Jim: *(Desperate)*
Rainbow visions which I used to see.

Both: All my dreams are broken and
            can't be mended.

Marilynn: Dancing time is all that is left
            for me.

Chorus: All her dreams of happiness are
            ended. (*bis*)

LONDON, DEAR OLD LONDON

(Jim)

(Burthen by George Grossmith Jr.)

Jim: I used to hate the strife
        And din of London life,
        But my tastes lately
        Have altered greatly.
        Yes, long past that day is,
        And now all I say is:

        London! brighter London!
        Save a place for me!
        You can make a note upon your
            cuff
        That I find London good
            enough:
        Remove all
        Doubts of my approval;
        If there's room in London,
        Put me anywhere.
        I'd prefer the Ritz; but failing
        That, I'll sleep against a railing:
        Just so long as it's in London,
            I don't care.
        London's foggy, also dirty,
        And they close it at twelve-thirty,
        But you'll find me right there.

        I think the old Metrop
        Is more or less tip-top.
        It's grey and musty,

But not so dusty
To speak more precisely,
It suits me quite nicely.

Burthen: London! dear old London!
            Save a place for me!
            I am told they want to brighten it:
            Well, I'm prepared to do my bit:
            Delighted
            If and when invited!
            When you brighten London
            Put me anywhere;
            If you want a man to do it,
            I'm the fellow; lead me to it,
            And I'll guarantee that I will do
                my share.
            You may spread the information
            That I've found my true vocation,
            And I've found it right there!

Men: Brighter London! That's the
                stuff!
            The place is not half bright
                enough;
            We'll have to lend a hand; it's only
                fair:
            Lead the way and you will find
            That we are following (trailing)
                close behind:
            Yes, we will be right there!

ORIENTAL DREAMS
FINALE—ACT 3

(Lyric by P. G. Wodehouse
and George Grossmith Jr.)

Ensemble: Oriental eyes that enrapture me
            On an Eastern Sea,
            Under Eastern skies,
            Oriental dreams
            In a golden Shrine
            Where a love like mine

So eternal seems.
Lo—Ho—O
Oh, your pale white arms,
Oh, your ruby lips,
From your honey charms
There the love-bee sips.
Oh, your snow-white breast
Oh, your silken hair,
In supernal rest,
Let me hide me there
Lo—Ho—O, Lo—Ho—O

(Marilynn appears at the top of the stairs)

DANCING TIME

(Marilynn, Jim and Chorus)

**(Lyric by Wodehouse
and George Grossmith Jr.)**

Marilynn: Dancing time is just when the
    music is playing,
    When the stars are shimmying
    up in the sky,
    Dancing time is just when
    your shoulders are
    swaying.

*(She catches sight of Jim and speaks to him,
then . . .)*

    Take me where the bees in
    the flowers are droning,

Jim: No! London is the only place
    to be!

Chorus: All the boys in London are
    telephoning.

Jim &
Marilynn: Dancing time's the time for
    you and me.

Ensemble: Dancing time is just when
    the music is playing,
    When the stars are shimmying
    up in the sky,
    Dancing time is just when
    your shoulders are swaying,
    When your feet have simply got
    to glide.
    You must lead me lightly,
    Hold me tightly;
    Take me where you hear all those
    saxophones,
    Where can those ukuleles be,

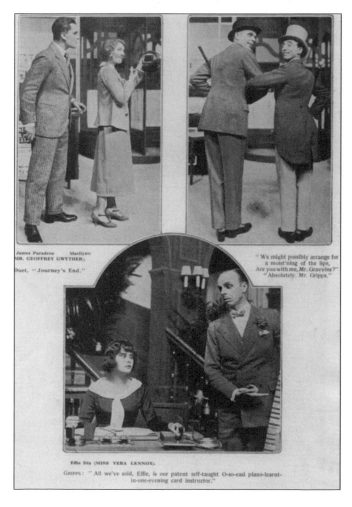

Top left: Geoffrey Gwyther (Jim) and Dorothy Dickson
(Marilynn). *Top right:* George Grossmith (Mr. Gripps) and
Norman Griffin (Mr. Gravvins). *Bottom:* Vera Lennox (Effie).

Ev'ry boy in London is telephoning,
   (All the lads and lasses are
     gramophoning,)
Dancing time is any old time
   for me.

In another version this number appears in Act 1 and is sung by Marilynn and Gravvins with the following additional material . . .

Verse 1
Marilynn: There's a tune I heard not very
           long ago,
          Whose haunting melody is
           dancing in my brain;
          Like the voice of someone that
           I used to know;
          That always whispers when it's
           time to dance again.

Verse 2
Gravvins: There was a philosopher who was
           not wrong;
          "There is a time and place to
           everything," said he,
          "Time for women, time for wine
           and time for song,"
          But when you dance, by gosh,
           it's time for all three!

Even though Kern followed his by now usual practice of recycling numbers from earlier shows—both "Chopin Ad Lib" and "First Rose of Summer" had their origins in *She's A Good Fellow* (1919)—the show was sufficiently well received by critics and public alike for the team to set to work on a successor for the following season.

THE BEAUTY PRIZE (1923)

(Originally, THE FIRST PRIZE)

Presented at the Winter Garden Theatre, London, on September 5, 1923 (214 performances).

PRODUCER
George Grossmith Jr.

BOOK
George Grossmith Jr.
and P. G. Wodehouse

LYRICS
George Grossmith Jr.
and P. G. Wodehouse

MUSIC
Jerome Kern

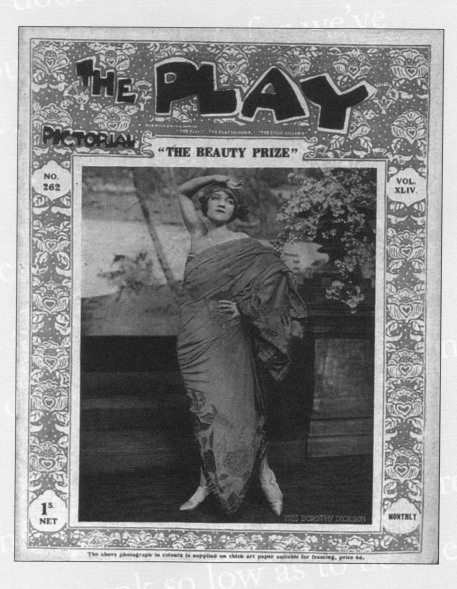

CAST

Hon. Dud Wellington:
PETER HADDON

Meadow Grahame:
DOROTHY FIELD

Mrs. Hexal:
SHEILA COURTNAY

Shinny Fane:
MARJORIE SPIERS

Gypsy Lorrimole:
DOROTHY HURST

Flutey Warboy:
GEORGE GROSSMITH JR.

John Brooke:
JACK HOBBS

Manicure Girl:
KOOKOO DUNCAN

Shoe Girl:
MONICA NOYES

Lingerie Girl:
PHYLLIS GARTON

Hairdresser:
DOROTHY DEANE

Flower Girl:
MIGNON MORENZA

Dressmaker Girl:
BERYL MURRAY

Glove Girl:
MINETTE CORDAY

Parasol Girl:
PHYLLIS SWINBURNE

Doreen:
EILEEN SEYMOUR

Hector:
ERNEST GRAHAM

Kitty Wren:
VERA LENNOX

Carol Stuart:
DOROTHY DICKSON

Lovey Toots:
HEATHER THATCHER

Jones:
CLAUDE HORTON

Mr. Odo Philpotts:
LESLIE HENSON

Quartermaster:
LEIGH ELLIS

James K. Stuart:
ARTHUR FINN

Pedro:
WILLIAM PARNIS

Servant:
FRED WHITLOCK

Marconi Boy:
WINIFRED SHOTTER

Steward:
JACK GLYNN

SYNOPSIS

Socialites gather in a supper club where a gypsy singer entertains them ("When You Take the Road With Me"). The girls discuss a beauty competition in which the first prize is a husband. John arrives and tells Flutey (his secretary) he is about to marry Carol, his American fiancée, and start a whole new life. He then sees her face in the ad for the beauty competition. In Carol's flat her servants are preparing for the wedding ("Now We Are Nearly Through"). Kitty (Carol's friend) is in charge of the presents ("Entrance Scene"). Kitty and Carol discuss what it feels like to be in love ("Honeymoon Isle"). Lovey, Carol's milliner, has entered her photograph without her knowing. Now it appears she has won and her prize, Odo, arrives ("I'm A Prize"). Flutey had hoped to win Carol and he meets Fannie, who now has lost hope of marrying John. They plot together to stop the wedding ("It's A Long, Long Day"). John now hears that not only has Carol won the competition but that she is very rich. He is her latest purchase. At which point his friends arrive for the festivities ("Joy Bells"). John and Carol meet and argue. She will marry Odo and John threatens to marry Lovey ("Act 1—Finale").

On the *S.S. Majestiana* on the way to the USA. To the annoyance of the Boys, the Girls are all busy playing mah-jong ("You'll Find Me Playing Mah-Jong"). Naturally—this being a musical comedy—all the principal characters are on board for one reason or another. Flutey tells Carol the news that her father is planning a party to celebrate her return. Isn't the wireless telegraph a wonderful thing? It can do almost anything ("You Can't Make Love By Wireless"). Odo is surrounded by the Girls. He tells them to get ready for the ship's Dancing Marathon ("Non-Stop Dancing"). Carol and John are clearly still in love—they argue every time they meet. They tell each other what they would do, if they were ever *really* in love ("That's What I'd Do For the Girl I Love"). Odo and Lovey are now attracted to each other ("Cottage in Kent"). Thanks to Flutey's intervention, both John and Carol have arranged for phony ship's telegrams to be delivered saying that each of them has lost everything, so money can no longer be an obstacle between them ("Act 2—Finale").

Carol's father's estate ("Opening Chorus"). Odo and Flutey arrive in fancy dress ("Meet Me Down on Main Street"). A lovelorn Carol sings to the Boys ("Moon Love"). Then a brisk happy ending with Carol and John confessing that they are not really ruined . . . Flutey being hired by Carol's father . . . and Odo and Lovey ready to find their cottage in Kent.

WHEN YOU TAKE THE ROAD WITH ME

(Gypsy)

Gypsy: There's a road that lies, shadow-
haunted,
Hard and rough with stone and briar,
Facing those who, all undaunted,
Seek the Land of Heart's Desire.
But though long it be and winding,
Swept by tempests fierce and blinding,
You and I will brave it, and
Travel o'er it hand in hand.

Refrain: We will take the road together,
Letting come what may;
We shall meet with stormy weather
As we go our way.
But no matter what betide us,
Safe at last we'll be,
For love will go beside us,
To guard our steps and guide us,
When you take the road with me.

All: For love will go beside us
To guard our steps and guide us,
When you take the road with me.

SCENE 2 OPENING CHORUS— NOW WE ARE NEARLY THROUGH

(Kitty, Hector, Maids and Footmen)

(Words by P. G. Wodehouse and George Grossmith Jr.)

Maids: Now we are nearly through,
I never thought—did *you*?
Such preparations
Could be effected
Just in an hour or two.

Footmen: Yes, it has been a strain,
And we must make it plain;
Our resignations

May be expected
If it occurs again.

Maids &
Footmen: Oh, dear!
Go away
We're busy!

Footmen: Still after all, well there!
Mind you, we've done a rare
Lot towards making
This little wedding
Quite a "re-*church*" affair.

All: Yes, though we're well aware,
We've had a lot to bear,
There's no mistaking,
This undertaking
Will be a smart affair.

Maids: And here are some
More things just come;
Where shall we, please,
Deposit these?

All: Just put 'em over there,
Just put 'em over there;
There's no mistaking,
This undertaking,
Will be a smart affair.

Kitty: Miss Carol asks me to convey
Her gratitude to everyone;
She hopes you'll wish her luck today
And thanks you all for what you
have done.

Hector: *This* has just arrived, miss,
It appears to be
A silver-plated cream jug
For afternoon tea:
I beg to state
The seventeenth—to date!

Kitty: The sky is gay
          And gleaming overhead
          Look where you may
          There's not a cloud in sight,
          Which must betide
          Good fortune, for it's said
          That happy is the bride
          On whom the sun shines bright.

Footmen: If you're requiring me,
          Down at the church I'll be,
          Watching with unction
          The little function
          Up in the gallery.

Kitty: And may she go up on her way
          As free from shadows as the day.

ENTRANCE SCENE

(Kitty and Girls)

Kitty: What lovelier things a bride could
              adorn
          Upon her happy wedding morn?
          Now here is one
          The fairies might have spun.

Girls: What lovelier things a bride could
              adorn
          Upon her happy wedding morn?
          Oh, just look there!
          Could anything be more rare?

Kitty: Oh, look! Just see this wonderful
              blue!

Girls: And this one here of lavender, too!
          And lots of others besides,

Kitty: To deck the happy bride.

All: Oh, happy bride,
          We are sure you ought to be satisfied

What more could heart desire?
For the sun shines bright and sky
    is blue
And Prince Charming waits at the
    church for you.
What more could a bride require?

HONEYMOON ISLE

(Carol and Kitty)

Carol: Somewhere, I know it,
          I was told so by a poet
          There's an island in a magic silver
              sea.
          It lies and dozes,
          Covered deep with Summer roses,
          And the orange blossom blooms on
              every tree.
          There 'neath a sky that's always blue
          Couples walk two by two;
          Or in some cool and quiet glade
          Sit whisp'ring in the shade,
          While the birds up above
          Murmur their songs of love.

Refrain: Honeymoon Isle
          Where lovers stray,
          Honeymoon Isle
          Lies far away;
          Many a mile
          O'er oceans uncharted,
          Only to some
          It's granted
          Ever to come there and
          Dwell in that dear, enchanted land.
          But if you try,
          And if you're stout-hearted,
          Love by and by
          May pilot you through
          And you may hope some day to
          Find at last your way to
          Honeymoon Isle, where dreams
              come true.

Kitty: Few people know it,
On the maps they never show it;
It's a place which no explorer ever
scanned.
It's barred to steamers,
And is only found by dreamers;
For to get there you must pass
through Fairyland.

Carol: Far, far beyond the rainbow's end,
On and on you must wend,
And only those may find it who
Set out by two and two.
If alone you set sail,
Always your quest must fail.

Refrain

I'M A PRIZE

(Odo and Carol)

Odo: I note with surprise
Not unmixed with *chagrin*
You don't realise
Just how lucky you've been.
I will therefore attempt to make
you see
What you have drawn in me.

Refrain: I'm a prize! I'm a prize that is simply
unique,
I can toot on the flute, play ping-pong
and *bézique*,
Can help you choose a frock or a hat,
I can shine your shoes and valet
the cat;
I'm so brave, if you gave but one cry
of alarm
I would fight like a knight to protect
you from harm,
You will snap such a chap up at once
if you're wise.
For no girl ever won such a prize.

Carol: You may have this string
Of great gifts, as you boast,
But *love* is the thing
That a girl yearns for most.

Odo: That's precisely where I come out
so strong;
Lucky I came along!

Carol: You're a prize!

Odo: I'm a prize!

Carol: That is simply unique.

Odo: Since a lad, I have had quite a name
as a Sheik

Carol: Would you clasp me tight and swear
to be true?

Odo: I may say that's quite the best thing
I do.

Carol: I love thrills!

Odo: You'd get chills!

Carol: I want shivers and shocks!

Odo: I'm no slow Romeo when I pull up
my socks.
You'll agree you can see without
any disguise

Carol: That no girl ever won such a prize.

IT'S A LONG, LONG DAY

(Flutey)

Flutey: Though up to the present
I've found life quite pleasant,
I'm a victim of the strangest malady.

No one healthier or fitter
As a general rule could be
Yet I get all in a twitter
If you mention work to me.
I shrink, I shy, I reel, I sway,
I don't know why, it seems to spoil
    my day.

Refrain: It's strange
I sleep quite well and my appetite's
All right at night.
I'll range thro' every drink that is on
    the list
If you insist.
Though I dine and sup, I dance and
    shimmy late;
Work in the daytime I can't assimilate.
When I get up every morning I say:
"It's a long, long day."

When I see my neighbours
Starting on their labours,
Sympathy and pity make my eyes
    grow dim.
Just to watch them turns me dizzy,
And my head begins to swim
Till I ring for something fizzy,
To restore my shattered vim.
I moan, I sigh, my hair turns grey,
I don't know why, it simply spoils
    my day.

Refrain: My case
Is one that doctors have probed
    in vain,
But they can't explain.
No trace of any microbe in me
    they find
Of any kind
Though at night I'm so bright and
    join in things chattily,
When I wake up I need Sal Volatile.
Though it be the loveliest morning
    in May,

It seems a long, long day.
If I have to walk just over the way
It seems a long, long day.

Encore
Refrain: I know sometimes I'd like to adopt
Old Rip Van Winkle's tip
And go to sleep for twenty odd years
And thus avoid all fuss.
Just follow his plan and safe in your
    bed you'll be
When tax collectors call round with
    their Schedule B.
No doubt about it, he knew the way
To pass the long, long day.

JOY BELLS

(Dud, Kitty, Men and Girls)

All: Cheer! We're here!
Whenever it's clear that a pal is
    in trouble,
We appear
Around him rallying, no dilly-dallying.

Dud: Far and near
We put on our spats and arrived at
    the double.

Kitty: John, we knew,
Would need a friend or two.

Men: Poor old crock,
He's jumping off the dock!

Girls: Still, of course, though time may
    bring remorse,
We're perfectly aware
It's quite their own affair.

Men: We can do no more than see him
    through
And heave a parting shoe.

Girls: Joy bells!

Men: We are the fellows to

Girls: Joy Bells!

Men: Do all there is to do;
          No need to make a fuss,
          Just leave it all to us

All: The job before us
          Is to sing in chorus
          Joy bells! Joy bells!
          Sing it happily
          Sing it snappily
          Not the sort of thing you want
             to whisper:
          Joy bells! Joy bells!

Boys: Not the sort of thing you want to
             whisper:
          For in efficiency,
          We yield to nobody,
          We'll see to ev'ry thing,
          Take care he's got the ring.

Girls &
Boys: Get some go in it,
          Put some flow in it,
          All you know in it,
          Make it crisper!
          Joy bells!

Boys: If there are one or two
          Trifles that puzzle you,
          Smooth out the furrowed brow,
          We'll fix 'em here and now.

Girls &
Boys: Put some grip in it!
          Shove some zip in it!
          Ask us and we'll show you how.

Girls: Wow!

FINALE—ACT 1

(Odo and Ensemble)

(Words by P. G. Wodehouse
and George Grossmith Jr.)

John: We will take the road together
          Letting come what may;

Carol: We shall meet with stormy
             weather
          As we go our way.

All: And no matter what betide them, safe
             at last they'll be:
          For love will go beside us and guard
             our steps and guide us
          When you take the road with me.

Odo: I'm a prize!

All: He's a prize!

Odo: Set misgivings at rest,
          We will coo, I and you, like two birds
             in a nest:

All: Yes, the Dunmow Flitch you'll win,
             we agree

Odo: Though you may be rich that won't
             worry *me!*
          I'm a prize!

All: He's a prize!

Odo: I'm too good to be true:
          You will find Fate was kind when it
             brought me to you

All: You will snap such a chap up at once,
             if you're wise,
          For no girl ever won such a prize.

ACT 2—OPENING CHORUS
YOU'LL FIND ME
PLAYING MAH-JONG

(Men and Girls)

Men: By tomorrow afternoon
        they say we'll be on
        shore.

Girls: Oh, dear! I wish you'd
        run along,
        You've gone and made me
        miss a pong.

Men: Makes one rather blue to
        think there's only one
        day more.

Girls: Oh, will you please keep
        quiet! Now,
        You've made me overlook
        a chow.

Men: When we've parted
        Broken-hearted we shall
        lose our reason.

Girls: Circle seven,
        Hand from Heaven!
        That's my first this season.

Men: Can't you stop this rotten game for
        just an hour or two?

Girls: But it's the only thing on earth we
        want to do.

Men: Have you got nothing else to do!

Girls: Pong, chow!
        Pong, chow!
        Pong all day long!

Lovey Toots (HEATHER THATCHER).   Odo Philpotts (LESLIE HENSON).

Odo: " Just in time."   Lovey: " In time for what ? "
        Odo : " To save you from falling on that bandbox."   *Photo, Stage Photo Co.*

Men: Yes, You've got it nowadays!
        That Mah-Jong craze!

All: While there's one tile that's left
        to pong,
        You'll find us playing this game
        of Mah-Jong.

Girls: Though you may travel for all you
        are worth,
        Though you may roam to the ends
        of the earth,
        You'll find you never are able for long

To get away from the game of
 Mah-Jong.

Men: Yes, there is nobody now
Who isn't bellowing "Chow!"
Or yelling "Pong!"
From Ponders End to Peru,
From Yokohama to Kew,
It's all Mah-Jong

Refrain

Bamboo
Girl: At all Swiss Mountain resorts,
They've given up winter sports;
They sit indoors all day long
And play Mah-Jong.
They think a Matterhorn climb
Is just a sheer waste of time;
The hotel lobby they throng
And play Mah-Jong

Men: Yes, there is nobody now,
Who isn't bellowing "Chow!"
Or yelling "Pong!"

Bamboo
Girl: From Waltham Green to Brazil,
From Cotopaxi to Rhyl,
It's all Mah-Jong.

All: Though you may travel for all you
 are worth,
Though you may roam to the ends of
 the earth,
You'll find you never are able for
 long
To get away from this game of
 Mah-Jong.

Circle
Girl: They say that bull-fights in Spain
Are very much on the wane;
They think they're lucky, I hear,

If they get two in a year;
For all the toreadors now belong
To special clubs where they play at
 Mah-Jong.
Yes, there is nobody now
Who isn't bellowing "Chow!"
Or yelling "Pong!"
From Gretna (Golders) Green
 to Rangoon,
From Potter's Bar to Kowloon,
It's all Mah-Jong.

Refrain

Character
Girl: There's no more dancing
And tender glancing,
There's no more moonlight
 bill-and-cooing,
And in the gloaming,
Instead of roaming,
You'll find us circling and
 bambooing.
We never wander in the shy light,
Of any scented summer twilight;
We're busy ponging
And gonging,
Discarding and Mah-Jonging.

For there is nobody now,
Who isn't bellowing "Chow"
Or yelling "Pong"
From Bexhill (Drury Lane) to Peru,
From Penge to Kalamazoo
It's all Mah-Jong.

Girls: While there's one counter (tile that's)
 left to pong,
You'll find us playing the game of
 Mah-Jong.

Men: Mah-Jong! Mah-Jong!
Life's just one long Mah-Jong!

Character
Girl: From Drury Lane to Peru,
        From Penge to Kalamazoo,
        It's all Mah-Jong.

Mah-Jong is a Chinese game for four, played with 136 or 144 pieces called "tiles," divided into five or six suits. It was all the rage at the time they were creating the show but Wodehouse apparently hated it. It amused Grossmith hugely that, when the rest of the family were happily playing it, the only place Wodehouse could work was on the kitchen porch among the garbage cans, where he would sit creating "Chinese-sounding lyrics."

YOU CAN'T MAKE LOVE BY WIRELESS

(Flutey and Carol)

(Lyric by P. G. Wodehouse and George Grossmith Jr.)

Flutey: Charles Augustus Chaytor,
         Wireless operator
         Loved the fair—
         Golden Hair'd Bessie Magee.
         She lived in Dargheeling
         Avenue, West Ealing,
         He was always out at sea.

Carol: Such was his devotion
         That when on the ocean,
         Every day
         He'd relay
         Greetings to Bess.

Flutey: But I'm told that sometimes
         There, alas, would come times
         When he moaned this S.O.S.:

Both: "You can't make love by wireless:"
         It's like bread without the jam.

Carol: There is nothing girls desire less
         Than a fond (cold) Marconigram.

Flutey: For it's something you can't speak to
         From a someone you can't see
         Like a village church that's spireless,
         Or a little home that's fireless
         Or a motor car that's tyreless,
         And it isn't any good to me!

Flutey: Mark the horrid sequel:
         It is hard to equal.

Carol: Fate with grim
         Tragic whim
         Upset his dream.

Flutey: For that maiden fickle
         Wed a man from Crickle
         Wood who kept a laundry (steam).

Carol: Charles, poor man, thus jilted,
         Naturally wilted;
         Soured he grew,
         Gloomy too,
         Quite lost his smile.

Flutey: Never more his jokes'll
         Entertain the foc'sle,
         He keeps muttering all the while—

Both: "You can't make love by wireless"
         It's like eggs without the ham.
         There's nothing girls desire less
         Than a fond (cold) Marconigram;
         For it's something you can't speak to
         From a someone you can't see;
         Like a Selfridge's that buyerless,
         (It's like a village church that's
             spireless)
         Or a taxicab that's hireless
         (Or a Selfridge's that's buyerless)
         Or a Pekinese that's sireless,
         And it isn't any good to me!

Reprise

Both: There's no present I require less
   There's no gift that I desire less
   Than a kiss sent off by wireless.

Flutey: It's like a friary that's friarless,
   It's like a Handling Rope that's
    flyerless;
   It's like a fishing club that's liarless
   But it's going to be a help to me.

In the same way that Wodehouse and Grossmith had seized upon the topicality of cabarets and Mah-Jong, they now determined to capitalize on the current craze for Non-Stop Dancing. The Wembley Exhibition of 1924–25 even held a competition, and lyricist Harry Graham wrote a verse to commemorate it . . .

  Fate moves in a mysterious way,
  As shown by Uncle Titus
  Who, unexpectedly, one day
  Was stricken with St. Vitus.
  It proved a blessing in disguise
  For, thanks to his condition,
  He won the Non-Stop Dancing Prize
  At Wembley Exhibition.

NON-STOP DANCING

(Odo)

Odo: Our home life once used to be
   quiet:
   Not a sign of bustle or riot,
   Ev'rything quite peaceable and
    serene.
   Ev'ry evening mother wrote letters,
   Grandma knitted stockings and
    sweaters,
   Father read the Parish Magazine.
   Now you'll find a different sort of
    scene.

Refrain: Since we got the non-stop dancing
    craze,
   We quite altered our domestic ways;
   Mother ev'ry evening may be seen on
    the floor,
   And no one's fed the baby for a
    fortnight or more.
   We don't ever go out nowadays,
   Life just passes in a sort of haze,
   Grandma's feet are getting tender,
   Father's burst his sock suspender,
   Since we got the non-stop dancing
    craze.

   Once the noise the tiniest mouse made
   Could be heard; but now when the
    housemaid
   Breaks the china, nobody hears a
    sound.
   Grandma is an absolute wonder,
   Tho' her ankle's buckling under,
   She'll beat all the girls for miles
    around.
   Does you good to see her cover
    the ground!

Refrain: Since we got the non-stop dancing
    craze,
   Life at home has changed in many
    ways
   Every night the friends we have in
    take to the game;
   The curate got a spavin and has since
    been quite lame.
   All day long the pianola plays:
   Grandma's worn out fourteen pairs
    of stays.
   Father pluckily continues,
   Though he's sprained eleven sinews,
   Since we got the non-stop dancing
    craze.

Refrain: Since we got the non-stop dancing
    craze,

We've quite altered our domestic ways.
Grandpapa, although he wheezes,
    knows how to step;
He shakes the old Waukeesis with
    abandon and pep.
With Aunt Mary, Uncle Percy sways
Father hasn't slept for seven days.
Even Cook, though stout's, no loafer
She's been shimmying with the
    chauffeur.
We're insured, for that's essential,
With the man from the Prudential,
Since we got the non-stop dancing
    craze.

Since we got the non-stop dancing
    craze
Life at home has changed in many
    ways.
Uncle James, who's eighty, hobbles
    round with the rest,
He's anxious to be matey, so he
    dances his best.
When we eat we take our meals
    off trays,
Just a bit of shrimps and mayonnaise.
If you want to be a winner
You've no time to stop for dinner
There is simply no concealing
We've all got that Kruschen feeling
Since we got the non-stop dancing
    craze.

THAT'S WHAT I'D DO FOR THE GIRL/MAN I LOVE (FOR THE MAN I LOVE)

(John and Carol)

John: Some day some girl I may love dearly
And she, I hope in all humility
May care for me.

Carol: Girls take strange fancies, so there
    clearly

Is just perhaps the possibility
That it might be:

John: You think it would be strange?

Carol: I quite agree
Still, if your dream came true
Pray tell me what you'd do.

John: I would take the girl that I loved and
    tell her gently
All the secrets burning within my
    breast
Down into the depths of her eyes
    I'd gaze intently
Till all my thoughts and dreams she
    had guessed;
Life would become a thing of wonder;
And, if Fate tore us two asunder,
Then I would search the whole world
    until I found her
Safe once more with my arms around
    her . . .
That is what I'd do for the girl I
    loved.

Carol: Somewhere I, too, may find love
    waiting,
As o'er the world we go a-wandering,
My heart and I.

John: But love's a thing, forgive me stating
Which, spite of all the wealth you're
    squandering,
You cannot buy;
For love's a thing that shops do not
    supply.
Still, if it came to you
Pray tell me what you'd do.

Carol: I would tell the man that I loved the
    same old story
Adam heard the day that he first
    met Eve:

Tell him that he filled all the world
  with golden glory
And ev'ry word that I said he'd
  believe;
Sometimes I'd scold him or I'd tease
  him,
Then, when I felt it time to please
  him—
"Dear, in your arms please take me,
  and if you're clever
Try to hold me in them for ever . . ."
That is what I'd say to the man I
  loved.

A COTTAGE IN KENT

(Odo and Lovey)

Lovey: Oh, how I'd love with you to stray
          Into the country far away.

Odo: If you were but my little wife
          I'd gladly lead the simple life.

Lovey: We'd take a tiny (cosy) cottage down
          In some place miles away from town.

Odo: And every evening I'd say "Hush!"

Lovey: (Spoken) What's that?

Odo: 'Tis Theodore, the local thrush.

Both: If we'd a little cottage down in Kent,
          An ivy-covered cottage down in Kent.

Lovey: We'd mow the corn and hoe the peas
          And grow tomatoes on the trees.

Odo: Which, when quite ripe, we'll sell to
            pay the rent.

Lovey: We'd stand and sniff the apple
            blossom scent

And pluck sweet roses ev'rywhere
  we went.

Odo: And Hilda, our resourceful hen,
          Would lay us omelettes now and then.

Both: If we'd a little cottage down in Kent.

Lovey: Each morning, if you showed me how,
          I'd go and milk Clarice, the cow.

Odo: Or for potatoes we would dig
          Or slaughter Paul, our genial pig.

Lovey: And if we found a snail or slug
          Or weevil or potato bug

Odo: I'd track them down and wring their
            necks
          Regardless of their age or sex.

Both: If we'd a little cottage down in Kent,
          A honeysuckle cottage down in Kent.

Odo: Belinda, our efficient bee,
          Would make the honey for our tea.
          Each day to an unlimited extent

Lovey: Our time in simple duties would
            be spent
          And we would know what perfect
            comfort meant.

Odo: When we sat up in bed at nights
          Comparing our mosquito bites
          In our commodious cottage down
            in Kent.

Extra Refrain
Both: If we'd a little cottage down in
            Kent,
          A thatched old red-brick cottage
            down in Kent,

Lovey: Each morn I'd let the
           chickens loose

Odo: While I served rice to
           Gus the goose.

Both: What life could be more
           suited to a gent?

Lovey: Just baking cakes would
           make me quite content

Odo: Which with a hatchet
           I would try to dent,

Both: And then we'd sleep till
           morning glowed
           And Reginald the rooster
           crowed
           Down in our little Paradise
           in Kent.

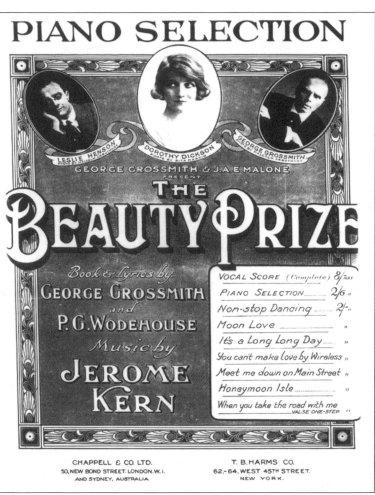

Never let it be said that Wodehouse didn't believe in "seconds." Knowing that *The Riviera Girl* (1917) had never been seen in London and that *The Beauty Prize* was unlikely to be Broadway-bound, "A Bungalow in Quogue"—with a slight change of geography—became "A Cottage in Kent." Reginald the Rooster and Clarice the Cow made encore appearances but Percival the Pig had been replaced by his brother, Paul.

FINALE—ACT 2

(Carol, John, Flutey, Boys and Girls)

Girls: Isn't it depressing?

Boys: Awfully distressing!

All: All their cash
           In a flash
           Swept right away!

Girls: Don't stand like a dumb thing,
           Go up and say *something* . . .

Boys: What on earth is there to say?

All: Tho' we're sympathizing,
           There is no disguising
           There is nothing one can say.

Flutey: My poor old friend
(to John)   I feel for you:
(to Carol)   Dear Lady,
           I'm broken-hearted.

All: How feeble
           Mere words can be
           When you would show your sympathy.

Carol: I can't say how sorry I am you've had
        this trouble!

John: I'm all broken up when I think of *you*.

All: Now that coldness vanishes like a
        broken bubble
    They feel that this was well worth
        going through.

(Carol and John release Odo and Lovey from their obligations)

Lovey: We'll have our little cottage down
        in Kent
    And we'll be oh, so cosy and content:

(But Odo sees it as their duty to fulfil their promises . . .)

Odo: Farewell! For us no nuptial knot:
    No Wilberforce the Wyandotte:
    We've lost our little cottage down
        in Kent.

ACT 3—
OPENING CHORUS

The stream flowing down to the sea
Sings—"She's near." Winds in the tree
Whisper to me—"Soon she will be here"
Hasten, my lady of night,
Put the dark shadows to flight,
Oh he, Oh la. Oh he—Oh la.
My lady of night.

MEET ME DOWN ON MAIN STREET

(Odo and Flutey)

(Lyric by P. G. Wodehouse and George Grossmith Jr.)

Odo: Yankee Doodle is no more
    He's (they've) been and changed
        his name.

Flutey: They call him George F. Babbitt now,
    But I guess he's just the same.

Odo: He's a great big husky buck-eyed guy,

Flutey: And his heart is simply great.

Odo: His *ad*dress is in Main Street

Flutey: In any town or state.

Both: So won't you meet me down on
        Main Street
    Where the George F. Babbitts
        grow;

Flutey: It is a place, as you're suggesting

Odo: That must be vurry (very) interesting;

Both: It's a great old burg, is Main Street,
    So I'm told by those who know;

Flutey: Are you with me, buddy?

Odo: I'm your man;

Flutey: We'll eat soft-shell'ed crabs

Odo: And breakfast bran;

Both: And we'll join the local Ku Klux Klan
    Where the George F. Babbitts grow.

Flutey: Now Main Street is a paradise of
        which I've heard men tell

Odo: Where boosters and Rotarians in
        sweet contentment dwell;

Flutey: They need a coupla live ones there,
        so brother, whatcha say?

Odo: Let's buy a hunk of chewing gum and
        go there right away

Both: Oh, won't you meet me down on
       Main Street
       Where the George F. Babbitts grow;

Flutey: It must be charming, if they're
         truthful;

Odo: Say, listen kid, you said a toothful;

Both: Yes, we'll go to dear old Main Street
       Soon as we can touch some dough.

Odo: We'll make our minds a perfect blank

Flutey: And we'll stand all day with Cy and
         Hank

Odo: Leaning up against the Farmer's
      Bank

Both: Where the George F. Babbitts grow

       Oh, won't you meet me down on
       Main Street
       Where the George F. Babbits grow.

Flutey: Say, guess the girls won't leap, bo.

Odo: When we're sighted at the dee-*pot*

Both: When we settle down in Main Street
       Reckon they won't find us slow.

Flutey: But if we get weary of being there

Odo: And of pork and beans we've had
      our share

Flutey: Then we'll both go back to Leicester
         Square

Both: Where the George F. Robeys grow.

Flutey: In Main Street they're determined to
         suppress what'er may come

Odo: The ravages created by the well-
      known Demon Rum.

Flutey: The Prohibition Officers would have
         you understand

Odo: The ice cream soda fountain is the
      bulwark of the land.

Both: Oh, won't you meet me down on
       Main Street
       Where the George F. Babbitts grow;

Flutey: All the police have full instruction

Odo: That they must curb your powers
      of suction;

Both: So, if you want a drink in Main Street
       We'll advise you where to go.

Odo: If you're seeking something strong
      and cool

Flutey: You can always buy it, as a rule

Odo: From the kindly village constabule

Both: Where the George F. Babbitts grow

George F. Babbitt was the hero of Sinclair Lewis's novel *Babbitt*, published in 1922. Its harsh indictment of middle-class American values made the term "Babbittry" a synonym for a rigidly conformist, materialistic, anti-intellectual way of life.

MOON LOVE

(Carol and Men)

Men: Our once austere morality
      (We're models of morality)
      The moon has softened quite:
      But though our souls are white,)

We ache
To take
Some girl in our arms tonight.

Carol: There are in this locality
A lot of girls, they say:
You'd better go and find them
    right away.

Men: Since our arrival at this fête
We've noticed one or two
But with regret, we beg to state,
That none of them will do—
There isn't one to compare anywhere
    with you.

Carol: Though you may think I'm lacking
    in tact,
Still I feel obliged to say
It's just the moon that's making
    you act
In this devoted way.
I fear
It's clear
You're not one bit sincere.

Men: At such a charge our pain and distress
We simply cannot express.

Carol: Though sentimental lovers (romantic
    poets) may sing
Of the magic silver moon,
This Moon Love is a gossamer thing
That passes all too soon.
It's plain
'Twill wane
When daylight comes again.

Men: Oh, don't treat our great passion,
    we pray,
In such a cynical way!

Carol: Moon Love!
    The stars are twinkling (gleaming)
    And life's a tinkling tune

Make haste
The moon is beaming
Don't waste
The hours in dreaming
Moon Love
Enjoy your playtime
It will be day-time
Soon.
Who misses
A few kisses
With no one to see but the
    moon!

Refrain (Amended)

Carol: Moon Love   Men: We love you.
    Above you

All: The stars are gleaming
And life's a twinkling tune.

Carol: Make haste   Men: And night
    time's The
    right time
    The moon   For lovers
    is beaming   dreaming
Don't waste   While high
    the hours in   in the
    dreaming   heavens
    the moon
    is beaming
Moon love   We're
Enjoy   yearning
    your   and
    playtime   burning
    And time is
    flying

All: It will be daytime soon

Carol: Vows spoken   Men: The vows are
    spoken
May be   Ne'er will
    broken   be broken

All: They've nothing to do with the moon.

PAT (1924)

A Musical Comedy in Three Acts (*Unproduced*)

BOOK and LYRICS   Guy Bolton and P. G. Wodehouse
MUSIC   Jerome Kern

CAST

(Notes in libretto)

"Pat" Holden:
MARILYN MILLER type
(*We have a girl*)
Bimbo, *General understudy in
Gus Sanders' tent show*:
JACK DONAHUE
Neil Fraser, *Gentleman-adventurer type,
was in the Canadian Mounted and
earned his discharge—possibly
wears their uniform coat*:
CHARLES KING
Wilfred Flack:
Pinckney Potter:
BERNARD GRANVILLE
Bella Weeks:
FRANCES HOWARD type
Uncle Ted, *Partners with
Neil* "Gabby" Johnson
In the Cross-Bar Ranch:

"Pug" Ferguson,
The bad man of Coldridge:
JOE ALLEN
Gus Sanders:
Peter van Alan,
Man of class Englishman:
Ernest Vaughn,
Stage Manager:
Jennie, *Chorus Girl*:
Rose, *Program, hat check and general
utility lady of the Benson
Opera House*:
MISS LAIRD
Two Kids:
Red Top, *A girl*, Hank, *A boy*

(Note: Jennie, Rose and Red Top can
all be *Folly* girls. Red Top must, of course,
be able to sing and dance. The other two
have no opportunity to do either.)

SYNOPSIS

A couple of kids are peeping through the fence at the circus ("Through the Fence"). The visitors are mostly typical mid-Westerners ("Circus Day"). Star of the show is Pat, "the girl who sings and dances standing on the back of a horse." We meet an assortment of characters. There's Pinkney Potter, a dude from the East out to impress the Girls ("Back East"). There's Plug Ferguson, the local bad man; Uncle Jed and Gabby Johnson, partners in a foundering ranch with hero, Neil, who is in love with Pat. Plug likes Pat's old songs ("Shufflin' Sam"), which causes the cowboys to call for Pat, who now appears. She tells them she knows her big break is just around the corner ("Pat's Going To Have Some Luck Today"). Neil feels his love is hopeless ("There Isn't One Girl in the World For Me"). Pat bursts in with the news that Mr. Potter has offered her a major booking in New York. If only she had the money to go. Jed and Neil offer it to her—even though it means giving up their ranch. She doesn't know this but in her gratitude vows to return every year on the same day, no matter how big a star she becomes ("A Year From Today").

Bimbo, the show's understudy, manages to con Plug out of his savings and tells himself he is a man of true greatness ("Julius Caesar"). Just as Pat is about to leave, she finds out about her friends' sacrifice. She will go to New York, make her fortune—and save the ranch!

In the New York rehearsal hall a dejected Pat is waiting to be called ("Worries"). Bimbo now arrives, posing as a millionaire playboy. He'll take her to a big society party and give her a foot on the ladder. They sing a duet from the old days ("Shufflin' Sam").

At the party the Girls and Boys sing the "Opening Chorus" ("Buy, Buy"). Mr. Van Zile, the party host, reminisces with Bimbo about life in Africa, which Bimbo has been claiming to know well ("Bongo On the Congo"). Neil is in town with the rodeo and runs into Pat. She admits she loves him. If all else fails, they can always live in her old wagon ("Covered Wagon"). Bella—Bimbo's on-and-off fiancée—arrives with news that he now really is wealthy through his investments. Now there is no reason why they can't get married ("Love's A Sort of Frenzy"). Pat auditions for Van Zile ("The Man in the Moon"). Seeing her success and not wanting to hold her back, Neil leaves.

A year later to the day, Pat is starring in a hit show in the nearby town. All the other characters have resolved their situations, except Neil. He is saddened to hear that Pat is to be married. The show over, Pat appears. She hears the ranch is doing fine. Won't a rancher need a wife? The only person she intends to marry is Neil ("Covered Wagon—Reprise").

Pat was a show with a somewhat ambiguous genesis. Wodehouse refers to it in a letter to his step-daughter, Leonora, dated February 4, 1924. When the letter was reproduced in a collection of his correspondence, the editor (Frances Donaldson) added a footnote to the effect that it had music by Vincent Youmans, book by Wodehouse and Bolton and lyrics by Wodehouse and Billy Rose. In this I believe she is mistaken and thinking of another (also still-born) collaboration, *Pat, The Gibson Girl* (1922).

The extant libretto for *Pat* is clearly dated February 23, 1924, and credits Bolton & Wodehouse & Kern in their accustomed roles. In addition, the appearance of so many of the songs in the subsequent *Sitting Pretty* would seem to put the matter beyond doubt.

According to Wodehouse's account to Leonora, the team were progressing both pieces in parallel for Ray Comstock and, presumably, The Princess:

We were going along nicely casting *Sitting Pretty* for Ray, when Jack Donahue (Marilyn Miller's long time partner)

suddenly called up and said he thought *Pat*, the other piece, a corker and wanted to play in it. So Ray instantly switched *Sitting Pretty* and started to cast *Pat*. Two weeks into rehearsal their director died And as for the piece, it knocked it cold. We tried three other directors and couldn't get them, and now we have switched back to *Sitting Pretty* again and are trying to cast that. . . . The nuisance is that *Pat* is complete, with all the lyrics done, and half the *Sitting Pretty* lyrics have to be written. . . . Oh yes, and I forgot to say that Ray has now gone cold on *Pat*, so we shall have to try and place it elsewhere. Ziegfeld wired from Palm Beach asking if it would do for Leon Errol, but that only evoked in us a faint, sad smile. We know those Ziegfeld commissions.

Not that the knowledge would prevent him from accepting one in the future. In fact, the impresario had been encouraging them to write *Pat* since December 1922, at which time Wodehouse noted "a rotten title."

THROUGH THE FENCE

Through the fence a magic world there lies
That's full of wonders most surprising.
Glimpses of it flash upon our eyes
To make the thing more tantalizing:
Hark to the music playing!
Hark to the barker braying!
Hear him shouting 'Hi! *ladees* an' gence,
Walk UP! The show will soon commence!
That's why we're creeping
Close and peeping
Through the fence, through the fence.

Here are the girls most attractive,
Dancers wonderful and active,
Clowns engaged to be funny
At great expense:
Come along now and see them;
We can strictly guarantee them;
It is worth all the money
To get through that fence.

CIRCUS DAY

Male   *(To Females)*
Visitors: Well, come on, kid! What'll it be?
You call the shots. I'm here to pay.
Take off the lid. Nothin' to me!
I'll blow my roll on Circus Day.

Female   *(Examining things for sale)*
Visitors: Well, ain't you sweet! *Oh*, what
a price!

Hot Dog
Man: They don't grow wienies
Nicer than mine is!

Peanut
Man: Buy, buy my peanuts!
Here's nuts that *be* nuts

Female
Visitors: It's much too much for you to pay!
This *is* a treat! Isn't it nice
To have a beau on Circus Day!

(Now all the CIRCUS PEOPLE join in . . .)

Walk up! For the show's about
to begin!
This way for the Wonder-Show!
Don't wait! Buy a seat and come
along in!
Astounding marvels you'll view
And bounding acrobats, too!

Visitors: We can't go wrong. Plenty to see.
The price is high, but we can pay;
So come along! Hang on to me!
For this is Circus Day.

BACK EAST

(Potter and Girls)

Girls: What a shame that we have got to
travel away:
This is just the place where I'd be
crazy to stay:

Potter: Yes, but dearie, when the cheery
William Harts around these parts
Start prodding one with a gun
That's not my idea of fun:

Girls: You must take that sort of thing for
granted, you know,
When into the great wide-open
spaces you go:

Potter: All this rough Wild Western stuff
Just bores me chilly. Seems a silly
Game to me,—for, you see,
I want to be . . .

Back East where
Taxis are hooting,
Boot-leggers booting,

Crap-shooters shooting,
Cuties patooting:
I want to inhale God's wonderful air
As it blows clean and sweet through
    Longacre Square:
Shoppers are shopping,
Traffic-cops copping;
Op'ras are opping,
Dagoes are wopping
Help take me back home and I'll
    never roam;
For I'll be contented then
Where Mickeys are Mikes and
    Ikeys are Ikes,
On Broadway where men are men.

Girls: No one can deny the West's a
        wonderful land;
    All the men you see are so romantic
        and grand:

Potter: They may be men, noble he-men,
    But I'll bet you they would get
    As mild as mush in the crush
    Of a good old Subway rush;

Girls: Cowboys always seem to me like
        heroes of old:
    Though they're rugged, still you
        know their hearts are of gold.

Potter: I can't mix with Western hicks,
    They may suit you, but I am through,
    And so today, hear me say,
    I'm on my way, etc.

Refrain

SHUFFLIN' SAM

(Plug and Jed)

(See *Sitting Pretty*)

Cowboys: We want Pat! We want Pat!
    We don't want the elephants—
    we want Pat!

We don't want the acrobats that come
    from Japan
We don't want Toto—nor the India-
    rubber man.
Pat! Pat! Pat, Pat, Pat.
WE—WANT—PAT!

PAT'S GOING TO HAVE
SOME LUCK TODAY!

(Pat and Men)

Lots of days are gloomy days, you get up feeling
    blue,
Don't know what to do,
Wish it wasn't true:
Other days are happy days, when all the world
    seems gay,
And that's the way it was when I woke today.

When I got up this morning,
The air was like a kiss.
Never was a morning
Half so fine as this.
All around the dew was glittering
Just like diamonds in the hay,
And the birds all started twittering
In the friendliest kind of way.
And oh, the sun was shining
As though it meant to say—
"Pat's going to have some luck today."

Crickets sang their morning song
As I went down the dell;
Somehow I could tell
They all wished me well.
Rabbits thumped their lucky feet as I went on
    my way.
Oh, everything was fine when I woke today.

When I got up this morning,
I knew the world was right.
I got up this morning,
Feeling gay and bright.

And I knew bad times were over
And good fortune was in store,
For I found a four-leafed clover
Growing right outside the door.
All Nature seemed to greet me,
As though it meant to say—
"Pat's going to have some luck today!"

THERE ISN'T ONE GIRL IN THE WORLD FOR ME

(Neil)

(See *Sitting Pretty*)

A YEAR FROM TODAY

(Pat and Neil)

(See *Sitting Pretty*)

Pat: When I come back I hope you'll be
The first of all to welcome me
And come and meet the train
That brings me home again.

Neil: I think you may rely on that.
I'll buy a brand new Stetson hat
In honor of the day,
However much I pay.
I'll stand right up and cheer
The moment you appear.

A year from today, dear, my dream
will come true.
The sun will be shining, the sky will
be blue,
The breeze in the rushes
Will join with the thrushes
To welcome the Springtime and
you—and you.
Bees in the clover will hum this
refrain—

Both: "The winter is over and Pat's home
again!"

And oh, what a lot we shall both have
to say
When I/you come back a year from
today.

Neil: And yet I fear that you may find
Old pals are hard to bear in mind
When all the men you met
Are falling at your feet.
Are you quite sure you won't forget
When you've become the public's pet
And love-sick millionaires
Camp daily on your stairs?

Pat: Please don't be so absurd.
You know I'll keep my word.
A year from today, dear, my dreams
will come true.
The sun will be shining, the sky will
be blue.
When roses are glowing
And soft South winds blowing
I'll come in the Springtime to you—
to you.
Bees in the clover will hum this
refrain—

Both: "The winter is over and Pat's home
again!"
And oh, what a lot we shall both have
to say
When I/you come back a year from
today.

Note: Although this song was also taken over into *Sitting Pretty*, the lyrics are significantly different, so both versions are included.

JULIUS CAESAR

(Bimbo and Girls)

Bimbo: In the days of Rome's great glory
Lived a wop renowned in story,
Known to every Roman flapper

As the nation's champion scrapper.
So that all the toughs for miles
    around
When they get to know his habits
Would try to burrow underground;
He'd got them scared like rabbits.

Girls: They tried to burrow underground;
    For he'd got them scared like rabbits.

Bimbo: Oh, Caesar!

Girls: Great Caesar!

Bimbo: He lived in ancient Rome.
    And things, you know, were never
        slow
    When he was round the home.
    If any guy got fresh with him
    He smote him on the beezer.
    He had the stuff
    He acted rough
    And I take after Caesar.

Girls: He had the stuff, etc.

Bimbo: All the ladies found him thrilling,
    For his work was raw but willing.
    He'd a smile that knocked them dizzy
    So his 'phone was always busy.
    If he met a girl along the block
    He would raise his Truly Warner
    And softly murmur '*Hic, haec, hoc*!'
    Which meant 'Come round the
        corner.'

Oh, Caesar! Great Caesar!
The girls, with joy would shriek
And gayly cry as he came by,
'Hey, Lizzie, pipe the Sheik!'
He'd meet a queen at five-fifteen;
At six o'clock he'd squeeze her.
For he'd a rep for zip and pep,
And I take after Caesar.

He was gay and bright and hearty
At a festive evening-party
For by twelve o'clock precisely
He was always going nicely
He had such delightful friendly
    ways
That the girls all called him 'Swifty.'
They'd stand around and burst their
    stays
When he sprang his latest nifty.

Oh, Caesar! Great Caesar!
They asked him everywhere
For he had stacks of snappy cracks
That made them gasp for air.
He'd grab a girl and tell her quick
A couple that would please her.
He knew just how to pull a wow
And I take after Caesar.

Extra
Verse: As a dancer he was noted.
    Quite a hoofer he was voted;
    For his style was brisk and breezy
    And he shook a mean waukeesi.
    All the girls to watch his work
        would rush
    But it never made him timid;
    And scores were injured in the
        crush
    Whenever Caesar shimmied.

Oh, Caesar! Great Caesar!
They liked the stuff he did.
When he cut in
They used to grin
And whisper 'At-a-kid.'
He'd greet a dame with 'Hello,
    Mame!'
And then he'd grab and squeeze
    her.
They'd all declare
The boy was *there*
And I take after Caesar.

You would always find him nightly
When the moon was shining brightly
In a scented garden, walking
With a lady, softly talking.
He would pull poetic stuff and rave
In a way that had them skidding;
So that some would say 'Now, you
    behave!'
And others 'Quit your kidding!'

Oh, Caesar! Great Caesar!
He used to make them reel;
For pretty quick
They got a kick
When he began his spiel.
Romantic mush that made them
    blush
He spouted like a geyser,
With snappy chat
He knocked them flat,
And I take after Caesar.

The resemblance to "Napoleon" in the 1917 *Have A Heart*—hardly needs underlining!

WORRIES
(In an early version—LOOK FOR THE SILVER LINING)

(See *Sally*)

BUY, BUY

(Girls and Men)

Men: In coming to this robbers' den we feel
    that we were rash
For something tells us we shall soon
    be parted from our cash.
If once a fellow falls among you
    female buccaneers

Girls: (Buy, buy! Hurry and buy! Walk up
    and buy!)

Men: He'd better kiss his roll farewell
    before it disappears.

Girls: Buy, buy! Hurry and buy! Walk up
    and buy!
We have ties you can wear around
    your neck
And a lot of cigarettes which are
    highly reccommended. They're
    splendid.

Men: 'Twill save a lot of bother, will it
    not,
If I hand over everything I've got.
It's no good trying to resist when
    once you hear that cry—

Girls: Buy, buy! Hurry and buy! Walk up
    and buy!
Our methods of barbarity
Are all in aid of Charity,
And that's why what we supply comes
    rather high.

Men: And that is why our cash goes
    winging
Just as soon as you start singing

All: Buy, buy! Hurry and buy! Walk up
    and buy!

BONGO ON THE CONGO

(Bimbo, Van Zile and Potter)

(See *Sitting Pretty*)

COVERED WAGON

(Pat and Neil)

Pat: We would get a wagon
We'd set out one day
Leave the world to drag on
In its foolish way.

Neil: We'd put behind us
         All warnings and advice

Pat: And none would find us
         This side of Paradise.
         From dawn to gloaming
         We'd go a-roaming,

Neil: With love beside us
         To cheer and guide us.

Both: Pioneers
         In our wagon faring
         To a land
         That is strange and new.
         Happy rangers,
         Making light of dangers,
         We would weather
         Dust and heat and storm
             together.
         Hopes and fears
         And disaster sharing
         Till the long, long journey was
         through.
         And my heart would not fail
         As I went down the trail
         In a Covered Wagon with you.

Neil: Past the plains and over
         Rocks and hills and streams,
         Beckoning to the rover,
         Lies the Land of Dreams.

Pat: You've but to wander
         Another mile or two,
         And see—out yonder
         It smiles to welcome you.
         A land of flowers
         And April showers;

Neil: Of rivers flowing
         And soft winds blowing.

LOVE'S A SORT OF FRENZY

(Bimbo, Bella, Potter and Daisy)

Bella: Oh, Love's a sort of frenzy
         That works in every clime

Bimbo: Like Spanish Influenzy
         It gets us all the time

Daisy: For though you're smart and clever
         You can't escape for ever

Potter: Yes. Soon or late you're bound to skid;
         And you'll be mighty glad you did.

All: For
         When Cupid comes along with his
             little bow and arrow
         Your worries and your troubles
             disappear.
         And you want to shout and dance
             a lot
         You feel just like Sir Lancelot
         When first he made a hit with
             Guinevere.
         You've a smile that's so seraphic
         That it nearly stops the traffic;
         On the Subway you keep bursting
             into song
         And your head, when love has hit you,
         Swells until your hats don't fit you.
         You may *be* no
         Valentino,
         But you think you are when Cupid
             comes along.

Bella: Oh, Love's a strange condition.
         Deny it if you can.

Daisy: 'Twill change the disposition
         Of nearly every man.

Potter: Head-waiters, if love's gripped 'em
         Will thank you when you've tipped
             'em.

Bimbo: Because he feels that life is sweet
         The janitor will send up heat.

All: For
         When Cupid comes along with his
             little bow and arrow,
         It gets you so you don't care what
             you do.
         You start buying things at Tiffany's
         And though the price is stiff in his
         Emporium, that doesn't worry you:
         All your cash you squander gaily
         Even though it means that daily
         At the Automat your meals you have
             to prong.
         For a bunch of flowers to send her
         You will hock your sock-suspender
         Though they soak you
         Till you're broke, you
         Never care a whoop when Cupid
             comes along.

THE MAN IN THE MOON

(Pat and The Boys)

The title was changed to "Shadow of the Moon" when it was used in *Sitting Pretty*.

So *Pat* was set aside while the team completed work on a show they had started some time earlier.

In mid-1922 they had agreed to provide a vehicle for the popular vaudeville act, the Duncan Sisters. Irving Berlin was to compose the songs, a fact which would normally have restricted Wodehouse to his share of the libretto. So great was Berlin's admiration for Wodehouse and his prior achievements, however, that he agreed to let him contribute some lyrics. The Duncans were to play the twin sisters who were the heroines of the Bolton/Wodehouse story.

Complications set in when Berlin was delayed on his previous commitment. This left the Duncan Sisters at a loose professional end, and they went off to fill in with an entertainment of their own devising, which proved unexpectedly popular. The result was that—with the twins no longer available—Berlin backed out and producer Ray Comstock persuaded Kern to join up with his old partners one more time. The Princess team was back together again—though not at the Princess, even though Comstock advertised it as "The Seventh of Their Series of the Princess Musical Comedies."

SITTING PRETTY (1924)

Presented by Ray Comstock and Morris Gest at the Fulton Theatre, New York, on April 8, 1924 (95 performances). (The Fulton had three times the seating capacity of the Princess.)

BOOK   Guy Bolton and P. G. Wodehouse
MUSIC   Jerome Kern
LYRICS   P. G. Wodehouse

Queenie Smith (*Dixie*) and the Boys in *Sitting Pretty*.

343

CAST

Mrs. Wagstaff, a teacher: MARJORIE EGGLESTON	Wilhelmina: JAYNE CHESNEY
James, a footman: ALBERT WYART	Otis: GEORGE SYLVESTER
Roger, a butler: HARRY LILFORD	Wilhelmina: MARIAN DICKSON
"Bill" Pennington: RUDOLPH CAMERON	Mr. Pennington: GEORGE E. MACK
Judson Waters, his friend: EUGENE REVERE	Horace: DWIGHT FRYE
Babe LaMarr, a chorus girl: MYRA HAMPTON	Joe, his uncle: FRANK MCINTYRE
May Tolliver: GERTRUDE BRYAN	Bolt, a coachman: GEORGE O'DONNELL
Dixie, her sister: QUEENIE SMITH	Jane, a housemaid: TERRY BLAINE
Jasper: EDWARD FINLEY	Prof. Appleby: GEORGE SPELVIN

SYNOPSIS

The Penningtons' summer house. Bill, old Mr. Pennington's nephew and heir, is entertaining some friends. The children from the Orphanage next door envy the setting but Mr. P is only concerned about his garden ("Is This Not a Lovely Spot?"). Babe—Bill's chorus girlfriend is also concerned . . . about Bill's prospects. But not Bill. Surely love is all they need! ("You Alone Would Do"). The guests gone, Bill runs into Dixie and May, twins from the orphanage. They exchange the stories of their lives. Dixie and May are worried they may not be adopted, but Bill tries to set their minds to rest ("Worries"). Mr. P gathers the family and tells them he has decided to disinherit them all and adopt a boy and girl. He still has to find the girl but he has the boy—and introduces Horace. Horace's Uncle Jo, a small time thief, has organized it, so that Horace can help him rob the house. They are discussing the caper when Bill's friend, Judson, arrives and they have to pretend they were discussing big game hunting in Africa ("Bongo On the Congo").

Dixie now meets Horace and they are attracted. Horace hopes Mr. P will adopt her, so that she can be his bride and help start the new Pennington dynasty ("Mr. and Mrs. Rorer"). But when Dixie does meet Mr. P, she is accidentally rude to him. He declares she is the *last* person he will adopt! Finding that Bill is disinherited, Babe dumps him. ("Gold diggers used to be forty-niners. Now they're perfect thirty-sixes!") ("There Isn't One Girl"). May hops over the wall and consoles him. It soon becomes clear that she is now the one girl. He tells her that he will go off and make his fortune, then come back for her ("A Year from Today"). But then Mr. P decides to adopt May—so both couples are to be separated! It's been quite an eventful morning at the Penningtons, but Dixie sums up how they should all feel by quoting the philosophy of an old man she once met ("Shufflin' Sam") ("Act 1—Finale").

Six months later at the Penningtons' Florida home. A costume ball is under way in the style of the 1850s to celebrate May's "coming out" ("Polka Dot"). A guest dressed as Princess Eugénie sings of the old times ("Days Gone By"). Bill arrives. He is now a successful private detective. He finds May and tells her she has been his inspiration ("All You Need Is a Girl"). Uncle Jo is planning to rob the house that night but Horace is having second thoughts. They might end up in jail—a nostalgic thought for Jo ("Tulip Time in Sing-Sing"). Dixie now arrives. She is a successful dress designer, here to arrange May's dresses. The sisters are reunited. If only they never had to be parted ("On a Desert Island With You"). Horace and Dixie decide to get married. So do Bill and May. After all, all you need is a little bungalow and the Long Island Railroad to take you home ("The Enchanted Train"). Horace now feels he must renounce his past ways to be worthy of Dixie and goes off, leaving her without a partner at the ball ("Shadow of the Moon"). Horace fulfills his pledge by foiling Uncle Jo. Now he and Dixie can be united ("Sitting Pretty"). Horace gives the credit to Dixie, who is forgiven by Mr. P. Happy endings all round . . . ("Finale Ultimo").

IS THIS NOT A LOVELY SPOT?

Orphans: Oh, glad the fate and bright the lot
Of him who owns this lovely spot!
To play all day about
This garden would not weary us;
It's full of shrubberies
All shady and mysterious;
But if we're caught inside
The penalties are serious;
Still, is it not a lovely spot?

Gardners: Good morning, sir!
Since the dawn we've been astir!
For honest work
Is a thing we never shirk!

Pennington: I see my roses have
Been nibbled by greenfly, and I'd
Suggest you go and mix
Some arsenic or cyanide
And squirt it over them
Before the creatures try and hide!

Gardeners: Oh, is this not a lovely spot?

Girls: Late nights and dancing in town
Have left us rather run-down
And alert and hearty
We'd be once more

Fresh air's the thing, so they say
That's why we've come here today
On a picnic party
In a coach and four!

Say, tell me, who do you think
Is this forbidding old gink?
Shall we vamp the glum thing
With our smiles that win?

I think this elderly guy
Has got a look in his eye
As if we were something
That the cat brought in!

Bill: Why, Uncle, this is fine!
I hope you're fit!
Come on, girls, form a line
And shake his mitt!

You've often heard me speak
Of Uncle Will
Step up and meet the sheik
And get a thrill!

Why, he shouldn't get sore if I
Start taking a whirl
At trying to glorify
The American girl!

We mustn't let him spoil our day;
So our lunch we'll take
Go on and find the way
Down to the lake!

Girls: Oh, glad the fate and bright the lot
Of him who owns this happy spot!

Judson: This lovely garden
Actually has a lake in it:
My gosh! It's simply just
An Eden with no snake in it!
Oh, gosh, we shall enjoy
The cocktails which we shake in it!

With Girls: Oh, is this not a lovely spot!

Bill and
Babe: Some day we'll seek a clergyman
who'll
Swiftly tie the knot
And then we'll bill and coo, just I
and you
In this delightful spot

This song is musically identical to "The Pergola Patrol" from *The Cabaret Girl* (1922). Once again Kern and Wodehouse were recycling material that only London audiences had heard.

Later in the first act there is a reprise:

Bill: A thirst like mine suggests
           somehow,
        A jug of wine, beneath the bough,
        I saw a doctor yesterday,
        He gave it then as his
        Opinion, that a thirst like mine
        To health a menace is.

Roper: We've Black and White, and Haig
           and Haig,
        And Three Star Hennesseys.

Bill: Oh, is this not
        A lovely spot!

YOU ALONE WOULD DO

(I'd Want Only You)

(Bill and Babe)

Bill: That verse that you have quoted
        As beautiful is voted
        As any in the writings
        Of Omar Khayyam.

        Yet though he was a wonder,
        I think he made a blunder
        On that one subject I must own
        Poor old Omar pulled a bone.

        A book beneath the bough
        A jug of wine and thou—
        I don't see why he needed all that
           stuff:
        For me the girl alone would be
           enough.

        If I could wander to
        Some desert spot with you
        I don't think I'd be needing
        Light works for summer reading.

        For you alone would do
        You wouldn't find me tippling
        Or reading Keats or Kipling
        For I'd want only you!

Babe: It's plain to any student
        That he was simply prudent;
        He looked into the future
        Did Omar Khayyam.

        That wine was to restore him
        In case the girl should bore him.
        He knew how boring girls could be!

Bill: No, you're wrong. I don't agree!
        If you were by my side
        I'd be quite satisfied
        In any kind of wilderness to stay.

Babe: You wouldn't stick it out for half
           a day!

Bill: If I could wander to
        Some desert spot with you

Babe: You'd say, "I'll see you later"
        And rush to find a waiter!

Bill: No, no, that isn't true
        I do not claim that I am
        A wiser man than Khayyam
        But I'd want only you!

WORRIES

(Troubles In A Box)

(A Great Big Box)

(Bill, Dixie and May)

May: Once upon a time, they say, in days of
           old a feller
        Gathered all the troubles lyin'
           round—

Dixie: Locked 'em in a cabin trunk
       and put it in a cellar
    Where he thought it never
       would be found—

May: But one day his wife—or
       p'raps his sister or his
       cousin
    Spied that box and opened
       up the lid.

Dixie: There was just one *whoosh*
       and out those troubles
       came a-buzzin'
    Nasty shock it gave that
       (the) silly kid.

Bill: And so the job we've got
       today, it's plain,
    Is just to catch the pesky
       things and put them
       back again.

All: Shove (slam) all your worries
       in a great big box,
    As big as any box can be:
    Shove (cram) all your worries
       in a great big box
    And lock it with a great
       big key.
    Cryin' never yet got anybody
       anywhere,
    So just stick out your chin,
    And shove (jam) all your worries
       in a great big box
    And sit on the lid and grin.

May: Doesn't matter where you go, old
       trouble's sure to find you.
    If you think you'll shake him off,
       you're wrong.

Dixie: If you try to hide, he just comes
       sneakin' up behind you.
    If you run away he trails along.

Queenie Smith.

Bill: Only one thing to be done when he
       starts to vex us:
    Just you turn around and call his bluff.

Dixie: Set your teeth and sock him one right
       in the solar plexus,
    That'll teach him not to play so rough.

All: And so's you won't be bothered
       any more,
    Just dump him in the cellar
    Where he used to be before

Shove all your worries in a great
    big box,
As big as any box can be:
Shove all your worries in a great
    big box
And lock it with a great big key.
Cryin' never yet got anybody
    anywhere,
So just stick out your chin,
And shove all your worries in a
    great big box
And sit on the lid and grin.

BONGO ON THE CONGO

(Horace, Uncle Jo and Judson)

Horace: Beneath the silver Afric moon
    A few miles south of C(K)ameroon,

Judson: There lies the haven which you ought
    to seek,
    Where cassowaries take their ease
    Up in the coca-cola trees,
    While crocodiles sit crocking in
    the creek.

Horace: Though on some nearby barren
    height
    The heat's two hundred Fahrenheit,
    Down in the valley it is nice and cool.

Uncle Jo: And yet . . . I don't know why it is . . .
    The girls of all varieties
    Wear little but a freckle as a rule.

All: In Bongo!
    It's on the Congo!
    And oh boy, what a spot!
    Quite full
    Of things delightful
    And few that are not.
    Have no misgiving,
    The cost of living
    Isn't cheaper anywhere.

Judson: If wifie needs another frock,

Horace: You needn't put your watch in hock:

Jo: You simply tell a native Chief
    To pick a poison ivy leaf.

All: In Bongo!
    It's on the Congo!
    And I wish I was there!

Horace: The girls in that vicinity,
    Are pearls of femininity.
    And mark you, all is friendly as
    can be.

Judson: If one thing's sure, old pal, it is,
    I'm tired of all formalities,
    So Bongo sounds the very place
    for me.

Horace: What's more, in this connection, it
    Just makes them more affectionate,
    If someone comes along whose face
    is white.

Jo: And something seems to urge a man
    To seek a local clergyman
    And start in marrying ev'rything
    in sight.

All: In Bongo!
    It's on the Congo!
    And oh boy! What a spot!
    Quite full
    Of things delightful
    And few that are not!
    There are no quarrels
    Because your morals
    Are not wholly on the square.

Judson: For when a visitor arrives,

Horace: They hand him half a dozen wives.

Jo: A man with less than twenty-four,
     Is looked on as bachelor

All: In Bongo!
     It's on the Congo!
     And I wish that I was there.
     In Bongo!
     It's on the Congo!
     And oh boy, what a spot!
     Quite full
     Of things delightful!
     And few that are not.
     There all the beaches
     Are full of peaches,
     Swimming gaily ev'rywhere.

Judson: The Summer girl is not a prude,
     Her tastes are simple, even crude.
     Her clothing, what there is of it,
     Is what you might call Poros-knit.

All: In Bongo!
     It's on the Congo!
     And I wish that I was there.
     In Bongo!
     It's on the Congo!
     And oh boy, what a spot!
     Quite full
     Of things delightful
     And few that are not.
     The native dances
     Are worth some glances.
     You can't beat them anywhere.

Judson: You ought to go and see them do

Horace: The one they call the Boola-Boo.

Jo: It's worth your while to make the trip,
     They haven't got a censorship.

All: In Bongo!
     It's on the Congo!
     And I wish that I was there.

In Bongo!
It's on the Congo!
And oh boy, what a spot!
Quite full
Of things delightful
And few that are not.
There no one collars
Your hard-earned dollars.
They've a system that's a bear:

Judson: When Government assessors call

Horace: To try and sneak your little all,

Jo: You simply hit them with an axe,
     That's the way (how) you pay your
      income tax.

All: In Bongo!
     It's on the Congo,
     And I wish that I was there.

MR. AND MRS. RORER

(Dixie and Horace)

Dixie: When Missis Rorer was a bride,
     She kept her husband well supplied
     With ev'ry appetizing dish
     That any hungry man could wish.
     And so when vamps came round
      his way
     And did their best to make him
      stray,
     She said that she'd do nothing rash
     She held him with her corned beef
      hash!
     When Mister Rorer felt a bit
      depressed,

Horace: Kind Missis Rorer acted for the best.

Dixie: She simply went and took a clam
     And served it with a ham that am

And made him tuck it underneath
   his vest!
When Mister Rorer came home
   feeling blue,

Horace: Kind Missis Rorer shined an egg
   or two.

Both: And modern husbands would not
   stray,
If only wives would act the way
That kind Missis Rorer used to do!

Dixie: And that's the way I too would do
To keep my husband fond and true,
I'd feed him all the time!

Horace: You would? Continue, kid, this
   listens good.

Dixie: We'd sit together hand in hand
And talk of

Horace: "Chicken Maryland."

Dixie: One sweet romance would never skid:
I'd do as Missis Rorer did!
When Mister Rorer came home
   feeling mad

Horace: Kind Missis Rorer wasn't scared or
   sad.

Dixie: With love-light beaming in her eyes,
She spoke to him of pumpkin pies,
And then went off and planked a
   wicked shad!
When Mister Rorer said that he
   was blue,

Horace: Kind Missis Rorer filled him up
   with stew.

Both: And there'd be no divorce today,
If only wives would act the way
That kind Missis Rorer used to do.

In *Bring On the Girls* Wodehouse indicates an "Omar Khayyam" song at this point in the show.

OMAR KHAYYAM

Old Omar Khayyam used to say
He liked to live the simple way:
For wealth and fame he did not wish;
Just cosy comfort was his dish.
To make life right, he had a hunch,
You need a girl and lots of lunch:
You have to hand it to the kid.
I'm feeling just as Omar did.
A steak and fried and lima beans and you!
That's all I need to make my life complete.

I'd be contented in a shack
Near the garbage dump in Hackensack
If you were there and I'd enough to eat.
Together in some faraway retreat
How sweet to settle down and bill and coo.
My lonely heart would cease to ache,
If only I'd a sirloin steak,
A steak and fried and lima beans and you.

Old Omar used to think it great
To phone a dame and make a date
And tell her to slip on her dress
And join him in the wilderness:
'I'm fixed up fine, old girl,' he said,
'With jugs of wine and loaves of bread:
We'll sit and neck while thousands cheer':
And Omar had the right idea.

A steak and fried and lima beans and you!
Apart from that I wouldn't need a thing;
With you my star, my hope, my guide,
And lots of gravy on the side,
I'll face whatever headaches life may bring.
Hard times will sort of kind of lose their sting:
Grey skies will kind of sort of turn to blue:
Oh, gee! Oh, gosh! Oh, joy! Oh, bliss!
I don't want any more of this,
A steak and fried and lima beans and you.

THERE ISN'T ONE GIRL

(Bill)

Bill: Oh, the world is wide and I've
          travelled it through
        From the Fiji Islands to Kalamazoo,
        And in ev'ry place I've found
        There were lots of girls around.
        But one and all they passed me by,
        Got married to some other guy!
        I'm so lonely, I don't know what
          to do,
        It's sad, but it's true . . .

        There isn't one girl in the world
          for me.
        There isn't one parson who needs
          my fee!
        Oh, every day some lovely belle
        Is packing up to go and dwell
        In the Niagara Falls hotel,
        But not with me,
        No not with me!
        It looks as though I wasn't
          going to see
        Another branch sprout on my
          family tree!
        I'm just an also-ran; I'm laid on
          the shelf.
        I've got to put my slippers on
          for myself,
        There isn't one girl in the world
          for me!

Extra
Verse: I know the job I'd be
           wonderful at
         Would be doing chores in
           a snug little flat:
         I've a natural talent for
         Bawling out a janitor:
         I'd love to put an apron on
         And wash the dishes till
           they shone;

Feed the goldfish and exercise the
  cat . . .
But what good is that . . .

There isn't one girl in the world
  for me,
You'll never find me getting
  housemaid's knee!
On every side I see a crush
Of happy brides who smile and blush,
And everywhere the ushers ush,
But not for me,
No, not for me!
I needn't put oil on the old latchkey,
For no one cares if I get home at
  three!
For all the punch that march of
  Mendelssohn's has

He might as well have written
    nothing but jazz,
There isn't one girl in the world
    for me!

(Now May climbs over the wall and joins him)

May: Hello.

Bill: Hello Humpty Dumpty. What are
              you doing on that wall?

May: Just sittin'. You're in trouble, aren't you?

Bill: I've been having a little unpleasantness
              with my rich uncle.
           And he has now said something to
              me which it is really impossible
              to overlook.

May: What's that?

Bill: Get out and stay out!

May: Oh, I *am* sorry. And . . . and that girl?

Bill: Oh, did you hear that?

May: I know I shouldn't have listened.

Bill: That's all right . . . she turned me down.
           Can't blame her.

May: *I* blame her. I know *I* wouldn't leave
           a man just when he needed me most.

Bill: That's the way with most girls.
           Never forget, my child—Poverty is
           the banana skin on the doorstep
           of romance.

I've always been a rover
I've roamed the wide world over.
From Singapore to Dover,
Back to Bombay
But, as my roll was slender
None of the female gender
Had time to cast their tender
Glances my way.

I've met with girls in millions,
Mabels and Kates and Lillians,
Helped them to dance cotillions,
Given 'em tea—
None of the whole collection
Showed me the least affection
After a brief inspection,
Goodbye to me!

There isn't one girl in the world
    for me,
There isn't one parson who needs
    my fee!
Oh, every day the bakers bake
Another stodgy wedding-cake
To give the bridegroom stomach-ache,
But not for me;
No, not for me
You'll never see me grope my way up
    the aisle
Without a friend on earth, but
    trying to smile.
There isn't one girl in the world
    for me.

When the song was intended for *Pat* it also
contained the following extra material:

I gave a box of candy
Once to a girl with sandy
Hair out in Tono-pandi: (Tonypandy)
What came of that?
She wed a wealthy fellow
That very week with yellow

Whiskers from Portobello,
Leaving me flat:

Girls in these modern ages
Don't reach the tender stages
Till Bradstreet in his pages
Lists you as 'A':
I've lost my last illusion:
Out of my life's confusion
I've reached the sad conclusion
That, as I say,
There isn't one girl in the world for me:

I know the job I'd be wonderful at
Would be doing chores in a snug little flat:
I've a natural talent for
Bawling out a janitor:
I'd love to put an apron on
And wash the dishes till they shone;
Feed the goldfish and exercise the cat . . .
But what good is that—?

A YEAR FROM TODAY

(Bill and May)

Bill: I'll only be away a year
         Then I'll come back and find
            you here.

May: Perched up upon that wall
         To greet you when you call;

Bill: I'll mention with a careless air
         That I've become a millionaire.

May: And I will answer "Good,
         I always knew you would."

Bill: And then we'll have our fling—
         Ice-cream and ev'rything!
         A year from today when I come
            back to you,
         The sun will be shining, the sky
            will be blue.

The wind in the rushes
Will sing with the thrushes,

Both: And doves in the tree-tops will
            coo-coo-oo
         Bees in the clover will hum this
            refrain,
         "Winter is over and Spring's here
            again!"
         And oh, what a lot we shall both
            have to say,
         When I/you come back a year from
            today.

Bill: A year! Why, that's no time at all!
         Just Summer, Winter, Spring and
            Fall,
         I'll be right back, just think!
         Before you've time to wink!

May: Then won't we have the grandest fun!
         I'll tell you everything I've done!

Bill: And when your story's through,
         Then I'll start telling you:
         I'll talk so fast I'll slip
         And dislocate a lip!

Both: A year from today

Bill: When I come back to you.
         The sun will be gay and the sky will
            be blue;

Both: The wind in the rushes, etc.

SHUFFLIN' SAM

(Dixie and Girls)

Dixie: Funny old Shufflin' Sam, his banjo
            a-strummin'
         Says: "This old world's no place to
            cry and be glum in:

If things are bad, you bet good
    luck is a-comin'.
Yes, comin' right quick it be:
You listen to me," says he.

Girls:
Shufflin' Sam
Says, "Hurry, honey, git yer shoes!
The only way to cure the blues
Is just to keep steppin'."
Shufflin' Sam
Says: "Trouble'll be leavin' soon.
You skeer him when you play a
    tune,
That's got some real pep in!
Don't you frown,
Be jolly and breezy
Put 'em down
And pick 'em up easy
Ain't a doubt.
You gotta keep on trippin',
    skippin', (skip-skip-skippin')
    like a lamb,
And you'll win out!"
Says Shufflin' Sam.

Dixie:
"Ain't no darn use," says Sam,
    "In anyone settin'
Wastin' the Lord's good time in
    worry and frettin':
If a thing's done there ain't no
    sense in regrettin',
(Jes' you get up right now and quit
    your regrettin')
No matter how bad things be
Start dancin 'em right," says he.

Shufflin' Sam says, "Hurry, honey,
    git yer shoes!
The only way to cure the blues
Is just to keep steppin'."
Shufflin' Sam says: "Trouble'll be
    leavin' soon.
You skeer him when you play a
    tune,

That's got some real pep in!
Don't you frown,
Be jolly and breezy
Put 'em down
And pick 'em up easy
Ain't a doubt.
You gotta keep on trippin',
    skippin', (skip-skip-skippin')
    like a lamb,
And you'll win out!"
Says Shufflin' Sam.

ACT 1—FINALE

(Spoken except where indicated)

Horace: Hey, Pop!

Pennington: Oh, there you are!

Horace: Listen, you can save yourself a lot of trouble. If you want a daughter you can be proud of, take that Tolliver girl.

Pennington: Tolliver girl?

Horace: She is the most talented girl I've ever met.
(sings) She cooks ragouts and casseroles and stews,
Things made with cheese and chicken fricassees!

Mrs.
Wagstaff: He must mean May. May is our best scholar. A really wonderful girl. Step forward, (come here) May.

(May comes forward, Dixie behind her)

Pennington: What? Why . . . this is the young person who was so rude to me just now.

May: Why, I was never rude to you!

Pennington: You certainly will never be adopted
              by me.

Dixie: Oh, it wasn't May, it was I who
           called you an old gazook.

Horace: Gee, what did you say that for?

Dixie: Oh, please, Mr. Pennington,
           don't be cross with us!
           May and I do so want to be
           adopted.

Pennington: Well, I want only one girl—and
              even if I *did* want two,
              I wouldn't take *you!*

May: Then I'm not coming either.

Pennington: Very well. I'll have to choose
              someone else.

Dixie: No, no, please. She'll go. I'll
           make her!

Horace: Haven't I got something to say
           about this?

Pennington: No, you haven't. This is the time
              I choose my own relative.

Dixie: *(To May)*
           You must take your chance.

May: But I'd feel so selfish going away
           on a lovely yacht and leaving
           you alone at the old Charity
           School!

Dixie: Don't you worry about me, honey.
           I don't mind the old school so
           much—and you'll be back
           before you know where you are.

May: A year from today, when I come
           back to you,

(Sings)   The sun will be shining the sky
           will be blue.
           The wind in the rushes
           Will sing with the thrushes
           And doves in the treetops will
           coo-oo-oo!

Dixie &
May: Bees in the clover will hum this
           refrain
           "Winter is over and spring's here
           again!"
           And oh, what a lot we shall both
           have to say
           When you/I come back a year
           from today!

Girls: She can't miss such a chance
           as this.
           Can't somebody make it plain
           That such luck won't occur again?

Boys: Do give her some good advice
           Opportunity won't call twice!

All: With this offer waiting
           You wouldn't find me hesitating
           I'd be too delighted if I were the
           person invited!

Dixie: *(To Horace)*
           Seems like our dreams ain't hardly
           coming true.
           Wish I could dish up a meal or
           two for you.
           But now I won't be there, you see,
           To cook you stew and fricassee,
           Like kind Missis Rorer used to do!

Chorus: Motoring's a silly game,
           monotonous and flat,
           Flying, too, is just the same, we get
           no kick from that!

We're agreed, we're tired of speed
And motor shops and traffic cops!
We want to do something new!
Coming with us, Bill?

Bill: No, thank you!

I've met with girls in millions,
Mabels and Kates and Lillians,
Helped them to dance cotillions,
    given 'em tea—
None of the whole collection
Showed me the least affection
After a brief inspection, goodbye
    to me!

I've always been a rover
I've roamed the whole world over.
From Singapore to Dover, back
    to Bombay
I've lost my last illusion,
Out of my life's confusion
I've reached the sad conclusion
    that, as I say,

There isn't one girl in the world
    for me.
There isn't one parson who needs
    my fee!
You'll never see me grope my way
    up the aisle
Without a friend on earth, but
    trying to smile
There isn't one girl in the world
    for me!

Dixie: Goodbye, Horace. Will you think
    of me sometime when you're
    away on the yacht?

Horace: You bet I will. Goodbye, Dixie.

Dixie: Goodbye, Horace.

May: Don't cry, Dixie.

Dixie: Shove all your worries in a great
    big box,
As big as any box can be;
Shove all your worries in a great
    big box
And lock it with a great big key.
Cryin' never yet got anybody
    anywhere,
So just stick out your chin
And . . .

(She breaks down)

OPENING ACT 2
(THE POLKA DOT)

Women: O'er the floor as we move to and fro
These dear old dresses billow quaintly.
Ancient tunes are tinkling soft and low
And far-off laughter echoes faintly.

And strong is the spell we're under.
Here in this world of wonder
Dreaming of the days of long ago
When hearts were young and life
    ran slow
Life was an easeful
Thing and peaceful
Long ago, long ago.

All: But though manners were stately,
Boys and girls don't alter greatly
There were frivolous glances
Even then, we know
Slyly we have suspected
That they might have been detected
Flirting during the dances
Seventy years ago!

DAYS GONE BY

(Empress Eugénie)

Hark! Through the music a whisper you'll hear
Soft and clear

Some come to look at our revels whom we
Cannot see.
Ghosts stand close at hand all the while,
And watch with a smile.
Tap time to the tunes which they too used to
    know
Long ago.

Dear gentle ghosts of bygone ages,
Come back again from hist'ry's pages.
Softly and wistfully
Calling you seem
Like a faint melody
Heard in a dream.
Hid from our sight you stand and listen
Watch us tonight with eyes that glisten.
Maybe you laugh at us, maybe you sigh,
Dear vanished ghosts of days gone by!
Ah! ah! ah! ah! ah

ALL YOU NEED
IS A GIRL

(Bill and May)

Bill: People tell you all the time
    Fame's a ladder hard to climb.
    Don't you go believing the things that
        they say:
    It is just a cinch, no less,
    Starting out to win success,
    If you've only discovered the way.

May: What is the way?
    Please, won't you say?
    What are the rules you have got
        to obey?

Bill: Though I'm confessing it
    Took some time guessing it,
    Here is the lesson I've learned
        today:

All you need is a girl,
Just one dear little girl
Standing near you to cheer you
When ev'rything seems going
    wrong,
Though the road may be
    rough
You'll win through sure
    enough:
All you need to succeed
Is a girl who will help you
    along.

Some day I shall find my name
In the Nation's Hall of Fame:

May: All you want is simply some
        patience and luck.

Bill: In another year or so,
    When I want to bank my dough
    I shall have to be hiring a truck.

May: I have no doubt,
    When you go out,
    By awe-struck crowds you'll be
        followed about.

Bill: And when they interview
    Me and would print a few
    Words of advice from me,
    I shall shout:

Both: All you need is a girl,
    Just one dear little girl
    Standing near you to cheer you
    When everything seems going
        wrong.
    Though the going is tough
    You'll win through sure enough:
    All you need to succeed
    Is a girl just to help you along.

TULIP TIME IN SING-SING

(Dear Old-Fashioned Prison of Mine)

(Uncle Jo and Horace)

Horace: Up the river there's a college
Which authorities acknowledge
Is a cosy sort of place to go and dwell:
And with joy each student chortles,
As he passes through its portals
And the faculty conduct him to
    his cell.

Jo: How I wish that there I'd waited,
Wish I'd never graduated,
For the memory of those days still
    stirs me so.
And the birdies every Spring sing:
"Aren't you coming back to Sing-Sing,
Where you used to be so happy long
    ago?"

Horace: When it's tulip, tulip, tulip time in
    Sing-Sing,

Jo: Oh, it's there that I would be.

Horace: There are gentle, gentle, gentle hearts
    in Sing-Sing,

Jo: Watching and yearning for me.
Oh, I wish I was back with a rock or
    two to crack,
With my pals of the class of
    ninety-nine.
How I miss the peace and quiet
And the simple wholesome diet
Of that dear old-fashioned prison
    of mine.

Oh, I'd give a lot to go there:
Life was never dull or slow there.
Ev'ry night there was a concert or
    a hop:

Or I'd sit discussing Coué
With my old pal Bat-eared Louie,
Quite the nicest man that ever
    slugged a cop.

Horace: We were just a band of brothers,
Each as good as all the others,
As the humblest sort of sneak thief
    you might rank
But when you'd been there a week,
    well,
You were treated as an equal
By the high and mighty swells who'd
    robbed a bank.
(By the swells who'd killed their wives
    or robbed a bank)
When it's tulip, tulip, tulip time in
    Sing-Sing,

Jo: Oh, it's there I would be.

Horace: There are gentle, gentle, gentle hearts
    in Sing-Sing,

Jo: Watching and yearning for me.
Oh, there's no place like home,
And I'm tired of having to roam
Through the world with its women
    and its wine.
So just bob my hair and shove me
Where I know the wardens love me
In that dear old-fashioned prison
    of mine!

In *Bring On the Girls* Wodehouse quotes an alternative lyric . . .

In Broadway, haunt of pleasure
Where they dine and tread the
    measure,
A young burglar was becoming
    slowly fried.
When the waiter saw this mobster

Sitting sobbing in his lobster,
He stole up and asked him softly
    why he cried.
And the egg said with a quiver
"There's a college up the river
Which I yearn for. That's the reason
    of my gloom.
For the little birds each Spring sing
Aren't you coming back to Sing-Sing
Now it's April and the tulips are
    a-bloom?
When it's Tulip Time in Sing-Sing,
Oh, it's there that I would be:
There are gentle hearts in Sing-Sing
Watching and waiting for me:
Take me back, take me back,
Give me lots of rocks to crack
With my pals of the class of '99:
For I'd rather have neuralgia
Than be tortured by nostalgia
For that dear old-fashioned prison
    of mine.

ON A DESERT ISLAND WITH YOU

(Desert Island)

(Dixie and May)

May: Some day when we've got money
    Across the sea we'll roam.

Dixie: And find an island, honey,
    Where we can build a home.

May: It mustn't be where steamers go,
    We want to be alone, you know.

Dixie: Well, listen then, what we will do,
    Is just hang up a sign or two,
    "Keep out! Yes, this means you!!!"

Both: We'll live on a dear little island,
    Where palm trees are waving,
    And drowsy winds croon.

And gently the ripples will whisper
All day as we dream by
The lazy lagoon.

May: Won't we have just fun,
    Far from ev'ryone?
    Think of all the things that we
    can do!

Dixie: No one cross or old,
    Comin' round to scold,
    On a desert island with you.

Both: We'll live on a dear little island,
    Where palm trees are waving,
    And drowsy winds croon.
    And gently the ripples will whisper

    All day as we dream by
    The lazy lagoon.

May: Each morning when we're waking
    I'll build a lovely fire.

Dixie: And breadfruit I'll start baking,
    As much as we require.

May: We'll keep a little private zoo,
    Like Mister Crusoe used to do.

Dixie: The monks and parrots soon will be,
    Just chummin' round with you and me
    Like one, big family!

Both: We'll live on a dear little island,
    Where palm trees are waving,
    And drowsy winds croon.
    And gently the ripples will whisper
    All day as we dream by
    The lazy lagoon.

May: All alone we'll be
    Simply you and me,
    Playing by ourselves the whole day
    through.

Dixie: Won't it just be grand
         Digging in the sand
         On a desert island with you?

Both: We'll live on a dear little island,
         Where palm trees are waving,
         And drowsy winds croon.
         And gently the ripples will whisper
         All day as we dream by
         The lazy lagoon.

THE ENCHANTED TRAIN

(The Magic Train)

(Bill and May)

May: There's a train that pulls out in the
             twilight,
         Quite the best on the list of all trains
             that exist;
         For it brings the commuters home.

Bill: When the stars above shed their
             shy light,
         Happy men come again
         Back to fair Flushing (Main),
         Auburndale, Little Neck, Plandome;
         Ev'ry day, if you are that way
         When shades of night are falling.

May: You can hear gentle voices a-calling:

Both: "All aboard, please! All aboard, please!

         All aboard! All aboard!"

May: Dear magic train that brings you
             home again,
         How I shall wish it could fly?
         How I shall worry and want it to
             hurry
         And stare at the clock as the minutes
             crawl by!
         Down at the gate I shall listen and
             wait:

         Oh! How excited I'll be!
         And how I'll cheer it each night,
         When I hear it,
         Bringing you back to me!
         It's quite a humble train, you know

Bill: And some people (folks) grumble that
             it's slow;

May: It stops to ponder now and then,

Bill: The air inside needs oxygen,

May: It's not like (some) trains known
             to fame,

Bill: But it's enchanted just the same.

May: It bumps as though the wheels
             were flat;

Bill: It rattles, too, but what of that?

Both: Every bump and every jump
         Seem but to whisper clearer
         "Getting near! Getting near!
             Getting nearer!
         Soon be home now! Soon be home
             now.
         Soon be home! Soon be home!"

Bill: Dear magic train, hear it sing that
             Refrain
         "Near! Getting near! Getting near."
         But while I'm in it I'll feel that
             each minute
         Is just about six times as long as
             a year:
         If cruel fate made me one second late,
         Goodness knows what I would do:
         No train could be quick enough to
             suit me,
         When I'm coming back to you.

Both: Dear magic train, hear it sing that Refrain
"Near! Getting near! Getting near!"

SHADOW OF THE MOON

(Dixie and the Men)

Men: Won't you be my partner, please?
(1st Group)   I shake a wicked toe.

Dixie: Thank you, (I'm sorry) no.

Men: Well, then if you won't be his,
(2nd Group)   Perhaps you will be mine?

Dixie: I must decline.
And if you want an explanation
Why I decline (refuse) your invitation,
There's someone else, forgive me stating,
Someone else for whom I'm waiting.

Oh, Man up in the Moon,
(Put on your silver shoes;)
Won't you be ready soon?
(We've got no time to lose:)
Don't keep me waiting, please!

The Ensemble in *Sitting Pretty*.

(Don't keep me waiting, please.)
Climb down here through the
　　trees,
Glide down here through the trees.)
Hark! Listen! Ev'rywhere.
Soft music's in the air
There's someone who
Wants to have a dance with you!

Can't think why he isn't here.
It's strange that he's (rude to be)
　　so late.

Men:　　I shouldn't wait—

Dixie:　　All our plans were made so very
　　　　　carefully, you know.
　　　　　(We arranged the time and place . . .)

Men:　　Ah! Let him go!
　　　　　Oh!

Dixie:　　Oh, no, I really shouldn't care to.
　　　　　In fact, I don't think I would
　　　　　　dare to:
　　　　　'Twould mean our friendship
　　　　　　would be ended,
　　　　　He's so easily offended.

　　　　　Oh! Man up in the Moon,
　　　　　Won't you be ready soon?
　　　　　Put on your silver shoes,
　　　　　(Hark! In each bush and bough)
　　　　　We've got no time to lose:
　　　　　(Breezes make music now.)
　　　　　I'm waiting on the lawn,
　　　　　Come quick before it's dawn,
　　　　　There's someone who
　　　　　Wants to have a dance with you.

SITTING PRETTY

(Horace and Dixie)

Horace:　　In my set, the chaps I've met
　　　　　Tell me sport's the one best bet

They say it's so low not to be keen
On tennis and polo, see what I
　　mean?
But I've found out more and more
All that kind of stuff's a bore.
With all the swells I'm getting
　　in wrong
Because I won't play Mah-jong
There is only one, just one
Game that I consider fun!

I want to sit
Just sit, and sit, and sit
With you the whole day through.

Dixie:　　Just sit?

Horace:　　That's it! Just sit and sit and sit

Dixie:　　With no one forbidding us.

Horace:　　And nobody kidding us
　　　　　I want to sit
　　　　　And hold your little mitt
　　　　　On chairs that fit just two
　　　　　For I'd give half the city
　　　　　If I were sitting pretty.
　　　　　Sitting pretty, little lady, with you.

Dixie:　　Smart frocks I stitch for ladies rich,
　　　　　Shut up all day inside a store
　　　　　I stitch and stitch and stitch.
　　　　　And then I start and stitch some
　　　　　　more
　　　　　Enjoyment this employment
　　　　　　doesn't bring, I'm here to say
　　　　　Believe me. I could use the time
　　　　　　in quite a different way.

I want to sit
Just sit and sit and sit
With you the whole day through.

Horace:　　Just sit?

Dixie: That's it! Just sit and sit and sit
          With nobody cutting in.

Horace: No smart alecks butting in

Dixie: I'd like to sit
          Before the lights were lit
          On chairs that fit just two.
          Other girls I would pity
          If I were sitting pretty.
          Sitting pretty, like a lady, with you

Additional verse:

(She dictates letter to an imaginary typist)

Dixie: "Dear Sir,
          Your favour just received,
          And though arriving rather late,
          My prompt attention will be given
                yours of even date.
          I hasten to reply and quote to you,
                a wholesale rate.
          I thank you for your order and in
                answer beg to state:

          I want to sit,
          Just sit and sit and sit
          With you the whole day through."

Horace: Just sit?

Dixie: That's it! Just sit and sit and sit,
          With nobody cutting in.

Horace: No smart alecks butting in.

Dixie: I'd like to sit
          Before the lights were lit
          On chairs that just fit two.
          Other girls I would pity
          If I were sitting pretty,
          Sitting pretty, like a lady with you.

FINALE ULTIMO

Dixie: I want to sit,
          Just sit and sit and sit
          With you the whole day through.

Horace: Just sit?

Dixie: That's it! Just sit and sit and sit
          With nobody cutting in.

Horace: No smart alecks butting in!

Dixie: I'd like to sit
          Before the lights were lit
          On chairs that fit just two
          Other girls I would pity
          If I were sitting pretty
          Sitting pretty like a lady with
                you.

May &
Bill: Dear magic train that brings you
                home again.
          How I shall wish it could fly!
          How I shall worry and want it to
                hurry
          And stare at the clock as the minutes
                crawl by!
          Down at the gate I shall listen and
                wait,
          Oh! How excited I'll be!
          And how I'll cheer it each night when
                I hear it
          Bringing you back to me!

All: Shufflin' Sam says "Hurry, honey, git
                yer shoes!
          The only way to cure the blues
          Is just to keep steppin.'"
          Shufflin' Sam says, "Trouble'll be
                leavin' soon
          You skeer him when you play a tune
          That's got some real pep in!

Don't you frown, be jolly and breezy.
Put 'em down and pick 'em up easy;
Ain't a doubt
You gotta keep on skippin', trippin'
    like a lamb
And you'll win out!" says Shufflin'
    Sam!

In researching the 1989 concert revival of
the show, conductor/musical director, John
McGlinn unearthed several unused numbers . . .

OPENING ACT 1
(original version)

(Chorus)

Motoring's a silly game, monotonous and flat!
Flying, too, is just the same, we get no kick
    from that!
We're agreed, we're tired of speed
And motor shops and traffic cops!

We want to do something new.
That is why we're going in for coaching.
Old-fashioned coaching.
That tally-hoing
Just gets you going.
It sets you tingling
And it makes you glad
That you were born.
That jingling to the cheery music
Of the horn!

Coaching, you can't beat coaching,
The horses clatter,
Your gloom will scatter.
And naught will matter
When the music starts to ring in your ear
As gaily bowling along the road you go!
I'll bet you will get right up
And let out a cheer
When once you're hearing
The coach horn blow!

ALL THE WORLD IS DANCING MAD
(No lyric)

I'M WISE (No lyric)

JUST YOU WAIT

(Billy, Uncle Jo, Horace and Judson)

Bill: Daily it grows harder
            For a man to be a bachelor.

Uncle Jo: Yes, things look black.

Judson: No use trying to dodge or hide
            You can't escape the blushing bride!

Bill: She's on your track!

Jo: Somewhere some girl's waiting to
            Put the ball and chain on you.

Horace: Oh, see the salesman with the ring.

Bill: The organist is practising

Judson: The wedding march!

Jo: Be a man and set your teeth,
            You'll soon be passing underneath
            That floral arch!

All: For some girl's going to come and
                grab you
            Sooner or late! Just wait! Yes, in a
                while
            With frozen smile along the aisle
                you'll stagger—
            That wedding cake will soon be
                sitting grimly
            Upon the plate.

Bill: You'll hear a voice

Judson: Say, "Wilt thou, Bill?"

Jo: And with a chill
           You'll say, "I will!"

All: For some girl's going to come and
               grab you
           Sooner or late! Just wait!

Bill: Maybe late or maybe soon,
           By daylight or beneath the moon.

Jo: It can't be stopped!

Judson: You will fall on bended knee
           And whisper, "Darling, marry me!"

Jo: And then you're copped!
           Then we'll see you, young and fair,
           Brushing rice out of your hair.

Horace: Oh, hear those bells, how loud they
               chime!

Bill: Brace up, my lad, you haven't time for
               vain regrets.

Jo: Take an older man's advice
           Go out at once and get a price
           On bassinettes!

All: For some girl's going to come and
               grab you
           Sooner or late! Just wait! Yes, in a
               while
           With frozen smile along the aisle
               you'll stagger.
           At the Niagara Falls Hotel, you're
               going to
           Have a date.

Bill: You're due to start

Judson: (Extremely soon)

Jo: A Honeymoon, goodbye, poor prune!

All: For some girl's going to come and
               grab you
           Sooner or late! Just wait!

The New York reviewers greeted the show respectfully and made generally pleasing comparisons with its Princess antecedents. Kern was hailed as "America's best writer of light music," while Wodehouse's lyrics were equally well received. "The love lyrics are soft without being mushy," Burns Mantle observed in the *New York Times* but, as usual, the comedy numbers attracted most attention. "'Dear Old-Fashioned Prison Of Mine' and 'Bongo On the Congo' . . . threatened to ruin the audience" with their many encores.

Despite this, the initially good business soon declined and the piece ran for only a disappointing 95 performances at the larger Fulton Theatre before touring. (It was subsequently revived in April 1989 for concert performances at Carnegie Hall's 300-seat Weill Recital Hall.)

Different explanations emerged as to why the show, which had one of Kern's best scores, should have failed so unexpectedly. In a letter dated August 30th, 1933, Kern wrote:

"*Sitting Pretty* as you know, flopped because the amusing complications due to the unrecognisability of twin sisters aborted, chiefly on account of the stupidity of casting for the girls, supposed to look exactly alike, Gertrude Bryan and Queenie Smith. Ignoring their racial differences, their linear measurements differed about eighteen inches."

Whether that was an accurate assessment of the position, or a mere rationalization with hindsight will never be known. Others have put the failure down to Kern's insistence that the music from the show should not be played in cabarets, the increasingly important radio stations or on phonograph recordings. (The sheet music carries the legend "The right to make arrangements or otherwise reproduce this composition is expressly reserved.") This ban was justified, so Kern claimed, in a statement in which he argued that "None of our music now reaches the public as we wrote it except in the theatre. It is so distorted by jazz orchestras as to be almost unrecognisable. A composer should be able to protect his score just as an author does his manuscripts." The result, of course, was that the general theatre-going public had no opportunity to sample the melodic songs which they would hear at the Fulton Theatre, and they stayed away.

Between the Detroit premiere and the Broadway opening a number of changes were made. At the opening of Act I three songs had been sung in succession—the first two, "Roses Are Nodding" and "Coaching," by the Chorus and "You Alone Would Do" by Bill and Babe. They were replaced by "Is This Not A Lovely Spot?"

"Just Wait" had been performed by the male principals part way through the act, while a second act trio for Horace, Bill & Dixie, "Ladies Are Present"—originally intended for *Ladies, Please!*—was also cut, as was Horace's number with the female Chorus—"A Romantic Man." (It is possible that these two songs are "All the World is Dancing Mad" and "I'm Wise" under different titles. Conversely, they may have nothing to do with each other.) Perhaps most surprisingly—since it was the culmination of Horace and Dixie's romance—the show's title song was sacrificed. The reason had nothing to do with the quality or relevance of the song itself. It was simply that the singer (Dwight Frye) experienced considerable difficulty pronouncing the word "sit"—something of a problem (of both linguistics and taste) considering the frequency with which it appeared in the lyric!

The year 1926 brought a strange assignment for Wodehouse. He was asked to adapt a Russian operetta, *The Orlov*. It became "A New Musical Play in Three Acts" called *Hearts and Diamonds*, the first work to be directed in Britain by the distinguished Russian director Komisarjevsky. Despite the program credits, there is evidence that Wodehouse did contribute one set of lyrics that make up the Act 2 Finale.

HEARTS AND DIAMONDS (1926)

Presented by Arthur Bourchier at the Strand Theatre, London, on June 1, 1926 (46 performances).

BOOK
Ernst Marischka and
Bruno Granichstadten

ENGLISH ADAPTATION
P. G. Wodehouse and
Laurie Wylie

LYRICS
Graham John
Act 2 Final: P. G. Wodehouse

MUSIC
Bruno Granichstadten
and Max Darewski

DIRECTOR, SCENIC
DESIGNER AND COSTUMER
Theodore Komisarjevsky

STRAND THEATRE

Licensed by the Lord Chamberlain to Arthur Bourchier

EVERY EVENING AT 8.15

Matinees : Wednesday and Friday at 2.15

First Matinee : Wednesday, June 9th

BY ARRANGEMENT WITH ARTHUR BOURCHIER

"HEARTS and DIAMONDS"

A New Musical Play in Three Acts

Adapted from "THE ORLOV"

By ERNST MARISCHKA and BRUNO GRANICHSTADTEN
English Adaptation by P. G. WODEHOUSE and LAURIE WYLIE
Lyrics by GRAHAM JOHN
Music by BRUNO GRANICHSTADTEN.   Additional numbers by MAX DAREWSKI

The Entire Production devised and directed, the Settings and the
Costumes designed by
THEODORE KOMISARJEVSKY

Characters in order of their appearance :

Hunter	Clerk at the Walsh Works ...	J. S. CARRÉ
Alexander Dorotchinsky	A Motor Mechanic ...	GEORGE METAXA
John Walsh	A Motor Manufacturer	CHARLES STONE
Jefferson	Walsh's Partner ...	LUPINO LANE
Mildred Harris ... }	Jefferson's Friends	DARLY AITKEN
Gladys Fayne ...		DOROTHY DAW
Dolly Watchett	A Typist	ANITA ELSON
Nadya Nadyakovska ...		LOUISE EDVINA
A Typist		LALA COLLINS
Purvis	Butler to Walsh ...	COLIN JOHNSTON
A Stranger		WALLACE LUPINO
Inspector Collins ...	A Detective	ERIC ROLAND
Stepanov		WILFRID CAITHNESS
Myra Clay	Stepanov's Friends ...	ENA EVANS
Esme Symes		KATHLEEN CARROLL
Douglas Roach		C. O'HARA
Victor	Maître d'hotel at "The Scarlet Circle" ...	HARRY HILLIARD

Orchestra under the direction of MAX DAREWSKI
Dances arranged by EDWARD DOLLY
Speciality Dances in ACT III. by ENA EVANS, LILIAN SMITH
and JACK STANFORD

CAST

Hunter:	A Typist:
J. S. CARRE	LALA COLLINS
Alexis	Purvus (Waksg's butler):
Dorotchinsky:	COLIN JOHNSTON
GEORGE METAXA	A Stranger:
John Walsh:	WALLACE LUPINO
CHARLES STONE	Inspector Collins:
Jefferson:	ERIC ROLAND
LUPINO LANE	Stepanov:
Mildred Harris:	WILFRID CAITHNESS
DARLY AITKEN	Myra Clay:
Gladys Fayne:	ENA EVANS
DOROTHY DAW	Esme Symes:
Dolly Watchett:	KATHLEEN CARROLL
ANITA ELSON	Douglas Roach: C. O'HARA
Nadja Nadyajivsja:	Victor:
LOUISE EDVINA	HARRY HILLIARD

SYNOPSIS

The main characters are:

Walsh & Jefferson, a motor-works established by Messrs. Walsh & Jefferson (the latter, now deceased, whose son inherited 60% of the business).

Walsh, an elderly business man who owns 40% of the motor-works Walsh & Jefferson. He is in love with Nadja Nadyajivsja, and in general will not permit pretty girls near the works, let alone be employed.

Dolly, is one of the rather ugly-looking stenographers employed at the works. Dolly Watchett is actually very pretty when she is allowed to take off her overalls and adjust her hair, and Walsh falls in love with her.

Alexis, Russian mechanic working at the factory who is not what he seems.

Nadja, Russian prima donna.

Walsh has invited Nadja to the works. When she arrives she rescues a kitten from under the wheels of a lorry, but needs to be rescued herself, by Alexis. She and Alexis click, and Jefferson warns Walsh, who invites Alexis to a party he is holding that night, the theory being that Nadja will see him humiliated in an environment outside his experience.

Meanwhile Jefferson proposes to Dolly who rejects him on the basis that he has only known her for half an hour. Alexis tells Jefferson that he will raise the money he needs to marry Nadja by selling the Orlov, the crown jewel of the Imperial Russian family, which he has in his possession, and asks Jefferson to handle the deal.

This responsibility causes Jefferson to pick Dolly up to take her to the party, and she is sore when they meet up. Walsh, meanwhile, is cross that Alexis is flirting with Nadja and also threatens to assault Jefferson. When Jefferson explains to Dolly in Walsh's presence, Walsh realizes that Alexis will be wealthy and decides to steal the jewel.

Jefferson and Dolly patch up their differences and while strolling in the grounds come across a stranger who purports to be a Scotland Yard detective sent down to guard the diamond. Jefferson passes it over into his safe-keeping.

Back in the house, Walsh announces he is going to buy the Orlov, but when the real Scotland Yard man comes on the scene, it becomes clear that it has been stolen. Alexis is suspected but is recognized by the detective's companion as the Grand Duke Alexis Dorotchinsky. Dolly, who seems to know who Alexis is, assumes that she is a cast-off. So Nadja agrees to marry Walsh. (The whole of this scene constitutes the finale of Act 2, including both spoken and sung lines, all written by Wodehouse.)

Act 3 is set at the Angry Cheese nightclub. Jefferson arrives to tell Dolly he spent the night in a cell and that he will have no money as he has lost the diamond. When Nadja arrives, Dolly explains she is engaged to Jefferson and had never seen Alexis before. The stranger with the diamond turns up to pass it over to Walsh, for whom he had been acting as agent, but is chased and caught by Jefferson. Not surprisingly, Alexis and Nadja are reconciled, and when Jefferson returns the diamond to Alexis he says it was only an imitation anyway; he had retained the original all the time.

ACT 2—
FINALE

Ensemble: The violins are sighing
Of love that you're denying
My name's a thing that came
by chance.
Like a glance!
Whilst we dance!
Forget what I have told you
And let my arms enfold you!
Together let us dance into
tenderness
Nameless in happiness!

Walsh: My friends, your attention!

All: *(Singing)*
What's this all about?

Walsh: *(Singing)*
The Orlov. You've heard that it's
now for sale.
Well, here is the fellow who's going
to buy it.

All: For whom?

Walsh: *(Speaks)*
For Madame Nadyajivsja

(Enter Nadja)

Men: *(As she enters singing)*—
Lovely! She's lovely!

*(Nadja comes down smiling. She sings with glances
toward Alexis who gazes at her, still overcome.)*

Nadja: For you, my sweet, for you
I smile and sigh tonight.

Walsh: *(Speaks)*
Splendid!

Nadja: There's no one else but you
In all the world . . . to be . . .

Walsh: *(Speaks)*
Is that so !!!
(Sings)
My friends, what you have heard
is true:
Our secret we won't hide:
Allow me then, to introduce to you
My lovely future bride!

Alexis: *(Stunned)*
Bride!!!

Chorus: Hip-hip-hurrah!
Hip-hip-hurrah!
Hip-hip-hurrah!
Hip-hip-hurrah!

Nadja: *(Speaks)*
I think you are rather premature.

Walsh: *(Sings)*
By no means
For I'm a man who knows his
mind;
My motto's do it now;
And when my chosen mate I find
No hesitation I allow.
To prove what I am saying,
(Speaks)
I'll pay for the Orlov in cash
Three hundred thousand pounds.

Alexis: No!
*(He seizes Nadja by the arm.
To Walsh)*—
You can keep your money
The Orlov will never belong to you.

Nadja: What do you mean
Perhaps you'll explain.

Alexis: That stone shall never belong to a
false woman.

Ensemble:	*(Speaks)* He's mad! Very sad! Shall we intervene?
Walsh:	*(Speaks)* Here, what do you mean by creating this scene?
Alexis:	*(To Nadja)* I beg your pardon if I have offended you.
Nadja:	Your manners were a little astray.
Alexis:	We Russians do not look on love as a joke.
Nadja:	Please make your meaning clearer.
Alexis:	Very well! I decline this offer. The Orlov belongs to me.
All:	To you. *(Laughter)*
Nadja:	To you? The claim you make is too absurd. How came you to have this Crown jewel?
Alexis:	It may seem impossible; but still it's true I think it is time you revealed who you are.
All:	Yes, yes.
Alexis:	Your humble servant!
Nadja:	Stop playing with words. Tell me the truth.
Alexis:	I am the man who is paid to mend your car.

All:	Yes, yes. *(Laughing)*
Nadja:	Are you laughing at me?
Alexis:	What if I am?
Nadja:	Oh! This is too much!
Walsh:	You, sir! Get out!
All Men:	Get out of here.
Nadja:	A mechanic and a general! *(All Laugh)*
Walsh:	And a waiter, too. *(All laugh)*
Nadja:	A waiter with the Orlov *(All laugh)* *(Sings)* I fear the truth is clear: You must have . . .
Alexis:	Stolen it . . . *(Sensation)* Answer me! You are silent. Now I know.
Nadja:	*(Sings)* We're living in a tinsel world of make believe Where Harlequin is mocking in his pointed sleeve And all the day he sips The honey-sweet from lips That wanton in the sun Of smiles from everyone
Nadja & Alexis:	For those who whisper passion till their dying day Are only in the fashion if they fly away

Forgotten is the word that once
was blazoned in the stars above.
The mocking balalaika sings the
knell of love.

Alexis: *(Speaks—laughs)*
What does it matter!
"Djiuli" etc.

(Enter Butler escorting Detective and Stepanov)

Butler: Excuse me, sir. This gentleman wishes to speak to you.

Detective: I am Inspector Collins from Scotland Yard, sir. We were telephoned that there was a valuable diamond from Russia to be guarded.

Walsh: Oh, yes, you're just in time. The diamond in question is the famous Orlov.

Detective: Ah! I thought so! We had already been notified that it was in this country; and, on receiving Mr. Jefferson's message, I immediately suspected it to be the missing jewel; and I have taken the precaution of bringing a former member of the Russian Imperial Court with me to identify it.

Walsh: *(Points to Alexis)*
Well, this man seems to have stolen it.

All: Yes, yes he has.

Walsh: He is a mechanic in my works.

Detective: *(To Alexis)*
Who are you?

Alexis: Who am I? I am a Russian and an officer of the Household Cossack Regiment.

(All laugh)

It was a labored effort and the subject matter was clearly something that had not fired Wodehouse's imagination. He makes no reference to it in any of his writings and of his several biographers only Lee Davis gives it passing mention. The run of only 46 performances tells its own story.

There was then an unusual (for them) three year hiatus, easily explained by Bolton's involvement in successive Gershwin hits—*Primrose* (1924), *Lady, Be Good!* (1924) and *Tip Toes* (1925). The successful run continued with *Oh, Kay!* (1926) (originally *Mayfair* then *Miss Mayfair*, then *Cheerio* before settling on its final Princess-reminiscent title) which was to give Gertrude Lawrence her first starring role in a "book" musical. Wodehouse collaborated with Bolton on the book but the lyrics were entirely Ira Gershwin's. It was not until the 1960 revival that Wodehouse lyrics would find a place in the show.

Precisely what persuaded the boys to undertake their next joint project—a musical dramatization of a supposed episode in the life of soprano Jenny Lind, "The Swedish Nightingale"—has never been made clear. Perhaps it was the flattery implicit in the offer of a "Shubert show." Certainly, by agreeing to work with composer Armand Vecsey, they were choosing to forget the earlier experience of *Rose Of China*. And at the end of the day they could always claim that *The Nightingale* was more than twice as successful. It ran for 96 performances, whereas *Rose of China* had only managed to scrape together a paltry 47!

THE NIGHTINGALE (1927)

A Musical Romance in Three Acts

Presented by the Messrs. Shubert at the Jolson Theatre, New York, on January 3, 1927 (96 performances), after a trial run starting in New Haven, Connecticut.

BOOK　　　Guy Bolton (based on the life of Jenny Lind)
LYRICS　　P. G. Wodehouse
MUSIC　　Armand Vecsey

Eleanor Painter (*Jenny Lind*) and Cast in *The Nightingale*.

CAST

Maj. Gen. Thomas Gurnee, Rex's grandfather
& Commandant of West Point:
LUCIUS HENDERSON
Mrs. Gurnee, Rex's mother:
SOPHIE EVERETT
Mr. Carp, understudy at Barnum's
Museum:
STANLEY LUPINO
Col. Wainwright, Alice's father:
JOHN GAINES
Mrs. Vischer Van Loo, a society lady:
CLARA PALMER
Alice Wainwright:
EILEEN VAN BIENE
Capt. Joe Archer:
ROBERT HOBBS
Piper, a Barnum employee:
THOMAS WHITELEY
Josephine, Jenny's companion:
VIOLET CARLSON
Cadet Officer:
DONALD BLACK
Jenny Lind, the Swedish Nightingale:
ELEANOR PAINTER
James McNeil Whistler:
HAROLD WOODWARD

Stephen Rutherford:
NICHOLAS JOY
Capt. Rex Gurnee:
RALPH ERROLLE
P. T. Barnum:
TOM WISE
Col. Robert E. Lee:
VICTOR BOZARDT
Dolly (maid):
EILEEN CARMODY
Susan (maid):
ARLINE MELBURN
Otto Goldschmidt,
Barnum's Musical Director:
WILLIAM TUCKER
Signor Belletti,
an opera singer:
IVAN DNEPROFF
Butler—Rutherford's:
JOHN GAINES
Footman—Rutherford's:
NEAL FRANK
Usher—Castle Garden:
ROBERT HARPER
Cornelius Vanderbilt:
VICTOR BOZARDT

SYNOPSIS

1851 . . . and the ball at West Point is in full swing ("West Point"). Everyone awaits the arrival of Capt. Rex Gurnee, hero of the Indian wars—none more than Alice, who has been in love with him for years. Their families expect them to marry, much to the disappointment of Joe, best friend to both, but also in love with Alice. Carp is a junior employee of P. T. Barnum, the famous impresario. He is sneaking time off. On the boat trip here he meets a "Miss Lamont" and her companion, Josephine. An instant musical comedy attraction has developed ("Breakfast in Bed"). A parade of cadets marches by. ("March Song"). Miss Lamont is already a hit with the soldiers and clearly enjoying herself ("Tonight the World Is Pleasure Bent"). We now learn that she is, in reality, the famous singer and Barnum's protégée, Jenny Lind. She had met Rex earlier and has come to West Point in the hope of seeing him again. His boat whistle is now heard ("Enough is Enough"); ("Homeland"). Rex and Jennie meet, though he still does not know who she is ("May Moon"). Alice can't understand why Rex doesn't rush to her side. Joe tells her *he'll* always be there for her ("Two Little Ships"). Barnum arrives but Jenny refuses to return to New York with him. He also discovers Carp and reprimands him. Carp bemoans his lot to the Girls ("He Doesn't Know"). Rex is reunited with his family and decorated by Gen. Robert E. Lee. He proposes to Jenny but Barnum reveals her true identity ("Finaletto"). Rex feels he has been deceived and made to feel foolish. Barnum takes Jenny off.

In her hotel suite back in New York, Jenny and her maids sing ("Fairyland"). Otto, her musical director, arrives and declares his own love for her ("I Know My Love Is You"). Now another suitor arrives—Signor Belletti, the famous opera singer ("Deep As The Ocean"). The three of them discuss the situation— not surprisingly, in song ("Love Is Calling"). Rex arrives to take her for a drive. He is to resign from the Army and work in an office for Cornelius Vanderbilt. Steve, another admirer, has persuaded the magnate to withdraw the offer. Carp arrives at Steve's apartment as part of the entertainment for a Christmas party he is giving ("Santa Claus"). Everyone is determined to break up the engagement between Rex and Jenny. Alice manages to convince Jenny that the relationship will be damaging to him. Only Jenny can turn him away ("Nightingale"). Only by pretending that she is living with Steve can she achieve it. Rex leaves and a heartbroken Jenny goes out on the balcony to face the public that truly loves her ("Jenny Lind").

Years later . . . all the principals meet at a Jenny Lind concert. Rex has married Alice, Carp married Josephine. When they have all gone, Jenny is left alone with Barnum. "It would never have done, Jenny. We're showmen, you and I, servants of the public. . . . We must keep on smiling and singing, even though our hearts are breaking."

OPENING CHORUS—WEST POINT

(Girls)

Along the river
The ripples quiver
And music jingling
Sets us tingling;
Absurd romances
And foolish fancies
Are in the air, so, girls, beware!
Behave demurely
Or you will surely
Find that your heart's been snared securely;
Men seek flirtations
At army stations
Upon the smallest provocations,
Be careful how you even let them fix your shawl,
For *anything* may happen at a West Point Ball.

West Point, West Point,
Gallant and gay,
How you steal our
Prudence away.
Our poor hearts you
Net in your snare;
You capture us,
Enrapture us;
It's something in the air;
For though we say,
Come what may,
Thoughts of folly we will banish
Soon or late,
Sure as fate,
Our good resolutions vanish;
West Point, West Point,
We're in your thrall;
And nothing seems to matter at a West Point Ball,
You can't help being foolish at a West Point Ball.

BREAKFAST IN BED

(Josephine and Carp)

Josephine: When we are married,
             When we are wed,

I'll bring you breakfast in bed;
Breakfast in bed.

Carp: Did I hear rightly
            Just what you said?
            You'll bring me breakfast in bed?

Josephine: Breakfast in bed?

            While you are still asleep
            Down to the kitchen I'll creep;
            Each day,
            My King,
            A tray
            I'll bring
            Of coffee, prunes and cereal!

Carp: And add,
            My pet,
            An omelette.
            My tastes are *so* material!

Josephine: I'll kiss you as you waken

Carp: And slip me eggs and bacon;

Josephine: And I'll be there
            And you'll be there

Both: And no one there but us.

Carp: "Say it with flowers,"
            Some people say.
            I know a better way,
            Far better way.

Josephine: Say it with flapjacks,
            That is the plan
            To win the heart of man.

Carp: I never knew—that (what) bliss
            Could be so blissful as this.

Josephine: Each day, my King,
            A tray I'll bring
            Heaped high with toast and
               marmalade

Carp: And eggs beside
         All certified
         The best that on the farm are laid.
         Outside the birds will chirrup
         While I eat cakes and syrup.

Both: And I'll be there
         And you'll be there
         And no one else (there) but us.

Josephine: I'll toil, my lamb,
         To broil you ham,
         Oh, won't I just take care of you.

Carp: And if you please,
         Some saus-a-gees,
         If our old pig can spare a few.
         You'll brush, my queen of charmers,
         The crumbs from my pajamas,

Both: And I'll be there
         And you'll be there
         And no one there but us.

MARCH SONG

(West Point Army Men)

All you millions
Of civilians,
You must forgive us if at times we seem to
    swagger.
Foemen near us,
Thousands cheer us
And not a girl will leave our side unless you
    drag her,
If we seem self-satisfied,
That is mere
Proper pride.
If we seem to own the earth,
We just know
Our true worth.
For, search the wide world through o'er land
    and sea,
And I think with me

You'll soon agree
That of all the mortals framed on human
    plan
There is none to beat an Army Man.

Army men
(Be ready),
Army men
(Be steady),
Shirk no duty anywhere,
We fear no man,
Friend or foeman.
When the trumpet sounds, we're there,
Love or war, you'll find us in the van.
It's been so since hist'ry first began.
When the shells are flying,
When the girls are sighing,
Trust an Army Man,
Trust an Army Man,
Trust to an Army Man,
Rah, Rah, Rah, Rah

Refrain

TONIGHT THE WORLD IS PLEASURE BENT

(Jenny and Men)

Jenny: Tonight the world is pleasure bent,
         There's music in the breeze,
         The rushes sway in merriment,
         The laughter shakes the trees.
         When hearts are merry making,
         Why should mine be breaking?
         Forget the thought of sorrow,
         Regrets may come tomorrow.
         Tonight—ah—grant me
         A moment's respite
         For dear delight—Ah.

         Her heart is throbbing
         Now with gladness;
         Her heart is almost full

To madness.
Lilacs so tender are bathed
In the moonlight of magical splendor.
Her lips are quivering now with
        laughter;
Who cares what fate may bring us
        after?
Her heart this lovely night
Longs to live and to love.

Rex arrives home . . .

ENOUGH IS ENOUGH

(Rex & Ensemble)

Rex: You've heard in song and
               story
           About the field of glory,
           Where heroes grit their teeth
               and breaths are bated.
           Well, now that I have seen it,
           I'll tell you, and I mean it,
           The field of glory's very
               over-rated;
           The poets have sung about
               the romance of war,
           But let me say as I have
               hinted before,
           The only single minute of
               real enjoyment in it
           Is, when you're safe back
               home once more.

Refrain
Ensemble:
           Home's the spot
           Where I would be.
           No more for me
           The battle's roar,
           And the gore and that sort
               of stuff.
           Oh, Home's the spot,
           For goodness knows I'm tired
               of foes

Who, when they fight
Are quite
Inclined to be rough.
I want to settle down,
My duty done,
And loaf and dance and laugh and
        have some fun;
For Home's the spot.
I don't deny when bullets fly you get
        a thrill,
But still,
Enough is enough.

HOMELAND

(Rex)

Now care and danger
Are left behind;
And friend for stranger
At last I find.
To greet you all
How good it seems;
You and my Homeland
Have filled my dreams.

Refrain: Homeland of mine,
My thoughts were of you;
Your spirit divine
Held my heart true.
Though storm and fear
A voice was ever near
That spoke from above
Of the land I love.
Just a fond thought of home!
That made my danger light,
Seemed to cheer the darkest night,
Home was calling to me in my heart.

MAY MOON

(Rex and Jenny)

Rex: The roving breezes kiss the
honeysuckle,
"Don't waste a night like this,"
They seem to chuckle.

Jenny: Regrets may come and sorrow,
And hearts may ache tomorrow;
Tonight life's all a tinkling tune,

Rex: Tonight we're minions of the moon.
Oh high, remote—a silver boat
On a sea of azure seems to ride
(Rides o'er a silver sea)

And there serene, sits throned
a Queen,

Who smiles to see me happy by
your side. (As kind as queens
should be.)

Rex: A fair enchantress, she,

Jenny: Who gives her subjects gladness,
(As kind as Queens should be)
And sweet midsummer madness,
(True friend of lovers)

Rex: From care and sadness she sets them
free. (She says, 'Be free.')

Jenny: And we say to her

Refrain

Jenny: May Moon,
Shining o'er field and dell,

Rex: May Moon
Lovers all love you well:

Both: May Moon
Gleaming and gay, bright star and
splendid
Until the night is ended,
Cast your old magic spell.

Rex: May Moon
Hark while we crave a boon;
Night flies,
It will be daylight soon (Dawn will
break o'er us soon);
May Moon
Oh, let our prayer be granted:
Hold us enchanted
For tonight, May Moon.

TWO LITTLE SHIPS

(Journey's End)

(Alice and Joe)

Joe: Life's like a stream
On which we seem,

Like little ships that on their trips
    go hurrying.
On current strong,
They race along,
Each moment faster,
Toward disaster.

Alice: But, as you glide,
If by your side
You chance to note another boat,
    stop worrying,
For someone's near to give you aid.
So you've no need to be afraid.

Refrain   We're just like

Joe: Two little ships
Sailing down where the river's
    flowing;
Two little ships,

And they both wonder where
    they're going.

Alice: Gliding side by side,
And in the roughest weather,
Still together,
One little ship
May get scared when the winds start
    blowing.

Joe: Poor little ship,
It need have no fear,

Both: The other ship is always near.

Joe: Two cockleshells,
They ride the swells
And pitch and roll with not a soul to
    pilot them;
And as they go
The tempests blow
And rapids thunder
To draw them under.

Alice: But one's a craft
Snug fore and aft;
No dangers grim can frighten
HIM—he'll smile at them;
And he'll protect his little friend
Until they come to journey's end.

Refrain

HE DOESN'T KNOW

(Another One Gone)

(Carp)

The stripling when he leaves his darling
    mother
Is like a little bird so blithe and gay;
His happy song he just begins to chirrup
And then some cat will get him right away.
He's for it, fate has caught him in the mill,
His chances of escape are almost nil.

Poor thing, some girl has got him,
Poor lamb, he doesn't know.
So innocently smiling to the end,
He doesn't know what's waiting round the bed,
Poor gink, he's just a rummy that some girl's got
    her clutches on.
She vamps him, then he's rattled, too late he
    finds he's grafted.
Poor nut, that's another one gone.

Scene two is some conservatory by moonlight,
The spider and the fly are seated there
But consciously he feels the net is closing,
The voice of doom is sounding in the air.
A sigh, a smile, he weakens for, the lunk,
One look, one tender word—he's sunk.
Poor thing, some girl has got him,
Poor thing, he doesn't know.
He's in his cell before he's counted three,
She locks him in and sits upon the key.
Poor sap, he's just some ninny that some girl's
    got her clutches on,

How her relations gloat, they've got him by
    the throat.
Poor fish, that's another one gone.

Scene three—they come and wake him from
    his slumber,
And drag him forth, all shivering, pale and
    cold.
His moment's come to face the firing party,
His little race is run, his tale is told.
He bids goodbye to all his weeping friends,
Just gasps, "I will" and then the trap
    descends.
Poor thing, some girl has got him,
Poor lamb, he doesn't know.
He'll never get another chance to talk,
He's got it where the bottle gets the cork.
He looks up as he places on the ring,
All the choir boys start to sing,
Poor stiff, that's another one gone.

(Encore)
Poor thing, some girl has got him,
Poor lamb, he doesn't know.
His waistcoat and his collar are too tight,
He'd love to tear the lot off, if he might.
Poor mutt, he's just a ninny that some girl's got
    her digits (didgets) on.
As he kneels upon his knees
There's a sound that makes him freeze—
My God, there's another one gone.

FINALETTO ACT 1—
LOVE IS ALL THAT MATTERS

(Rex and Jenny)

Rex: And so it seems
          Our comedy of love is ended!
          No doubt it proved exciting for
            you.
          Win my heart and then break it
            in two.
          It can't be mended,

          I was foolish to care
          But I loved you;
          Could you not play fair?

Jenny: Oh, what are names to lovers?
          Is mine so much to you?
          Who cared when you caressed me,
          When in your arms you pressed me?
          My heart is yours,
          Tonight is ours.

Rex: No, deceit all romance shatters.

Jenny: Love to me is all that matters.

MAY MOON (Reprise)

(Rex)

When around me the world is all gladness,
Why must I be weary with sadness?
The one that I care for is missing and
    therefore—
The night, tho' fair it seems—
Just made for dreams
Is all in vain—in vain.

FAIRYLAND

(The Sun's in the Sky)

(Dolly and Susan)

Dolly &
Susan: The sun's in the sky,
          Morning's creeping, creeping,
            creeping by;
          With feet the street is ringing;
          And birds so gaily singing
          A chant of welcome make
          To greet you as you wake.
          Winds that gently blow
          Whisper to and fro
          Throughout the summer scene
          Soft tales of love relating;
          And outside your door

Subjects by the score
For their sleeping queen
Are waiting.

I KNOW MY LOVE IS YOU
(LOVE LIKE YOURS
IS RARE INDEED)

(The Sun Is Far Above Me)

(Otto)

Otto: Just as the sun is far above me,
You may never love me.
Still, it seems
You fill my dreams.
To clasp your hand so slender,
Hear your voice so tender,
Must suffice for me.
We meet in friendship day by day,
And yet in heart
So far apart.
I thrill with gladness through
Yet filled with sadness, too.
To love you
Is bitter sweetness,
Still, I would not choose
One fond thought to lose,
Though I know my love is vain . . .

Jenny: Why beg the sun so far above you?
Other maids will love you,
All your dreams
Are vain, it seems,
When other hands are slender,
Other hands are tender.
Do not sigh for me.
We meet in friendship day by day
And yet in heart so far apart.
To thrill with gladness through
Brings only sadness, too
For loving is bitter sweetness.
Still, I would not choose
One fond thought to lose,
Love like yours is rare indeed.

DEEP AS THE OCEAN

(Love Like Mine)

(Belletti)

(Recitative: Very Florid)

Love like mine for thee
No power can check,
No prayer can alter,
Love must conquer soon or late,
So why defy your fate?
Deep as the ocean,
Fierce as a fiery flame
Whose burning breath
Even death
Cannot tame
Is my devotion;
I'd sack a city
Without remorse or pity,
Rob monarchs of their treasure
To give you passing pleasure;
Did you implore
I would soar
To Heaven's bars
And silver stars
Pluck down—ah
For your crown—ah!

LOVE IS CALLING

(Josephine, Otto and Belletti)

Josephine: It's most confusing;
How shall *you* start choosing
When you both plead in this
eloquent way?
What can a poor girl say?

Belletti: Hear me speak!

Otto: My pleading hear!

Belletti: He's too weak.

Otto: It's surely clear.

Belletti:	Much too meek.
Otto:	He's insincere.
Belletti:	Let doubts and fear disappear.
Both:	Love is waiting for you, dear!
All:	Love's voice my/your choice
Belletti & Josephine:	Is urging
Otto:	Love in my heart is surging
All:	Love is calling. Love is calling
Otto:	Do not spurn me, do not spurn me.
All:	I/you am/are left no chance for 　　silence or evasions
Otto:	Nor unheeding, hear my pleading.
All:	Words are a waste of time, For love brooks no persuasion. Love is calling, is calling, So why delay When love points out the way?

SANTA CLAUS

(Carp)

'Twas Xmas night and Baby Flo
Said to Cousin Joe—
"Last night, it's true, I told you so,
Santa Claus came here, I know.
I lay awake all night," she said,
"Whilst he tiptoed around my bed."

"Santa Claus brought me a dolly
Whilst I was watching for him,

A rattle for dear sister Molly
And a horse for my wee brother Tim.
He brought a new go-cart for Polly
And some candies in a jar.
He gave all these toys to us girlies and boys—
Then he got into bed with Mama."

Josephine enters and they bicker as usual . . .

JOSEPHINE

(Back to Nature)

(Carp and Josephine)

Carp:	Someday, if I should steal you, Somewhere, dear, I'll conceal you, Far from the glare of the crowd—
Josephine:	Happy by sunny calm seas, Dreaming mid waving palm trees,
Carp:	Trespassers there not allowed.
Josephine:	In some far-off Tropical Isle, We could love—jungle-style;
Carp:	'Back to Nature' just for a while.
Josephine:	Love like Adam And his Madame.
Refrain Carp:	Josephine—Josephine Come with me—cross the sea, Josephine—Josephine.
Josephine:	You'll be King, I'll be Queen There we'll both defy convention.
Carp:	Do the things we mustn't mention; No one near to interfere;
Josephine:	For we will love Primitive.

Carp: Josephine—Josephine
There with you—we can do
Everything—anything;

Josephine: I don't know what you mean.

Carp: Josey, life will be so rosy,
Cosey in the jungle, Josey;

Both: Josephine
(Be my Josephine)
(I'm your Josephine)

Josephine: Sundays as well as Mondays
We'll need no heavy undies,
We'll dress in leaves, that is all.

Carp: Though fleas may
tantalize us,
No one will criticize us,
Two extra beads in the fall.

Josephine: We will climb the tropical
trees,

Carp: Just like the chimpanzees
Branch to branch go
leaping with ease.

Josephine: Dining well on
Nuts and melon.

Barnum arrives and Jenny tells him she wants to give up her career. Alice meets Rex and reminds him of the happy early days they had.

ONCE IN SEPTEMBER

(Alice and Rex)

Rex: Do you recall when we
were small,

Alice: I used to fancy I was quite
in love with you?

What fun we had, a girl and lad,
And sometimes you would make
believe you loved me, too,
All our toys we shared together.

Rex: Childish joys in sunny weather;

Alice: And today with twilight falling,
Comes a voice enthralling—calling,

Refrain
Both: Once in September,
Do you remember?
Love in a garden?
Our hearts were beating
In our glad refrain,
Can you forget, dear?

MAY MOON

The Messrs. Shubert
Present

The Nightingale

A MUSICAL ROMANCE BASED ON
THE LIFE OF JENNY LIND

BOOK & LYRICS BY
GUY BOLTON
AND
P.G. WODEHOUSE
MUSIC BY
ARMAND VECSEY

STAGED BY
LEWIS MORTON
DANCES STAGED BY
MAX SCHECK

THE ENTIRE PRODUCTION STAGED UNDER THE
PERSONAL DIRECTION OF MR. J. J. SHUBERT

HARMS
NEW YORK

How I regret, dear,
You and I will never meet in that
   garden again.

Alice: Those pirates bold in search of gold
Would often capture me and bind me
   to a tree.

Rex: Then unafraid my trusty blades
I draw in battle slaying twenty-two
   or three.

Alice: Bricks I'd take out and most sedately

Rex: You would make a mansion stately

Alice: All complete with turrets flashing

Rex: Then I came and sent it crashing,
   smashing.

General Gurnee arrives with Barnum and
tells Rex he disapproves of the marriage
to Jenny. Later Alice pleads her own case with
Jenny and persuades her to try to turn Rex away
from her for his own good.

NIGHTINGALE

(Jenny and Rex)

Rex: I shall hear your song
The whole day long
Within my heart,
Nightingale—my Nightingale
Trill each note to hear
That whispers clear.
"We'll never part,"
Nightingale—my Nightingale.

Jenny: Oh, say once more you love me,
Even though tomorrow
Maybe fate will bring us sorrow.

Rex: Dear, why are you sad and pale?
Our love ever shall prevail.

Jenny: All my heart tonight is full to
   breaking.

Rex: Will my vain   Jenny: Dearest,
   regret be   There is
   ever waking?   fear in
Dearest, if   my heart
   you love me,   What do
   though you   we care
   love me,   for fate
Till tonight!   For tonight.

JENNY LIND

(Jenny and Ensemble)

Jenny: I'll sing to them all with gladness,
For songbirds sing better thru
   gladness
For plaudits and fame and the
Wide world's acclaim
Our hearts flame.

Girls: Songbird, we adore you today,
Songbird, we implore you to stay,
Jenny Lind, Jenny Lind, Jenny Lind,
Jenny Lind!

Boys: Nightingale, we love you,
Nightingale, you seem to set our
   hearts on fire,
Nightingale, you know that we
   adore you—
Sing again, we beg you, sing again,
That is our fervent desire
Every man as but a soldier can
Would serve you heart and hand:
We are your loyal band
At your command.
Jenny Lind, Jenny Lind, Jenny Lind,
   Jenny Lind!

Once again, the songs came and went. A number that does not appear in the New York Library libretto was another duet for Jenny and Rex. From its content it would appear to fit in Act 1 as the lovers meet after Rex's homecoming. It was presumably felt to be too similar to "May Moon."

WHEN I MET YOU

(Rex and Jenny)

Rex:
All about me the world's
    pleasure making
While I wait with a heart sad
    and aching.
No comfort taking
In the dance and the revelry.
Gay and bright
Is the night
Laughter light
Echoes waking,
But no matter how gay it be,
It is empty for me.

Violet Carlson (*Josephine*) and Stanley Lupino (*Mr. Carp*) in *The Nightingale*.

Jenny:
Love, my senses enthralling
Brought me here to your calling.
Prudence struggled to aid me,
But my heart has betrayed me.
Love called clear in the distance
Broke my feeble resistance,
Night winds cool and caressing.

Rex:
My secret guessing
Whispers life was made for love.

Jenny:
And the moon seems to smile
    above
As it hears me confessing:

Refrain
Jenny:
Life began for me when I met you,
Life was all a golden mist;

Rex:
Ev'ry flow'r and tree when I met you
By sunshine from above was kissed.

Jenny:
Rough had been the road o'er which
    I'd passed,
But I had come to journey's end
    at last.

Both:
And I seem to waken
In a world all strange and new,
When I met you.

Jenny:
Life began for me when I met you
Underneath a summer sky.

Rex:
O'er a magic sea when I met you,
I floated and the world went by.

Jenny: Floated till my boat had crossed
                the bar
            And reached the Isle where no
                storms are.

Both: Life was like a gray day,
            When the sun came smiling through,
            When I met you.

The piece was not considered a success. The critics greeted it politely—perhaps in recognition of its frail state of health. Clearly, a musical based on a famous real life singer requires superb singing from the lead and, unfortunately, Eleanor Painter's voice was no longer up to the vocal demands of the part— "Miss Painter's voice has lost something of its once deep-piled velvet . . . and her single attempt at coloratura failed to enhance the illusion of Jenny Lind."

Next came the show that brought together in glorious practice all the theories Bolton & Wodehouse & Kern had ever articulated—except that Bolton was to have nothing to do with it and Wodehouse's connection, though visible, was at best accidental and peripheral. It was called *Show Boat.*

SHOW BOAT (1927)

Presented by Florenz Ziegfeld Jr. at the Ziegfeld Theatre, New York, on December 27, 1927 (575 performances).

BOOK Oscar Hammerstein II (based on the novel by Edna Ferber)
LYRICS Oscar Hammerstein II
MUSIC mostly by Jerome Kern

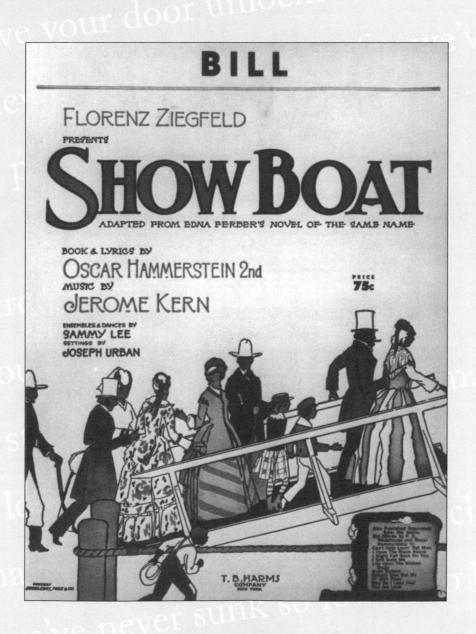

CAST

| Charles Winniger, Helen Morgan, | Edna May Oliver, |
| Norma Terris, Howard Marsh, | Jules Bledsoe |

Show Boat was the culmination of everything Bolton & Wodehouse & Kern had been striving for for the last decade by way of integration of song and story, and it was ironic that only one of the trio—Kern—was principally involved in it. The history of the American Musical Theatre, quite simply, is divided into two eras: "everything before *Show Boat* and everything after *Show Boat*," as one writer put it.

Despite Ziegfeld's efforts to "lighten" this story of bigotry, miscegenation, gambling and domestic violence, Hammerstein and Kern stuck to the dark side of Ferber's novel. Admittedly, later revivals and the two film versions softened that impact and exchanged its edge for greater romanticism. Only the Hal Prince revival of the late 1990s was truly faithful to the original intention.

It was in this unlikely setting that a Wodehouse "orphan" finally found a home. "Bill"—originally intended for *Oh, Lady! Lady!!* and subsequently also rejected for *Sally*—was sung by torch singer Helen Morgan, perched on top of a grand piano in the scene where Julie, whose mixed blood now makes her unacceptable to her old friends on the show boat *Cotton Blossom*, rehearses in a Chicago night club.

The lyric finally used in the show ran as follows . . .

BILL

Credited to P. G. Wodehouse and Oscar Hammerstein II. The italicized lyrics are Hammerstein's.

I used to dream that I would discover
The perfect lover
Some day.
I knew I'd recognize him if ever
He came 'round my way.
I always used to fancy then
He'd be one of the God-like kind of men;
With a giant brain and a noble head,
Like the heroes bold
In the books I read.

Refrain   *But along came Bill,*
Who's not my type at all,
You'd meet him on the street
And never notice him;
His form and face,
His manly grace
Are not the kind that you
Would find in a statue.
Oh, I can't explain,
It's surely not his brain
That makes me thrill.
I love him
Because he's wonderful,
Because he's just old Bill.

He can't play golf or tennis or polo,
Or sing a solo
Or row.
He isn't half as handsome
As dozens of men that I know.
He isn't tall and straight and slim,
And he dresses far worse than Ted or Jim.
And I can't explain why he should be just
The one, one man in the world for me.

eefdfffffewfesdewedwsdexeeeeeeeeeeexdsew

Refrain: He's just my Bill,
An ordinary guy,
He hasn't got a thing that
    I can brag about;
And yet to be
Upon his knee
So comfy and roomy
Seems natural to me.
Oh, I can't explain,
It's surely not his brain
That makes me thrill.
I love him
Because he's—I don't
    know,
Because he's just my Bill.

Helen Morgan (*Magnolia*) in *Show Boat*, who introduced "Bill."

While the two original verses had survived from the version dropped from *Oh, Lady! Lady!!* and subsequently auditioned for Ziegfeld, the two choruses had been slightly but subtly amended. At that stage Kern had no inkling that he would be working with Hammerstein.

Wodehouse himself was in no doubt that Hammerstein's amendments were relatively minor. In a letter to Guy Bolton (September 3, 1945) he is complaining:

> My God, if there is one thing that makes me froth, it is these fellows changing a couple of lines in a lyric and then calling themselves part-authors. Clifford Grey used to do it incessantly. If any changes had to be made in "Bill," Jerry should have asked me to make them, and only if I had been too busy to do it would Oscar have had any right to touch the lyric.

In a subsequent letter to his friend, Denis Mackall (January 14, 1946) he continues:

> That "Bill" thing is quite a drama. As you say, I wrote it in 1917 for *Oh, Lady! Lady!!* Right. But, as always happens when you get a real winner, it was cut out. I think it was considered too slow or something and I wrote a lousy waltz thing instead. All straight so far. Well, when *Show Boat* was in preparation, Jerry asked me if he could use "Bill," and I said yes, and he did. But Oscar Hammerstein went and changed about three

words in it and for twenty years has been getting half the publishing royalties. I didn't pay any attention to this, not being particularly interested in lyrics during those years . . . but a few days ago I heard from America that Oscar has now relinquished all rights to the thing and in addition has coughed up $5,000 for back payments.

In this he was being less than fair to Hammerstein by implying that the latter had given way grudgingly. Apart from the financial restitution, Hammerstein insisted on Wodehouse receiving full credit. When the show was successfully revived in that year, he declared—"I am particularly anxious to point out that the lyric for the song 'Bill' was written by P. G. Wodehouse. Although he has always been given credit in the program, it has frequently been assumed that since I wrote all the other lyrics for *Show Boat*, I also wrote this one, and I have had praise for it which belongs to another man."

All of which might seem to put the debate to rest. Except . . . except Wodehouse's recollections in tranquillity have been known to reflect the version of events he'd have *preferred* to have happened. The lyric he claims was sung on Ziegfeld's yacht in 1926 was the one he remembered in 1954 in *Bring On The Girls*—a book he himself admitted to being an "odd" one. ("I think we shall have to let truth go to the wall if it interferes with entertainment.") And in his biography of Wodehouse, Barry Phelps specifies countless examples of personal letters that were significantly doctored before they were finally published.

The italicized lines do not appear in any Wodehouse version that we have seen to date, and one conclusion, therefore, must be that these are Oscar Hammerstein's "about three words." On the other hand, musicologist Benny Green argued persuasively that "the deft rhyming of

'That you' with 'statue,' where the stress is on the first syllable, and then following the logic of the situation and rhyming only the first syllable, was something pioneered by Wodehouse and copied by all the great lyricists who followed him." Was it Wodehouse? Or was it Hammerstein being Wodehousean? The jury is likely to remain out.

And despite Hammerstein's generous attribution, there was to be a further sour note. One of the effects of Wodehouse's wartime "problem" was that the BBC refused for a while to allow his lyrics to be sung on their radio programs—with the result (as he wrote, far from gruntled, to Bolton in 1946) "they went and featured 'Bill' and attributed it to Oscar!" He was sure of a sympathetic audience, since he had long ago ceded half the song's royalties to his colleague, even though Bolton had not had a finger, let alone a hand, in it.

In late December 1927 Ziegfeld took Bolton aside and told him that he had signed the popular team of Marilyn Miller and Jack Donahue for the following season. Could Bolton and Wodehouse write a show for them in time?

Within ten days they not only had the complete libretto for something called *The Gibson Girl* but the enthusiastic agreement of the two stars. All they had to do now was sell it to Ziegfeld, who happened to be on vacation in Palm Beach.

With memories of their last abortive trip in 1918 Bolton and Wodehouse retraced their steps. Ziegfeld listened without any real show of interest and a few days later the reason became clear. The impresario had become enamoured with another idea dreamed up by his favorite book writer, Bill McGuire. It was a "topical" story, based on the recent U.S. visit of Queen Marie of Roumania and her daughter. In Maguire's version the princess is in love with a West Point cadet, who has flown the Atlantic with a pal (the Donahue role) and landed in—guess where?—Roumania.

The show was to be called *Rosalie* and it was not destined to be a particularly happy experience for Wodehouse. In fact, it was to plague him on both stage and screen.

Ziegfeld was no respecter of persons or professional relationships; he tossed talents together as if he were mixing a salad. Ignoring Bolton & Wodehouse's track record as librettists entirely, he teamed Bolton with Bill McGuire. He then proceeded to fire the original composer and lyricist and hire *two* composers for good measure—Sigmund Romberg and George Gershwin. Since even Ziegfeld couldn't separate the Gershwin brothers by this time, that gave him Ira, too. At that point—like Noah—he had *two* of everything . . . librettists, composers, lyricists.

Recalling the events in a letter to his friend Bill Townend (November 28, 1927), Wodehouse goes on to describe how Ziegfeld "asked me to do the lyrics with Ira. I wrote nine in a week and ever since then have been sweating away at the rest . . . and all is well—or will be until Flo wants all the lyrics re-written, as he is sure to do. We open the Bolton-McGuire-Ira Gershwin-Wodehouse-George Gershwin-Romberg show in Boston next week. It's called *Rosalie,* and I don't like it much, though it's bound to be a success with Marilyn and Jack Donahue in it."

Particularly interesting from the historical point of view are the Gershwin-Wodehouse-Gershwin numbers. It would be another thirty years—and the 1960 revival of *Oh, Kay!*—before Wodehouse words were again set to a Gershwin tune.

ROSALIE (1928)

Presented by Florenz Ziegfeld Jr. at the New Amsterdam Theatre, New York, on January 10, 1928 (335 performances).

BOOK

William Anthony McGuire and Guy Bolton

LYRICS

Ira Gershwin and
P. G. Wodehouse

MUSIC

George Gershwin and
Sigmund Romberg

CAST

Capt. Carl Rabisco:
HALFORD YOUNG

Michael O'Brien:
CLARENCE OLIVER

Mary O'Brien:
BOBBE ARNST

Prince Rabisco:
A. P. KAYE

HRH King Cyril:
FRANK MORGAN

HRH Queen:
MARGARET DALE

Sister Angelica:
KATHERINE BURKE

Bill Delroy:
JACK DONAHUE

Lieut. Richard Fay, USA:
OLIVER MCLENNAN

Princess Rosalie:
MARILYN MILLER

Marinna:
ANTONIA LALSEW

Steward:
CHARLES GOTTHOLD

Corps. Lieutenant:
JACK BRUNS

Superintendent of
West Point:
CHARLES GOTTHOLD

Capt. Banner:
CLAY CLEMENT

Ex-King of Portugal:
CHARLES DAVIS

Ex-King of Bulgaria:
CLARENCE DE SILVA

Ex-King of Prussia:
HENRI JACKIN

Ex-King of Greece:
MARK SHULL

Ex-King of Bavaria:
HARRY DONAGHY

Ex-King of Turkey:
EDGAR WELCH

SYNOPSIS

Taking advantage of America's fascination with Lindbergh's record-breaking solo flight to Paris, the story deals with the exploits of West Point pilot Lt. Dick Fay, whose love for Princess Rosalie of Romanza causes him to fly the Atlantic to be near her. She, of course, can't marry a commoner unless her father, King Cyril, abdicates—which, conveniently, he decides to do.

THE HUSSARS' MARCH

(Music by Sigmund Romberg)

Musical theatre historian and Gershwin expert Robert Kimball believes that the original sheet music attributing the whole lyric to Wodehouse is in error and that, while he wrote the verse, Ira Gershwin was responsible for the refrain. However, notice the marked similarities between this and "West Point Song" from *The Nightingale* of the previous year.

Rosalie: I lead a regiment bold,
Each man, (just) like those knights
of old,
Of whom the poets tell
In moonlight parties, or
When out on the dancing floor
They cast a magic spell.

Men: But, tho' they're fine at cotillions,
And quite outshine all civilians,

Rosalie: Don't you think these gentlemen
Are mere ornamental men
They're made for use as well
For . . .

Refrain
Rosalie: When they hear the war drum
sound.

Men: (We're a very lucky band
With a princess in command)

Men: Rataplan! Rataplan!

Men: (Ev'ry regimental man
Ev'ry member of your clan)

Rosalie: On guard, and at his post, is found

Men: Every man, every man.

Rosalie: Yes, clustered, keener than mustard,
You'll find them there,
Prepared to do and dare,
And tho' they know when fights
grow warm,

Men: Ratatat! . . . Ratatat.

Men: (It's a pleasure fighting for
A commander we adore)

Rosalie: One's apt to crease one's uniform:

Men: What of that? What of that?

Men: (Though the crease we
don't retain,)

Rosalie: If, fighting for all their ladies,
(for old Romanza)

Men: (Your Hussars will not complain)

Rosalie: Their boots chance to lose their shine
They don't repine, these soldiers fine
of mine.

WEST POINT SONG

(Dick and Boys)

(Music by Sigmund Romberg)

Dick: There's a sound you wot of,
You hear a lot of
In West Point barracks today
(each day);
When the morn is pearly
It wakes us early,
And jerks us out of the hay.
Oh, it's far from sweet and musical,
And it makes us grouse, and yet,
Till they drop the curtain,
There's one thing certain,
That sound we'll never forget.

Refrain: For you may journey here and yonder
To where the ends of nowhere start,
But, however far you wander,
It still will echo in your heart.
Yes, till the last gray shades are falling
And life's long, long hike is thru!
You'll hear the West Point bugle
   calling
Across the world to you.

Boys: When we want to sleep
It won't let us sleep
It wakes us up with its din.
It says "Show a leg,
Come on, show a leg
For work, work, work, work must
   begin."

Refrain

Dick: Tho' today its music
Makes me and you sick
Just wait till forty years on,
When you're old and tubby
And stout and chubby
And hair and waistline have gone.
As you doze, who knows, quite
   suddenly,
You will hear it sound and then,
All the long years shedding
You'll find you're treading
That dear old spot once again!

Refrain

OH, GEE! OH, JOY!

(Bill and Rosalie)

(Words by P. G. Wodehouse & Ira Gershwin)

(Music by George Gershwin)

Bill: Yea bo, but isn't love great!
Gee whiz!

Rosalie: Heigh-ho!
I'm willing to state it is!

Both: Don't know who the chap was
Who first began it,
But it's the only thing
On this planet.

Refrain: Oh, gee! Oh, joy!
The birds are singing:
Because why?
Because I am in love!
Oh, gee! Oh, joy!
The bells are ringing
Because why? Because I am in love.

Rosalie: And all the while I seem
In a dream,
I never was so happy!

Bill: Folks complain I'm insane,
Because I act so sappy.

Both: Oh, gee! Oh, joy!
The birds are singing:
Because why?
Because I am in love.

SAY SO!

(Rosalie and Dick)

(Words by P. G. Wodehouse and Ira Gershwin)

(Music by George Gershwin)

Dick: When your eyes look into mine
There's something they would say:
Is it "No" or "Yes"?

Rosalie: Surely you can guess?
Look again and quickly then,
Your doubts will fly away.

Dick: If their secret you'd tell,
Words are needed as well.

Refrain

Dick: Say so!
          Say you love me.
          None above me
          In your heart
          Pining, I'll be pining till you do.

Rosalie: Say so!
          Don't resist me,
          Say you've missed me
          From the start.
          Say so, for I pray so that it's true.

Both: There are just three little words I
              sigh for,
          Crazy about them;
          Three little words I'd die for;
          Can't live without them.

Rosalie: Say so!
          Change the gray sky
          To a gay sky,
          Ever blue.
          Say so!

Dick: I should say so!
          I love you.

WHY MUST WE ALWAYS
BE DREAMING?

(Music by Sigmund Romberg)

Rosalie: On a day not far away,
          But, oh! How distant it seems!
          I began to shape and plan
          A golden palace of dreams.
          Gallant and shining and splendid,
          It grew and grew and grew so
              beautiful;
          Soaring high, it touched the sky,
          All bright and new,
          And now in smoke it's ended,
          As castles of dreams always do!

Refrain: I built it of moonlight and madness.
          Each stone was a true lover's vow,
          And ruin and heart ache and
              sadness
          Are all that is left of it now.
          Oh! Why should love set us
              a-scheming
          If love is to melt like the dew?
          And why must we always be dreaming
          If dreaming can never come true?

THE KING CAN DO NO WRONG

(Music by Sigmund Romberg)

Gershwin scholar Robert Kimball believes
this is "probably" a collaboration between
Wodehouse and Gershwin, though "there is
some possibility that the lyric to the earlier version is by Wodehouse."

Though the cares of state are ever so
    troublesome,
Yet my spirits manage to bubble some,
For I make up when I take up
Women, wine and song.
Doesn't matter what I do, ev'rything is
    right;
There's a law says: Always, a king is right.
Let me stress it and impress it:
I am diff'rent from the throng—
For the king can do no wrong.

Refrain 1: If a maid I chance to dandle,
            She must not fly off the handle.
            Just remember that the king can do
                no wrong.
            Never criticize His Highness—
            Give him plus and never minus.
            If with you I go a-Maying,
            And by chance my arm is straying
            Please recall that splendid saying:
            That the king—that the king—that
                the king can do no wrong!

Refrain 2: He's at liberty to squeeze a
            Girl in his Hispano-Suiza—
            For remember that the king
            can do no wrong.
            Though a girl who with a
            boy rides
            Often walks home from her
            joyrides,
            When the kingly arms enfold
            her,
            She grows warmer—never
            colder.
            For her mother's often told
            her
            That the king—that the
            king—that the King can
            do no wrong!

Refrain 3: Although Mrs. Grundy
            eyes him,
            She may never criticize
            him—
            Please remember that the
            king can do no wrong.
            If a husband without
            warning,
            Comes home early in the
            morning.
            Wifey says, "Don't fret, because it
            Was the *king* inside that closet!"
            And the husband says, "Oh, *was* it?
            Well, the king—well, the king
            —well, the king can do no
            wrong!"

Encore
Refrain: Though his conduct may seem
            sprightly,
            You must not condemn him
            lightly—
            Just remember that the king can
            do no wrong.
            If you come upon him creeping
            Up the stairs when all are sleeping,

Marilyn Miller as *Rosalie*

Bear in mind that it is treason
To inquire what business *he's* on
(Though he's only B.V.D.'s on).
For the king—for the king—for the
king can do no wrong.

Verse 2
(Unused):   I'm a king who feels that it doesn't
            hurt a bit
            If I fool 'round and maybe flirt a bit
            So I call for—and I'm all for
            Women, wine and song.
            'Way back home I always have the
            gang around,
            So I'm asking you girls to hang
            around.

Please come closer—Don't say
  "No, Sir!"
Don't be shy—but come along—
For the king can do no wrong.

Earlier Version (Unused)

Verse 1: There's just one thing about a king
      that makes his job worth trying
    And separates him from the common
      throng
    And that's the ancient legend,
      which has shown no signs of
      dying
    That the king can do no wrong.
    Oh, it helps him get along.

    For though persons staid and steady
    There may be around him *who* wish
    That he wasn't quite so ready
    With a story that is blueish.
    Though he may shock Mrs. Grundy
    With behavior of a pattern
    Which is criticized each Sunday
    By the Reverend Doctor Stratton—

Refrain 1: Still, the king can do no wrong!
    No, the king can do no wrong!
    And he finds the fact consoling
    When he starts the ball a-rolling
    With women, wine, and song—
    For if husbands without warning,
    Come home early in the morning,
    He need never worry long;
    Wives say, "Do not fret, because it
    Was the *king* inside that closet!"
    And the husband says, "Oh, *was* it?"
    For the king can do no wrong.

Verse 2: A king's existence nowadays, there's
      no denying, is hard
    It's not so pleasant as it used to be.
    He never knows when somebody
      won't bump him in the gizzard

With a charge of T.N.T.
It's a wearing life, you see.
For although it's no use whining,
Still, he does feel rather shaken
When he finds a bomb reclining
In his morning eggs and bacon;
And remorse and agitation
Like a dagger seem to strike him
When he gets the information
That Bill Thompson doesn't like him.

Refrain 2: Still, the king can do no wrong!
    No, the king can do no wrong!
    He's at liberty to squeeze a
    Girl in his Hispano-Suiza—
    And squeeze her good and strong.
    Though a girl who with a boy rides
    Often walks home from her joyrides
    On a road that's rough and long;
    When a monarch's arms enfold her
    She just nestles on his shoulder,
    For she knows that Mother told her
    That the king can do no wrong.

But Wodehouse was not done with *Rosalie*—or, rather, the lady was not done with him. 1930 found the Wodehouses in Hollywood on what turned into a two-year, $2,000-a-week contract for MGM. One of the projects he was given was the task of turning *Rosalie* into a starring vehicle for his old friend Marion Davies. ("It was a pleasant little thing, and I put some three months into it. When it was finished, they thanked me politely and remarked that, as musicals didn't seem to be going so well, they guessed they would not use it.")

At one surrealistic point Wodehouse was summoned by Irving Thalberg, "the big boss (and a most charming fellow incidentally, about the nicest chap I've run into out here"), who proceeded to dictate a complete scenario of his own. He then suggested that Wodehouse should go away and "write it not in picture form but as a novelette, after which, I suppose it will be turned into a picture. The prospect of this appalls me, and I am hoping that the whole thing will eventually blow over, as things do out here."

The novelized version was written and the story line was substantially, but not wholly, changed.

When Wodehouse returned to Hollywood for a second stint in 1936, the first assignment he was given was to work on a musical version of *Rosalie*. His efforts were overshadowed by those of the chief scriptwriter, Bill McGuire, joint author with Guy Bolton of the original book of the musical,

and McGuire eventually took over the project in its entirety. Some of the footage of the unreleased Marion Davies film turned up in this 1937 version which starred Nelson Eddy and Eleanor Powell. The whole of the original score was excised and replaced with one by—Cole Porter.

When Ziegfeld signed Wodehouse to write the lyrics of *The Three Musketeers* (book by the ubiquitous Bill McGuire), he was throwing him a bone to make up for losing out on *Rosalie*. It turned out to be a fairly meaty bone, since the Broadway production ran for 318 performances and the subsequent London one for 242.

THE THREE MUSKETEERS (1928)

Presented by Florenz Ziegfeld Jr. at the Lyric Theatre, New York, on March 13, 1928 (318 performances).

BOOK
William Anthony McGuire
(based on the novel by
Alexander Dumas)

LYRICS
P. G. Wodehouse and
Clifford Grey

MUSIC
Rudolf Friml

Dennis King as D'Artagnan in *The Three Musketeers*.

CAST

Sergeant Jussac:
ROBERT D. BURNS

Comte De La Rochefort:
LOUIS HECTOR

Innkeeper:
HARRISON BROCKBANK

Zoe: NAOMI JOHNSON

Lady De Winter:
VIVIENNE OSBORNE

Porthos:
DETMAR POPPEN

Athos:
DOUGLASS R. DUMBRILLE

Aramis:
JOSEPH MACAULAY

Constance Bonacieux:
VIVIENNE SEGAL

Planchet: LESTER ALLEN

D'Artagnan: DENNIS KING

Anne, Queen of France:
YVONNE D'ARLE

M. De Treville:
JOHN M. KLINE

The Duke of Buckingham:
JOHN CLARKE

Cardinal Richelieu:
REGINALD OWEN

Louis XIII:
CLARENCE DERWENT

Brother Joseph:
WILLIAM KERSHAW

Premier Danseuse
of the Court:
HARRIET HOCTOR

Auberiste:
AUDREY DAVIS

The Bo'sun:
JOHN MUCCIO

Patrick, valet to
Buckingham:
NORMAN IVES

Cardinal's Guards:
CHARLES SUTTON &
GERALD ROGERS

The King's Attendant:
GERALD MOORE

Presented by Felix Edwardes at the Theatre Royal, Drury Lane on March 28, 1930 (242 performances).

DIRECTOR Alfred Butt

CAST

Sergeant Jussac:
JOHN ROBERTS

Comte De La Rochefort:
LOUIS HECTOR

Innkeeper:
GORDON CROCKER

Zoe: MOYA NUGENT

Lady De Winter:
MARIE NEY

Porthos:
ROBERT WOOLLARD

Athos: JACK LIVESEY

Aramis:
RAYMOND NEWELL

Constance Bonacieux:
ADRIENNE BRUNE

Planchet:
JERRY VERNO

D'Artagnan:
DENNIS KING

Anne, Queen of France:
LILIAN DAVIES

M. De Treville:
STEPHEN T. EWART

The Duke of Buckingham:
WEBSTER BOOTH

Cardinal Richelieu:
ARTHUR WONTNER

Louis XIII:
GEORGE BISHOP

Brother Joseph:
ERIC J. HODGES

Premier Danseuse
of the Court:
ULA SHARON

Auberiste:
ALINE AVERY

The Bo'sun:
ERNEST LUDLOW

Patrick, valet to
Buckingham:
WALTER WEBSTER

Cardinal's Guards:
WALTER CUTLER and
JOHN DELANEY

The King's Attendant:
A. J. WILLARD

SYNOPSIS

D'Artagnan comes to Paris, where he soon joins the daredevil band of Athos, Porthos and Aramis. He falls in love with Constance Bonacieux. When the Duke of Buckingham steals the French queen's jewels, the Musketeers take off for England to recover them before their loss is discovered and the queen embarrassed.

MARCH OF THE MUSKETEERS

(D'Artagnan, Athos, Porthos, Aramis and Chorus)

(Words by P. G. Wodehouse and Clifford Grey)

D'Artagnan: In days of yore,
A score of heroes there have been
With quite a claim to name and fame.

All: Men of skill and might,
Handy in a fight!

Aramis: And long in song
With fervent admiration,
Poets have extolled their doings bold.

All: Very bold,
So we're told,
Were those men of old.

Athos: And yet (still), one and all,
They seem small,
Do these men of whom one hears.

All: True for you, true for you, true for you!
(True for you! Very true! So they do!)

D'Artagnan: Placed beside the King's own Musketeers.

Refrain
D'Artagnan, Athos, Porthos & Aramis: We are the Musketeers,
Bold, dashing Musketeers;
Stout comrade Musketeers,

All: Bound to ride side by side, true and tried.

D'Artagnan, etc.: We've found for years and years
No foe can hide his fears,
When faced by Musketeers:
He wisely disappears.

All: War and daring
We are ever sharing,
Strangers to dangers indeed.

To laugh and love and serve the king,
And live for his renown,
To kiss a maid or sack a town
Or ride a foe-man down.
As One for All and All for One,
We stand or fall (face) united,
We are the Musketeers,
Bold, dashing Musketeers,
Stout, comrade Musketeers,
Come what may, stand or fall
All for One!
And One for All.

YOUR EYES

(D'Artagnan and Constance)

Constance: Though the road that you must
    tread
Is full of dread and dark and
    drear,
A light will be shining to guide
    you, guide you, guide you
Going for ever beside you,
Casting out your fear.

Refrain
Constance &
D'Artagnan: Your eyes, your eyes like beacons
    will light me
By night and day.
Your eyes, your eyes to glory
    invite me
To carve my way;
As they gleam I'll dream
    you're there,
What e'er may betide,
Fortune dark or fortune
    fair,
To share at my side, dear.
No storms that rise shall
    ever affright me,
Though far I roam,
And at last, dangers past
Your dear eyes will lead
    me home.

From 1928 the musical theatre took a back seat as far as Wodehouse was concerned. Perhaps the relatively minor role he had been asked to play in *Rosalie* and *The Three Musketeers* had something to do with it and certainly the two year Hollywood "sabbatical" proved distracting. But the main reason was undoubtedly that in the late 1920s and early 1930s he was in the middle of his fictional *age d'or*.

Between mid-1928 and mid-1934 he published *Money For Nothing; Mr. Mulliner Speaking; Summer Lightning; Very Good, Jeeves; Big Money; If I Were You; Dr. Sally; Hot Water; Louder and Funnier; Mulliner Nights; Heavy Weather;* and *Thank You, Jeeves* (the first novel in which Jeeves and Bertie Wooster appeared together).

Furthermore, he was developing his involvement with the non-musical theatre. Starting with *The Play's The Thing* (1926), he was author or joint author of *Her Cardboard Lover* (1927); *Good Morning, Bill* (1927); *A Damsel in Distress* (1928); *Baa Baa Black Sheep* (1929); *Candlelight* (1929); *Leave It To Psmith* (1930); *Who's Who* (1934); and *The Inside Stand* (1935), all of which had New York and/or London productions.

Program
LYRIC THEATRE
DENNIS KING

It was at this point that Bolton arrived bearing an offer from producer Vinton Freedley (1891–1969) to write a show with a shipboard setting with a score to be composed by Cole Porter. ("That means I'm out," was Wodehouse's first reaction, "What pests these lyric-writing composers are! Taking the bread out of a man's mouth.")

The show began life as *Crazy Week*, which became *Hard To Get* and ended up as *Anything Goes*. As *Hard To Get* the piece was largely a Hollywood satire—a concept Freedley firmly rejected. Both it and its successor script then involved a shipwreck. While the subject itself was not taboo, the sinking of the *S.S. Morro Castle* with the loss of over a hundred lives caused immediate sensitivity.

Broadway legend insists that this was the reason Bolton & Wodehouse were removed from the project but theatre historian Lee Davis argues that the real reason was that—with rehearsals imminent—Bolton was stricken with appendicitis and an already over-committed Wodehouse prevented by tax problems from entering the U.S.

Freedley turned to his director, Howard Lindsay (1889–1968), who in turn enlisted as collaborator his friend Russell Crouse (1893–1966). The new team "fixed" the book around a score that had already been partly written and the show—still crediting Bolton & Wodehouse as the principal authors—opened at the Alvin to great acclaim, running for 421 performances and a further 250 for the London production. The fact that they continued to receive their original fee went some way—but only some of the way—toward softening the blow. ("Just got the *Anything Goes* script from America," Wodehouse would write. "There are two lines of mine left in it, and so far I am receiving £50 a week apiece for them. That's about £3.10s. a word, which is pretty good payment, though less, of course, than my stuff is worth.") But the fact remained that it was not *their* show the town was talking about. It was also to be their last (produced) collaboration in the musical theatre, although such "straight" productions as *Don't Listen, Ladies* (1948) were still to come.

ANYTHING GOES (1934)

Presented by Vinton Freedley at the Alvin Theatre, New York, on November 21, 1934 (421 performances).

BOOK   Guy Bolton and P. G. Wodehouse
                       Revised by Howard Lindsay and Russell Crouse
LYRICS and MUSIC Cole Porter
DIRECTOR   Howard Lindsay

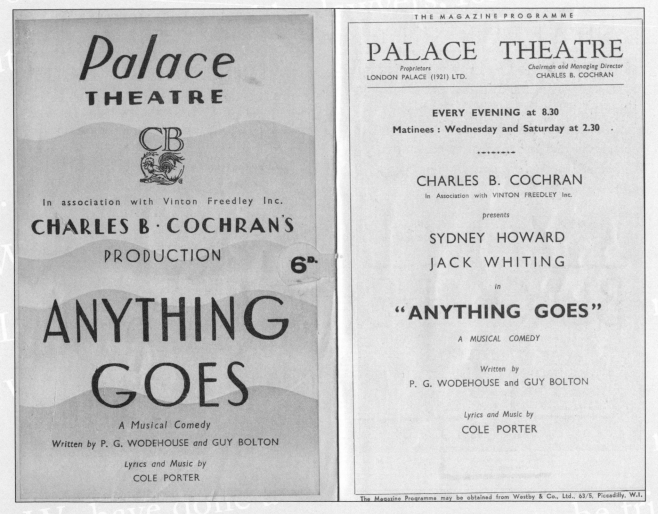

Cast of the London production of *Anything Goes* (1935).

CAST

William Gaxton,	Victor Moore,
Ethel Merman,	Bettina Hall

UK production presented at the Palace Theatre, London, on June 14, 1935 (261 performances).

CAST

Jeanne Aubert,	Peter Haddon, Jack Whiting,
Sydney Howard,	Adele Dixon

There was to be one more bite of this particular cherry—at least, as far as Wodehouse was concerned. As with *Oh, Kay!* he became more involved with the revival than the original.

When the show was subsequently produced in London, Wodehouse was the author responsible for eliminating the particularly American references in the book and lyrics and generally making the revisions necessary for an English audience. The revisions (*italicized on the following pages*) were done "with Porter's enthusiastic approval."

ANYTHING GOES

Cole Porter:
Verse:
Times have changed
And we've often rewound the
clock
Since the Puritans got a shock
When they landed on Plymouth
Rock.
If today
Any shock they should try to stem
'Stead of landing on Plymouth
Rock
Plymouth Rock would land
on them.

1st Refrain:
In olden days, a glimpse of
stocking
Was looked on as something
shocking
But now, Lord knows,
Anything goes.

Good authors, too
Who once knew better words
Now only use four letter words
Writing prose
Anything goes.
If driving fast cars you like
If low bars you like
If bare limbs you like
If old hymns you like
If Mae West you like
Or me, undressed you like
Why nobody will oppose
When every night, the set that's
    smart is in—
Dulging in nudist parties in
Studios,
Anything goes.

2nd Refrain
P. G.
Wodehouse:

When maiden Aunts can freely
    chuckle
At tales much too near the knuckle
The facts disclose
Anything goes.
When in the House our Legislators
Are calling each other, "Traitors"
And "So and So's"
Anything goes.
The world's in a state today
Like Billingsgate today
We are each today
For free speech today
Nothing's blue today
Or taboo today
Or meets with scandalized "Oh's"
But while we hope for days more
    sunny,
The Government gets our money
'Cause Neville knows
Anything goes.

3rd Refrain:

When Grandmamma, whose age
    is eighty

In night clubs is getting matey
With gigolos
Anything goes
When mothers pack and leave
    poor father
Because they decide they'd rather
Be tennis pros
Anything goes.

Cole Porter:

The word has gone mad today
And good's bad today
And black's white today
And day's night today.

P. G.
Wodehouse:

In Colney Hatch today
We ought to snatch today
A little rest and repose
When ladies fair who seek affection
Prefer gents of dark complexion
As Romeos
Anything goes.

4th Refrain:

The dogs chase fleas
The bees chase honey
And we all are chasing money
And when it shows
Anything goes.
The Duke who owns a moated
    castle
Takes lodgers and makes a parcel
Because he knows
Anything goes
It's grab and smash today
We want cash today
Get rich quick today
That's the trick today
And the Great today
Don't hesitate today
But keep right on their toes
And lend their names, if paid to
    do it
To anyone's soap or suet
Or baby clo's
Anything goes

Cast of the London production of *Anything Goes.*

YOU'RE THE TOP

Verse 1

He: At words poetic
          I'm so pathetic

          That I always have found it best
          Instead of getting them off my chest
          To let 'em rest
          Unexpressed.
          I hate parading my serenading
          As I'll probably miss a bar,
          But if this ditty
          Is not so pretty
          At least it'll tell you
          How great you are.

Refrain 1

He: You're the top

          You're the Colosseum
          You're the top
          You're the Louvre Museum
          You're a melody from a symphony
              by Strauss,
          You're an Ascot bonnet,
          A Shakespeare sonnet,
          You're Mickey Mouse.
          You're the Nile
          You're the Tower of Pisa
          You're the smile
          On the Mona Lisa.

I'm a worthless cheque—a total
   wreck—a flop.
But if, Baby—I'm the bottom
You're the top!

Verse 2

She: Your words poetic
       Are not pathetic

       On the other hand, boy—you shine
       And I can feel after every line
       A thrill divine
       Down my spine.

       Some gifted fellow—like young Novello
       Might think that your song is bad
       But for a person—who's just
          rehearsin'
       Well, I gotta say this, my lad.

Refrain 2

She: You're the top
       You're Mahatma Gandhi
       You're the top
       You're Napoleon brandy
       You're the purple light—of a summer
          night in Spain.
       You're the National Gallery
       You're Garbo's salary
       You're cellophane.

       You're the grace of the Brontosaurus
       You're the pace of a Cochran chorus

       I'm a toy balloon—that's fated soon—
          to pop
       But if, Baby—I'm the bottom
       You're the top!

Refrain 3

He: *You're the top*

You're a Russian Salad
You're the top
You're a Gershwin ballad

She: *You're the boy I'd swipe for the perfect*
       type of male.

He: *You're an old Dutch Master*
       You're Lady Astor
       You're Chippendale

She: *You're supreme*
       You're the Gates of Heaven

He: *You're the Cream from the shire of*
       Devon

       I'm just in the way, as the French
          would say
       'De trop.'

Both: But if, Baby, I'm the bottom
       You're the top!

Refrain 4

He: *You're the top!*

       You're a dress by Patou

She: *You're the top!*
       You're an Epstein statue

       You're the nimble tread—of the feet
          of Fred Astaire.

       You're Mussolini

He: *You're Mrs. Sweeney*

       You're Camembert

She: *You're the run*

Of a film by Arliss

He: *You're the sun*
        On the Crystal Parliss

        I'm a lazy lout that's just about to stop.

Both: But if, Baby—I'm the bottom
        You're the top!

Refrain 5

She: You're the top
        You're a Ritz hot toddy

        You're the top!
        You're a Rolls-Royce body

He: You're the boats that glide—by the
            sleepy Zuider Zee.

She: *You're a bed of roses*

PGW: *You're Holy Moses*
        You're Jubilee
        You're a prize—
        You're the Hula-Hula

He: *You're the eyes of the fair Tallulah*

        I'm a broken doll—a fol-de-rol—
            a blop.

Both: But if, Baby—I'm the bottom
        You're the top!

Refrain 6

She: *You're the top!*

        You're a new invention
        You're the top!
        You're the fourth dimension

He: *You're the green and gold—and the*
            mauve
        Of the old school tie.
        You're the Brothers Western
        You're Harry Preston
        You're Custard Pie.

She: *You're an ode*
        By a leading songster

He: *You're a road*
        Where there's not a gongster

She: I'm a frog—without a log—on which
            to hop.

Both: But, if, Baby—I'm the bottom
        You're the top!

Refrain 7

She: You're the THOIST
        You're a Tangee lipstick,

He: You're da FOIST
        In da Irish SWIPSTICK

She: By the River Rhine
        You're a sturdy stein of beer.

He: *You're the Firth of Forth*

        You're the Cock of the North
        You're Stratosphere

        You're a rose
        You're Inferno's Dante

She: You're the nose
        On the great Durante

He: *I'm a son of a gun—an underdone—*
            chump chop.

Both: But, if, Baby—I'm the bottom

         You're the top!

Note: While many of the lines are completely Wodehouse, several others involve small word changes to sharpen the references—for instance, "Mrs. Astor" became "Lady Astor"— a convenient happenstance!—"a Waldorf salad" becomes a "Russian salad"; "a Berlin ballad" "a Gershwin ballad"; " a dress from Saks" a "dress by Patou"; and "gifted humans like Vincent Youmans" becomes "some gifted fellow like young Novello." Notice, too, the way Wodehouse tips his lyrical hat to Porter by using *Jubilee*, the name of Porter's 1935 show.

In the light of Cole Porter's initial generosity, it is disappointing to find Wodehouse himself behaving somewhat ungenerously when he found himself engaged in further revision for the 1962 revival.

On October 28th, 1961, he is writing to Bolton—"Here is the revised 'You're the Top' lyric. It was a pretty difficult job, as the lines were short and one was confined to nouns and no chance of using adjectives, plus all those double rhymes . . . I'm not satisfied with some of the couplets like Cole's 'Arrow collar', 'dollar', which seem flat to me and the poor devil got exhausted after doing five refrains. Fancy letting a line like 'You're the baby grand of a lady and gent' get by. Not to mention 'Inferno's Dante.' What the hell does *that* mean?"

If the complexity of the verse form had bothered him twenty-five years earlier, he had failed to mention it. The taste of slightly sour grapes carries over into his appraisal of the show itself— "I have always disliked *Anything Goes* . . . because the wrongness of the balance offends my artistic sensibilities . . . the score is so thin. Apart from the three hit songs, we have almost nothing. . . . In your letter you ask me to send you a 'list' of Cole Porter songs but I don't know any except

the well known ones. I think what we ought to do is go entirely for the melody. If you find one with a good tune, I can write an entirely different lyric and one that will fit the situation . . ."—and later—"I feel I would like to rewrite every lyric in the show—at any rate to cut out some of the lines and substitute others."

He then goes on to report progress on "Anything Goes":

When the courts decide, as they did latterly,
We could read *Lady Chatterley*
If we chose
Anything goes.

"Darned sight better than anything old King Cole ever wrote."

We now come to an area of considerable grey. In 1947 Wodehouse wrote that he had revised the lyrics for a new version of the popular 1909 operetta *The Chocolate Soldier*. Originally produced in Vienna in 1908 as *Der Tapfere Soldat* and loosely based on Shaw's anti-war satire *Arms and the Man*, the piece had a book and lyrics by Stanislaus Stange and music by Oscar Straus. It ran for 296 performances at New York's Lyric Theatre and for 500 in its London production, before becoming a staple item in the repertory of amateur companies.

Stange diluted Shaw's pacifist sentiments and turned it into a story of the peace loving Lt. Bumerli, who would rather eat chocolate than fight, and his love for Nadine, the daughter of the comic Colonel Popoff and ex-fiancée of Major Alexis Spiridoff, who sees Bumerli as his deadly rival.

In 1947 Guy Bolton rewrote the book and the new production was put on at the Century Theatre in New York on March 12th. Hans Bartsch produced a cast that included Frances McCann (Nadine), Keith Andes (Bumerli) and comedian Billy Gilbert (Popoff). The choreography was by George Balanchine. Despite good reviews, it ran for only 70 performances. In December 1948 there was a production at the Manchester Opera House, but there is no evidence that it ever came to the West End.

In the area of grey lies Wodehouse's contribution. Although he claims to have rewritten the lyrics—and the lyrics *are* substantially rewritten—he receives no credit in the libretto.

I am venturing to include the revisions for two reasons—first, that Bolton revised the book at a time when he and Wodehouse were constantly debating another joint venture, and second, because he did so at a time when Wodehouse's reputation was emerging from the cloud of wartime. The producer may well have considered it politically unwise, if not precisely incorrect, to advertise his presence. To be fair, that is pure speculation. So—*caveat lector . . .*

THE CHOCOLATE SOLDIER (1947)

Presented by Hans Bartsch at the Century Theatre in New York on March 12, 1947 (70 performances).

BOOK　　　　　Guy Bolton
CHOREOGRAPHY　George Balanchine

CAST	
Nadine: FRANCES MCCANN	Popoff:
Bumerli: KEITH ANDES	BILLY GILBERT

WE ARE MARCHING
THROUGH THE NIGHT

(Nadine, Aurelia, Mascha and Soldiers)

Soldiers: We are marching through the night,
             Marching left—marching right.
             We are tramping out the story
             Of another page of glory,
             Yet we need a girl to kiss.
             Oh, it's this that we miss.
             At the call to arms—we fight!
             For the right! Day or night!
             But the stars above remind us
             Of the girls we left behind us.
             Oh, we wonder where and when
             We shall see them again.

Nadine,
Aurelia &
Mascha: Doing your duty, longing for beauty—
             Poor soldier boy!
             No hand that presses, no soft caresses,
             No moments of joy.
             But we remind you girls left behind
                 you
             Find war is lonely, too.
             Oh, how we're waiting it through,
                 for you.

WE ARE ROUNDING UP THE FOE

(Life Is Lonely If You Haven't Got a Man)

(Nadine, Aurelia, Mascha and Soldiers)

Soldiers: We are rounding up the foe
             As we go—high and low.
             Like a rat he may be hiding
             But his fate is past deciding,
             When we find him he shall die.
             He shall die.

Nadine: They have gone!

Mascha: And we wait on!

Aurelia: Now we are sad.

Nadine: Sad.

All: As can be
             Life is so lonely,
             Oh, so lonely,
             If you haven't got a man.
             You can try it but deny it if you can.

Nadine: Oh, how sad a woman's plight is!

Mascha: What a waste of naughty nighties

Aurelia: Ev'ry day it's getting tougher
             And the birthrate's bound to suffer.

Mascha: For a kiss I'm almost frantic!

Aurelia: I feel even more romantic!

Nadine: From whatever way you're viewing,
             It appears there's nothing doing.

Nadine &
Mascha: What a life!

Nadine: Why don't you close the shutters?
             Lock them up and bar them tight!

Aurelia: My heart with terror flutters

Nadine: Lock up and say "Goodnight."

Aurelia: Lock up and say "Goodnight."

Nadine: He is not here!

Mascha: He is not here!

Aurelia: He is not here!

Nadine: Gone!

Mascha: Gone!

Aurelia: Gone!

All Three: Yes, gone.

Reprise
Nadine: Life is so lonely, oh, so lonely,
          If you haven't got a man.

Mascha: Like a dance without a partner,
          Like a flirt without a fan.

Aurelia: Like a summer without roses,
          Like a world without a plan.

All: Life is lonely if you haven't got a man.

SYMPATHY

Nadine and Bumerli

Bumerli: A woman should be sympathetic,
           A woman should be soft and
               sweet.
           But you are hard and energetic;
           You'd turn me out upon the street.
           You'd bid me go where shots are
               flying
           And you bid me leave, instead
               of love.
           If I am shot, it's no good crying
           When next we meet 'twill be
               above!

Nadine: Up in the sky,
          You fly too high, sir!
          You'll go below . . . so now,
              good-bye, sir
          Oh, noble soldier, go away . . .
              away . . . don't stay.

Bumerli: Oh, life is sweet when you're
               in love,

There's music in the sky above.
On nights like this I treasure
My life beyond all measure.
Each moment I'm with you, dear
And all I need on earth is here
And though we part I know
    that we
Are heart to heart in sympathy.

Nadine: It cannot be . . . I am not free
          It is my duty to bid you go . . .
          Go now! Away! Oh, sire, I beg
              you.

Bumerli: Farewell! . . . Farewell!
           I'm on my way.
           A bullet waits me there
           But don't pretend that you care.
           Outside they wait,
           The hounds of fate . . .

Nadine: Farewell! Farewell! Away. Away.
          Farewell! Farewell! . . . Away.

Bumerli: Farewell! Farewell! It's as you say
           Farewell! Farewell! . . . Away.

Nadine: No, stop!

Bumerli: What for?

Nadine: For me!

Bumerli: For you?

Nadine: For me!

Bumerli: My thanks, dear lady kind.

Nadine: Oh no, please no!

Bumerli: I am sure you had a noble mind,
           A gracious noble mind,
           It is a burden sweet to carry,
           The burden of a woman's heart.

Nadine: Remember, I'm engaged to
               marry—
            I saved your life, but we must
               part.

Bumerli: My life is sweet, I hold it dear,
            All death is gruesome, dark and
               drear.
            I love beyond all measure;
            My life, therefore, I treasure.
            I love to live, and live to love,
            So do not care to go above.
            Though we must part and you
               leave me,
            For you I feel some sympathy.

SEEK THE SPY

(Massakroff and Soldiers,
Nadine, Aurelia, Mascha)

Massakroff &
Soldiers: We are searching, searching for
               the spy.
            When we find him he shall
               surely die.
            The spy is here, is hidden;
            By law that is forbidden
            Seek him, seek everywhere,
            Track the rascal to his lair.

            Oh, Barbarians,
            Yes, Barbarians
            Are the fighting fierce Bulgarians.
            We have proved in blood and
               battle
            That it's not mere tittle tattle.
            Don't annoy a big bad Bulgar
            Or he may do something vulgar.

            With a lunge we'll sometimes
               stab you!
            By the throat we'll sometimes
               grab you!

            By the hair we'll sometimes
               grip you,
            With a foot we'll sometimes
               trip you,
            When at last we swing our sabres,
            It's the end of all your labours!

Massakroff: Make no trouble for us here,
               my beauty.
            Massakroff does his duty.
            If we find him here, he'll die.
            I'll massacre the spy, ha!

Nadine: For whom do you search here?

Massakroff: For a man we search—that is
               clear!

Nadine: So?

Massakroff: A foe!

Nadine: He is not here . . .
            Go search below.
            I am your greatest hero's bride,
            So now perhaps you'll be satisfied.
            Had any spy sought refuge here,
            It would have cost him very dear.

Massakroff: He's somewhere, though!

Nadine: I tell you "No" and what I say
               is so!
            I am your greatest hero's bride,
            My honour must not be defied.

Massakroff: I cannot go, Miss,
            Until I know, Miss,
            He is not here.
            If we find him he shall die—
            I'll massacre the spy, ha!

Soldiers: Ha!

Oh, Barbarians,
Yes, Barbarians
Are the fighting fierce Bulgarians.
If the spy is here we'll spot him
And he'll never know what got
      him!

Aurelia: Who was that,
            In heaven's name?
            I heard a voice.
            Who could it be?

Mascha: A revolver.

Aurelia: A revolver?

Massakroff: Look at it!

Aurelia: A Serb revolver.

Massakroff: If he's caught, this will involve
            her!

Aurelia &
Massakroff: A revolver . . . His revolver.

Massakroff: Where's the spy?
            Has he been found?
            I'm sure he's somewhere here
               around.
            One, two, three, four

Soldiers: He's not hidden on this floor.

Massakroff: Five, six, seven, eight.

Soldiers: He's not here, we came too late.

Massakroff: Nine, ten, eleven, twelve

Soldiers: No one here

Nadine: (to portières)
            You're safe, my dear.

Massakroff: Ha! The bed! He's under that!

Aurelia: Don't look there, you are much
               too fat.

Nadia: The balcony you have neglected.
            It should be at once inspected.

Massakroff: He shall die when detected!
            Ha! Ha! Ha!

Mascha &
Aurelia: There's something very fishy, dear,
            Or how come that revolver's here?
            Nadine has concealed the spy
            But they'll not find him . . . she's
               too spry!

Nadine: (*To Bumerli behind portières*)
            Be careful, I will fool them yet!

Bumerli: I kiss your hand, my little pet!

Mascha &
Aurelia: If Massakroff should see that gun,
            The spy would find his game is
               done,
            And that would rather spoil
               our fun.

Massakroff: (*Re-enters*)
            He must have vanished into
               thin air.

Nadine: A pity you're not a ballooner.
            You'd massacre him sooner.
            Ha!

Massakroff: Pray pardon this intrusion,
            It's not been very nice.
            I'm covered with confusion—
            I'll kill that dam' spy . . . twice.

            Fall in! Are you all in?

Soldiers:	Yes!
Massakroff:	Forward!
Soldiers:	Oh, Barbarians, Yes, Barbarians Are the fighting fierce Bulgarians. We have proved in blood and battle That it's not mere tittle tattle. Don't annoy a big bad Bulgar Or he may do something vulgar.
Mascha & Aurelia:	There's something very fishy, dear, Or how come that revolver's here? Nadine has concealed the spy.
Aurelia:	But they'll not find him, he's too sly.

Mascha &
Aurelia:
	The spy brought that revolver
	    here,
	The spy brought that revolver
	    here,
	That revolver, that revolver here.

THE FATHERLAND IS FREE

(Mascha and Chorus)

Mascha & Chorus:	Give a loud Hurrah And a proud Hurrah. What a blessing peace will be, For the battle's won. The war is done And the Fatherland is free. Give a long hurrah And a strong hurrah That our boys will fight no more. And raise a shout,

Let bells ring out,
For we have won the war.
Hurrah! Hurrah!
Come on and cheer. Hurrah!
Hurrah!
For peace is here.

FINALE

Chorus:	Everybody's coming in, Tell us when the drinks begin! Hear those wedding bells so gay— Our Nadine weds today. Hurray! Hurray!
Aurelia:	My mother's heart goes bump! Goes thump—goes jump!

Popoff:	My father's heart with joy
	    expands.
	The girl will soon be off our
	    hands.

Aurelia &
Popoff:
	(Mother's) (My father's) heart
	    goes jump!
	Goes thump! Goes jump!
	(Father's) (My mother's) heart is
	    full of thrills—
	Now someone else can pay the
	    bills.

Chorus:	Everybody's coming in, Tell us when the drinks begin. Hear those wedding bells so gay. Our Nadina weds today. Hurray! Hurray! The church bells are ringing, Of love they are singing, Hail to the bride! The fond happy groom!

Soldiers: Oh, Barbarians—yes, Barbarians
Are the fighting fierce Bulgarians.
We have proved in blood and
battle
That it's no mere tittle tattle
Don't annoy the big bad Bulgar
Or he may do something vulgar.

Massakroff: Respected sirs—and honoured
misses—
What a lovely party this is.
The bridegroom I must
congratulate,
I envy him his fate. Ha!
Ei . . . Ei . . . But this is very
queer,
How comes it that this man is
here;
The spying, lying Serb for whom
I searched in this young lady's
room?

Bumerli: Forgive, forgive, forgive
Why was I there?
I wished to live.
I little knew what fate was
shaping.
My only purpose was escaping.
I climbed up there to save my
skin,
That's why I refuge sought
within.
She gave me hope my life to
save
And that I swear is all she gave.
She kept me there so I may live—
Forgive, forgive, forgive.

Chorus: Forgive, forgive, forgive.
Why was he there?
He little knew what fate was
shaping,
His only purpose was escaping.

He climbed up there to save his
skin,
That's why he refuge sought
within.

Bumerli: She let me sleep the whole night
through,
And that is all she let me do.
She kept me there, so I may live.
Forgive, forgive, forgive.

Alexius: In dreams I once was your hero
Long, long ago.
Love burned, now it's at zero
Yes, that is so.
But now you have betrayed me,
You have deceived me,
You have dismayed me.
But I loved you . . .

Nadine: Yes, once I thought you my hero
And I was true.
Love burned—now it's at zero—
I'm done with you.

Bumerli: Come, come.
He would disgrace you,
My arms are yearning now to
embrace you.
I love but you.

Nadine: Where, where, where is my hero?
Where is my ideal?

Massakroff: (*To Alexius*)
Come, come, now be my hero—
My true ideal!

Aurelia: Where, where, where is her hero,
Where her ideal?

Alexius: He, he, now is her hero,
Her new ideal!

Popopff:	He, he, now is her hero Her new ideal!
Massakroff:	He, he, now is her hero Her new ideal!
Bumerli:	I, I would be your hero, Your true ideal.
Chorus:	See, see, see her new hero, Her new ideal. We came here to a wedding feast, This interests us not the least. A wedding we would celebrate— Must we condole or congratulate?
Nadine:	That quickly you shall see (*She pulls ring from finger and* *throws it at Alexius's feet*) I set you free!
Alexius:	You set me free? End all that binds me to you, You to me?
Nadine:	I dreamt that he was my hero, Yes, my ideal.
Mascha:	I'll dream that you are my hero, Yes, my ideal
Aurelia:	She dreamt that he was her hero, Yes, her ideal!
Alexius:	Once her ideal!
Bumerli:	I'll dream I am your hero, Yes, your ideal!
Popoff:	She dreamt that he was her hero, Yes, her ideal!
Massakroff:	She dreamt that he was her hero, Yes, her ideal!
Chorus:	She dreamt that he was her hero, Yes, her ideal!

Although Wodehouse and Bolton wrote the book for *Oh, Kay!* it was—musically speaking—a Gershwin show. A story Wodehouse and Bolton *don't* tell about its origins in *Bring On The Girls* is how it got its name.

Gertie Lawrence was in great demand after her success in the 1924 *Charlot Revue* in which she had starred in New York with Beatrice Lillie and Jack Buchanan. There were many offers for her to choose from on the day Wodehouse, Bolton and George Gershwin paid a visit to her apartment.

When they had auditioned some of the material for her, Gertie asked: "What are you going to call it?" "The thing we are waiting breathlessly for you to say," Bolton replied. "OK," said Miss Lawrence, "very much OK." At which Gershwin struck up—"Oh, Kay, you're OK with me."

The original 1926 Broadway production was a triumph for Lawrence in her first book musical. She played the part of Kay for 256 performances at New York's Imperial Theatre and a further 213 at His Majesty's Theatre, London. Wodehouse's contribution—apart from his share in the book—was to anglicize some of the lyrics for the 1927 London production.

For the 1960 off-Broadway revival—with the permission of Ira Gershwin—he wrote new lyrics to two songs that had originally been heard in *Primrose* (1924) in London—"The Twenties Are Here To Stay" ("When Toby Is Out of Town") and "The Pophams" ("The Mophams"). In addition, "Home" used the melody from "Don't Ask" and "You'll Still Be There" from "Dear Little Girl," both from the original production. None were retained for David Merrick's 1990 all black Broadway revival (77 performances).

OH, KAY! (REVIVAL 1960)

Presented by Leighton K. Brill, Frederick Lewis Jr. and Bertram Yarborough at the East 74th Street Theatre, New York, on April 16, 1960 (89 performances).

BOOK	Guy Bolton and P. G. Wodehouse
LYRICS	Ira Gershwin
	(Additional lyrics by P. G. Wodehouse)
MUSIC	George Gershwin

CAST

The Cotton Tails:
Phil:
ROSMARRI SHEER
Izzy: LINDA LAVIN
Polly:
PENNY FULLER
Jean:
FRANCESCA BELL
Odile:
LYNN GAY LORINO
Molly: SYBIL SCOTFORD
Larry Potter:
EDDIE PHILLIPS
Earl of Blandings:
MURRAY MATHESON

McGee:
BERNIE WEST
Chauffeur:
JAMES SULLIVAN
Jimmy Winters:
DAVID DANIELS
Constance:
EDITH BELL
Revenue Officer:
MIKE MAZURKI
Kay:
MARTI STEVENS
Judge Appleton:
JOSEPH MACAULAY

SYNOPSIS

Kay helps her aristocratic brother—who also happens to be a bootlegger—to hide his illegal booze on the Long Island estate of the young and wealthy Jimmy Winters, whose social life means that he hardly ever visits the place. When, inconveniently, he does, Kay has to pretend to be a housemaid before true love untangles all the complications of the plot.

THE TWENTIES ARE HERE TO STAY

(Earl of Blandings, Larry and McGee)

Earl: *(Spoken)*
Oh, I love this country!
It's so full of excitement!

Larry: *(Spoken)*
It's the Twenties!

Earl: *(Spoken)*
The madcap days in anybody's life
(Sings)
Columbus had the right idea,
The right idea,
The bright idea
When first he put this country on
the map.
There's something in the air, you know,

That makes you glad you're there,
    you know—
I mean, it sort of braces up a chap.

Larry: Just an earthly heaven
And no need to wonder why—
It's 1927
And the goose is hanging high!

McGee: Things are on the boom today,
No room today
For gloom today
So bring your plate and get your slice
    of pie . . .

Larry: No one has a thing on their mind
And every cloud is silvery-lined—
The Twenties are here today!

McGee: Ev'rything is go-as-you-please,
And dollar bills are growing on trees—

All: The Twenties are here—hooray!

Earl: Whole world is making whoopee
And it's one long "Hey! Hey!"

McGee: All the boys are having a drink
And all the girls are smothered in
    mink—
The Twenties are here today!

Earl: Life is just a marathon dance
And anyone can tell at a glance
The Twenties are here today!

Larry: Ev'rything is merry and bright
And stocks are rising as high as
    a kite—

All: The Twenties are here—hooray!

McGee: Gaily the sun is shining
And we're all making hay—hey!

All the boys are chasing the girls
And all the girls are gathering
    pearls—

All: The Twenties are here to stay!

HOME

(Jimmy and Girls)

Jimmy: Doesn't matter where you tour to—
Bali or Manila or Spain.
Here's the funny thing you're sure to
Find when you have got back again.
There is nothing like the dear old
    places
Where you see the old familiar
    faces . . .

I've been around,
Covered some ground,
But no place ever found
Like home.
People you meet
Rave about Greece
Say there's nothing to beat
Old Rome.
Naples, Cannes,
Isle of Man,
Lake of Lucerne,
Florence, Venice,
Take 'em in turn
And—
What have you got
Out of the lot?
There is never a spot
Like home.

Girls: You'll hear that thing—
Paris in Spring,
It has not got a thing
On home.
People are wrong
Saying they long

For a trip to Hong Kong
Or Nome.
No Madrids, pyramids, or Bunds
    of Shanghai—
Really rate and I'll tell you why
Isn't it natch? None of the batch
Is as much as a patch
On home.

Jimmy: Girls I have met
Pretty and yet
They are not like what you get
Back home.
Right down the line
None were for mine,
Though I searched with a fine
Tooth comb.
Mademoiselles,
Spanish belles,
Girls everywhere,
Nice enough but couldn't compare
With Polly and Phil
Molly and Lil,
Betty, Dolly or Jill
My girls back home.
Oh, I love you all!

THE POPHAMS

(Earl of Blandings and Girls)

Earl: *(Spoken)*
The Pophams were really quite
    something but I'm afraid they
    rather petered out at the end.

Girls: Oh, no, they haven't!

Do tell us, if you're willing,
For I know it will be thrilling,
All the daring deeds your family
    have done.
Search the history books and that'll
Show that on the field of battle

All the many kinds of honor they
    have won.

Earl: Well, of course, we Popham blighters
Always have been doughty fighters;
Through the ages that has been our
    special line.
One could hardly count the foemen
We have spiked in the abdomen
Or have cloven to the chine.
For a Popham is always a Popham . . .
We're never known to turn our
    backs.

Girls: Such courage!

Earl: When bounders attack us, we bop 'em.

Girls: You bop 'em?

Earl: Yes, clean on the bean with a
    battleaxe.
My ancestors in batches
Have been mentioned in dispatches
In campaigns of all descriptions
    everywhere.

Girls: Really?

Earl: Indubitably.
When things were getting messy
At Agincourt or Crecy,
You'd always find a Popham there.
But though so very martial,
To the ladies we've been partial
In the intervals of leaping to the fray.

1st Girl: Don't begin apologizing;
2nd Girl: It's not at all surprising:

Both: That has always been the military
    way.

Earl: With their husbands on vacation,
Wives could have the consolation

428 THE COMPLETE LYRICS OF P. G. WODEHOUSE

Of reflecting that a friend in need
    was near:
When they wept, there'd be a
    Popham
Looking in on them to stop 'em
And to dry the starting tear.
For a Popham is always a Popham.
When dealing with the other sex . . .

Girls: You mean us?

Earl: Who else?
At necking no rival could top 'em
And nature contrives that all wives
    have necks
So when husbands who'd been
    roaming
Come back homing
In the gloaming,
It would give the little woman quite
    a scare . . .

Girls: Naughty boy!

Earl: For when like Mother Hubbard,
They looked inside their cupboard,
They'd always find a Popham
    there!

YOU'LL STILL BE THERE

(Jimmy and Kay)

Kay: *(Spoken)*
If you can't weep over the grave of
    love, what are our tears for?

Jimmy: I should have known that I would
    find you,
I can see that it was fated
Now that it's too late . . .

Kay: The promises that you've made that
    bind you.

Jimmy: If I'd only waited . . .

Kay: But you didn't wait
And so once again our ways have
    parted—
Try not to be downhearted.

You'll take your road,
I'll take mine
And yet—
You'll still be there.
Time will pass but I shall not
    forget—
You'll still be there.

Jimmy: Your dear face I'll see again
All the long years through;
You will smile at me again
As you used to do.

Both: Every hour of every day
I'll see you everywhere,
Though you're half a world away
To me—
You'll still be there.

Kay: Your dear voice I'll hear again
In each breeze of Spring
And I'll know you're near again
And my heart will sing.

Both: Every hour of every day
I'll see you everywhere,
Though you're half a world away
To me—
You'll still be there.

There were other Wodehouse contributions to the show that were not used.

On March 8, 1959, he is writing to Ira Gershwin to tell him he believes that Bolton's revised book is "twice as good as it was in 1926" and to report progress on his own songs. Can they, he asks, have Ira's permission to use "that

Muddling Through number" ("Stiff Upper Lip")? (Used by Gershwin in the 1937 film *A Damsel in Distress,* based on a Wodehouse novel.)

The permission duly given, Wodehouse writes again (April 9, 1960) as the show evolves: "I wouldn't be a bit surprised if (it) didn't turn out the hit of the show. . . ." He describes where the song will be used and then reprised and goes on—"for the Shorty-Jimmy spot I have written a new refrain, though feeling that I was tampering with sacred writ. Shorty first sings your refrain, then Jimmy sings a verse to the effect of 'There's a lot of sense in what you say.' I'd like to brood on it at my leisure. Would you mind repeating it?" They then sing the following—

> Stiff upper lip. Stout fella.
> Carry on, old sox.
> Chin up, keep muddling through.
> Stiff upper lip. Stout fella.
> When they're throwing rocks,
> Just let the bounders see it means nothing
>   to you.
> Never make a bally fuss
> When you find you're in a spot.
> Simply raise an eyebrow—thus—
> And say "I say, I say! What, what?"
> Stiff upper lip. Stout fella.
> That's the thing to do.
> Sober or blotto . . . etc.

It isn't Ira G., but I think it's all right."

At first glance it would seem that Wodehouse is copying Gershwin copying Wodehouse, since "a stiff upper lip" is a phrase that recurs frequently in his fiction. In fact, Ira—in his *Lyrics On Several Occasions* (1973) traces it back to an *American* origin, the *Massachusetts Spy* (1815) and claims lexicographer Eric Partridge reports the phrase made its first appearance in the UK as late as 1880.

Ira further recorded his stylistic debt to his friend:

When I did this lyric (for the 1937 film version of Wodehouse's *A Damsel In Distress.*) I remembered 'muddle through' as a Briticism, sometimes of criticism, sometimes of resolution, much used at the time of World War I and almost as prevalent as World War II's term of approval, "good show." Then, from various characters in Wodehouse came phrases like "pip-pip," "toodleoo" and "stout fella."

Just to underline the depth of his affection for his old partner, Ira prefaced one of the secondary songs, "Things Are Looking Up," as follows: "Sung by Fred Astaire to Joan Fontaine on the downs of Totleigh Castle located in Upper Pelham-Grenville, Wodehouse, England."

Another suggestion to Ira—handwritten from the Hotel Sylvania, Philadelphia—was for the "green light mysterioso" scene, "if it would help any"—but it was not used:

> Let's pull ourselves together,
> For there's not a thing to be frightened at.
> *(Crash)*
> What's that?
> It must have been a bird we heard
> A-twittering in a tree,
> Or the cat
> On the mat.
> I think I need a tonic
> Or a cocktail on a tray,
> For I'm not myself today.

Refrain: Oh, I feel so ner-ner-nervous
> I dud—don't know what to do.
> For my heart is going bump,
> My pulse is going thump,
> At every sound
> I leap and bound
> And jer-jer-jer-jump.
> All the while I'm quivering and
>   shivering
> And my legs go round in curves.

Do not thuh-thuh-think
It's due to der-der-drink,
It's simply ner-ner-nerves.

Let's pull ourselves together.
We'll regard this by-and-by
As a joke
(Crash)
Holy smoke!
There's nothing to be scared at;
It just happened that a fly

On my coat
Cleared his throat
I thought it was a dynamite
Explosion 'cross the way,
For I'm not myself today.

Wodehouse had clearly forgotten—or chosen to ignore—that the number had substantially been used as "Nerves" in *The Cabaret Girl* (1922)—not to mention even earlier in *See You Later* (1918).

TO BE CONTINUED . . .
(1945–1975)

After *Anything Goes* there were to be no more original Wodehouse musicals—with or without Bolton—to reach the public stage.

Not that there was any lack of ambition. Though separated by the Atlantic—by the end of the 1930s Wodehouse was living in Le Touquet and Bolton in New York—their letters reveal the old itch was waiting to be scratched.

In the real world, however, the plot was getting a little out of hand. In a letter to Bolton dated December 23, 1939—well into the Phoney War—Wodehouse writes: "I'm frightfully keen to come over and work with you. Can you get me a commission? . . . It would be fine if we could revive the old B-W-Kern combination. Has Jerry abandoned Hollywood?"

Time and the arrival of German troops on his doorstep settled that question.

During his internment by the Germans Wodehouse typically kept on writing but concentrated on his fiction.

There was, however, at least one occasion in 1940 when, as he put it in *Performing Flea,* "the lyricist in me awoke and I sat down at a table in the upper dining-room and wrote a song hit." . . .

DEAR OLD PNIBW

A young man was sipping soda in a gilded
    cabaret,
When a song of home sweet home the
    orchestr*ah* did start to play:
And he thought he ought to tie a can to dreams
    of wealth and fame
And go right back to the simple shack from
    which he once had came.
And as for his soda he did pay,
To the head waiter these words he then did say:
"Goodbye, Broadway."

There's a choo-choo leaving for dear old Pnibw
Where the black-eyed susans grow
(I wanna go, I wanna go).
There's a girl who's waiting in dear old Pnibw
(Oh, vo-de-o-de-o-de-o)
Tender and dreamy,
Yearning to see me.

There are girls in Koppienitz and girls in
    Peiskretscham
And possibly in Slupska too,
But the honey for my money is the one who's
    sitting knitting
Underneath the magnolias in dear old Pnibw.
America, I love you with your eyes of blue
But I'm going back, back, back to the land where
    dreams come true.
P-n-i-b-w spells Pnibw,
And, as Ogden Nash would say,
What the hell did you think it was going to do?

"It is a little rough at present, as I have not
had time to polish it, but the stuff is there.
It has the mucus."

By the end of 1945, however, he is beginning
to feel the old lyrical stirring and he writes from
Paris to Bolton:

> I am concentrating now on writing lyrics, of
> the type that will fit in anywhere, but I find
> it awfully hard to get anything done without

a book and a composer to inspire me.
Somehow when you have the scene in front
of you that has to be topped off with a duet,
there is always something in the characters
that gives you an idea, whereas doing a He
and She duet cold is tough. Still, I'm at least
getting what [Rudolph] Friml used to call
sketches. I used to go and see him, yearning
for a completed tune so that I could make a
dummy, and he would play a couple of bars
and then wander off into a lot of vague notes.
"Just a sketch," he used to say, blast him! By
the way, do you think the modern lyric has to
be very different from the old ones? I mean
are there any new tricks one has to learn?
It seems to me, listening to the radio, that
verses seem to have disappeared. At least, on
the radio the singer simply charges straight
into the refrain. But in a show, I imagine,
you still need a verse, though probably a
short one. Do you realise that I haven't seen
a musical show since 1937! What do you
think are the prospects of your being able to
get a commission for a B and W show? I am
longing to get going on one.

Only a few days later he returns to the theme:

> I have abandoned all other forms of work
> and am spending my whole time working on
> lyrics and am pleased to report that the old
> Muse is in the real 1916–1918 form. So far
> I have completed three really good ones, a
> couple of light comedy duets and one of
> those trios for three men which used to go
> so well. I am hoping before long to have a
> large reserve into which we can dip when the
> moment arrives. Of course, the difficulty is
> that one is so handicapped, working this way
> without having a story and characters, and
> I have to stick to stuff that can be fitted in
> anywhere.
>
> A fear that haunts me, of course, is that
> I may be thirty years behind the times and be

turning out stuff that would have been fine for 1917 but no good for 1946. But I don't believe there is any reason to feel like this. The numbers I hear on the radio sound exactly like those of twenty and thirty years ago. My theory is that the business of keeping up to date is entirely the headache of the composer. If he is modern and the lyricist does his lyric to the music the lyricist can't go wrong. Where I may be out of date is in writing a thing like that trio for three men, for it is *quite* possible nowadays they are as much a back number as the old story song like "Yip-i-addy." What do you think? Can you get away today with trios like *Sir Galahad* and *It's A Hard World For A Man?* As regards the duets, I feel happier. The only change there has ever been in the light comedy love duet is in the rhythm of the music. Anyway, I'm working away like the dickens.

From letters to Bolton in that immediate post-war period it is clear that in 1946 he worked—however briefly—on at least two shows in addition to *The Chocolate Soldier*. One (of which nothing further is known) was called *Saratoga Chips* and he assured Bolton that it had "a pippin of a lyric." The other—in May of that year—was an assignment for book and lyrics for a musical about Madame de Pompadour to star Grace Moore. The producer was to be Hassard Short.

He writes to his old friend, Ira Gershwin:

I was torn between the desire to get in on what will presumably be a big production and a hit, especially as I was an old beachcomber trying to make a come back after thirty years, and the desire to put on a false beard and hide somewhere till the thing had blown over. I imagine you probably feel the same as I do when asked to work on a 'period' musical show—a sort of deadly feeling that you are

going into a fight with one arm strapped to your side and hobbles around your ankles. Because you won't be able to use anything in the nature of modern comedy lines or ideas and so are robbed of your best stuff. When I write a lyric I want to be able to work in Clark Gable and Grover Whalen's moustache and corned beef hash, and you can't when you are dealing with La Pompadour.

That particular project seems to have fallen through because Wodehouse still didn't have his U.S. visa.

There were other offers—a few of which we know about only because Wodehouse happened to mention them in letters to friends. He was asked—also in 1946—to make a musical out of a play called *Enter Madame* in collaboration with Ogden Nash ("I'm damned if I can see how you can make (it) into a musical"). . . . In 1950 there was the suggestion of a musical version of J. M. Barrie's *The Admiral Crichton* ("Now it seems like a turkey of the first water"). Then, showing that his own judgment was not always of the best, he writes that "the best bet for a musical would be *The Cave Girl*"—a Bolton show that had been an also-ran even in 1920.

In 1947 he is lamenting to Bolton: "I can't get used to the new Broadway. . . . Apparently you have to write your show and get it composed and give a series of auditions to backers, instead of having the management line up a couple of stars and then get a show written for them."

Hans Bartsch was apparently sufficiently encouraged by the reception of the 1947 *The Chocolate Soldier* to commission a "sequel." He supposedly asked Wodehouse to rewrite the book and provide a completely new set of lyrics for *The Waltz Dream* (1908), although nothing appears to have survived, if, indeed, it was ever written.

In 1950 Wodehouse was asked to play the role of "show doctor" for Vinton Freedley's production of *It's Great To Be Alive* but, having worked on the first act, he was told that the

authors refused to have anyone else work on
the project. No show of that name was ever produced either.

By 1951 he is even more disenchanted: "I
am feeling an absolute loathing for the Broadway
stage now . . . everyone raves about *The King And I*
and I still can't see what can be the attraction.
I saw a photograph in the paper the other day
of the ballet "The Small House of Uncle Thomas"
. . . a lot of bloody Siamese leaping about and
looking perfectly awful. . . . What Oscar has done
to the good old American musical."

In time of comic need it was the work of an
instant to improvise a song lyric. To illustrate an
anecdote about beards in his 1956 volume of
American reminiscences (*America, I Like You*—a
loose reassembly of *Over Seventy*) he writes . . .

MEN WITH WHISKERS

The world is in a mess today,
Damn sight worse than yesterday,
And getting a whole lot worser right along.
It's time that some clear-thinking guy
Got up and told the reason why
America has started going wrong.
If laws are broke and homes are wrecked,
It's only what you might expect
With all the fellows shaving all the time.
Yes, sir, the moment you begin
To crop the fungus from the chin
You're headed for a life of sin
And crime.

What this country needs is men with whiskers
Like the men of an earlier date.
They were never heels and loafers
And they looked like busted sofas
Or excelsior in a crate.
Don't forget it was men with whiskers
Who founded our New Yorks, Detroits and
     San Franciskers.
What this country needs is men with whiskers
Like the men who made her great.

The pioneers were hairy men,
Rugged devil-may-care-y men,
Who wouldn't have used a razor on a bet.
For each had sworn a solemn oath
He'd never prune the undergrowth;
Their motto was "To hell with King
     Gillette!"
And when they met on country walks
Wild Cherokees (Indians armed) with
     tomahawks,
I'll say those boys were glad they hadn't
     shaved.
When cornered by a redskin band,
With things not going quite as planned,
They hid inside their whiskers and
Were saved.

What this country needs is men with whiskers,
For the whisker always wins.
Be it war or golf or tennis
We shall fear no foeman's menace
With alfalfa on our chins.
Whitman's verse, there is none to match it,
But you couldn't see his face unless you used
     a hatchet.
What this country needs is men with whiskers
Out where the best begins.

What this country needs is men with whiskers
Like the men of long ago:
It would all be hunkadory
With the nation's pride and glory
If we let our grogans grow.
Grants and Shermans and Davy Crocketts
Never used to go around with razors in their
     pockets:
What this country needs is men with
     whiskers
Like the men it used to know.

What this country needs is men with whiskers
Like the men of Lincoln's day.
At the Wilderness and Shiloh
They laid many a doughty guy low,

They were heroes in the fray.
Theirs is fame that can never die out,
And if you touched their beards, a couple of birds
    would fly out,
So let's raise the slogan of "Back to whiskers!"
And three cheers for the U.S.A.

In a 1947 letter to lyricist Arthur Schwartz he claimed that he had originally written it "in case Guy and I ever got around to doing a show with a Civil War ball scene in it."

The fact of the matter was that, no matter what he was writing, he was always apt to burst into song at the most unlikely moments. In *Over Seventy*, for instance, he recounts an unexpected and unwelcome visit to Evelyn Waugh from Lord Noël-Buxton and the journalist Nancy Spain. Wodehouse had only read about it in a newspaper account but "the episode so impressed me that I reached for my harp and burst into song about it."

THE VISITORS

My dear old dad, when I was a lad
Planning my life's career,
Said 'Read for the bar, be a movie star
Or travel around in lands afar
As a mining engineer,
But don't, whatever you do', he hissed,
'Be a widely read, popular novelist.'
And he went on to explain
That if you're an author, sure as fate,
Maybe early or maybe late,
Two jovial souls will come crashing the gate,
Noël-Buxton and Nancy Spain.

Noël-Buxton and Nancy Spain, my lad,
Noël-Buxton and Nancy Spain.
They're worse, he said, than a cold in the
    head
Or lunch on an English train.
Some homes have beetles and some have mice,
Neither of which are very nice,

But an author's home has (he said this twice)
Noël-Buxton and Nancy Spain.

Well, I said 'Indeed?' but I paid no heed
To the warning words I quote,
For I hoped, if poss, to make lots of dross
And to be the choice of the old Book Soc.,
So I wrote and wrote and wrote.
Each book I published touched the spot,
There wasn't a dud in all the lot,
And things looked right as rain,
Till as one day at my desk I sat
The front-door knocker went rat-a-tat,
And who was it waiting on the mat?
Noël-Buxton and Nancy Spain.

So all you young men who hope with your pen
To climb to the top of the tree,
Just pause and think, 'ere you dip in the ink,
That you may be standing upon the brink
Of the thing that happened to me.
That stern, stark book you are writing now
May be good for a sale of fifty thou',
But it's wisest to refrain.
For what will it boot though it brings to you
A car and a yacht and a page in *Who's Who*,
If it also brings, as it's sure to do,
Noël-Buxton and Nancy Spain.

Noël-Buxton and Nancy Spain, my lads,
Noël-Buxton and Nancy Spain.
They'll walk right in with a cheerful grin
And, when they are in, remain.
I wouldn't much care to be stung by bees
Or bitten, let's say, by a Pekinese,
But far, far better are those than these,
Noël-Buxton and Nancy Spain

And even in the middle of a short story you could easily stumble over the occasional fragment in "The Coming of Gowf" (1919)—the servile courtiers of King Merolchazzar sing a song in praise of his supposed golfing prowess . . .

OH, TUNE THE STRING

Oh, tune the string and let us sing
Our godlike, great, and glorious King!
He's a bear! He's a bear! He's a bear!

Oh, may his triumphs never cease!
He has the strength of ten!
First in war, first in peace,
First in the hearts of his countrymen.

Oh, praises let us utter
To our most glorious King!
It fairly makes you stutter
To see him start his swing;
Success attend his putter!
And luck be with his drive!
And may he do each hole in two,
Although the bogey's five!

Aside from his beloved golf, a subject painfully close to the Wodehouse heart was income tax. Over the years he had many an altercation with the authorities in both the US and the UK—which impelled him (in *Louder and Funnier*) to write . . .

THE INCOME TAX SONG

Treble Solo: We have heard it hinted darkly
That your leisure you employ
Drinking cocktails at the Berkeley,
Having lunch at the Savoy;
So if you will tell us clearly
What's your total income yearly
We will thank you most sincerely:
At-a-boy!

All: God rest you, merry gentlemen,
Let nothing you dismay:
We're needing stacks of income tax,
So pay—pay—pay!

But, as far as the real theatre was concerned, 1953 and *Guys and Dolls* brought the *coup de grâce* and perhaps the real insight into what

bothered him most—"I can't stand this modern practice of never bringing on the girls."

Is there likely to be a major revival of general interest in Wodehouse lyrics? Probably not, since most of them were expressly designed to be integrated into the context and to fit the characters of particular long ago shows, and time has been notoriously unkind to musical comedy "books."

Nonetheless, the last few years have seen the occasional song finding its way into the repertoire of leading cabaret artistes or popping up in a CD anthology of recycled material, and an ambitious project (sponsored by the Packard Foundation) to record the entire musical theatre output of Jerome Kern means that we shall have the opportunity to hear the original orchestrations of at least the "Princess shows"—all of which may well trigger the reaction: "I didn't know Wodehouse wrote *that*. . . ."

Well, now you do . . .

And there was to be one more piece of unfinished business: the "Jeeves musical."

By 1951 Wodehouse was comfortably nesting once more in the US and anxious to renew his collaboration with Guy Bolton. The first thought was a straight play to feature Jeeves, "something a bit risky with a lot of sex in it," he suggested in a letter to Bolton.

The initial draft had a racing theme and was to be called *Derby Day*, but the release of the Anna Neagle–Michael Wilding film of 1952 caused them to change it to *Come On, Jeeves*. When the play failed to score in an out-of-town tryout, Wodehouse turned it into the 1953 novel *Ring For Jeeves* (*The Return of Jeeves*, 1954 in the U.S.).

There matters rested until the success of the 1965 BBC TV series *The World of Wooster* caused them to speculate on the possibility of a revival starring the TV leads Ian Carmichael and Dennis Price. This presented a logistical problem, since Bertie had been relegated to a minor role in the play. Instead, Wodehouse and Bolton did a total rewrite with the new title *Win With Wooster*.

It was at this point that fate—or, rather, their neighbor, song writer Frank Loesser of *Guys and Dolls* fame—took a hand. Why didn't they turn the piece into a musical and revive the old Princess tradition? The boys were intrigued—but who would write the music? There was no longer a Jerry Kern in their world.

Loesser suggested the team of Robert Wright and George Forrest (whose musical credits included *Song Of Norway* and *Kismet)* and arranged a preliminary meeting for the five of them. Although he went along with it, Wodehouse experienced considerable heart searching. In August 1966 he is writing to Bolton: "I still feel a Singing Jeeves is all wrong, but with the proviso that it would be all right with Stanley Holloway as Jeeves."

(A later version has pencil suggestions for Carmichael as Bertie, Holloway "or younger" as Jeeves, Derek Nimmo as Pongo, Eve Arden "or younger" as Brenda and Susan Watson as Zenny.)

Two years later he is still concerned as to how the public would react to a terpsichorean Jeeves and prepared to consider quite radical alternative solutions: "It occurs to me as a possibility to jettison the Bertie-Jeeves set-up and make Bertie Lord Something and his butler some other name. Then it wouldn't matter the butler being young and lively and an eccentric dancer. We would lose the Jeeves publicity but people have got such a fixed idea of Jeeves as an elderly, grave, orotund character that that might not matter." (There exists, in fact, a 2-page undated treatment called *Leave It to Larry* in which Tommy Steele is cast as Larry Lumpit, a "Broker's Man," and there is a character called Bill (Lord Dillingham), the "Bertie character," as well as Fern, the maid and a love interest for Larry.

The action takes place in Athelston Abbey, Bill's family home, which is up for sale—hence Larry's presence tagging the furniture. Larry laments the fact that society is being leveled

down . . . a kitchen sink world . . . where's the romance? . . . what about love turning chorus girls into duchesses? "He might sing a song on the subject," says a note.)

A further note—presumably by Bolton—adds that "Plum has written to Fielding [UK producer, Harold Fielding] telling him of the new angle which would permit the character of JEEVES to be exchanged for a singing and dancing comic. Of course, it means a complete rewrite of the role and of some portions of lyrics. . . . We are very open to suggestions." Nothing came of it.

Despite his provisos, work went on with Loesser acting initially as an informal impresario. As they established a *modus operandi*, Wright and Forrest noticed something about Wodehouse. He was doing what many a musically illiterate lyricist does—he was putting the words in his head to music that was already there. All of his lyrics were being set to old Jerome Kern music before being handed to his new colleagues to find new melodies for them!

Wodehouse was relieved to find that the old brain had not lost its lyrical cunning—but then he *had* been keeping in practice for the last several decades. Nonetheless, he did encounter a few unexpected problems as work progressed. When the first redraft was completed, he realized that they would need seven solo songs, "which are always the devil to write lyrics for. Have you ever seen a musical with seven solos?"

Nor was he particularly impressed with some of the melodies Wright and Forrest had come up with for his lyrics. He was, he pointed out, in the habit of writing four or five alternative lyrics before he found one that satisfied him, whereas his collaborators seemed to be in the habit of settling on their first. He should, perhaps, have considered that their earlier successes had been based on the music of others—i.e., Grieg and Borodin.

Eventually the piece was finished—and there it stayed. Several managements toyed with the idea of putting it on. In 1968 Wodehouse is writing to playwright John Chapman that impresario Tom Arnold will be staging his Jeeves–Bertie musical. "The first lyrics I have done for forty years and they have come out well." Despite his optimism, nothing came of it.

Then in 1971 Wodehouse and Bolton received a visit from Andrew Lloyd Webber and Tim Rice. At this point they had written just two shows but already the phenomenal success of *Joseph and the Amazing Technicolor Dreamcoat* (1968) and *Jesus Christ Superstar* (1969) had made them both wealthy and powerful in musical theatre circles.

Lloyd Webber, in particular, was an avid Wodehouse fan and arrived with a proposal that he and Rice should write a Jeeves musical. He even had a prior production commitment from the Stigwood organization. Putting aside for the moment the legal complexities of *Betting On Bertie*, Wodehouse signed away the rights for the new musical—known initially as *Leave It To Jeeves* and, later, simply *Jeeves*, when it was finally staged in 1974.

Before that several things were to happen. To placate Wright and Forrest, the rights to *Betting On Bertie* were ceded to them. By this time Wodehouse is more concerned with how the "Jesus Christ boys" (Lloyd Webber and Rice) are getting on. "Probably something frightful," he writes in 1973. "Not that that means it won't be a hit. . . . They are evidently quite exceptional in the way of talent. (But I wish one of them, I can't remember which it is, would get his hair cut.)"

But it isn't long before his underlying concerns emerge again. "I'm afraid the difficulty is that the boys regard Jeeves as sacred writ and think that the more of the stuff in the stories they can cram in, the better." Wodehouse's own experience has taught him otherwise. "I'm sure that CLARITY is the essential thing. Get a clear script and never mind how much good material you have to leave out."

Before long Tim Rice backed out. Wodehouse commented that Rice "said the subject beat him!

I was pleased, as I never thought the venture could prosper. . . . I bet nothing comes of it." But something did come of it. Rice was replaced as lyricist by playwright Alan Ayckbourn, and *Jeeves* opened at Her Majesty's Theatre, London, on April 22nd, 1975, after a provincial tryout which showed that the original production lasted over four hours! Wodehouse's own reservations, however, were confirmed by critics and public alike and the show only ran for a handful of performances.

The show was Lloyd Webber's only failure up to that point, and he did not take it lightly. Neither did Ayckbourn and in 1996 the two men produced a totally reworked show called *By Jeeves*, which was given a much better reception.

Opening at Ayckbourn's Stephen Joseph Theatre in Scarborough—where almost all of his plays first see the light of stage—it transferred first to London's Lyric Theatre and then to the Duke of York's, enjoying a successful London run.

During the next few years it was performed—in a production that evolved as it went along—in a series of provincial American venues, finally coming to Broadway in October 2001 at the Helen Hayes Theatre, where it created little stir. Perhaps a post–September 11th New York audience was not in the mood for English eccentricity . . . perhaps it was simply too slight a piece to bear the weight of Broadway expectations.

Meanwhile, the Wodehouse-Bolton-Forrest-Wright *Betting On Bertie* remained in a state of suspended animation, as it does to this day, having had a handful of staged readings but no professional production. Of the four collaborators only Robert Wright is alive at the time of this writing and, while admitting Wodehouse's authorship of many of the lyrics, he retains the rights and refuses permission for their publication. The most one can offer, under the circumstances, therefore, is the hope that in future editions of this book Mr. Wright may be persuaded that a taste of the Wodehouse lyrics will help rather than hinder the show's chances of a production.

Appendix A

The "Lost Shows"

Not surprisingly—in a theatrical career that lasted so long—and started so long ago—there are gaps in the record and a number of questions that may never be fully answered.

Different commentators have mentioned several early shows in connection with Wodehouse, yet such records as have come to light fail to validate his participation. Which is not to say that he did not participate—simply that the fact remains at this date non-proven.

For example . . .

The Girls of Gottenberg

Presented by Charles Frohman at the Gaiety Theatre, London, on May 15, 1907 (303 performances), followed by a further short run (12 performances) at the Adelphi from August 10, 1908.

BOOK	George Grossmith Sr. and L. E. Berman
LYRICS	Adrian Ross and Basil Hood
MUSIC	Ivan Caryll and Lionel Monckton

In his autobiography *GG* (1933), George Grossmith Jr. mentioned that when the Kaiser visited the Gaiety Theatre, the cast were instructed by the German Embassy (through the Lord Chamberlain's office) to remove all the Eagles from the various German uniforms.

P. G. Wodehouse's personal writing paper at the time includes a song from the show entitled "Our Little Way" as being amongst his "recent successes." This did not appear in the show's libretto.

It would be amusing to report that he was also responsible for one of leading lady Gertie Millar's principal songs—"Mitzi—the Titsy Bitsy Girl"—but, alas, there is no such evidence!

In June of that same year a production called *The Hon'ary Degree* appeared at the New Theatre, Cambridge and supposedly included one Wodehouse song, "My Grassy Corner Girl." Again, the British Library text does not include it and the show does not appear to have made the transfer to the West End.

Nor is there much more to be said for *The Bandit's Daughter*—"a musical sketch by Herbert Westbrook and P. G. Wodehouse, music by Ella King-Hall." Produced at the Bedford Music Hall, Camden Town, on November 11, it was—according to its co-author's diary—"a frost!"

Over in the U.S. February 25, 1916, saw the production of a musical called *Pom Pom*. Supposedly, Wodehouse was called in by Savage to "doctor" the show and was to share credit for both libretto and lyrics with Anne Caldwell. In his biography *P. G. Wodehouse: A Portrait of a Master* (1974) David Jasen refers to the collaboration as a matter of fact and even includes Bolton as part of the act. However, there is no mention of Wodehouse's participation in any extant theatre program. The show was produced at the Cohan Theatre in New York and ran for 114 performances.

In the fall of 1921—according to Lee Davis in his *Bolton and Wodehouse and Kern* (1933)—Bolton and Wodehouse "managed to outline" the libretto for a musical to be called *The*

Blue Mazurka. Savage was to have produced, and the music was to have been written by Franz Lehar and Jerome Kern. Wodehouse went as far as to write two dummy lyrics—"The Hickey Doo" and "If You've Nothing Else To Do." Neither appears to have survived.

A year later we have something of a puzzle. Jasen lists a show called *Pat (The Gibson Girl)* as being "written 1922—never produced." The book was supposedly by Bolton & Wodehouse, the lyrics by Wodehouse and Billy Rose and the music by Vincent Youmans.

Where the confusion arises is in the fact that the boys *did* write a show called *Pat* at that time—but it was for Ziegfeld and had music by Kern. It was later discarded in favor of the show that became *Sitting Pretty*, and many of the songs ended up in that show. Wodehouse's collaboration with Rose and Youmans—such as it was—was to happen in 1929, when Ziegfeld had them all working on yet another musical adaptation of the play *East Is West*—and that never saw the lights of Broadway either! Wodehouse wrote to his friend William Townend that he and Rose completed a few lyrics before the project was abandoned but neither the Rose nor the Wodehouse archive has any record of them.

Then—confusion worse confounded—in December 1927 Ziegfeld asks Bolton and Wodehouse to write a Marilyn Miller vehicle for the 1928 season. In two weeks they turn one out—but by this time the mercurial producer has decided to go with a different idea, which ends up as *Rosalie*. The rejected script was called—*The Gibson Girl.*

A fascinating but frustrating announcement appeared in the March 21, 1930, edition of *Radio Times.*

On the following Thursday, March 27, there would be a program called "A Café in Vienna" and part of it would be "A Viennese Operetta" entitled *Zara.* The details were as follows:

BOOK   Leonora Wodehouse & C. Dents Freeman
MUSIC   Tony Lowry
LYRICS   P. G. Wodehouse

CHARACTERS
(in order of speaking)

An habitué of the Café
The New Proprietor
Fritz, a Waiter
Zara Korngold, a famous Viennese singer
Lord Michael Grange, an English diplomat
The Old Proprietor
An Austrian Secret Service Agent
Count Wachan, an Austrian Nobleman
Students

Scene: A Café in Vienna
Time: Present day and before the War

And that, frustratingly, is all we know of this unique collaboration between Wodehouse and his step-daughter, "Snorky" (Leonora)—except that the three contributors received a fee of £30 *among them*!

Finally, there are those tantalizing "lost" songs from the existing shows—many of them, perhaps, songs-that-never-were, some of them indicated by name in a libretto as an intention but apparently never written. Others were included in a theatre program that appeared in an out of town try-out or early in the run, but were then dropped from the score and, consequently, never published. It's perfectly possible that some of them may turn up, in which case they will be included as an Appendix in a subsequent edition of this book.

Piecing together the various clues I have found references to the following . . .

Have A Heart . . . "What Would You Do For $50,000?" . . . "The Whirlwind Trot" . . . "That's The Life."

Leave It To Jane . . . "I've Never Found a Girl Like You."

Kitty Darlin' . . . "Am I To Blame?" . . . "The Blarney Stone" . . . "The Dawn of Love" . . . "Dear Bath" . . . "Dear Curracloe" . . . "I'd Do the Same" . . .

"Just We Two" . . . "The Maid and the Valet" . . . "The Mother of the Regiment" . . . "Peggy's Leg" . . . "Spread the News" . . . "Swing Song" . . . "The Sword of My Father" . . . "Tick, Tick, Tick" . . . "Vanity" . . . "You'll See."

Miss 1917 . . . "The Honor System."

See You Later . . . "If You Could Read My Mind" . . . "No One Ever Loved Like Me" . . . "Rally Around" . . . "Run Away" . . . "Josephine" . . . "Happy Pair" . . . "Make the Best of Tonight."

The Canary . . . "Hunting Honeymoon."

The Rose of China . . . "American Jazz" . . . "The Land of the White Poppy" . . . "Ling Tao's Farewell" . . . "Proposals" . . . "Little Bride" . . . "Spirit of the Drum" . . . "My China Rose."

Sitting Pretty . . . "Roses Are Nodding" . . . "Coaching" . . . "Ladies Are Present" . . . "A Romantic Man" . . . "I'm Wise" . . . "All the World Is Dancing Mad."

How many of these are Wodehouse alone . . . how many are the same song with different titles (since he, Bolton and Kern were musical recyclers of renown) . . . and how many are specialty musical numbers with no lyrics (perhaps, for example, "The Whirlwind Trot" or "The Clog Dance")? . . . All of these remain unresolved questions, at least for now.

APPENDIX B

On the Writing of Lyrics by P. G. Wodehouse

The musical comedy lyric is an interesting survival of the days long since departed, when poets worked. As everyone knows, the only real obstacle in the way of turning out poetry by the mile was the fact that you had to make the darned stuff rhyme.

Many lyricists rhyme as they pronounce, and their pronunciation is simply horrible. They can make "home" rhyme with "alone," and "saw" with "more," and go right off and look their innocent children in the eye without a touch of shame.

But let us not blame the erring lyricist too much. It isn't his fault that he does these things. It is the fault of the English language. Whoever invented the English language must have been a prose-writer, not a versifier; for he had made meager provision for the poets. Indeed, the word "you" is almost the only decent chance he has given them. You can do something with a word like "you." It rhymes with "sue," "eyes of blue," "woo," and all sorts of succulent things, easily fitted into the fabric of a lyric. And it has the enormous advantage that it can be repeated thrice at the end of a refrain when the composer has given you those three long notes, which is about all a composer ever thinks of. When a composer hands a lyricist a "dummy" for a song, ending thus,

Tiddley-tum, tiddley-tum
Pom-pom-pom, pom-pom-pom,
Tum, tum, tum,

The lyricist just shoves down "You, you, you" for the last line and then sets to work to fit the rest of the words to it. I have dwelled on this, for it is noteworthy as the only bright spot in a lyricist's life, the only real cinch the poor man has.

But take the word "love."

When the board of directors, or whoever it was, was arranging the language, you would have thought that, if they had a spark of pity in their systems, they would

443

have tacked on to that emotion of thoughts of which the young man's fancy lightly turns in spring, some word ending in an open vowel. They must have known that lyricists would want to use whatever word they selected as a label for the above-mentioned emotion far more frequently than any other word in the language. It wasn't much to ask of them to choose a word capable of numerous rhymes. But no, they went and made it "love," causing vast misery to millions.

"Love" rhymes with "dove," "glove," "above," and "shove." It is true that poets who print their stuff instead of having it sung take a mean advantage by ringing in words like "prove" and "move"; but the lyricist is not allowed to do that. This is the wretched unfairness of the lyricist's lot. The language gets him both ways. It won't let him rhyme "love" with "move," and it won't let him rhyme "maternal" with "colonel." If he tries the first course, he is told that the rhyme, though all right for the eye, is wrong for the ear. If he tries the second course, they say that the rhyme, though more or less ninety-nine percent pure for the ear, falls short when tested to the eye. And, when he is driven back on one of the regular, guaranteed rhymes, he is taunted with triteness of phrase.

No lyricist wants to keep linking "love" with "skies above" and "turtle dove," but what can he do? You can't do a thing with "shove"; and "glove" is one of those aloof words which are not good mixers. And—mark the brutality of the thing—there is no word you can substitute for "love." It is just as if they did it on purpose.

"Home" is another example. It is the lyricist's staff of life. But all he can do is to roam across the foam, if he wants to use it. He can put in "Nome," of course, as a pinch-hitter in special crises, but very seldom; with the result that his poetic soul, straining at its bonds, goes and uses "alone," "bone," "tone," and "thrown," exciting hoots of derision.

But it is not only the paucity of rhymes that sours the lyricist's life. He is restricted in his use of material, as well. If every audience to which a musical comedy is destined to play were a metropolitan audience, all might be well; but there is the "road" to consider. And even a metropolitan audience likes its lyrics as much as possible in the language of everyday. That is one of the thousand reasons why new Gilberts do not arise. Gilbert had the advantage of being a genius, but he had the additional advantage of writing for a public which permitted him to use his full vocabulary, and even to drop into foreign languages, even Latin and a little Greek when he felt like it. (I allude to that song in *The Grand Duke*.)

And yet the modern lyricist, to look on the bright side, has advantages that Gilbert never had. Gilbert never realized the possibilities of Hawaii, with its admirably named beaches, shores and musical instruments. Hawaii—capable as it is of being rhymed with "higher"— has done much to sweeten the lot—and increase the annual income of an industrious and highly respectable but downtrodden class of the community

Vanity Fair
June 1917

SELECT BIBLIOGRAPHY

BORDMAN, Gerald
Jerome Kern: His Life and Music
    OUP 1980
American Musical Theatre: A Chronicle
    OUP 1978

CAZALET-KEIR, Thelma
Homage to P. G. Wodehouse (Ed.)
Barrie & Jenkins 1973

CONNOLLY, Joseph
P. G. Wodehouse: An Illustrated Biography
London 1979

DAVIS, Lee
Bolton and Wodehouse and Kern:
The Men Who Made Musical Comedy
James H. Heineman (NY) 1993

DAY, Barry & RING, Tony
P. G. Wodehouse: In His Own Words
Hutchinson 2001
Overlook 2003

DONALDSON, Frances
P. G. Wodehouse: The Authorized
    Biography
Weidenfeld & Nicolson 1982

"Yours, Plum": The Letters of
    P. G. Wodehouse (Editor)
Hutchinson 1990

GREEN, Benny
P. G. Wodehouse: A Literary Biography
Rutledge Press (NY) 1981

GROSSMITH, George
"G.G."
Hutchinson 1933

JASEN, David A.
P. G. Wodehouse: A Portrait of a Master
Mason & Lipscomb (NY) 1974

The Theatre of P. G. Wodehouse
Batsford 1979

KREUGER, Miles
Show Boat: The Story of a Classic
    American Musical
De Capo 1990

PHELPS, Barry
P. G. Wodehouse: Man and Myth
Constable 1992

RING, Tony
You Simply Hit Them with an Axe
Porpoise Books 1995

SUSKIN, Steve
Show Tunes (1905–1991):
The Songs, Shows and Careers of
    Broadway's Major Composers
Limelight Editions (NY) 1992

USBORNE, Richard
Wodehouse: At Work to the End
Penguin 1975

WODEHOUSE, P. G.
Performing Flea
Herbert Jenkins 1953
Over Seventy
Herbert Jenkins 1957

WODEHOUSE, P. G. &
Guy BOLTON
Bring On the Girls:
The Improbable Story of Our Life in
    Musical Comedy,
With Pictures to Prove It.
Herbert Jenkins 1954

SELECTED RECORDINGS

It seems pointless to even attempt to list 78 r.p.m. recordings of the original shows, since they are now collectors' items. Such modern recordings as there are originated with recent revivals.

- *Leave It To Jane*—(STET 15017 – DRG Records 1991): An original cast recording of the 1959 revival. The same CD also includes the 1960 revival of . . .
- *Oh, Kay!*
- *Sitting Pretty*—(New World Records—0387-2 1990): A studio recording based on 1989 performances at Carnegie Hall's Weill Recital Hall
- *The Land Where the Good Songs Go*—(Harbinger Records—*HCD 1901* 2001): A recital by Hal Cazalet and Sylvia McNair with Steven Blier (Piano) & Laura Cazalet, which includes "Oh, Gee!, Oh, Joy!"; "Tell Me All Your Troubles, Cutie"; "You're the Top"; "Rolled Into One"; "Sir Galahad"; "The Land Where the Good Songs Go"; "If I Ever Lost You"; "Go Little Boat"; "You Can't Make Love By Wireless"; "Bill" (*original version*); "You Never Knew About Me"; "Shimmy With Me"; "Non-Stop Dancing"; "My Castle in the Air"; "The Enchanted Train"; "Anything Goes." (The recital was also performed live in 2001 at the Library of Congress in Washington and in 2002 at both the Wigmore Hall, London, and New York's Carnegie Weill Hall.)
- *Broadway Through the Gramophone: The Musical Stage in the War Years, Volume III: 1914–1920—Pearl—Pavilion Records—Gems 0084—2 CD set 2002*): Original recording selections from *Have A Heart, Oh, Boy!, Leave It To Jane* and *Oh, Lady! Lady!!*
- *The Packard Humanities Institute's Recordings:* Intended primarily for archival purposes, this ambitious project set out to record the complete theatrical output of composers Jerome Kern and Victor Herbert. Of the Kern-Wodehouse shows it would include *Have A Heart, Oh, Boy!, Leave It to Jane*, and *Oh, Lady! Lady!*

SONG LIST

NOTE ON CREDITS:

Wodehouse songs were published in England and America—and sometimes in both. Since many of them were published almost a century ago, it has not always been possible to verify details. In this American edition I have only attempted to deal with publication as it affects US copyright in which all material published before 1923 is now in the public domain. The situation in the UK is significantly different and, to complicate matters further, a song published by one house in the US may have different UK parentage, even though the original company has an office there. Songs without attribution have not been claimed by either of the two principal publishers: Warner/Chappell and Universal Music. And all the songs in a particular show were not necessarily published All of which is an attempt to say that, should any of the attributions prove incorrect, this will be rectified in subsequent editions. Any previously unpublished lyrics are hereby now copyright of the Trustees of the P. G. Wodehouse Estate.

Ain't It a Grand and Glorious Feeling!, 84
US: Public Domain

All Full of Talk (When You're Full of Talk), 46
US: Public Domain
UK: © Warner/Chappell

All the Time For You (You're the Little Girl I've Waited So Long For), 147
US: Public Domain

All You Need Is a Girl, 358
Words and Music by Jerome Kern and P. G. Wodehouse
US: © 1924 Universal—Polygram Int. Publ., Inc. (ASCAP) 100.00%
UK: © Warner/Chappell

And I Am All Alone (I See You There), 53
US: Public Domain

Annette, 185
© 2004 the Trustees of the Wodehouse Estate

Anything Goes, 409
(Lyrics by Cole Porter & P.G. Wodehouse)
US © 1934 (Renewed) Warner Bros. Inc. (ASCAP) (All rights reserved.)
(Cole Porter lyrics used by permission of Peter H. Felcher, Trustee of the Cole Porter Music and Literary Property Trusts)

Anytime Is Dancing Time, 207
US: Public Domain

Ask Dad, 233
US: Public Domain

Back East, 336
© 2004 by the Trustees of the Wodehouse Estate

Back To the Dear Old Trenches, 209
US: Public Domain

Barcarolle, 28
© 2004 by the Trustees of the Wodehouse Estate

Be A Little Sunbeam, 84
US: Public Domain

Before I Met You, 159
US: Public Domain
UK: © Warner/Chappell

Behind the Scenes, 10
© 2004 the Trustees of the Wodehouse Estate

Bill *(Oh, Lady! Lady!!),* 390
US: Public Domain
UK: © Warner/Chappell

Bill *(Show Boat),* 164
(Lyric by P. G. Wodehouse & Oscar
    Hammerstein II)
US: © Copyright 1928 Universal—Polygram
    Int. Publ., Inc. (ASCAP) 100.00%
UK: Warner/Chappell

Bongo On the Congo, 349
Words and Music by Jerome Kern and P. G.
    Wodehouse
US: © 1924 Universal—Polygram Int. Publ.,
    Inc. (ASCAP) 100.00%
UK: © Warner/Chappell

Breakfast In Bed, 377
UK: © Warner/Chappell

Bright Lights, 55
US: Public Domain

Bring On The Girls, 168
US: Public Domain

Broken Blossoms, 268
US: Public Domain

Bunny, Dear, 263
US: Public Domain

But Its Meaning, Who Can Tell?, 180
© 2004 the Trustees of the Wodehouse Estate

Buy, Buy *(Pat),* 340
© 2004 the Trustees of the Wodehouse Estate

Buy! Buy! Buy! *(Ladies, Please!),* 214
© 2004 the Trustees of the Wodehouse Estate

Calico, 14
© 2004 the Trustees of the Wodehouse Estate

Can the Cabaret, 66
US: Public Domain

Cantata, 182
© 2004 the Trustees of the Wodehouse Estate

Chancellor of the Exchequer, The, 28
© 2004 the Trustees of the Wodehouse Estate

Childhood Days, 240
US: Public Domain

Chopin Ad Lib (Opening Chorus), 300
UK: © Warner/Chappell

Church 'Round the Corner, The *(Oh, Lady!
    Lady!!),* 218
US: Public Domain

Church 'Round the Corner, The *(Ladies,
    Please!),* 215
© 2004 the Trustees of the Wodehouse Estate

Church 'Round the Corner, The (*The Little Thing*), 216
© 2004 the Trustees of the Wodehouse Estate

Church 'Round the Corner, The (*Sally*), 216
US: Public Domain
UK: © Warner/Chappell

Cinderella (Once Upon A Time), 42
US: Public Domain

Circus Day, 336
© 2004 the Trustees of the Wodehouse Estate

City of Dreams, 234/241
US: Public Domain

Cleopatterer, 101
US: Public Domain
UK: © Warner/Chappell

Clog Dance, The (The Low Back'd Car), 142
US: Public Domain

Cochin China, 183
© 2004 the Trustees of the Wodehouse Estate

College Spirit, 265
US: Public Domain

Come Where Nature Calls, 234
US: Public Domain

Cottage In Kent, A, 328
UK: © 2004 the Trustees of the Wodehouse
    Estate

Country Life (*see* The Finest Thing in the Country), 238
US: Public Domain

Covered Wagon, 340
© 2004 the Trustees of the Wodehouse Estate

Crickets Are Calling, The, 102
US: Public Domain

Daisy, 65
US: Public Domain

Dancing M.D., A (Tell All Your Troubles to Me), 138
US: Public Domain

Dancing Time (*Oh, Lady! Lady!!*), 169
US: Public Domain

Dancing Time (*The Cabaret Girl*), 313
UK: © Warner/Chappell

Dartmoor Days (Dear Old-Fashioned Prison of Mine), 288
US: © Warner/Chappell Music Inc.
UK: © Warner/Chappell

Days Gone By, 257
Words and Music by Jerome Kern,
    P. G. Wodehouse
US: © Copyright 1924 Universal—
    Polygram Int. Publ., Inc. (ASCAP)
    100.00%

Dear Eyes That Shine (The Miniature), 289
US: © Warner/Chappell Music Inc.
UK: © Warner/Chappell

Dear Old Church Bell, 184
© 2004 the Trustees of the Wodehouse Estate

Dear Old Dublin, 114
US: Public Domain

Dear Old Pnibw, 432
© 2004 the Trustees of the Wodehouse Estate

Dear Old Prison Days, 163
US: Public Domain

Dear Old Stage Door (At A Moving Picture Show), 146
US: Public Domain

**Lovers' Quarrels (*See You Later—
    Version 1*), 188
US: Public Domain
UK: © Universal Music

Loving By Proxy, 90
© 2004 the Trustees of the Wodehouse Estate

Magic Melody, The, 165
US: Public Domain

Man, Man, Man, 125
US: Public Domain
UK: © Universal Music

March of the Musketeers, 405
US: © Warner/Chappell Music Inc.
UK: © Warner/Chappell

March Song, 378
© 2004 the Trustees of the Wodehouse Estate

May Moon, 380
UK: © Warner/Chappell

Meet Me Down on Main Street, 330
UK: © Warner/Chappell

**Melodrama Burlesque (The Old-Fashioned
    Drama),** 45
US: Public Domain

Men With Whiskers, 434
© 2004 the Trustees of the Wodehouse Estate

Moon Love, 331
UK: © Warner/Chappell

Moon Song, 157
US: Public Domain
UK: © Warner/Chappell

Mother Paris (*See You Later—Version 1*), 185
US: Public Domain
UK: © Universal Music

Motor Car, The, 11
© 2004 the Trustees of the Wodehouse Estate

Mountain Girl, The, 118
US: Public Domain

Mr. Gravvins—Mr. Gripps, 301
© 2004 the Trustees of the Wodehouse Estate

Mr. and Mrs. Rorer, 350
Words and Music by Jerome Kern,
    P. G. Wodehouse
US: © 1924 Universal—Polygram Int. Publ.,
    Inc. (ASCAP) 100.00%
UK: © Warner/Chappell

Music Hall Class, The, 23
© 2004 the Trustees of the Wodehouse Estate

My Castle in the Air, 43
US: Public Domain
UK: © Warner/Chappell

My Girl, 280
US: © Warner/Chappell Music Inc.
UK: © Warner/Chappell

My Grassy Corner Girl (Queen), 1
© 2004 the Trustees of the Wodehouse Estate

My Little Place in the Country, 305
UK: © Warner/Chappell

My Tango Maid, 23
© 2004 the Trustees of the Wodehouse Estate

My Wife—My Man, 60
US: Public Domain

Napoleon, 63
US: Public Domain

Nero, 274/309
© 2004 the Trustees of the Wodehouse Estate

Nerves!, 198
US: Public Domain
UK: © Warner/Chappell

Nesting Time in Flatbush, 81
US: Public Domain
UK: © Warner/Chappell

New York Girl, The, 147
US: Public Domain

Nightingale, 386
© 2004 the Trustees of the Wodehouse Estate

Non-Stop Dancing, 327
UK: © Warner/Chappell

Not a Word, 26
© 2004 the Trustees of the Wodehouse Estate

Not Yet, 152
US: Public Domain
UK: © Universal Music

Now That My Ship's Come Home, 18
© 2004 the Trustees of the Wodehouse Estate

**Now We Are Nearly Through
  (Opening Chorus),** 318
© 2004 the Trustees of the Wodehouse Estate

Nurse, Nurse, Nurse, 145
U.S. Public Domain

Nuts In May (Gathering Nuts in May), 291
UK: © Warner/Chappell

Oh, Daddy, Please, 80
US: Public Domain
UK: © Warner/Chappell

Oh, Gee! Oh, Joy!, 397
US: © 1928 WB Music Corp. and Warner Bros.
    Inc. (Renewed)
UK: © Warner/Chappell

Oh, How Warm It Is Today, 254
US: Public Domain

Oh, Lady! Lady!!, 155
US: Public Domain
UK: © Warner/Chappell

Oh, Mr. Chamberlain!, 8
© 2004 the Trustees of the Wodehouse Estate

Oh, That Yankiana Rag, 30
© 2004 the Trustees of the Wodehouse Estate

Oh, Tune the String, 436
© 2004 the Trustees of the Wodehouse Estate

Old-Fashioned Wife, An, 74
US: Public Domain
UK: © Universal Music

Omar Khayyam, 351
© 2004 the Trustees of the Wodehouse Estate

On A Desert Island With You (Desert Island),
  360
Words and Music by Jerome Kern,
    P. G. Wodehouse
US: © 1924 Universal—Polygram Int. Publ.,
    Inc. (ASCAP) 100.00%
UK: © Warner/Chappell

Once in September, 385
© 2004 the Trustees of the Wodehouse Estate

Opening Chorus Act 2—*The Riviera Girl,* 123
US: Public Domain

Opening Chorus Act 3—*The Riviera Girl,* 129
US: Public Domain

Opening Chorus Act 1—*See You Later
  (Version 1),* 175
© 2004 the Trustees of the Wodehouse Estate

Sometimes I Feel Just Like Grandpa, 119
US: Public Domain

Sun Is Far Above Us, The, 383
(*See* I Know My Love Is You)

Sun Shines Brighter, The (I'm So Happy), 104
US: Public Domain
UK: © Warner/Chappell

Sun Starts to Shine Again, The, 162
US: Public Domain
UK: © Warner/Chappell

Sunrise Intermezzo (Opening Chorus), 262
US: Public Domain

Sympathy, 418
© 2004 the Trustees of the Wodehouse Estate

**Tao Loved His Li (A Chinese Adam and Eve/
The Legend of the Tea-Tree),** 264
US: Public Domain
UK: © Universal Music

Tell Me All Your Troubles, Cutie, 136
US: Public Domain
UK: © Universal Music

That Ticking Taxi's Waiting At the Door,
211/258
US: Public Domain

**That's the Kind of Man I'd Like to Be
(The Bachelor),** 85
US: Public Domain

That's What I'd Do For the Girl I Love, 327
© 2004 the Trustees of the Wodehouse Estate

That's What Men Are For, 226
US: Public Domain

There Goes a Married Man, 176
© 2004 the Trustees of the Wodehouse
Estate

There Isn't One Girl, 351
Words and Music by Jerome Kern,
P. G. Wodehouse
US: © 1924 Universal—Polygram Int. Publ.,
Inc. (ASCAP) 100.00%
UK: © Universal Music

**There It Is Again (When Your Favorite Girl's
Not There),** 100
US: Public Domain
UK: © Universal Music

There'll Never Be Another Girl Like Daisy,
120
US: Public Domain
UK: © Universal Music

There's Life in the Old Dog Yet, 207
US: Public Domain

There's A Light In Your Eyes, 257
US: Public Domain

**There's Lots of Room For You (There's Lots of
Chance For You),** 218
© 2004 the Trustees of the Wodehouse
Estate

They All Look Alike, 66
US: Public Domain
UK: © Universal Music

This Is the Existence, 42
US: Public Domain

**Those Days Are Gone Forever (Long Years
Ago),** 308
UK: © Warner/Chappell

Thousands of Years Ago, 225
US: Public Domain

Through the Fence, 336
© 2004 the Trustees of the Wodehouse
Estate

You, You, You, 20
© 2004 the Trustees of the Wodehouse Estate

You Alone Would Do (I'd Want Only You), 347
Words and Music by Jerome Kern,
    P. G. Wodehouse
US: © 1924 Universal—Polygram Int. Publ.,
    Inc. (ASCAP) 100.00%

**You Can't Keep a Good Girl Down
    (Joan of Arc),** 278
US: Public Domain
UK: © Warner/Chappell

You Can't Make Love By Wireless, 325
UK: © Warner/Chappell

**You Found Me and I Found You (I Found You
    and You Found Me),** 155
US: Public Domain
UK: © Warner/Chappell

You Never Knew About Me, 73
US: Public Domain
UK: © Warner/Chappell

You Never Know, 237
US: Public Domain
UK: © Warner/Chappell

You Said Something, 62
US: Public Domain
UK: © Universal Music

You Want the Best Seats, We Have 'Em, 300
UK: © Warner/Chappell

You Whispered It (You—You—You!), 182
US: Public Domain
UK: © Universal Music

You'll Find Me Playing Mah-Jong, 323
© 2004 the Trustees of the Wodehouse Estate

You'll Still Be Here, 428
US: © Warner/Chappell Music Inc.
UK: © Warner/Chappell

You're Here and I'm Here, 164
US: Public Domain

You're Here and I'm Here (*Alternative version*),
    169
US: Public Domain

You're The Top, 411
Lyrics by Cole Porter & P. G. Wodehouse
US: © 1934 (Renewed) Warner Bros. Inc.
(Porter lyrics used by permission of Peter H.
    Felcher, Trustee of the Cole Porter Music
    and Literary Property Trusts)

Young Man (*See You Later—Version 1*), 182
© 2004 the Trustees of the Wodehouse Estate

Young Man (*See You Later—Version 2*), 196
US: Public Domain
UK: © Universal Music

Your Eyes, 406
US: © Warner/Chappell Music Inc.
UK: © Warner/Chappell

Photo Credits

Thanks are given to the following institutions for use of the photos on the pages listed below:

The Billy Rose Theatre Collection at the New York Library for the Performing Arts at Lincoln Center: pp. 47, 86, 93, 106, 112, 128, 153, 233, 279, 343, 362, 387, 399

The Museum of the City of New York: frontispiece, pp. 39, 69, 260

The Shubert Archive: pp. 146, 374

The Mander & Mitchenson Collection: p. 411

All other illustrations are from private collections, the majority from the personal collection of Tony Ring, to whom I am most grateful for permission to reprint.

INDEX

ABOUT THE AUTHOR

Barry Day is the author or editor of numerous books and plays with particular emphasis on theatre—and musical theatre in particular. In his twenty-plus years working with the Noel Coward estate, he has produced Coward's *Complete Lyric; Collected Sketches and Parodies; Theatrical Companion to Coward, Updated Edition; A Life in Quotes;* and *The Unknown Noel: New Writing from the Coward Archive,* as well as concert versions of the Coward musicals *After the Ball* and *Pacific 1860*.

He has also edited a series of literary "autobiographies" in the *A Life . . . in His Own Words* series, including those of Oscar Wilde, P. G. Wodehouse, and Dorothy Parker. He was part of the team that rebuilt Shakespeare's Globe playhouse on London's Bankside, and his *This Wooden 'O': Shakespeare's Globe Reborn* is the official account of that historic project. He and his wife, Lynne, divide their time between New York, Palm Beach, and Weston, Connecticut.